D0983767

THE OUTLAWED PARTY

SOCIAL DEMOCRACY IN GERMANY

1878–1890

THE OUTLAWED PARTY
SOCIAL DEMOCRACY
IN GERMANY, 1878-1890

VERNON L. LIDTKE

PRINCETON, NEW JERSEY
PRINCETON UNIVERSITY PRESS
1966

Library of Congress Catalog Card Number: 66-14311

Publication of this book has been aided by
the Whitney Darrow Publication Reserve Fund
of Princeton University Press.

The initials at the beginning of each chapter
are adaptations from *Feder und Stichel*
by Zapf and Rosenberger.

Printed in the United States of America by
Vail-Ballou Press, Inc., Binghamton, New York

PREFACE

Many of the problems of modern Germany have been integrally related to the history of the Social Democratic movement. Questions concerning the advancement of political democracy in the Bismarckian Reich, the integration of the working classes into German society and politics, the possibilities of peaceful reform and the expectations of violent revolution, all have been affected in varying degrees by the theory and practice of Social Democracy. For this reason the study of Social Democracy has been essential as one approach to understanding Germany in the nineteenth and twentieth centuries, and the existing scholarly literature has already clarified many of the fundamental problems.

This book seeks to make a further contribution by providing a narration and analysis of the Social Democratic experience under the Socialist Law (1878–1890), the years known as the "heroic epoch" in the traditions of the party. To the Social Democrats, the heroism and excitement of clandestine activities stood out as the most memorable features of their experience under the Socialist Law; expulsions, arrests, and imprisonment gave them a heightened sense of being revolutionaries. From the perspective of the 1960's, however, the less exciting aspects of the period appear to be equally significant, perhaps revealing even more about the fundamental nature of the movement. Without overlooking the illegal and secret labors of the Social Democrats, I have given more attention to their lawful political endeavors in the Reichstag and the state diets, an aspect not usually stressed in the studies of this period. Much of my emphasis has been on the interaction between the practical political activities and the theoretical searchings of the Social Democrats, an approach that is intended to elucidate the meaning of the ideological shift that took place from the time of the Gotha program of 1875 to the adoption of the Erfurt program in 1891. More particularly, I have attempted to show how the following themes and changes were interrelated in the theory and practice of the movement: the shifting relationship of the Social Democrats to their traditional ideals of political democracy; the parallel issue of parliamentarism as it concerned their theory and practice; the search for guidance in matters of socialist economic theory; the various meanings they gave to the concept of revolution and their

expectations about revolution; and the gradual penetration of Marxism as it displaced the reliance of the Social Democrats on Lassalle and other thinkers. Some very fundamental changes occurred within the Social Democratic movement during the Socialist Law, and it has been my objective to show how these came about and how they affected Social Democracy as a political party of the working classes.

Writing the history of the Social Democrats under the Socialist Law has been an enjoyable task, for it was an era in which courage and success overcame despair and failure. Equally pleasant is the opportunity to express my gratitude for the advice and cooperation I have received from numerous persons and institutions in the course of writing this book. I should like especially to thank Professors Carl Landauer, Raymond J. Sontag, and Werner T. Angress for their thoughtful suggestions and guidance as I wrote an earlier version of this study at the University of California, Berkeley. My colleagues at Michigan State University, Professors Norman Rich and Herbert Kisch, gladly agreed to read the manuscript and offered ideas for its improvement. Although Professors Carl E. Schorske and Guenther Roth were not directly concerned with the manuscript, I have benefited considerably from discussions with them on problems of Social Democracy. To the late Professor Dr. A. J. C. Rueter, formerly director of the Internationaal Instituut voor Sociale Geschiedenis, Amsterdam, I am grateful for permission to use the archive of the German Social Democratic party. Other members of the staff of the Instituut generously assisted my research, notably the late Werner Blumenberg, then director of the German division, and Dr. Horst Lademacher. My experience in Amsterdam would not have been complete without the fruitful discussions with a fellow researcher, Dr. Shlomo Na'aman, now at the University of Tel Aviv. A grant under the Fulbright program made possible my research in Amsterdam. I wish to thank the Department of History, Michigan State University, for giving me leave from teaching duties for one quarter so that I could complete the revisions of the manuscript and to the university's research fund for financial assistance. My research was expedited by the staff members of numerous libraries; in particular, I wish to thank Dr. Kurt Koszyk, director of the Westfaelisch-Niederrheinisches Institut fuer Zeitungsforschung, for guiding me to several newspaper sources; the library of the Freie Universitaet in Berlin for the use of the special "Stein

Bibliothek"; and the staff of the library at the University of California, Berkeley, for cooperation at all times. The publishers of the *International Review of Social History* have given me permission to use, in slightly modified form, the content of an article, "German Social Democracy and German State Socialism, 1876–1884," which originally appeared in that journal (Vol. IX, Part 2, 1964). To the editorial advisor of the same journal, Dr. Frits Kool, my thanks for his careful scrutiny of the substance of that article and for rewarding conversations at other times. Of all the persons associated directly or indirectly with this book, none deserves more appreciation than my wife; for her understanding, patience and encouragement, I am deeply grateful.

East Lansing, Michigan
May 1966

Bibliothek") and the staff of the library of the University of California, Berkeley, for cooperation at all times. [illegible]

[illegible]

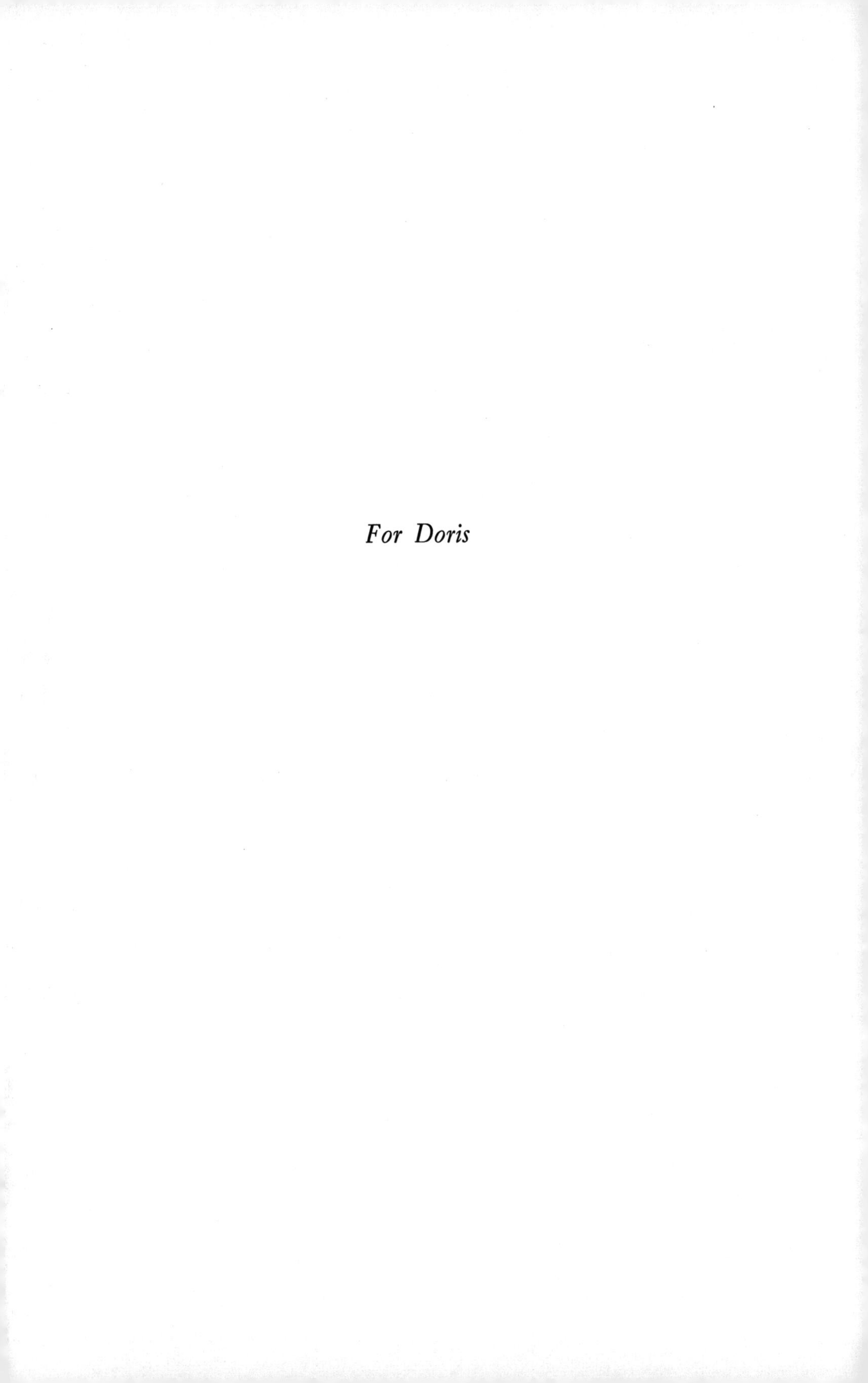

For Doris

CONTENTS

THE OUTLAWED PARTY

SOCIAL DEMOCRACY IN GERMANY

1878–1890

CHAPTER I · THE EMERGENCE AND EARLY ORIENTATION OF WORKING-CLASS POLITICAL ACTION

The German Social and Political Context

THE SOCIALIST movement burst forth vigorously on the German political scene in the early 1860's. It emerged at a time when the whole of central Europe was in a process of rapid industrial expansion and political reorganization. These developments stimulated the rise of the labor movement and also created the conditions that defined the nature of its future growth. To be sure, organizations of workingmen had appeared in the revolution of 1848, and some with socialist tendencies, but the victory of the counter-revolution frustrated their ambitions. On the surface, all was quiet during the reactionary fifties. Isolated groups of socialists and workers continued to exist, but they were fragmented and without influence. That changed in the sixties, and so rapidly, and with such energy, that the socialist movement was a dynamic political reality before many Germans were truly aware of what had taken place.[1]

The initial characteristics of the labor movement were fashioned by the interplay between three salient factors: the take-off of German industrialization from about the 1830's, the failure of the bourgeois liberals to achieve the unification of Germany on liberal principles, and the formation of a German state under Prussian hegemony by 1871.[2] As

[1] It may be debated for some time whether the beginnings of the modern German labor movement, as a political force, should be dated from the sixties or from an earlier date, especially the revolution of 1848. The question has many complexities, arising out of the problems of organizational, ideological, and personal continuity. The present study is concerned with specifically socialist organizations, and therefore begins in the sixties, from which time there is a definite continuity. For the literature on this question, see Frolinde Balser, *Sozial-Demokratie 1848/49–1863. Die erste deutsche Arbeiterorganisation* (Stuttgart, 1962), I, pp. 22–40. On the basis of extensive archival research, Balser argues for a much greater continuity in the labor movement between 1848–1849 and the sixties than has generally been recognized.

[2] Although W. W. Rostow, *The Stages of Economic Growth* (Cambridge, 1960), initiated the use of the "take-off" concept, he dates it from the eighteen-fifties for Germany. A more convincing case for dating the German take-off from 1830/35 to 1855/60 has been made by Walther G. Hoffmann, "The Take-Off in

industrialization restructured and enlarged the working population, the inclusion of universal suffrage in the constitution of the new state offered the lower classes a crucial instrument for the enlargement of their political role. But the bourgeois liberals, capable of making great economic gains through industrialization, were incapable of directing the unfolding political events to their definite political advantage. Thus, in Germany, the working classes thrust themselves into the political arena before the bourgeoisie had succeeded in ordering the constitutional structure according to its own conceptions.

Numerous indices indicate the rapid pace of German industrialization in the fifties and sixties, even before the famous *Gruenderjahre* (founding years) of the early seventies. Capital for industrial investment was mobilized through the establishment of banks especially designed for this purpose. A basic railroad system for Germany was completed by 1870, serving not only to facilitate trade and communications but also to add a significant element to the unity of the new state. Joint-stock companies emerged in many trades and industries. These changes were especially apparent in the Rhineland-Westphalia, Saxony, Silesia, and in scattered areas throughout north and middle Germany. After the founding of the Reich in 1871, a boom period of nearly three years took place, witnessing a rapid rise in investment and an increase in the number of joint-stock companies. Germany's economy then reached a stage of sustained economic growth marking its full transformation into an industrial society.

Although German industrialization began its determined take-off before the mid-century, the old feudalistic conceptions of social organization died slowly. For several decades after industrialization had begun, Germans, and not merely Junkers, continued to think in terms of a society organized around estates (*Staende*) rather than classes. When the traditional categories of nobility (*Adelstand*), peasantry (*Bauerntum*), and bourgeoisie (*Buergertum*) no longer sufficed to include the new forms of the lower class, a so-called fourth estate (*vierter Stand*) or Workmen's Estate (*Arbeiterstand*) was added to this concept of social organization. These categories were easy to apply, but they were not entirely appropriate to the emerging industrial society, for most of the legal realities that had provided each "estate" with certain privileges were rapidly vanishing.[3] Although the landed aristocrats continued to

Germany," in W. W. Rostow (ed.), *The Economics of Take-Off into Sustained Growth* (New York, 1963), p. 96.

[3] Cf. Karl Erich Born, "Der soziale und wirtschaftliche Strukturwandel

enjoy certain inherited privileges, the "fourth estate" had only disadvantages. But in the flux of a period of industrialization these concepts served a purpose, and even Ferdinand Lassalle (1825–1864) spoke of the "Workmen's Estate" and its future mission in European society. As Eduard Bernstein has commented, Lassalle's use of this concept reflected not only its place in common parlance but also Lassalle's juridical framework of thought.[4]

There were material reasons why the German nobility continued to view society in the traditional "estate" framework. Despite the rapid pace of German industrialization in the second half of the century and the ensuing restructuring of the middle and lower classes, the landed aristocracy preserved its traditional pattern of life and most of its social prestige and political power. It was decades before industrialization, in full maturity by the seventies, brought with it a social revolution that could shake the stability of the old, pre-industrial ruling class of the Prussian state. Although the German nobility varied widely in cultural and social development, it preserved a sense of "estate" solidarity. The refined Rhineland aristocrat was a noticeable contrast to the boorish, half-literate east Elbian Junker. And, in contrast to the aristocratic classes of France and Britain, all the German nobility was typically less cultivated.[5] But this did not mean that the German aristocrats were less capable of preserving their own social prestige and material interests. With its economic base on the land, the aristocracy for the most part looked disdainfully upon business and industry as forms of human endeavor that lacked cultivation and honor. Even in an age when the east Elbian Junkers had become agrarian capitalists, competing for their markets like other businessmen, they liked to think of their estates in terms of historical right and social eminence rather than in terms of quantitative production and income. Despite the lofty contempt for business of some aristocrats, a few became involved with industry, and all were keen in defense of their own economic interests. When they felt the competitive pinch in grain from foreign agriculture, they unified to turn Germany away from free trade in the late seventies. In times of trouble, the German landed aristocracy was capa-

Deutschlands am Ende des 19. Jahrhunderts," *Vierteljahrschrift fuer Sozial- und Wirtschaftsgeschichte*, L (Nov. 1963), pp. 364–65.

[4] Eduard Bernstein, *Ferdinand Lassalle as a Social Reformer* (London, 1893), pp. 101–02.

[5] Robert H. Lowie, *Toward Understanding Germany* (Chicago, 1954), pp. 83–93.

ble of achieving a solidarity that was matched by very few other social classes.

The wealth of the German landed aristocracy in the second half of the nineteenth century declined relative to that of the commercial and industrial bourgeoisie. Nonetheless, the aristocrats were able, not only through the protection of their markets but through other means, to preserve their political and social eminence in the Reich. For generations they had been closely linked to the leadership of the Prussian army, and they maintained that stronghold of power. Equally significant, they had unlimited entrance into the highest offices of the civil service, and from these places could influence directly the policies of the government to favor their own interests. There were, in effect, no doors closed to German aristocrats with even the most limited talents, and it must be said, perhaps to their credit, that they remained energetic and ambitious as a class.[6]

An important reason for the continued strength and prestige of the German aristocracy must also be sought in the nature of the German professional, commercial, and industrial bourgeoisie. A brief account of the German social structure in the second half of the nineteenth century, like the present description, may give the impression that class lines were sharply drawn, excluding the possibility of social mobility. We need not assume such a class cleavage, not even between the working classes and the bourgeoisie; but few reliable generalizations can be made until lower-class mobility is more accurately studied. One generalization is beyond dispute—that is, that in their search for social prestige, the upper levels of the commercial and industrial bourgeoisie imitated the chief features of the landed aristocracy. If possible, these members of the upper bourgeoisie literally joined the aristocracy, through marriage or the acquisition of landed estates and noble titles. Short of that, there was a distinct tendency to accept the cultural and social ideals of the aristocracy, to become aristocrats in mind, if not in fact. This process of feudalization of the upper bourgeoisie, taking place gradually throughout the nineteenth century, buttressed the conservative landed class in a period when it no longer had an economic hegemony.[7]

[6] Werner Sombart, *Die deutsche Volkswirtschaft im neunzehnten Jahrhundert und im Anfang des 20. Jahrhunderts* (5th ed.; Berlin, 1921), pp. 464ff.

[7] *Ibid.*, p. 470. Ludwig Beutin, "Das Buergertum als Gesellschaftsstand im 19. Jahrhundert," in his *Gesammelte Schriften zur Wirtschafts- und Sozialgeschichte*, edited by Hermann Kellenbenz (Cologne and Graz, 1963), pp. 312–13.

The feudalization of the upper bourgeoisie was stimulated not only by the search for social prestige but also by the fact that the two groups had some economic interests in common. The first expression of this community of interests came with the founding of the North German Confederation in 1867, when some landed aristocrats and industrialists joined together in the "Free Conservative Union," a pro-Bismarck political association. Later, after the crash of 1873, a greater number of landed aristocrats and industrialists felt the need for protection from foreign competition and so together they pushed for a change in government policy from free trade to protectionism. The community of interests between aristocrats and industrialists extended to a mutual hatred of the burgeoning labor movement; they eagerly endorsed all of Bismarck's plans in the seventies for its suppression. The fusion of aristocratic and industrialist interests served as an important social-political base for Bismarck's politics from the late seventies through the eighties.[8]

The feudalization of a major portion of Germany's upper bourgeoisie makes it apparent that, as a class, the bourgeoisie—including here, its upper, middle, and lower segments—did not possess the same degree of solidarity enjoyed by the aristocracy. In the 1840's, one could speak of a bourgeoisie (*Buergertum*) as it had a place in the pre-industrial society, that is, a socially self-conscious and fairly cohesive commercial and professional urban grouping. After Germany's industrial take-off, however, diversification in business and industrial enterprises introduced a corresponding diversification of social and economic goals, leading to a further fragmentation of the bourgeoisie.[9] Thus, although the bourgeoisie often appeared as a solid bloc of capitalist exploiters to the socialist workingman, the reality within the total German social structure was characterized more by disunity.

The German bourgeois classes also lacked unanimity on the issue of national unification in the sixties. A large part of the bourgeoisie in the middle and south German states refused to endorse the ideal of a uni-

[8] Johannes Ziekursch, *Politische Geschichte des neuen deutschen Kaiserreiches* (Frankfurt am Main, 1925), I, p. 202. On the promotion of protectionism by industrialists and agriculturalists in the later seventies, see especially Ivo N. Lambi, *Free Trade and Protection in Germany 1868–1879* (Wiesbaden, 1963), pp. 113–49, *Beiheft* No. 44 to *Vierteljahrschrift fuer Sozial- und Wirtschaftsgeschichte*.

[9] Born, "Der soziale und wirtschaftliche Strukturwandel Deutschlands," pp. 370–71. The uncohesive nature of the German bourgeoisie in the nineteenth century is stressed by Beutin, "Das Buergertum als Gesellschaftsstand im 19. Jahrhundert," pp. 287, 292.

fied Germany under the leadership of a liberalized Prussian state. This solution was embraced by bourgeois liberals in Prussia; and by founding the National Society *(Nationalverein)* in 1859 they sought to push it forward. The National Society did not succeed, however, in coordinating the German bourgeois classes behind its scheme for unification. Instead, the non-Prussian bourgeois democrats from the middle and south German states peeled off from the liberals in the National Society and the Progressive party and formed their own *Volkspartei* (People's party), devoted to the achievement of a parliamentary democratic state including all Germans on a federal principle. The bourgeois liberals were further split when one group accepted Bismarck's indemnity bill in 1866 and formed the National Liberal party, while those who refused remained as the Progressive party. Thus, although it appeared in the early sixties that the bourgeois liberals were on the threshold of an era of political power capable of toppling the absolutist system and replacing it with an effective parliamentary constitutionalism, compromise and division frustrated such an achievement. Not even the unification of Germany in 1871 could revive a sense of unity among bourgeois liberals; the fissures sustained themselves, preventing German liberalism from achieving decisive political success.[10]

The diversity within the category "bourgeoisie" becomes even clearer if one includes the lower levels in the discussion, that is what the Germans commonly called the *Kleinbuergertum* (petty bourgeoisie). The frequent use of the term "petty bourgeoisie" in the nineteenth century, by socialists and non-socialists alike, implied the existence of a well-defined class with social cohesion and a degree of ideological unity. Significant social-economic differentiations, however, were perhaps more characteristic than unity. Composed as it was of petty traders, master craftsmen, small independent farmers, and the lower levels of clerical staffs in government and business, the petty bourgeoisie reflected a pre-industrial social grouping, bound to undergo changes in a era of industrialization. The process of industrializa-

[10] On these party developments, see the various sections of Arnold Bergstraesser, *Geschichte der politischen Parteien in Deutschland* (10th ed.; Munich, 1960), and Thomas Nipperdey, *Die Organisation der deutschen Parteien vor 1918* (Duesseldorf, 1961). An interpretive account of the liberals in the sixties, stressing their "capitulation," in Friedrich C. Sell, *Die Tragoedie des deutschen Liberalismus* (Stuttgart, 1953), pp. 184–226. Stressing the rise of the "middle class interest" as a detriment to the traditions of "intellectual idealism," Leonard Krieger, *The German Idea of Freedom* (Boston, 1957), examines the numerous liberal societies in the sixties in terms of the "rise and decline of institutional liberalism" (pp. 398–457).

tion, however, did not affect all the segments of the petty bourgeoisie in the same manner. For some, industrialization brought economic insecurity and ultimate ruin in their traditional occupations. This was particularly true in those handicraft trades, notably in textiles, where factory production had been introduced, creating a competitive level beyond the reach of the small producer. At the same time, skilled master craftsmen, if forced to abandon their roles as independent producers, could sometimes find employment in larger shops as foremen or trained technicians. Although technically proletarians, their real economic positions may have been hurt only slightly. On the whole, however, the workers in a threatened handicraft trade had to face the prospects of frequent unemployment and geographic dislocation. On the other hand, the growth of the German population and the rapid urbanization of the second half of the nineteenth century also created new markets for some of the traditional tradesmen. Butchers, bakers and similar tradesmen involved in the distribution of food supplies could sustain themselves and even prosper in a period of industrialization and population growth. On the basis of general statistics, Heinrich Bechtel argues that the number of master craftsmen grew more rapidly than the general population between 1816 and 1895. In another respect, the growth of the transportation system, the increase in industrial plants, the enlargement of government services, and the need for more schools created an increased demand for clerical staff and teachers on the lower levels. All of this leads to the conclusion that for the various segments of the petty bourgeoisie, industrialization certainly created insecurity and dislocation for many, but also a chance for different kinds of employment and an upward as well as downward mobility. As thorough studies on the problems of social mobility are lacking, no final judgment can be made.[11]

For the emergent socialist movement in the sixties and seventies, the petty bourgeoisie had a special significance—from its ranks came a large percentage of the political leaders of German labor. Educated in the elementary schools (*Volksschule*) and then trained as artisans in various trades, many of them either became master craftsmen or used their skills and talents in some other field to achieve a limited proper-

[11] On the *Kleinbuergertum* and master craftsmen, see Sombart, *Die deutsche Volkswirtschaft*, pp. 458ff.; Heinrich Bechtel, *Wirtschaftsgeschichte Deutschlands im 19. und 20. Jahrhundert* (Munich, 1956), pp. 27–28. Evidence that skilled workers could rise to become entrepreneurs is given by Wolfgang Koellmann, *Sozialgeschichte der Stadt Barmen im 19. Jahrhundert* (Tuebingen, 1960), p. 107.

tied status. In some cases, the nascent trade unions or the party organization itself offered them a chance to free themselves from manual labor and become paid agitators, newspaper editors, or even Reichstag deputies. In almost all cases, however, the opportunity to engage in political activity depended upon an individual's having secured a social-economic status well above that of the journeyman artisan or the propertyless worker. Other leaders of the early socialist movement came from still higher strata of German society, so that they had enjoyed the benefits of a Gymnasium education or its equivalent.[12] The lower and middle levels of the German bourgeoisie thus supplied the socialist movement with one of its most valuable elements—a leadership with skills and sometimes a fair degree of education.

[12] The following leaders, as some examples, either came from or achieved a petty bourgeois status in society. Ignaz Auer (1846–1907) began as a saddler and rose largely through activity in labor organizations; August Bebel (1840–1913), born into a family of lower military rank, trained as a wood-turner, actually became a fairly successful businessman on a small scale (Robert Lowie cites Bebel as an illustration in describing the petty bourgeoisie, in *Toward Understanding Germany*, pp. 116–19); Eduard Bernstein's (1850–1932) father started as a plumber and rose to be a railroad engineer, while Eduard worked for nearly a decade as a bank clerk; Johann H. W. Dietz (1843–1922) rose as a printer so that he could become a small publisher; Joseph Dietzgen (1828–1888), the self-taught philosopher of Social Democracy, was born into an old family of Blankenburg near Cologne, opened a grocery, bakery, and tannery in the early fifties and worked as a fairly successful tanner throughout his life; Carl Grillenberger (1848–1897), trained as a locksmith, became a foreman in a gas factory in 1873 and then went into socialist journalism; Julius Motteler (1838–1908), studied cloth-making and business and by the late fifties was a foreman and bookkeeper in an Augsburg cloth factory; and Julius Vahlteich (1839–1915) was already an independent shoe maker in Leipzig when he played a leading role in founding the Lassallean movement in 1863. In the above cases, and many others, the leaders had achieved either an independent existence or clerical rank by the time they began political activity; it was only after 1890 that both the trade union and party organizations were sufficiently secure and widespread to offer a great many of their members permanent jobs and also a means to achieve higher social status.

Other leaders of the socialist movement from the sixties through the eighties came from a more established and prosperous level of the bourgeoisie. Among these, Karl Kautsky (1854–1938) was raised in Vienna by parents with artistic and literary ambitions, and he enjoyed a university education; Wilhelm Liebknecht's (1826–1900) ancestry in Hesse included a long list of officials and educated persons, and he himself studied at several universities; Max Kayser (1853–1888) came from a Jewish business family in Breslau (similar to Lassalle), and the young Kayser went to the Gymnasium and into business; Paul Singer (1844–1911), from a Berlin commercial family, was himself part-owner of a ladies' clothing factory by the end of the sixties; and finally, Georg von Vollmar (1850–1922) was rather unique with his aristocratic lineage and a father who held a high ministerial post.

Convenient biographical sketches of the German socialists may be found in the following: Werner Blumenberg, *Kaempfer fuer die Freiheit* (Berlin and Hannover, 1959), and Franz Osterroth, *Biographisches Lexikon des Sozialismus*. Band I: *Verstorbene Persoenlichkeiten* (Hannover, 1960).

From its beginning, the socialist movement rested on a working-class base, but that base was no more homogeneous than the other classes of the society. To be precise, one should speak of working classes rather than class, but even this is not adequate to indicate the diversity rising from occupational, regional, and religious differences. Most important, the socialist movement could not arouse or organize the laborers on the land, in the smallest villages, or even in certain occupations. As late as 1871, almost 64 percent of the German population lived in a rural environment, that is, in villages of less than 2,000 inhabitants. In 1882, 42 percent of the labor force was still agricultural; by 1895 it had dropped to slightly over 36 percent. These rural workers remained outside the effective realm of socialist influence, but so did many of the artisans who lived in innumerable villages of limited population.[13]

In origin, the members of the urban working class came from rather diverse backgrounds, but chiefly from apprentice and journeymen artisans, displaced domestic producers, surplus rural laborers, or unpropertied peasants. Despite the progress of German industrialization and the increase in factory production, the functions of a great part of the German working class preserved something of the artisan character through the 1880's. As of 1882, no less than 59 percent of German laborers worked in shops that employed less than five employees. The percentage dropped steadily, until by 1895 it was only slightly over 46. At the same time, plants employing between six and fifty and between fifty-one and one thousand workers rose in the percentages. In the sixties, the decade of the emergence of the socialist movement, the small shops still predominated in the employment of the urban working classes.[14]

The accumulation of laborers from differing backgrounds meant that internal differentiations continued to characterize the working class in the decades after the middle of the century. In many cases, the new industrial forms could absorb the handicraft worker easily and use his skill and training to advantage. But for the displaced rural worker

[13] Juergen Kuczynski, *Die Geschichte der Lage der Arbeiter unter dem Kapitalismus* (Berlin-East, 1962), II, p. 131; Gerhard Bry, *Wages in Germany 1871–1945* (Princeton, 1960), pp. 24–26.

[14] On the formation of the working classes, see Werner Conze, "Vom 'Poebel' zum 'Proletariat.' Sozialgeschichtliche Voraussetzungen fuer den Sozialismus in Deutschland," *Vierteljahrschrift fuer Sozial- und Wirtschaftsgeschichte,* XLI (1954), pp. 333–64, and Wolfgang Koellmann, "Politische und soziale Entwicklung der deutschen Arbeiterschaft 1850–1914," in *ibid.*, L (Jan. 1964), pp. 482–83. The figures on size of shop and factory are derived from Kuczynski, *Die Geschichte der Lage der Arbeiter unter dem Kapitalismus,* III, p. 253.

the transition was much more difficult. It involved almost a complete change of environment, from the farm village to the city, and it brought the rustic into a system of production that was quite foreign to him. There were equalizers, however, that gradually erased many of the original differences. Regardless of previous training or occupation, the urban workers, whether skilled artisans in small shops or unlearned laborers in larger factories, tended to live in the same districts of the city. Common features distinguished these working-class neighborhoods in city after city from the more prosperous bourgeois life around them. Chiefly, overcrowded and miserable housing conditions provided a common denominator of social deprivation. Differences in backgrounds, wage rates, and occupation seemed to be minor as workers viewed their situation in the totality of the German social structure. The mobility of many workers with respect to a place of residence worked as another social equalizer of the laboring class. In the system of handicraft production, journeymen artisans had always wandered for a few years in search of experience, training, and adventure, but then settled down again to make a permanent home and achieve a propertied status if possible. As Germany began to industrialize, a significant internal migration of laborers took place, especially after unification in 1871; a part of the labor force was permanently mobile, seeking work where it could be found.[15]

The difficulty in analyzing the exact social-economic composition of the working classes between the sixties and the nineties is compounded by the fact that in terms of labor organizations these decades formed a transitional period. In the sixties, and even later, artisans were still grouped according to the traditional pattern of master, journeyman, and apprentice, but the guild system that had given rise to this structure was no longer a vital organizational institution. Although some efforts were made as late as the eighties to reestablish some of the legal base of the guild system, the time had passed when this could succeed completely. On the other hand, craft unions were hardly known in Germany in the sixties, although some beginnings were made. In the seventies the concept of the craft union took hold, but the Imperial In-

[15] See Koellmann, "Politische und soziale Entwicklung der deutschen Arbeiterschaft 1850–1914," pp. 484–85, for the equalizing effect of working-class neighborhoods. On the internal migration, Wolfgang Koellmann, "Industrialisierung, Binnenwanderung und 'Soziale Frage' (Zur Entstehungsgeschichte der deutschen Industriegrossstadt im 19. Jahrhundert," *Vierteljahrschrift fuer Sozial- und Wirtschaftsgeschichte*, VII. (March 1959), pp. 45–62.

dustrial Code (*Gewerbeordnung*), although it allowed the right of free association, severely restricted the unions in their pursuit of economic gain. The only figures available indicate that as of 1877 about 49,000 workers were organized into trade unions; this constituted perhaps about one-half of 1 percent of the estimated non-agricultural labor force (on the basis of the industrial census for 1882). The suppression of socialist trade unions in 1878–1879 then cut off this growth; not until the last years of the eighties were trade union organizations again allowed on a wide scale.[16]

Whether they were factory workers, domestic servants, or even independent artisans, a salient problem for the working classes was their integration into the German society. Encumbered with archaic values and ancient arrogance, many Junkers viewed the members of the "fourth estate" as the unfortunate byproducts of an undesirable industrial capitalism. Given their social values and their traditional eminence, the Junkers found it difficult to see by what means the fourth estate could be integrated into German society. To permit this would destroy much that the aristocrat valued in German society. The bourgeois liberals at least perceived that the workers had to be brought to the borders of the society, if not fully integrated. For that reason, educational societies for workers could be sponsored; but the idea that the workers should have a share in political power was unacceptable to most liberals. Even the most advanced bourgeois liberals hoped to retain the workers as economic and political subsidiaries, always useful and never troublesome. In this context, it was certainly logical, if not inevitable, that the German workers should become more and more estranged from the dominant culture of the society. The social estrangement of the working class was a condition into which it was reared, and which increased rather than diminished in the period through the eighties. The first fruits of that estrangement were harvested in the sixties with the founding of an independent political labor movement. In that development, both the ineptitude and shortsightedness of the liberal bourgeoisie played a decisive role.

The late 1860's were the finest years of nineteenth-century European liberalism, but when the showdown came, the German bourgeois liberals were found wanting. To achieve their goals—a unified Germany with a limited monarchy controlled by parliament—they needed

[16] On the early history of the craft unions, W. Kulemann, *Die Berufsvereine* (2nd ed.; Jena, 1908), II, pp. 1–39, and Bry, *Wages in Germany*, pp. 29–33.

to apply the full impact of the forces on the left against the Prussian absolutism. The speed of the industrialization, the spread of liberal ideals, and the sentiment for national unification created dynamic forces that could be thrust into the struggle. The key to the whole issue was to break the grip of the Prussian Junkers on the political power of the state. Only in that way could the bourgeoisie achieve a political influence that corresponded to the rapid increase of its material wealth. But for that task, the bourgeoisie needed not only its own unity but also the wholehearted support of all the segments of society that were hostile to the old regime. With the memory of 1848 still fresh in their minds, the bourgeois liberals drew back from unleashing the full force of the radical elements in German society. Perhaps their fears were justified. In the uncoiled force of the working class, the bourgeois liberals could see a great danger to their economic power. Thus, they preferred to move cautiously in their dispute with the Prussian Monarch and Bismarck between 1862 and 1866, hoping that their role and influence would be accepted without destroying the stability offered by the continuance of aristocratic influence in the state.

The timidity and tardiness with which the bourgeois liberals pushed their own political cause encouraged their opponents above and disenchanted their potential cadres below. Had the bourgeois liberals approached the workingmen with greater generosity, the two groups might have fused to achieve many of the interests of both. The working class would gladly have remained in the bourgeois political fold if the latter had offered a truly protective shelter. In Germany, however, the possibility of an effective alliance by liberals and labor was frustrated from the beginning. Even before the liberals were out-played by Bismarck in 1866, many of the German workers, under the leadership of Ferdinand Lassalle, had concluded that the bourgeois liberals were a sad lot and that nothing could be gained by cooperation with them.

Thus, the first salient feature of the German labor movement—its emergence as an independent political force—was determined by the interplay between Germany's rapid industrialization and the political ineptness of the bourgeois liberals. At a time when the working class was still comparatively formless in terms of organizations for economic gains, some of its members were already maturing to independent political activity. Most historians of the socialist movement have interpreted that as a great leap forward, but in retrospect it seems clear that it had consequences that were detrimental for the socialists as well as for the liberals. The mutual isolation of the two most progressive movements in German society permitted the conservative aristocrats to retain political influence and control far beyond their appropriate time. And for the labor movement, the liberal-socialist cleavage meant that the social estrangement of the working class from the dominant German society was now reenforced by a political isolation. Thus, the social integration of the working class was hindered significantly by these initial developments in the sixties. But the dominant classes in a society determine the possibilities of social integration, and the failure of the working class to achieve integration in the sixties must be laid at the doorstep of the bourgeois liberals and the aristocratic conservatives.[17]

The constitutional structure of the new German state, as it was first unveiled in the North German Confederation (1867) and then given a final form in the German Empire (1871) is the other factor that created the channels in which the nascent labor movement had to operate. After the successful campaign against Austria in 1866, it was possible for Bismarck to build the new political structure on a compromise between the old Prussian government and the liberal bourgeoisie as represented in the National Liberal party. But perhaps the group that best illustrates the sociological base of the new political system was the so-called "Free Conservative Union" which took the name of *Reichspartei* in the Reichstag. It was composed of those landed aristocrats who, abandoning the narrow Prussian particularism of many of their class, enthusiastically endorsed Bismarck's program, and a large number of upper bourgeois industrialists and capitalists, who were more conservative than the bourgeois members of the National Liberal party. This was the perfect amalgam of the new with the old, the economically powerful industrialists with the traditionally powerful aris-

[17] The problem of the political and social integration of the German working class is skillfully examined by Guenther Roth, *The Social Democrats in Imperial Germany. A Study in Working-Class Isolation and National Integration* (Totowa, New Jersey, 1963). Sweeping over the whole period from the sixties through World War I, Roth shows how a "Social Democratic Subculture" emerged in response to the exclusiveness of the dominant German culture and the authoritarian political system. Summarizing his fundamental thesis, Roth says: "Class cleavage pervaded Imperial Germany because the authoritarian state and the liberal bourgeoisie were unwilling to integrate the labor movement into the national community through compromises resulting in far-reaching democratization" (p. 136).

tocracy. It was also an amalgam of those groups which were most determined to rebuff the political and economic ambitions of the working class.[18]

The aspect of the new constitution that most directly affected the political development of the labor movement was the establishment of an Imperial parliament elected on the basis of universal manhood suffrage. This created both opportunities and problems for the young socialist movement. The adoption of universal suffrage was a great boon, the one decisive element that offered the working classes a chance for some political integration into German society. Despite the fact that Bismarck had introduced universal suffrage for his own tactical reasons—to balance off the strength of the bourgeois liberals with votes from the lower classes—this was an instrument that the working classes could not fail to use for their own purposes. Universal suffrage, decreed in 1867 while the working-class movement was still ill-formed, guaranteed in effect that workers would never be obligated to rely on the bourgeois liberals for entrance into politics. Here was the base on which they could develop their own political ambitions, and from 1867 a slow process took place by which the socialists—only a loose movement to that time—emerged after some agonizing decades into a parliamentary party. All of this seems so obvious that it should hardly be repeated, except that it is also so fundamental.

The particular features of the Reichstag also created problems. The system of which it was a part was not one of parliamentary responsibility, wherein the representatives of the people controlled the formation of the ministry. Germany was not a monarchy with a ministry based upon parliamentary sanction, but a constitutional monarchy that of necessity tolerated a form of popular representation as one appendage to the basic structure.[19] This is not surprising, because the German Reichstag was brought into existence by Bismarck, one of Germany's most bitter anti-parliamentarians. Bismarck had introduced universal suffrage in the hope not that it would make the Reichstag a better par-

[18] Bergstraesser, *Geschichte der politischen Parteien in Deutschland*, pp. 124–25; George W. F. Hallgarten, *Imperialismus vor 1914* (2nd ed.; Munich, 1963), I, pp. 146ff.

[19] A thesis has recently been presented that the Reichstag and the government were actually equally powerful in the balance of forces in the Imperial constitution. In view of the evidence offered by the author, this interpretation is too optimistic about the impact that the Reichstag had. Cf. Ernst Rudolf Huber, *Deutsche Verfassungsgeschichte seit 1789* (Stuttgart, 1963), III, pp. 775–77.

liamentary institution, but a worse one. Effective parliamentary influence—even within the limits of the monarchical structure—was completely incompatible with his objectives. His first goal was a parliamentary majority that would be a docile tool of his own will. But, failing that, fragmentation and instability were preferable to a solid political opposition in the Reichstag.[20]

The result, due in large part to the military strength behind Bismarck's desires and the built-in weaknesses of the liberals, was a Reichstag which did not meet the requirements of the bourgeois liberals in two respects. First, the Reichstag was too weak in relation to the other branches of the government (Monarchy, Ministry, Bundesrat), and second, the liberals would have desired a restricted suffrage. Universal suffrage undermined the strength of the bourgeois liberals even within a weakened parliament. Since German parliamentarism did not meet the requirements of the more advanced bourgeois liberals—those in the Progressive party, for example—what position could a socialist and democratic working-class movement take in respect to it?

The comparatively weak and ambiguous role of the German Reichstag contributed immensely to a problem of the socialist movement that emerged already in the late sixties—parliamentarism. It was a problem fraught with confusion and uncertainty, but one that was of the greatest importance for Social Democracy and the German working class. The approach of the Social Democrats to parliamentarism was an indicator both of their relationship to the traditions of political democracy and of the degree of their political integration into German society.

The subsequent chapters of this study are a commentary on the fact that the German workers found it impossible to integrate themselves into the traditional mainstream of their society. The rapid expansion of the Social Democratic party was an expression of that political, social, and cultural isolation. Throughout the nineteenth century, the isolation increased, but especially during the years under the Socialist Law (1878–1890), when the dominant classes of the society legalized the exclusion of a great part of the working class from the traditional soci-

[20] Interpreters of all shades of opinion have almost always agreed on the fundamental incompatibility between Bismarck and an effective parliamentarism. Cf. Gustav Adolf Rein, *Die Revolution in der Politik Bismarcks* (Goettingen, 1957), pp. 264ff.; Roth, *The Social Democrats in Imperial Germany*, pp. 59ff.; Erich Eyck, *Bismarck. Leben und Werk* (Erlenbach-Zurich, 1943), II, pp. 325–41.

ety. The German working-class movement thus matured into a self-contained and inner-directed Social Democratic party within a hostile environment.

Ferdinand Lassalle and the Socialist Movement: An Ambiguous Heritage

The intriguing story has been told many times, of Lassalle's adventurous life, of his knightly rescue of Countess Hatzfeldt's honor, of his brilliant mind and his unlimited personal ambition, and of his crucial role in crystalizing the working class into political activity. A legend emerged, stimulated by his romantic flamboyance, his personal daring, and his enormous energy, that in two short years Lassalle created the German labor movement. Perhaps the legend will never die, because it fits so snugly into the theory of the hero in history. Nevertheless, for the German workingman—even for those who were not strictly Lassalleans—the image of Lassalle was a great inspiration. He ranked as the "founding father," and the honor he received from posterity equaled that of all men in this category.[21]

Lassalle did not create the politically conscious labor movement, he simply gave it a special organizational form and a programmatic substance. That was a significant contribution, and even today those who despise his name do not fail to recognize the meaningful achievements of this paradoxical man. A fighter for the cause of the modern industrial working class, he died, not at the barricades, but in a duel for the love of a young lady, in the style of a feudal aristocrat. A remarkably able student in philosophy and law, he impatiently abandoned his study

[21] Hermann Oncken, *Lassalle. Eine politische Biographie*, 4th ed.; Stuttgart and Berlin, 1923); Eduard Bernstein, *Ferdinand Lassalle as a Social Reformer* (London, 1893), see also the later edition, *Ferdinand Lassalle. Eine Wuerdigung des Lehrers und Kaempfers* (Berlin, 1919); David Footman, *Ferdinand Lassalle. Romantic Revolutionary* (New Haven, 1947). Lassalle's honor as a "founding father" has been challenged by the scholars in the German Democratic Republic, just as his role was often condemned by the radical wing of Social Democracy in the last century. Cf. Heinz Huemmler, *Opposition Gegen Lassalle* (Berlin-East, 1963) and Hans Juergen Friederici, "Zur Einschaetzung Lassalles und des Lassalleanismus in der buergerlichen und rechtssozialdemokratischen Geschichtsschreibung," *Beitraege zur Geschichte der deutschen Arbeiterbewegung*, II (1960), pp. 294–313. On the other hand, writers in the German Federal Republic almost always approach Lassalle with more generosity. Cf. Carlo Schmid, "Ferdinand Lassalle und die Politisierung der deutschen Arbeiterbewegung," *Archiv fuer Sozialgeschichte*, III (1963), pp. 5–20, and Thilo Ramm, "Lassalle und Marx," *Marxismusstudien*, III (1960), pp. 185–221

when the opportunity for practical action appeared. A "friend" and student of Marx, he emerged nonetheless as the fountainhead of a non-Marxist current in the stream of German socialism. Nothing was clear cut in the complexity of Lassalle's intellectual or personal make-up, except, perhaps, the drive to be at the top of the greasy pole.

The record of Lassalle's valuable service to the labor movement is offset by the fact that some of his ideas and many of his tactics left an ambiguous heritage. Although he hastened the creation of an independent labor party by drawing many workers away from the bourgeois liberals, he bred the disastrous illusion that this party could at times do business with Bismarck and the feudal aristocrats. While he was himself a democrat, and focused the workers' attention on the need for universal suffrage, he fashioned a non-democratic constitution for the General Association of German Workingmen (*Allgemeiner Deutscher Arbeiterverein, ADAV*) that bestowed dictatorial powers on him as president. In almost every respect, Lassalle was himself a social and political revolutionary, but his Hegelianism, with its implicit glorification of the existing state, tempted many of his followers to compromise with the anti-democratic Bismarckian militarist state and to forget about the pressing need for its democratization. The powerful statist tradition in the Lassallean movement undermined much of its democratic thrust. Although Lassalle taught the workers to throw off the tutelage of the bourgeois liberals, to plot their own political destiny, he failed to outline more than a fragmented program of thought and action. He offered them slogans—they could not understand more, he thought—when they needed a reasoned statement of their over-all goals. No doubt, Lassalle sacrificed some things for the cause of democracy, socialism, and the working class, but his ambitious grasp for power and prestige overshadowed the nobler side. The "founding father" of the German labor movement, with his ambition to hobnob with the great and well-born, his passion for a luxurious and flashy life, and his penchant for intrigue and amorous escapades, was hardly a model for the future leaders of a democratic and socialist movement.

The revitalization of the bourgeois liberals in the last years of the 1850's offered the workers the first chance for organizational developments after the collapse of the revolution in 1849. In their emerging struggle with the absolutist system in Prussia, the bourgeois liberals wanted working-class support. In this context, it was necessary for the liberals to offer some proposals for a solution of the "social question."

The substance of the liberal formula had two aspects, neither of which envisaged the workers as political partners: Education for cultural advancement and cooperative self-help for economic improvement. To encourage education, many liberals participated in the founding of Workmen's Educational Societies (*Arbeiterbildungsvereine*), many of which sprang up in the very first years of the sixties. To foster economic improvement, the workers were exhorted to save their earnings and to organize self-help cooperatives of various kinds, for credit, production, and consumption. The cooperatives never prospered as the Workmen's Educational Societies did. In the early sixties, at the beginning of the great constitutional struggle in Prussia, these societies were the most advanced form of working-class organization.[22]

The leaders of the Workmen's Educational Societies themselves grew impatient with the condescending attitudes of the bourgeois liberals toward the aspirations of the working class. Bound to a *laissez-faire* conception of economics, the liberals in the National Society and the Progressive party rebuffed all suggestions that political intervention should be applied to reduce the misery of the working classes. Believing that property and education were reasonable prerequisites to political activity, the bourgeois liberals also rejected the idea that the Workmen's Educational Societies should be active partners in the National Society. When a deputation from the Leipzig Central Committee of the Workmen's Educational Societies presented that proposal in 1862, the leaders of the National Society replied that the workers in the society could look upon themselves as "honorary members."

The rebuff irritated the members of the Central Committee, Otto Dammer, Friedrich Wilhelm Fritzsche, and Julius Vahlteich. Frustrated in their appeals to be accepted as partners in the political work of the bourgeois liberals, they cast about for a new tactic. Some of them, such as Vahlteich, already believed that through the educational societies the workers should constitute themselves as a political movement. Others were reluctant, still accepting the liberal concept that the workers lacked the education necessary for political activity. In their search, it was natural that the Central Committee should turn to Ferdinand Lassalle, as one man who might have ideas about what course of action they could follow. Thus, on February 11, 1863, they

[22] Franz Mehring, *Geschichte der deutschen Sozialdemokratie* (8th and 9th eds.; Stuttgart, 1919), III, pp. 9–12; R. Meyer, *Der Emancipationskampf des vierten Standes* (2nd ed.; Berlin, 1882), I, pp. 197–208.

addressed a letter to Lassalle, requesting that he should express his views "upon the working-class movement, and the tactics it should pursue, and especially upon the value of the associations for the entirely unpropertied classes of the people." [23]

Lassalle jumped enthusiastically at the opportunity to influence directly the Workmen's Educational Societies and the working class in general. The appeal implied a willingness of the Central Committee to move to the left, for Lassalle was known as a radical democrat and socialist whose contempt for the bourgeois liberals was no secret. Now he was in a position to gather a popular following of workingmen, something new and exciting in his already eventful life. From February 1863 to August 1864, the greatest part of his time was taken up in some way with the labor movement and the General Association of German Workingmen, which was founded under his leadership in May 1863.

Lassalle's great impact on the German labor movement was both organizational and ideological. Sensing the disenchantment of some of the labor leaders, he pushed them into an organizational break with the bourgeois liberals. The ADAV was then organized as a working-class party, whose highly centralized structure provided the president with nearly dictatorial powers. After Lassalle died in 1864 and the presidency finally was passed to Johann Baptist von Schweitzer (1833–1875), the anti-democratic implications of this structure were the cause of much dissension. Thus, the specific organizational pattern of the ADAV was transitional, passing from the scene in 1875 when the Lassalleans merged with the Eisenachers, the other labor party that emerged in the sixties.

The ideological impact was more durable and much more responsible for creating the ambiguous Lassallean heritage. Lassalle had composed an important part of that ideology in 1862 in a speech specifically directed to workingmen. The speech was entitled, significantly, "On the Special Relationship of the Idea of the Workers' Estate to the Present Historical Epoch" (commonly known as the "Workers' Program").[24] The address had a twofold message. In conjunction with a rather extensive historical analysis of the social and economic development of Europe, Lassalle announced that the "workers' estate" had

[23] Bernstein, *Ferdinand Lassalle as a Social Reformer*, p. 120.

[24] Ferdinand Lassalle, *Gesammelte Reden und Schriften*, edited by Eduard Bernstein (Berlin, 1919), II, pp. 147–202.

now reached a point where its principles could begin to change society. Each of the dominant estates in the past, the feudal nobility and the capitalist bourgeoisie, had embodied certain concepts that had structured the nature of the state in the periods of their hegemony. In the sixties, it was the bourgeois conception of the state as a night watchman that still dominated the pattern of constitutional development. The idea of the state embodied in the workers' estate contrasted in the most drastic manner to the bourgeois conception.

The second aspect of Lassalle's message thus spelled out the concept of the state that was appropriate to the working class. From these passages arose the Lassallean cult of the state. In sharp contrast to Marx, who analyzed all states as the political instruments of class rule, and therefore as the representation of concrete material interests, Lassalle approached the problem in a truly Hegelian fashion, viewing the state at any time as the embodiment of abstract principles associated with particular dominant estates. And, in contrast to the liberal and democratic political tradition in Europe which suspected the state as a potential instrument of tyranny, Lassalle saw only the idea that the state had not yet realized its full ethical mission. The arrival of the workers' estate into historical significance brought with it the principles that would permit the state to realize its great mission, the "development of the human race to freedom." The highest ethical goals of the state would be achieved through the instrumentality of the workers because the latter were a disinherited people, with no special privileges to impose for themselves. The practical principle of the workers' estate was therefore universal suffrage, for this would bring all people into union with the state. Through the union of all individuals, the state would achieve levels of "education, power, and freedom" that the individual could never achieve on his own. This was the "true moral nature of the state" which both the feudal nobility and capitalist bourgeoisie failed to recognize. But even in the face of their failure, the state itself had striven toward these ultimate goals. With the arrival of a new historical epoch, there was no longer any doubt but that the workers' estate "would carry out its task with the greatest clarity and complete awareness of this moral nature of the state." Under the influence of this abstract principle, the state would achieve the highest ideals of all humanity.[25]

It is obvious that Lassalle reserved his highest praise for the state as it

[25] *Ibid.*, pp. 197–98.

would realize the humanitarian, ethical, and democratic principles borne by the working class. But it is also clear that he saw all of the beneficial aspects immanent, if not realized, in the state as it already existed. It was this that compromised his democratic republicanism and undermined the opposition of some of his followers to the clearly anti-democratic Bismarckian state. Lassalle wrote this speech for workers, and he had no reason to assume that they would make the sophisticated differentiations that he could make on the basis of his far superior historical and philosophical knowledge. If the glorification of the state were to be reserved strictly for the final achievements of the democratic and socialist working class, Lassalle did not make this clear. "The cult of the State as such," as Eduard Bernstein wrote years ago, "means the cult of every State, and even if Lassalle's democratic and socialistic views made it impossible for him to support directly the existing State, it did not prevent this cult from being exploited later on by the advocates of the existing State in its interest. . . . Lassalle's concept of the State is the bridge [Bernstein now alludes to Lassalle's flirtation with Bismarck and other Junkers] that was one day to bring together the Republican Lassalle and the men fighting for absolute monarchy, the Revolutionist Lassalle and the out-and-out reactionaries." [26] In truth, the Lassallean cult of the state was the most detrimental part of the ambiguous heritage.

It is difficult to understand how Lassalle, committed to political democracy from the days of his youth, could also approach the absolutist Prussian state in a mood of compromise. A satisfactory answer to the problem would demand a complete examination of his personality and his philosophy.[27] While it is clear that Lassalle did not intend to endorse unreservedly the Prussian absolutism as it existed, it is equally apparent that he had never dropped the Hegelian view of the state as the highest creation of man and history. He simply disagreed with Hegel on the issue of when and under whose guidance the state would achieve its lofty mission. For Lassalle, the high ethical values that were immanent in the state had not yet been realized, but he was equally certain that they would be. Perhaps Lassalle's personality is also cru-

[26] Bernstein, *Ferdinand Lassalle as a Social Reformer*, p. 106.

[27] Such an analysis has been provided by Shlomo Na'aman, "Lassalle—Demokratie und Sozialdemokratie," *Archiv fuer Sozialgeschichte*, III (1963), pp. 21–80. See also the discussion by Carl Landauer, *European Socialism. A History of Ideas and Movements from the Industrial Revolution to Hitler's Seizure of Power* (Berkeley and Los Angeles, 1959), I, pp. 239–50.

cial. Full of personal ambition and confidence that he could deal advantageously with the great and the powerful, he was ready both in theory and in practice to do business with the Prussian absolutism.

The revolutionary implications of the "Workers' Program" caught the attention both of the leaders in the Workmen's Educational Societies and the Prussian police, who prosecuted Lassalle for "inciting the non-possessing classes to hatred and contempt of the possessing classes." Despite the statist assumptions, Lassalle had called upon the workers to recognize that they had a role in history, and that the key was universal suffrage. For Prussia in April 1862 those were revolutionary demands. In the remaining months of the year, Lassalle threw himself into his own legal defense, using each appearance before the court as an opportunity to present a commentary on the Prussian constitutional crisis and the role of the workers. Then, in February 1863, he received the request from the Central Committee and immediately set to work drafting the "Open Reply Letter to the Central Committee for the Summoning of a General German Workers' Congress in Leipzig." Although the "Open Reply Letter" did not equal the thunderous effect of Luther's Ninety-Five Theses—as Lassalle dreamed it would—it nonetheless proved to be one of the most significant documents for the history of the German labor movement.

The "Open Reply Letter" was lucid, simple, and pugnacious. It commenced with a sharp rebuttal of the idea that workingmen had little reason to concern themselves with politics, the favored nostrum of the bourgeois liberals. On the contrary, Lassalle argued that "the working class must constitute itself as an independent political party and must make the demand for universal, equal, and direct suffrage the battle cry of the party, written on its banners. The legitimate interests of the workers can only be satisfied through working-class representation in all the legislative bodies of the German states. A peaceful propaganda for this objective, conducted with all legal means, should be the political program of the party." That was the first blow at the bourgeois liberals, but there was more to come.

Lassalle turned to demolish the liberal prescription for self-help cooperatives. The creation of such cooperatives within the capitalist system, Lassalle argued, could never benefit the workers. The reason was simple—the so-called iron law of wages. As a consequence of that law, every effort of the workers to improve their condition through self-help was doomed to failure. The iron law of wages could be broken only if the wages of the workingman were replaced by his possession of the products of labor, i.e. if the working class employed itself. But for this purpose, self-help cooperatives were inadequate, for they could never accumulate the necessary capital. If, on occasion, a self-help cooperative succeeded, the consequences would be equally regrettable, for the leading participants would assume the mentality of employers. Lassalle did not drop the cooperative idea, however, but simply modified it. Cooperatives could contribute significantly to a solution of the social question, he believed, if they were given sweeping financial support by the state. State-help should replace self-help. Thus, the cooperative system with state-help should be built on a vast scale, including not merely handicraft production (typical of the self-help cooperatives) but also factory production. This would provide the first decisive step toward the socialization of production. How could the workers push the state in this direction? Once again Lassalle came back to his key political idea, universal suffrage. If universal suffrage were achieved, then the workers would have the leverage for pressuring the government to provide state-help on a vast scale.[28]

There was much more to Lassalle's own philosophical thinking than is contained in the above summary. But the labor movement had no reason to concern itself with everything that Lassalle had written, although most of it might be relevant in some way. Within the historical context of the young socialist movement in Germany, Lassalleanism meant essentially these leading ideas: the high moral purposes of the state, the key role of universal suffrage, and the demand for cooperatives with state-help necessitated by the iron law of wages. The slogan that all classes apart from the workers formed "one reactionary mass" was not specifically initiated by Lassalle, but it was generally consistent with his program and became a popular belief among the Lassalleans. It said simply and erroneously that the bourgeois liberals and democrats were as reactionary as the Junkers.

Popularly understood, Lassalleanism could not pretend to be a total theoretical system in the manner of Marxism. Although Lassalle, unlike Marx, did not strive to rid his thought of Hegelian idealism, the two held many ideas in common. But differences on such matters as the theory of the state and the tactics of the working class became the basis for a genuine differentiation. The program that Lassalle designed in 1862–1863 was intended simply to coalesce the workers into a party,

[28] Lassalle, *Gesammelte Reden und Schriften,* III, pp. 41–92.

with specific goals for the immediate future. It was composed of easily grasped ideas around which he could rally the working class. He preferred not to trouble the workers with the over-all theory. Thus, for example, he himself did not believe that the fragmented program presented in 1863 was truly socialist or that it would necessarily lead to socialism.[29] This created problems. After Lassalle's death, most of his followers took his outline program as a kind of finished product which offered a comprehensive solution for the whole of the social question. What Lassalle had fashioned as a relatively effective program for the period of crisis in 1863 was absolutized by many of his followers. Decades passed before the idea of cooperatives with state-help lost its appeal, and his view of the state haunted the Social Democratic movement throughout the nineteenth century.

Lassalle's tactical contribution to the socialist movement was equally ambiguous. On the one hand, he encouraged the workers to enter into legal parliamentary activity in their own interests as an independent political party. Designed as a rebuff to the class-conscious and ineffective bourgeois liberals, that was a fruitful direction for the practical endeavors of the working class. On the other hand, Lassalle's own tactics were based on the assumption that he could bargain and negotiate with Bismarck and the reactionaries to the benefit of the working class. That was a contradiction of the view, implicit in his call for independent political activity, that the working class must emancipate itself. Thus, in 1863–1864, Lassalle entered into secret discussions with the Minister President of Prussia, Bismarck, notorious in those years as the unrelenting foe of the liberals and extremely doubtful as a friend of labor. This is not the place to probe the details of the contact between Lassalle and Bismarck, but simply to point out some of the heritage it left. Although the discussions were secret, the German public could not miss the fact that Lassalle glanced flirtatiously at Bismarck. The most famous case arose when the mayor and constable in Solingen dissolved a meeting at which Lassalle was speaking. Instantaneously, Lassalle sent off a telegram to Bismarck, appealing "for the severest, promptest, legal satisfaction" against the "Progressive Burgomaster." The public did not know it, but even before this famous telegram Lassalle had held his first discussions with Bismarck. By 1864 there

[29] Cf. Gustav Mayer, "Zum Verstaendnis der politischen Aktion Lassalles," *International Review for Social History*, III (1938), pp. 89–106; Landauer, *European Socialism*, I, p. 249.

were vague rumors among the leaders of the labor movement that some kind of contact between Bismarck and Lassalle existed. Even without the details, it was possible to guess that Lassalle's tactics had drawn him into associations with reactionaries.[30]

Lassalle thus left a heritage that was both full of promise and fraught with ambiguities. His concentrated campaign against the bourgeois liberals had stimulated the self-assertion of many workers, but it also mislead many Lassalleans into believing that they had to hate and reject the liberals under all conditions. Their great hatred of the bourgeois liberals, and Lassalle's own flirtations with Bismarck, created the danger that the Lassalleans would fall into transitory alliances with the real reactionaries, the feudal Junkers. This possibility was all the more attractive due to the Lassallean glorification of the state. In that way the Lassalleans often failed to recognize that, however pusillanimous and anti-labor the bourgeois liberals might be, they were still a much more progressive element within German society than the pre-industrial Junkers.

Political and Social Democracy in the Eisenacher Tradition: The "People's State"

Many workers in the Workmen's Educational Societies did not shift their membership to the Lassallean organization when it was founded in May 1863. The activities of the Workmen's Educational Societies continued much as before, especially in the middle and south German states. In June 1863, less than a month after the Lassallean party was founded, representatives of the Workmen's Educational Societies met in Frankfurt am Main, where they formed a Union of German Workmen's and Educational Societies (*Verband deutscher Arbeiter- und Bildungsvereine, VDAV*). Here, working-class members continued to work in unison with the bourgeois liberals and democrats of middle and south Germany for several years. They shared a strong Prussophobia and desired the unity of all German peoples in a federated, liberal, parliamentary state, not under the dynastic headship of any royal house. They had a deep commitment to the advanced democratic ideals

[30] On Lassalle's contacts with Bismarck, see, in addition to Gustav Mayer's *Bismarck und Lassalle, ihr Briefwechsel und ihre Gespraeche* (Berlin, 1928), Shlomo Na'aman, "Lassalles Beziehungen zu Bismarck—ihr Sinn und Zweck," *Archiv fuer Sozialgeschichte*, II (1962), pp. 55–85; Wilhelm Mommsen, "Bismarck und Lassalle," *ibid.*, III (1963), pp. 81–86.

that had emerged in the revolution of 1848. Some of the most distinguished German democrats worked in the Union, including Leopold Sonnemann and Friedrich Albert Lange. Among those from the working class, August Bebel (1840–1913) participated from the beginning and soon became one of its leading spirits. In 1865, Wilhelm Liebknecht also joined, after growing deeply suspicious that the Lassalleans, with whom he had been working, were compromising with Bismarck. Together, Liebknecht and Bebel began to reorient the Union, and thus it became the organizational base on which they founded the Social Democratic Labor party in 1869, more popularly known as the Eisenachers.[31]

The Union was not a political party, but paralleling its development the bourgeois democrats in south Germany founded a party that would work for the realization of a federation of all German peoples in a democratic, non-dynastic state. Known as the People's party (*Volkspartei*), it was accepted by most of the workers in the Union as their political mouthpiece. Thus, after Koeniggraetz, when Prussian military power was threatening to destroy all the hopes of the anti-Prussian democrats, Bebel and Liebknecht took the leadership in founding a Saxon People's party as an affiliate of the People's party. However, by that time, serious antagonisms had arisen between the bourgeois democrats and the workers, and it was only two years before they parted ways.

The fundamental cause of the ultimate split between the workers in the Union and the bourgeois democrats in the *Volkspartei* differed somewhat from the reason for the departure of the Lassalleans from the bourgeois liberals in Prussia. In the south, the bourgeois democrats had no objections to giving the workers a partnership in their party; in fact, they welcomed it. But they did object to the social demands that the workers, particularly under the leadership of Liebknecht and Bebel, wanted the People's party to endorse. Although men such as

[31] August Bebel, *Aus meinem Leben* (Stuttgart, 1911), I, pp. 81–100; Karl-Heinz Leidigkeit, *Wilhelm Liebknecht und August Bebel in der deutschen Arbeiterbewegung 1862–1869* (2nd ed.; Berlin-East, 1958), pp. 61–72. To date, neither Bebel nor Liebknecht is the subject of a scholarly and comprehensive biography. For the bibliography on Bebel, the reader may be referred to Ernst Schraepler (ed.), *August-Bebel-Bibliographie* (Duesseldorf, 1962), and a popular sketch of his life by a group of scholars in the German Democratic Republic under the direction of Horst Bartel, *August Bebel. Eine Biographie* (Berlin-East, 1963). On Liebknecht, see Edward Aveling, *Wilhelm Liebknecht and the Social-Democratic Movement in Germany* (London, [1896]), and Kurt Eisner, *Wilhelm Liebknecht. Sein Leben und Wirken* (2nd ed.; Berlin, 1906).

Lange and Sonnemann were sincerely concerned about the social question, they still represented a pure political democracy. On the other side, Bebel and Liebknecht were unquestionably devoted to the democratic political ideal, but they wanted the People's party to embrace the whole of a social program as they conceived it. They wanted the People's party to become an organ of social democracy, as well as of political democracy.

The conflict sharpened in 1868 when the Union of Workers' Societies, following the recommendation of Liebknecht and Bebel, voted to affiliate with the International Association of Workingmen, the First International. The International had been in existence only four years, but in everyone's mind it was associated with Karl Marx and working-class socialism. For most bourgeois democrats, it was much too radical, and they immediately dropped their association with the Union. It was only a matter of time until all organizational connections between the bourgeois democrats and the working-class societies would be severed.[32]

The final break came in 1869, when the Union transformed itself into the Social Democratic Labor party at its annual conference at Eisenach. The new party was founded in conjunction with a group of Lassalleans who were completely disenchanted with the dictatorial leadership of Schweitzer. In this way, the Workmen's Educational Societies took steps similar to those taken by the workers who had followed Lassalle in 1863. They were now an independent political party. They reaffirmed their affiliation with the First International, and for that reason were often referred to as Marxists. To a limited degree, in the context of the sixties, they were Marxists, for, in contrast to the Lassalleans, the Eisenachers put considerable emphasis on the international nature of the labor movement. Likewise, the International, along

[32] The best account of the development of the People's party and its relationship to the Union of Workers' Societies is still Gustav Mayer, "Die Trennung der proletarischen von der buergerlichen Demokratie in Deutschland (1863–1870)," *Archiv fuer die Geschichte des Sozialismus und der Arbeiterbewegung*, II (1912), pp. 1–67 (hereafter cited as *Gruenbergs Archiv*). Cf. also, Bebel, *Aus meinem Leben*, I, pp. 132–85; Leidigkeit, *Wilhelm Liebknecht und August Bebel*, pp. 73–152; Franz Mehring, "Aus der Fruehzeit der deutschen Arbeiterbewegung," *Gruenbergs Archiv*, I (1911), pp. 101–33. In a detailed and careful study that was not yet available as I wrote my text, Roger Morgan, *The German Social Democrats and the First International 1864–1872* (Cambridge, 1965), presents convincing evidence to challenge the idea that Liebknecht worked seriously on behalf of the International before 1868 (pp. 98–128). Nonetheless, Liebknecht had tactical reasons, arising out of his conflict with Schweitzer, for helping to bring about the adherence of the Union to the First International in September 1868 (pp. 141–44).

with Marx and Engels, expected that the economic position of the workers could be improved to a degree through the efforts of trade unions, an attitude not shared by the Lassalleans. Beyond this, however, the socialism of the Eisenachers was not distinct from that of the Lassalleans. The specific socialist content of the Eisenacher program was almost identical with that of the Lassalleans, that is, the call for "state advancement of the cooperative system and state credit for voluntary productive cooperatives with democratic guarantees." [33]

However, the roots of the Eisenachers in the political democracy of the People's party overshadowed all their other ideological sources. The Eisenachers preserved intact the political views of the People's party, although they demanded much more in the way of social reform. They continued to share the passionate hatred of the Prussian system, and even after the founding of the Reich in 1871, their hostility to the existing state was built in great part on Prussophobia.

The Eisenachers' program clearly stated that the political goal was the "Free People's State" (*Freie Volksstaat*). They understood that to mean a completely democratic state, obviously including a parliamentary system of representation. They also understood it to mean a republic. They failed to use the term "republic" simply because of the dangers this would involve within the highly charged monarchical system of their time. "People's state" was a euphemism for republic. In its subordinate parts, the program called for the following: the extension of universal, direct, and secret manhood suffrage in all elections for parliament, state diets, and municipal bodies; per diem allowances for elected representatives; the introduction of direct legislation by the people, meaning initiative and referendum; the abolition of privileges derived from class, property, birth, and confession; the establishment of a people's militia to replace the standing army; the separation of the church from the state and the school from the church; obligatory education in primary schools and free instruction in all public educational institutions; the independence of the courts and industrial courts with juries and free legal council; and, finally, the abolition of the restrictive laws on the press and association.[34]

The Eisenachers sought to differentiate themselves from both the Lassalleans and the People's party. No one was more conscious of the

[33] "Programm der Sozialdemokratischen Arbeiterpartei," reprinted in *Der Leipziger Hochverratsprozess vom Jahre 1872*, edited by Karl-Heinz Leidigkeit (Berlin, 1960), p. 525.

[34] *Ibid.*, pp. 524–25.

need for these distinctions than August Bebel, who wrote a series of articles for the *Volksstaat* (the organ of the Eisenachers) which then appeared as a pamphlet entitled *Unsere Ziele* (*Our Goals*). It deserves attention, because it was one of the most accurate statements of the Eisenachers' views and it became a very popular propaganda piece throughout the seventies.

Bebel distinguished the future "People's state" (*Volksstaat*) of the Eisenachers from that of the People's party by insisting that it would provide for the social needs of the people in addition to guaranteeing political liberty. German workers were still under the illusion, he believed, that once they had gained political liberty all their needs would be satisfied. To counter this error, Bebel leaned to the other side, insisting that "mere political liberty" was in no way sufficient for the emancipation of the working class. If political liberty were sufficient, he argued, then the workers in the United States and Switzerland (where they enjoyed such political benefits) would have nothing more to work for. That was obviously not the case, since the workers in these countries also suffered economic and social exploitation. It was true, he added, that the labor movement in a Free State (*Freistaat*) could achieve influence and make social gains more rapidly than in a "half-free or despotic state." Political liberty was therefore desirable, and possibly necessary, but chiefly as a means to the ultimate goal, the "establishment of economic equality." [35]

To distinguish the Eisenachers' endorsement of cooperatives with state-help from that of the Lassalleans, Bebel insisted that a state under the capitalist system would not introduce measures that would bring about the decline of capitalism and the class struggle. In a capitalist society, he argued, the ruling classes would set up cooperatives only when these would reenforce their own economic and political power.[36] From that it followed for Bebel—and here he was consistent with the position of Marx and the First International—that the socialization of society through cooperatives could be undertaken only when the political power of the existing ruling classes had been undermined. The acquisition of political power by the workers and the democratization of the state were preconditions for the implementation of socialist measures. Thus, the Eisenachers focused their attention on the demo-

[35] August Bebel, *Unsere Ziele. Eine Streitschrift gegen die "Demokratische Korrespondenz"* (9th ed.; Hottingen-Zurich, 1886), pp. 16–17.
[36] *Ibid.*, pp. 10–11.

cratic political principles as the immediate objectives of their party. In the Eisenachers' People's state, the social transformation would not be instituted by an alien ruling class from above, but by all the people from below. "In such a state," Bebel summarized, "self-help is people's-help, people's-help is state-help; self-help and state-help therefore are identical, there is no contradiction." [37]

Bebel did not expect the working class in Germany to acquire political power in the near future. First, the party had to undertake to "enlighten the masses" about their social and political conditions. On this educational task, Bebel put great emphasis throughout his life; it was as if he never completely dropped the assumptions of the educational societies. He did not fail to add that trade unions were also significant for the emancipation of the working class, a point that distinguished the Eisenachers from the Lassalleans, who actually discouraged the trade union movement. After the educational phase had succeeded, Bebel expected that the working class would come into political power, but whether by legal or violent means he found it impossible to predict. Only if absolutely necessary would the working class use violence.[38]

Although Lassalleans and Eisenachers both originated in the movement of bourgeois political democracy, the commitment of the Bebel-Liebknecht party to these beliefs was more pronounced, despite the emphasis of the Lassalleans on universal suffrage. The Eisenachers had none of the statist cult in their tradition, so the attraction of making bargains and deals with Bismarck did not appeal to them. Hostile to the bourgeoisie, they nonetheless recognized that the feudal aristocracy was a greater enemy to the principles of the working class. Although the Eisenachers had severed their organizational connections with the bourgeois democrats, the two groups could still communicate on the basis of a common political heritage. The democratic ideal, summed up in the "People's state," provided them with a clear and definite political program for the immediate and long-range goals of the party.

Principles and Tactics: Parliamentarism as an Issue of Socialist Politics

Two mutually hostile working-class parties, both socialist-oriented and organizationally independent of their liberal progenitors, seeking

[37] *Ibid.*, p. 15.
[38] *Ibid.*, p. 15.

to sustain themselves in an inimical environment, faced the practical problem in the late sixties of what tactical procedures corresponded to their over-all principles. To a large extent, the problem itself was in a state of flux until after the founding of the Reich in 1871. The practical work of the socialist parties had to be carried out until that time largely within the context of the North German Confederation. But, because the fundamental structure of the Confederation was transferred to the Reich, it is possible to define one of the most persistent of tactical problems as it emerged in the late sixties, and to carry over that formulation of the problem into the Reich. This was a question of what means to use to achieve their goals. This in turn resolved itself fundamentally into a problem of how to approach parliamentary practice.

Given the roots of the two working-class parties in the soil of political democracy, it was natural for each to engage in the parliamentary process as a normal part of its development. With the founding of the North German Confederation and the elections to its Reichstag on the basis of universal suffrage, these workers' movements for the first time had a chance to become parliamentary parties. This pattern began to emerge when, in 1867, Bebel won a seat to the constituent assembly of the North German Confederation as a deputy of the Saxon People's party, and, later in the same year, two Lassalleans and four candidates of the Saxon People's party won seats for the first regular legislative period.

On the surface, it appeared that participation in the Reichstag should create no difficulties, but it was not long before this became a hotly debated issue with implications for both the tactics and the principles of the working-class movement. Much of the difficulty in the late sixties arose from the fact that Liebknecht and Bebel rejected on principle the new German state. That, in turn, led them to look upon the Reichstag with considerable contempt, as the parliament of a system that violated the true national and democratic aspirations of the German people. After 1871, the Eisenachers reconciled themselves to the fact that their ideal of German unity would never be realized and therefore accepted the Reich as a *fait accompli.* On the other side, the president of the Lassalleans, Schweitzer, accepted the North German Confederation as a *fait accompli* from the beginning, and, if he did not greet the whole structure with enthusiasm, he nevertheless approached it without recriminations. Whereas Bebel and Liebknecht approached the Reichstag in a mood of alienation, distrust, and hatred, Schweitzer approached it in a mood of compromise, acceptance, and practicality.

Schweitzer's every move in the Reichstag enraged Liebknecht and Bebel, adding to their conviction that he intended to betray the working class into the hands of the reactionaries. They had some reason for suspicion because Schweitzer, like Lassalle, was a political bargainer, willing to use any parliamentary tactic to achieve some practical end. In the elections, he had led the Lassalleans into trading votes with the conservatives, and in the Reichstag he used various forms of tactical opportunism to make some minor point. To Bebel and Liebknecht it appeared that Schweitzer implicitly endorsed the policies of Germany's reactionary forces.[39]

Liebknecht and Bebel were so uncompromising in their total rejection of the new system that they accused Schweitzer of treason to the working class when he tried to introduce a Workmen's Protection Bill in the Reichstag of the North German Confederation.[40] There was absolutely nothing in the specific content of the bill that they could disagree with, but Liebknecht was particularly incensed, seeing in the introduction of such a measure a way by which Schweitzer was trying to add prestige to the Prussian-dominated state. Although some of his tactics may have been unfortunate, Schweitzer threw himself into all parliamentary discussions on the labor question with the greatest energy. In the debate on the Industrial Code *(Gewerbeordnung)*, he spoke at length on the principles of socialism. Just prior to this debate, Friedrich Engels, writing in the organ of the Saxon People's party, had appealed to the socialists to present their position on the Industrial Code from the principles presented in Marx's *Capital*. "What Engels demanded," Franz Mehring wrote decades later, "Schweitzer did word for word and in the most brilliant manner; it requires no special proof that his speech was based completely on Marx; the hastiest glance at it suffices to show this connection." [41] If Liebknecht and Bebel did not see the value of what Schweitzer did in that debate, their blindness stemmed from their conviction that everything associated with the North German Confederation had to be opposed and, probably, from

[39] Mehring, *Geschichte der deutschen Sozialdemokratie*, III, pp. 283–88; J. B. von Schweitzer, *Politische Aufsaetze und Reden*, edited by Franz Mehring (Berlin, 1912), pp. 190, 248.

[40] The bill is reprinted in "Der erste socialdemokratische Arbeiterschutzgesetzentwurf in Deutschland," *Documente des Socialismus*, I (1902), pp. 180–85.

[41] Mehring's editorial comment, in Schweitzer, *Politische Aufsaetze und Reden*, p. 306.

the fact that they had not yet studied Marx's *Capital* as well as Schweitzer had.

The intensely hostile approach of the Eisenachers to the North German Confederation thus inadvertently created the source of a current of anti-parliamentarism within the German socialist movement. Liebknecht, more than Bebel, gave expression to this original anti-parliamentarism. Although both of them condemned almost everything that Schweitzer undertook, they did not agree among themselves about the emerging issue of parliamentarism. They agreed in their contempt for the Reichstag of the North German Confederation, but Liebknecht absolutized this attitude into a general principle of anti-parliamentarism. From the beginning, the issue suffered from a lack of clarity, and Liebknecht initiated a considerable part of the confusion by his hasty, flamboyant, and categorical denunciation of all parliamentarism.

Liebknecht's furious outburst against parliamentarism came in a speech to a workers' club on May 31, 1869; immediately printed as a pamphlet and reissued many times, it played an influential role in the Social Democratic movement throughout the following decades. The focus of the speech was on tactics, but it spilled over into principles, for throughout his life Liebknecht was wont to talk majestically about principles. Simply put, Liebknecht sought to refute all arguments in defense of any socialist participation in the Reichstag of the North German Confederation. Neither gains for the workers nor propaganda value for the socialists could be expected from such participation. Out of tactical matters, considerations of principle arose. Debating and negotiating in the Reichstag, he admonished, could lead only to a "sacrifice of principles." With absolutist conceptions, Liebknecht declared that "principles are indivisible, they can either be *maintained completely or sacrificed completely*." [42] There was no middle ground. Once elected, the only honorable action for a socialist deputy was to go to the Reichstag, make a series of courageous protests, and then leave the building before his principles could be compromised. From there a deputy should go out to the masses, because "*socialism is no longer a question of theory, but simply a question of power, which, like any other question of power, cannot be decided in parliament, but only in the streets, on the battle-field.*" [43]

[42] Wilhelm Liebknecht, *On the Political Position of Social-Democracy Particularly with respect to the Reichstag* (Moscow, no date, but 1959), p. 26.
[43] *Ibid.*, p. 28.

To Bebel's mind, Liebknecht's intransigent anti-parliamentarism was much too impulsive and negative, unnecessarily cutting off the socialists from all attempts to influence legislation and from the full tactical use of the Reichstag for propaganda. No doubt Bebel detested the Bismarckian state as much as Liebknecht did, but it did not follow that the Reichstag was therefore useless to the socialists.[44] Almost from the first days of his political career, Bebel acted on the assumption that parliamentary tactics—for legislation and propaganda—constituted a fundamental policy of his party. Entering the constituent assembly in 1867, at twenty-seven, Bebel began one of the longest parliamentary careers in the history of any nation, for until his death in 1913 he failed to win a seat in only one election, 1881.

In retrospect, it seems important that Bebel's political activity began as a leader of the educational societies and as a parliamentarian. Liebknecht, on the other hand, had entered political action in the revolutions of 1848, followed by a decade in exile, and neither his past experience nor his personal sentiments prepared him for the routine of parliamentary work by 1869. Perhaps, too, the "Soldier of the Revolution"—as Liebknecht liked to be called—suffered greater disappointments at the form of German unity than did Bebel, who was separated almost a full generation from the democratic forty-eighters. By nature enthusiastic, impetuous, and impatient, Liebknecht did not adapt easily to the demands of the legislative process, although he delivered speeches in the plenary sessions with the greatest delight. By contrast, Bebel's patient, persistent, and deliberate nature meshed more smoothly with the parliamentary routine. In parliamentary debates, this self-educated wood-turner, always sensing his need for more education, would first study the questions carefully and then speak. But Liebknecht, the university-educated journalist, never insecure about his knowledge or his abilities—he was truly a talented man—would speak and then study, or not study at all. As a consequence, Bebel soon emerged as the far more effective parliamentarian of the two. Liebknecht did not follow his own anti-parliamentarian tactics, but remained in the Reichstag—even supporting Bebel's amendments to the Industrial Code in 1869—and thus added more confusion to the issue of parliamentarism.[45]

[44] Bebel's comments on Liebknecht's position, in *Aus meinem Leben*, II, pp. 163–66.

[45] *Ibid.*, pp. 158–59, 164.

Despite the inconsistency in his own actions, Liebknecht's speech expressed the underlying disgust of the Eisenachers with the "sham" Reichstag, and marked the beginning of sporadic anti-parliamentarian grumblings in the whole Social Democratic movement. In subsequent decades, however, anti-parliamentarism meant different things to different people. Liebknecht's anti-parliamentarism in 1869 grew out of his fervid commitment to the ideal of a unified Germany on the best democratic principles, something that the new Reichstag in no way embodied. Had Germany been unified on the basis of an effective parliamentary democracy, it is most unlikely that Liebknecht would have raised objections. Later, in the seventies and particularly in the eighties, anti-parliamentarism came to have very different meanings, although its spokesmen often quoted Liebknecht as a source. On the tactical level, anti-parliamentarism expressed the conviction of some that direct revolutionary action offered the only honorable course for the Social Democrats. On the level of principles, anti-parliamentarism often implied a rejection of the whole democratic tradition as it had been proclaimed by the People's party and the Eisenachers. When this was implied, it was clear that the Social Democratic party was shifting its political convictions, and this, in part, is the story of the eighties. In still another way, the anarchists used anti-parliamentarism as a means by which to undermine the prestige of the Social Democratic leaders with the rank-and-file. In sum, by the 1880's, there were few among the Social Democrats who were anti-parliamentarians for the same reasons as Liebknecht in 1869.

To summarize, the economic and political dynamics at work in Germany had shaped the initial features of the labor movement. The combination of industrialization and political unification taking place at the same time created conflicting pressures on the new working-class movement. On the other hand, the social and political exclusiveness of the landed aristocracy and the upper bourgeoisie, in conjunction with the political weakness of the bourgeois liberals, forced the working class into a self-conscious isolation and quite naturally toward independent political activity. As the working-class organizations peeled off from the main body of bourgeois liberals and democrats, first in 1863 and then in 1868–1869, the social-political fissure became permanent and thus created a basis for an enlarged working-class activity. On the other hand, the problem of German unification had created a divisive dynamic that subsided only with the formation of the Reich in

1871. After that ideological disagreements and personal hostilities continued to feed the conflict between Lassalleans and Eisenachers for several years. The formation of the German state created serious tactical problems, especially for the Eisenachers. Rooted in the democratic tradition, their ideal was a parliamentary democracy with a strong social program, and thus they condemned the German Reich in principle. But Bismarck had included universal suffrage in the new constitution, and this offered the opportunity for parliamentary politics but it also gave rise to the confused and hazy issue of parliamentarism. The formative period of the sixties had thus defined the initial organizational structure, the ideological tendencies and an underlying question of tactics. It was the work of the seventies to overcome many of the divisive elements and to probe the questions of principles and tactics.

CHAPTER II · THE MATURATION OF THE SOCIALIST MOVEMENT IN THE EIGHTEEN-SEVENTIES

THE EVENTS of 1870–1871—the Franco-Prussian War, the final unification of Germany, and the Paris Commune—confronted the young socialist movements with major crises and produced conditions that transformed their outlooks and organizations. The outbreak of the Franco-Prussian War in July 1870, with Prussia's annexationist intentions blatantly obvious after September, compelled the two socialist groups to clarify their relationship both to wars of acquisition and to the Prussian-created Reich. Before the war ended, an amazing degree of unanimity on both these issues was reached by the Lassalleans and Eisenachers. At the same time, the unification of 1871 destroyed the last hopes of bourgeois democrats and Eisenachers that a democratic federation of all Germans could be achieved. With that stroke, the Eisenachers had no alternative but to accept in practice the new state as a *fait accompli*, and thus the unification of Germany created the political framework for the unification of the labor movement. Finally, the appearance of the Commune in Paris, spreading a wild fear of the red specter throughout Europe, offered the German socialists an opportunity to avow their own revolutionary commitment by identifying their cause with that of the communards. When both Lassalleans and Eisenachers embraced the communards as their brothers in the international struggle of the working class, the image of the socialists in Germany acquired new colors and contours, dotted with suggestions of screaming mobs, rising barricades, and burning buildings. The upheaval of 1870–1871 thus created the objective-political and subjective-ideological conditions that favored a merger of the two socialist parties. The same cluster of events intensified the alienation of the socialist-oriented workers from the dominant social-political system and quickened the desire of the masters of the new state to root out the evil that had beset German society. The fruition of 1870–1871 came in 1875, with the unification of the Lassalleans and Eisenachers, and in 1878, with the official suppression of the Social Democratic movement by means of the Socialist Law.

The Quest for Revolutionary Identity and Organizational Unity

It was by no means clear when the Franco-Prussian War broke out in July 1870 that the ensuing events would cultivate the ground for a closer cooperation between the Eisenachers and Lassalleans. Although everyone in Europe believed that Prussia was the innocent party, Bebel and Liebknecht, motivated by their Prussophobia, abstained from voting in the Reichstag when Bismarck requested war credits. They would not give Bismarck a vote of confidence in any form. On the other hand, the two Lassallean deputies, Schweitzer and Wilhelm Hasenclever, readily cast their votes for the credits, and thus the disagreements between the two groups seemed to persist. But the situation changed very rapidly after Napoleon III's Empire collapsed in September and the bourgeois liberals in Paris proclaimed a republic. The defensive objectives of Prussia had been achieved, but the war continued, and all the signs indicated that the ultimate objective was annexation of some French territory. Thus, when Bismarck requested further credits at the end of November, Schweitzer and Hasenclever firmly endorsed a Bebel-Liebknecht resolution calling upon the Reichstag to refuse the credits and to compel Bismarck to renounce all annexationist intentions. It was a momentous step for the socialists. As one body they courageously declared their fundamental hostility to the policies of Bismarck at a time when he stood at the peak of popularity, as the German people screamed delightedly at the prospect of great military victories and political unity.

The wrath of the Prussian government turned immediately against the socialists, but especially against Bebel and Liebknecht, who from the beginning had made no secret of their intentions to thwart the aims of Bismarck. Certainly they posed no real threat to Bismarck in 1870–1871. Nonetheless, for their bitter political criticisms, the Prussian government initiated legal proceedings against them—along with Adolf Hepner, an assistant on the *Volksstaat*—on the charge that they had made "preparations for high treason." In the following months the members of the Eisenachers' Central Committee were tried and sentenced to several months in prison on charges of violating the laws of association.[1] Soon after that Lassalleans received the same treatment.

The prosecution of Liebknecht, Bebel, and Hepner, because of the high treason charge, captured the center of attention among the socialists. But before their trial took place before the Court of Assizes, March 11–26, 1872, the Commune rose and fell in Paris (March 18—end of May 1871). No other event since 1848 was so significant for the European socialist movement in the nineteenth century as the cataclysmic life of the Commune. Almost instantaneously it leapt forward as the issue that divided the most radical revolutionary reds from all other liberal and radical groups, for, a simple word spoken in sympathy for the communards sufficed to make one a dangerous revolutionary in the eyes of most. For most Europeans, the Commune appeared as an outrageous episode of terror, destruction, and disorder; but, for its sympathizers, it inspired visions of heroic struggles against bourgeois exploiters and political tyranny in the cause of freedom, justice, and socialism. Through Marx's interpretation, the Commune emerged as a potent ideological factor, as a beginning of the proletarian revolution, and as an incomplete model of a socialist society harboring profound lessons for the future of the working-class socialism.

Enthusiastic expressions of support for the Commune were heard throughout Germany from the Eisenachers and the Lassalleans, but Bebel's passionate defense in the Reichstag made the most lasting impression. At the time, Bebel was the only socialist-oriented deputy in the Reichstag, for, in the midst of the nationalist fervor in the elections of March 1871, the two parties did badly. On May 25, as the communards waged their last tragic battles, Bebel praised the Commune, as he had on previous occasions. "Gentlemen," Bebel warned, "even if the efforts of the Commune in your eyes are so reprehensible or . . . insane, you may be convinced that the whole European proletariat and everyone who still loves freedom and independence looks to Paris. Gentlemen, if in this moment Paris is suppressed, then remember this much, that the struggle in Paris is only a minor outpost skirmish, that the great issue in Europe is still before us and that before a few years pass the battle cry of the Paris proletariat 'War on the Pal-

[1] These above events are covered in some detail in Bebel, *Aus meinem Leben*, II, pp. 178–213; Mehring, *Geschichte der deutschen Sozialdemokratie*, IV, pp. 5–25.

aces, Peace for the Cottages, Death to misery and laziness!' will become the battle cry of the whole European proletariat." [2] Socialists throughout Germany echoed Bebel's pugnacious sentiments. They blended their hostility to the annexationist war with the desperate struggle of the communards and in this way sharpened the sense of their own revolutionary role. In their own eyes, and in the eyes of their countrymen, they too were dangerous revolutionaries.[3]

The identification with a revolutionary tradition intensified when the Leipzig court sentenced Bebel and Liebknecht to two-year prison terms in 1872. The trial had lasted for two weeks, long by the practice of the day, and the prosecution had entered almost everything in the history of the Eisenachers as evidence against the defendents—party programs, articles, poems, and their connections with Karl Marx.[4] By the time Bebel and Liebknecht went off to the Hubertusburg Castle, confined under "honorable custody," to serve their time, the socialists had a lively awareness of their revolutionary commitments and of their role as the pariahs of German society.

In nearly every way the events of the early seventies encouraged the cause of socialist unity. A personal reason for antagonism vanished in 1871 when Schweitzer, facing harsh opposition from within his own organization and failing to win a Reichstag seat in March, resigned as president of the Lassallean party in July and then severed all of his connections. Internal tranquility never returned to the Lassalleans, suggesting to many of them that union with the Eisenachers would be advantageous. Then, in 1874, the Prussian government unleashed a barrage of prosecutions against the Lassalleans, culminating in the dissolution of the whole party organization in June. Faced with these persecutions—Liebknecht and Bebel were still in "honorable custody" —the old antagonisms lost meaning. Already in February 1874, shortly after the elections had returned three Lassalleans and seven Eisenachers to the Reichstag, the two groups merged to form one parliamentary *Fraktion.* In every way the groundwork for unity had been built.[5]

[2] Germany, Reichstag. *Stenographische Berichte ueber die Verhandlungen des Deutschen Reichstages.* I Legislative Period, i Session (1871), vol. II, p. 921. Hereafter these debates will be cited as *SB* with the legislative periods in upper-case Roman numerals and the sessions in lower-case Roman numerals.

[3] For the details of the response to the Commune, see Hans Juergen Friederici and Jutta Seidel, "Der Widerhall der Pariser Kommune in der deutschen Arbeiterbewegung," *Beitraege zur Geschichte der deutschen Arbeiterbewegung,* III (1961), pp. 280–98.

[4] *Der Leipziger Hochverratsprozess vom Jahre 1872, passim.*

[5] Erich Kundel, *Marx und Engels im Kampf um die revolutionaere Arbeiterein-*

The Gotha Program as a Synthesis of Traditional Social Democratic Ideas

The organizational merger of the Lassalleans and Eisenachers, achieved at the Gotha congress in May 22–27, 1875, grew out of two preliminary conferences in December 1874 and February 14–15, 1875. Unification faced some obstacles, but the strong sentiment in favor of close cooperation had grown so vigorously that it overrode all difficulties with amazing ease. This sentiment had been at work throughout 1874, and thus, when representatives of the two parties met in February 1875 to write a preliminary draft of a unified party program, serious frictions did not come to the surface. When one recalls the heritage of bitter rivalry, the comparative ease with which an acceptable program was written emerges as an important fact in an evaluation of the Gotha program. In light of the fact that Marx and Engels expressed such bitter contempt for the program but that it nevertheless served as the official ideological guideline for the Social Democratic party until 1891, some careful evaluation is necessary.[6]

Despite arguments to the contrary, it is clear that the Gotha program reflected rather accurately the ideological outlook of the unified party and that it contained very few ideas that either side found intensely obnoxious. At the program discussions in February, each party was well represented: for the Eisenachers Liebknecht, Julius Motteler, Julius Vahlteich, August Geib, Ignaz Auer, and Eduard Bernstein; and for the Lassalleans Hasenclever, Wilhelm Hasselmann, Klaus Reinders, Georg Hartmann, and the brothers August and Otto Kapell. Obviously, each side had to make some concessions, but the charge by Marx and Engels that the Lassalleans dominated and won more than the Eisenachers is too sweeping. The Lassalleans' organizational pattern was completely dropped, and on all ideological matters the Eisenachers had an equal voice.[7]

heit. Zur Geschichte des Gothaer Vereinigungskongresses von 1875 (Berlin-East, 1962), offers a detailed, if one-sided, account of the unity movement.

[6] Mehring, *Geschichte der deutschen Sozialdemokratie*, IV, pp. 83–88; Eduard Bernstein, "Zur Vorgeschichte des Gothaer Programms," *Die Neue Zeit*, vol. XV, part I (1896/97), pp. 466–72.

[7] Kundel, *Marx und Engels im Kampf um die revolutionaere Arbeitereinheit*, pp. 127–33. Kundel has also argued (pp. 308–09) that the Eisenachers were much closer to Marxism by 1875 than has often been recognized, and that they were theoretically much more advanced than the Lassalleans. While there is specific

In the Gotha program, the socialists in fact synthesized—perhaps rather awkwardly—the traditional political and economic ideas of the working-class movement in Germany. As Marx and Engels correctly complained, the program contained many Lassallean ideas, but that stemmed in great part from the fact that the Eisenachers had drawn many of their conceptions from Lassalle. The slightest examination of the contents of the Gotha program reveals immediately that it contained nothing which had not already become part of the traditional attitudes of the working-class movement. Thus, all the political points harmonized completely with the 1869 program of the Eisenachers, especially the statement that the new party aimed for the "free State," which meant essentially the same thing as the "free people's State." The other political demands came directly from the ideas of the bourgeois democrats in the People's party and the Eisenachers. The program simply reaffirmed the new party's loyalty to the principles of political democracy.

The economic aspects of the program had the mark of Lassalle, and it is clear that, although some of the Eisenachers expressed their objections, they did not press the issue for fear that the cause of unity would be shattered. Thus, the Eisenachers' program had called for cooperatives with state-help under democratic control, but Wilhelm Bracke had already attacked that idea in a pamphlet of 1873 and called instead for the Eisenachers to put more stress on trade unions. He had necessarily combined this suggestion with a criticism of Lassalle's conception of the iron law of wages and its consequences. Bebel too had changed his mind, writing in the preface to the fourth edition of *Unsere Ziele* in 1872 that he no longer advocated cooperatives with state-help. Bracke and Bebel made no secret of their objections to these Lassallean ideas, but at the same time they too wanted unity and did not initiate a vigorous campaign against the program.[8]

It has usually been assumed that Marx's famous *Critique of the Gotha Program* (composed in March–April 1875) exerted no influence on the Social Democrats until Engels first published it in the *Neue Zeit* in 1891 because in 1875 Liebknecht had returned it to London without using it as a guide to modify the draft of the Gotha program

evidence to support this conclusion, if limited to certain individuals, it can not be taken to mean that the Eisenachers had actually dropped their adherence to many of the Lassallean ideas about specific socialist measures.

[8] *Ibid.*, pp. 159–60, 224–28, 250–56.

and without showing it to Bebel.[9] This assumption is only partially correct. It is true that in 1875 only Liebknecht and Bracke could have read the *Critique* before it was returned to Marx, and also that neither studied the *Critique* seriously or attempted to use it in their future expositions of socialism. But the fact has been overlooked that although Bebel did not see the *Critique* in 1875, he did receive a long letter from Engels at the end of March that contained many of the same ideas found in Marx's glosses. Furthermore, it is clear that the letter to Bebel was written while Marx and Engels were jointly discussing their criticisms of the Gotha draft. They first saw the proposed Gotha program when they received the March 7th issue of the *Volksstaat*, containing a verbatim reprint. Immediately they set to work composing their criticisms of the new program, and the result was, first, Engels' letter to Bebel, completed by March 18 but not sent until the 28th because Bebel could not leave prison until April 1, and Marx's *Critique*, which was sent on May 5 to Bracke, who was requested to pass it on to Liebknecht, August Geib, Ignaz Auer, and Bebel. When Bebel received the letter from Engels, he studied it carefully for possible future use, but not for making demands for immediate changes in the program draft; when Liebknecht received the *Critique* from Bracke he put it out of circulation, although he did not completely forget about it.[10]

Two problems thus arise. Why did Liebknecht put the *Critique* out of circulation without showing it to the others—Bebel, Geib, and Auer? Second, what did Bebel do with the letter from Engels, and what influence did it exert on his thinking?

Both practical and ideological reasons account for Liebknecht's refusal to make use of Marx's *Critique* early in May 1875, just two weeks before the opening of the conference that would climax all endeavors for unity. The practical considerations are quite clear. Liebknecht had put considerable energy and enormous enthusiasm into the preparatory work for unification, and even in later years he looked upon this as a major achievement. Although the sentiment in both parties favored unification, experience had shown that the Lassalleans had to be ac-

[9] See, for example, Peter Gay, *The Dilemma of Democratic Socialism: Eduard Bernstein's Challenge to Marx* (New York, 1952), p. 37; Roth, *The Social Democrats in Imperial Germany*, p. 57.

[10] Kundel, *Marx und Engels im Kampf um die revolutionaere Arbeitereinheit*, pp. 137–39; Bebel, *Aus meinem Leben*, II, pp. 316–24, 329; Gustav Mayer, *Friedrich Engels. Eine Biographie* (The Hague, 1934), II, pp. 274–78.

cepted as honorable brothers, without personal recriminations or intransigent ideological objections. Under these circumstances, Liebknecht believed that the proposed program was the best that could be achieved, as he wrote to Engels on April 21 (before receiving the *Critique*) that it was a choice between "this program or no unification." Thus, as a practical matter, when Liebknecht read the bitter attacks on the Lassalleans in the *Critique* he knew that its public use or endorsement by the Eisenachers would almost certainly cripple the move for unity. In fact, as late as 1891, when the personal influence of the old Lassalleans had been destroyed in the party, Bebel still complained privately to Engels that it would have been better if the "violent invectives against Lassalle" had been omitted from the *Critique* because many would believe that they stemmed from "personal hatred and jealousy" on the part of Marx and Engels. If this was so clear to Bebel in 1891, how much more striking must it have been to Liebknecht in 1875? In the practical cause of unity, Liebknecht had one reason to keep the *Critique* out of circulation.[11]

The evidence for Liebknecht's ideological objections to the *Critique* is not so clear, but they may be interpolated from what is known about his political beliefs. That Liebknecht took serious exception to Marx's criticisms of the Lassallean economic ideas may be doubted. There is no evidence from Liebknecht's previous speeches and writings that he had committed himself to the Lassallean social program, although he no doubt accepted, as did most of the Eisenachers, the call for cooperatives with state-help. But Liebknecht was sufficiently hostile to everything specifically connected with Lassalle to have rejected these ideas on personal grounds, without even probing their theoretical shortcomings.

What Liebknecht must have found disturbing, however, were the sweeping attacks that Marx launched against the political ideals in which all Eisenachers had believed from their earliest days in the People's party. Liebknecht's whole career had been devoted to the ideals of political democracy as well as to socialism. The Eisenachers' goal, as expressed in the "*freie Volksstaat*" (note that their newspaper was also called the *Volksstaat*), was a democratic republic, as Bebel and Lieb-

[11] Liebknecht's letter of April 21, 1875, quoted in Kundel, *Marx und Engels im Kampf um die revolutionaere Arbeitereinheit*, pp. 138–39. Bebel expressed his sentiments in a letter to Engels on Jan. 21, 1891, in Werner Blumenberg (ed.), *August Bebels Briefwechsel mit Friedrich Engels* (The Hague, 1965), pp. 406–07 (hereafter cited as Bebel, *Briefwechsel*).

knecht affirmed under cross-examination in the Leipzig trial. There had been nothing in Liebknecht's intellectual or political background to raise doubts in his mind about the complete appropriateness of the ideal of the "People's state" for a socialist society. But now Marx offered criticisms of almost everything that the Eisenachers believed in, for Marx denounced not merely the Lassallean points, but just as vigorously the endorsement of political democracy. In a crucial passage, Marx observed that the program's "political demands contain nothing beyond the old democratic litany familiar to all: Universal suffrage, direct legislation, popular rights, a people's militia, etc. They are a mere echo of the bourgeois People's party, of the League of Peace and Freedom. They are all demands which, insofar as they are not exaggerated in fantastic presentation, have already been *realized.* Only the state to which they belong does not lie within the borders of the German Empire, but in Switzerland, the United States, etc. This sort of 'state of the future' is a present-day state, although existing outside the 'framework' of the German Empire." [12]

According to Marx's criticism, the program confused the whole question of socialism's final goals, for it tacitly implied that the party sought nothing more than the achievement of a democratic republic. Marx did not deny that the socialists had to aim for the democratic republic, but only as a transitional stage to the communist society. Thus, his attack on the "old democratic litany" had been preceded by an explanation of the nature of the whole transitional period: "Between capitalist and communist society lies the period of the revolutionary transformation of the one into the other. There corresponds to this also a political transition period in which the state can be nothing but *the revolutionary dictatorship of the proletariat.*" And finally, in the same context, Marx argued that as long as the socialists were unwilling to state openly that they aimed for the democratic republic—which he admitted would not be wise under the circumstances—then they should not have made demands that were only "appropriate in a *democratic republic.*" By making these demands of the existing state, they had erroneously implied that genuine democratic features could be realized within the framework of the German Empire.[13]

The meaning and purpose of Marx's criticism of the "old democratic

[12] Karl Marx, *Critique of the Gotha Program,* in Karl Marx and Friedrich Engels, *Selected Works in Two Volumes* (Moscow, 1955), II, p. 33.
[13] *Ibid.,* pp. 32–33.

litany" is quite clear, and there is no reason to assume, as has sometimes been implied, that Liebknecht dropped the *Critique* simply because he could not understand it.[14] On the contrary, there is more reason to believe that Liebknecht understood the meaning and the implications of Marx's exposition and disagreed with significant parts of it. Given everything we know about Liebknecht, before and after 1875, it seems unlikely that he ever believed that the "democratic republic" would be only the "last form of state of bourgeois society" and therefore only a transitional goal of the socialists. In fact, Liebknecht and every other Eisenacher assumed that the final political goal of the socialist movement was a democratic republic, or, as their euphemism had it, a "People's state." They saw no reason why the "People's state" could not implement the full measure of socialist objectives for which they struggled. No doubt this indicates, as others have said, that in 1875 Liebknecht was far from being a Marxist, but it does not mean that he capriciously rejected Marx's advice. He often sought advice genuinely, but he reserved the right to disagree. Had Liebknecht agreed with everything contained in the *Critique*, it would still have required a sweeping ideological reorientation of the socialist movement to have brought the program in line with the wishes of Marx and Engels. For Liebknecht, it was sufficient if a program reflected the political and economic goals generally accepted by the party members; for Marx, a program could stand ahead of the generally accepted ideas, as a guideline for intellectual developments, even if only partially understood. In the circumstances of 1875, it no doubt seemed to Liebknecht much wiser to fashion the program from ideas that were already accepted in the socialist movement as a whole.

With regard to the second problem raised above—Bebel's response to Engels' letter of March 18–28, 1875—it becomes clear that Bebel was no better prepared than Liebknecht to absorb and adjust to the political criticisms of Marx and Engels. Along with many points similar to those in the *Critique*, Engels scornfully lampooned the "heap of rather confused *purely democratic demands*" which, he assumed, the Eisenachers had included in the program to counter the Lassallean ideas. In the heart of his criticism, Engels directed his Marxist analysis at the idea of the "free state," with the recommendation that all talk

[14] See, for example, Franz Mehring, *Karl Marx: The Story of his Life* (Ann Arbor, 1962), p. 509, who says that the intellectual content of the *Critique* soared over the heads of all the Eisenachers.

about the "state," the "people's state," or the "free state" be dropped from socialist programs.[15] This he built on the analysis that political structures are the instruments of class rule. One of the crucial passages explained this to Bebel. "As, therefore, the state is only a transitional institution which is used in the struggle, in the revolution, in order to hold down one's adversaries by force, it is pure nonsense to talk of a free people's state: so long as the proletariat still *uses* the state, it does not use it in the interests of freedom but in order to hold down its adversaries, and as soon as it becomes possible to speak of freedom the state as such ceases to exist. We would therefore propose to replace *state* everywhere by 'community' [*Gemeinwesen*] a good old German word which can very well represent the French word '*commune*.' "[16] If Engels' exposition very neatly encapsuled the Marxist theory of the state, it also struck at the very heart of the Eisenachers' political traditions. Precisely as in the *Critique*, Engels asked them to dump their commitment to the "People's state" as a final goal of their socialist movement, and thus to re-think the whole matter of immediate, intermediate, and final goals. Beyond that, with his reference to the Commune, he had given a specific suggestion about what would be appropriate as a slogan or phrase to define the final goal. The letter that Engels wrote is thus almost as full of meaning as Marx's *Critique*, and Bebel's response to it was also significant for the ideological development of the Social Democratic movement in Germany.

Bebel did not seek to alter the proposed program to correspond with Engels' suggestion, in part because he had many personal obligations, having just left prison on April 1, and also because, as he said, "the unification was also dear to me" and he hoped that the "errors" could be repaired later.[17] He might have added that some of the ideas in Engels' letter were foreign to him, not the prescriptions against Lassalleanism, but the criticism of the "People's state" as a socialist goal. Bebel did not dismiss the arguments that Engels had presented, but in some measure tried to incorporate them into his own thought. He could understand that Engels had offered a theoretical framework that would provide the reasons for shedding the political democracy of the People's party and would present concepts and ideals to give democracy a more appropriate meaning for the socialist movement. Like Marx, Engels made it

[15] Friedrich Engels to Bebel, March 18–28, 1875, in Marx and Engels, *Selected Works*, II, pp. 41–42.
[16] *Ibid.*, p. 42.
[17] Bebel, *Aus meinem Leben*, II, p. 324.

amply clear that for socialists a democratic republic could only be a transitional or intermediary goal on the road to the final socialist society. These distinctions had to be clear, Marx and Engels believed, if the socialists were ever to achieve an ideological foundation that would distinguish them from the bourgeois democrats and guide them in their role as the leaders of the working class.

Two tasks were involved in Engels' recommendations, one negative the other positive. On the negative side, the easier of the two to implement, the task was simply to omit all reference to the "People's state" as the political goal of socialism. There were two reasons for this, first, socialism would have no use for the state in any form, and, second, the "People's state" embodied the aims of the bourgeois democrats and therefore it could be only a transitional state. On the positive side, Engels advised that instead of "People's state," the socialists think in terms of the Commune as the final goal, because it had embodied several essentials—it had not been a state, it had a working-class character, and it had embarked on a socialist course.

It is obvious that Bebel paid close attention to Engels' suggestions, and that in the following years he made some efforts to incorporate them into his own thinking.[18] Thus he used the term "People's state" less frequently, although in the first edition of *Die Frau und der Sozialismus* (1879) he employed it almost precisely as he had ten years earlier in *Unsere Ziele*.[19] In later editions, however, he dropped all reference to the "People's state," and one can hardly find it mentioned in any of his other speeches and writings.

The ease with which Bebel shed the traditional cloak of the "People's state" contrasts to the difficulties encountered in tailoring a new garment from the materials offered by the Commune. The obstacles that arose were both practical and theoretical. As a practical matter, Engels realized that in 1875 Bebel and his comrades, living in a monarchical authoritarian state, could not embrace the Paris Commune as the model of their own goals without bringing down upon themselves the harshest retribution. The defenders of law and order, the courts and the police, would never understand the great ideals in the Commune, but only the specter of bloody barricades and belligerent masses. In Germany, even the open espousal of the democratic republic would

[18] In a letter to Engels of September 21, 1875, Bebel said that he agreed with the criticisms, but did not indicate that he had yet thought through the political recommendations. *Ibid.*, pp. 334–36.

[19] August Bebel, *Die Frau und der Sozialismus* (Hottingen-Zurich, 1879), p. 106.

have invited bitter retaliation, and, as Marx had agreed, the socialists had no need to create more dangers for their movement than already existed.[20] In the same spirit, Engels had suggested that, rather than using the term "Commune," the socialist cause could be well served by the completely harmless concept of *Gemeinwesen* (community), which he thought of as an adequate equivalent.

In view of later developments, one cannot avoid the conclusion that this cautious approach, necessitated by the overwhelming power and burning hostility of the authoritarian Reich, negatively influenced the ideological development of the Social Democratic movement. Open and free discussion among the socialists of their possible ultimate goals was obstructed when they feared that this would invite brutal police retaliation that might endanger the life of the movement. Thus, they had used the more neutral "People's state" when they meant "democratic republic." Now in 1875 Engels offered *Gemeinwesen* for "Commune," and this created a problem. Grammatically the two terms may have been equivalent, but historically and politically they were by no means the same. *Gemeinwesen* had none of the revolutionary and socialist connotations commonly associated with "Commune"; by comparison it was not only harmless but vague and insipid. It could inspire neither anxious fears in the hearts of the propertied classes nor revolutionary fervor in the souls of the socialist-oriented workers. It is not surprising that Bebel made little use of *Gemeinwesen* and that it did not become the slogan of the socialist movement. On the other hand, Bebel continued to praise the Paris Commune after 1875, and in 1876 wrote of the "Commune" adding the term *Gemeinde*, i.e. community, in parentheses—as the basic unit of a future socialist society. Later, in the second edition of *Die Frau und der Sozialismus* (1883) he dropped "People's state," but only hinted at the idea of the Commune.[21] The fact is that Bebel's efforts were not sufficient to give the Social Democrats a comprehensive understanding of what was in-

[20] At the founding congress of the Eisenachers in 1869, Liebknecht and others specifically endorsed the "democratic republic" but also advised that it not be used in the program because of the dangers it would create. *Protokoll ueber die Verhandlungen des Allgemeinen Deutschen Sozialdemokratischen Arbeiterkongresses zu Eisenach am 7., 8. und 9. August 1869*, reprinted in *Der Leipziger Hochverratsprozess*, pp. 468–69.

[21] The second edition carried the title, *Die Frau in der Vergangenheit, Gegenwart und Zukunft* (Zurich, 1883); see pp. 178–79. His earlier use of "Commune" is in *Die parlamentarische Taetigkeit des deutschen Reichstages und der Landtage und die Sozialdemokratie von 1874 bis 1876*, reprinted as Part II of *Die Sozialdemokratie im deutschen Reichstage* (Berlin, 1907), p. 157.

volved if the Commune were introduced as the final goal of the movement. But the meaning of this relates to the late eighties and not to the middle seventies.

As of 1875, the large issues embodied in the criticisms of Marx and Engels had no immediate impact on the writing of the Gotha program or on the ideological tendencies of the socialist movement. The party thus adopted a program that was a rather clumsy synthesis of the traditional ideas of the Lassalleans and the Eisenachers. The delegates left the congress with the unchallenged certainty that socialists had to struggle for the achievement of a "free state," or, more specifically, a democratic republic based on a parliamentary system with universal suffrage controlled by initiative and referendum. On this basis, they looked forward to fashioning a practical parliamentary tactic for their deputies in the Reichstag and to the possibility that socialists would soon hold seats in many state diets and municipal councils.

Certain about their political objectives, the Social Democrats had less confidence in their economic program. Although many Lassallean ideas had been included, they had been challenged by Eisenachers in the past (by Bracke and Bebel specifically), and the delegates were aware in 1875 that the trade unions had a more important role to play in the emancipation of the working class than the Lassalleans had recognized in the sixties. In many ways, the Lassallean ideas about the economics of socialism had already lost their dynamism by 1875, and this left the arena open for further ideological combat. Such were the ideological highlights of the remaining period before the Socialist Law dropped unmercifully on the Social Democrats in 1878—full of conviction about their demand for a parliamentary democratic republic, but lacking in knowledge, certainty, and confidence in the economic aspects of socialism.

Unity between Social Democratic Theory and Practice in Politics

If, in the seventies, the Social Democrats were still comparatively weak in theory—Marxist or any other—their Gotha program nonetheless had the virtue that for the party members its goals related directly to their practical politics. In the context of the authoritarian Reich, the political goals of the Social Democrats were truly revolutionary, for the democratic make-up of the ideal "free state" was incompatible with both the political structure and the social base of the German state. It did not follow from this that the Social Democrats had to pursue their goals by illegal or violent means, commonly thought of as the ingredients of a revolutionary tactic. On the contrary, given the fact that the Social Democrats envisaged a democratic republic or, in another way, a parliamentary democracy, it was entirely consistent that they should pursue this goal through the parliamentary and legal means offered to them in the Reichstag, the state diets, and municipal councils. Although some dissenting voices were heard from within the party, the great majority accepted the assumption that Social Democracy stood for parliamentarism both in theory and practice. They could not in principle accept what passed for parliamentarism in Germany, because in their view the Reichstag was a sham, but they intended to use it both for agitation and for influencing legislation. They often adopted a posture of intransigent opposition in the Reichstag, but just as often they pursued positive legislative goals on such issues as the political democratization of the Reich and the social-economic improvement of the working class.

The parliamentary tactic, however, made up only one part of the practical activity of the Social Democrats. Equally important in their over-all plan were the tasks of strengthening, extending, and tightening the party organization and its affiliates. By its traditionalist and conciliatory nature, the Gotha program served the Social Democrats well as they sought to build a solid organizational base for the political ambitions of the working class.

Almost immediately, however, the German government initiated policies to obstruct the organizational development of the Social Democrats. In the fall of 1875, the government presented the Reichstag with a bill, aimed obliquely at the Social Democrats, calling for a tighter version of the Penal Code's prescriptions against inciting the classes of society against each other or attacking the institutions of marriage, family, and property (Article 130). When the Reichstag refused to pass the government bill early in 1876, the Prussian state dissolved by legal process the Social Democratic party on the ground that its organization violated the 1850 law of associations. Unable to constitute themselves as a legal organization in the largest and most powerful state of the Reich, the Social Democrats had to modify the official structure of the party. Henceforth, the party no longer had an official Central Executive elected by the congresses, but only a Central Election Committee, seated in Hamburg and elected by the Social Democrats in that area. Officially, this Central Election Committee had no connections with the other local organizations, but in fact it had greater power over party policy than the former Executive Committee. To circumvent legal restrictions further, the congresses of the party were recorded merely as general meetings of socialists, with no official connections with the local organizations.[22]

Although the hostile policy of the Prussian government obstructed the efficiency of the Social Democratic organization, it could not impede the momentum that unification had stimulated. The 98 delegates at the party congress of August 19–24, 1876, represented a total of 38,254 members from 291 locals, a sizable increase in membership over the 24,443 of 1875. Although the recorded membership dropped slightly in 1877, the political strength of the Social Democrats is more accurately reflected by their returns in elections to the Reichstag. Thus, in 1877 they received 493,447 votes, or almost 10 percent of the total; and in the election of July 1878, in the midst of the national panic over the assassination attempts on the life of Emperor Wilhelm I, they dropped only to 437,158, almost 8 percent of the total.[23]

A party that is built on a working-class following can hardly expect to be rich, but the Social Democrats nonetheless had an adequately supplied treasury. From June 1875 to August 1876, the treasury received 58,763 marks; from August 1876 to April 1877, 54,217 marks; and from February to October 1878, 64,218 marks. From these funds, the party could pay its officials (i.e. the members of the Central Election Committee), support professional agitators, and subsidize the publication of newspapers and periodicals. As of 1876, the party paid the secretaries of the Central Committee 150 marks a month, the treasurers 135 marks, and the other members 45 marks. In addition, it offered full financial assistance to eight agitators and partial support to fourteen others, with occasional contributions to 123 trained and ready speakers. The party's Reichstag deputies also received per diem allowances up to nine marks daily.[24]

The Social Democrats placed great emphasis on the publication of newspapers and periodicals for the agitational, educational, and political activity of the party. Between 1876 and 1878 the Social Democratic

[22] Mehring, *Geschichte der deutschen Sozialdemokratie*, IV, pp. 102–04; Nipperdey, *Die Organisation der deutschen Parteien vor 1918*, p. 304.
[23] Mehring, *Geschichte der deutschen Sozialdemokratie*, IV, pp. 104, 108, 145.
[24] *Ibid.*, pp. 104–07, 111, 145.

publishing business flourished in an unprecedented manner and no doubt contributed significantly to the impression that the movement posed an increasing danger to the order and tranquility of German society. In 1876, the former party organs of the Lassalleans and Eisenachers were merged into the *Vorwaerts,* henceforth the official organ of the Social Democrats until it was suppressed two years later. At the same time, the party founded a literary journal, *Die neue Welt,* edited by Bruno Geiser, Liebknecht's future son-in-law. Then at the congress of 1877, the delegates endorsed the establishment of *Die Zukunft,* the first "scientific" periodical of the German Social Democrats. It was made possible by a considerable financial subsidy from Karl Hoechberg, the wealthy son of a Jewish banking family from Frankfurt am Main who played a significant role in party affairs for several years. As of 1876 the Social Democrats had twenty-three political newspapers, but within a year eighteen more were added, and by the time the Socialist Law was passed there were forty-seven. Collectively these newspapers, about a fourth of which appeared as often as six times weekly, created a tremendously effective system for the dissemination of party news, election propaganda, and socialist thought.[25]

The Social Democrats encountered their first opportunity to throw the full force of their new party organization into a national election in January 1877. At the party congress of August 1876, the delegates made systematic preparations for the election, deciding where to focus their campaign energies by labeling those districts as "official" in which the Social Democrats had the greatest chance of victory. Forty out of the 397 Reichstag districts appeared to the Social Democrats to be worthy of concentrated campaigning. However, the party did not limit itself to these districts, but ultimately Social Democratic candidates campaigned for Reichstag seats in 175 districts. At the end of the run-off balloting, the Social Democrats had captured twelve seats. They sent eight former Eisenachers, Auer, Bebel, Wilhelm Blos, Bracke, Liebknecht, Johann Most, Julius Motteler, and Moritz Rittinghausen, and four former Lassalleans, Demmler, Fritzsche, Hasenclever, and Kapell, to the Reichstag. In the eyes of Germany's propertied and educated classes, they were all notorious agitators, but some such as Bebel, Liebknecht, and Johann Most, caused more consternation than

[25] *Ibid.*, pp. 105–06, 111–12, 155; Bebel, *Aus meinem Leben,* II, pp. 375, 389–90; Karl Kautsky, *Erinnerungen und Eroerterungen,* edited by Benedikt Kautsky (The Hague, 1960), pp. 404–07.

the others. In 1877, however, the Social Democratic deputies turned their minds to the serious work of parliamentary legislation.[26]

This Social Democratic Reichstag *Fraktion* planned an active legislative program for the 1877 session, mixing it with generous amounts of negative criticism. Their greatest attention, however, focused on a Workmen's Protection Bill which they introduced in the Reichstag in April. In many ways, this bill closely resembled the bill that Schweitzer had wanted to introduce in the late sixties but could not for lack of signatures. Apart from the contents of the bill, it is notable as the first piece of comprehensive labor legislation introduced by the unified Social Democratic party.[27] The introduction of this measure reflected a conviction among many Social Democrats that they should use parliamentary activity to bring about reforms within the existing system. Other Social Democrats, however, continued to harbor deep reservations about cooperating positively in a parliamentary body for which they had such contempt because of its inability to challenge the real base of power in the Reich.

A spirit of anti-parliamentarism thus persisted among the Social Democrats, as an expression of an underlying sectarian mood that feared a corruption of the party's principles if its tactics linked it too closely to the hated Bismarckian system. To a degree, the former Eisenachers reflected these sentiments more strongly than the Lassalleans, and one suspects that it was derived more from their roots in south German bourgeois democracy than from their specifically socialist principles. Thus, Liebknecht still insisted at the Gotha congress in 1876 that "if Social Democracy participates in the [Reichstag] farce, it will become an official socialist party." If Liebknecht felt that way,

[26] Mehring, *Geschichte der deutschen Sozialdemokratie*, IV, pp. 106–08, 110.

[27] The Social Democrats' bill introduced a far-reaching regulation of all industry, including the handicraft trades, through the establishment of an Imperial factory inspection. It also provided a general plan for an Imperial Health Office to regulate the physical conditions of work; district Industrial Boards, composed of elected members equally divided between employers and employees; and a series of Industrial Courts to arbitrate labor disputes. Supplementing these regulatory agencies, it set a maximum working day of ten hours (eight hours for persons under eighteen) and called for the abolition of the truck system (payment in goods), of certain kinds of work for women and of all work for children under fourteen, and of Sunday work except in trades where it was absolutely necessary. Finally, it envisaged obligatory education until eighteen, with special attention to trade and continuation schools. *SB*, III, i (1877), vol. III, *Anlagen*, No. 92, pp. 316–21. Several articles in the party organ explicated the various features of the bill; cf. "Die Socialisten im Reichstag," *Vorwaerts*, No. 42, April 11, 1877, and "Das Arbeiterschutzgesetz im Reichstag," *Vorwaerts*, No. 48, April 25, 1877.

August Dreesbach, a former Lassallean, pointed out, then he ought to resign his Reichstag seat just as Johann Jacoby (the famous forty-eighter who had joined the Eisenachers in 1873) had done in 1874 because on principle he would not participate in a sham parliament.[28] But Liebknecht knew that he had no alternative tactic to offer the party. Since Liebknecht had no intention of planning insurrections, the only alternative was to emphasize building up the organization and educating the workers; but each of these meshed harmoniously with the parliamentary tactics.

The work of the deputies in the Reichstag session that began early in 1878 is the best evidence that the Social Democrats intended to pursue a parliamentary tactic to democratize the Reich and to bring about social-economic reform. At the party congress in May 1877, the Lassallean Fritzsche emphasized the need for the Social Democrats to introduce legislation "in a positive sense" and even suggested that the party's Reichstag deputies ought to form a unified *Fraktion* with the most radical "middle-class democrats." [29] The delegates did not accept the latter recommendation, but in the 1878 session many Social Democratic bills were in fact signed and supported by deputies from the People's party. In conjunction with these democrats, the Social Democrats introduced a whole series of bills designed to increase the political and civil rights of Germans. The number of bills a party introduces in a single session may not be too meaningful, but in the case of the Social Democrats it bears directly upon the party's tactical assumptions. It is significant, therefore, that the Social Democrats introduced more bills in the first session of 1878 than did any other party. Equally significant, these bills aimed chiefly at reforms of the German political system. The nature of these bills, and the political assistance the Social Democrats received in presenting them (two National Liberals undersigned one measure!), demonstrates rather strikingly that just prior to the Socialist Law the party seriously devoted itself to political reform and that anti-parliamentarian sentiments had little practical effect.[30]

[28] *Protokoll des Socialisten-Congresses zu Gotha vom 19. bis 23. August 1876* (Berlin, 1876), pp. 30–31.

[29] *Protokoll des Socialisten-Congresses zu Gotha vom 27. bis 29. Mai 1877* (Hamburg, 1877), pp. 30–31, 34.

[30] The following list of bills, presented by the Social Democrats in the first session of 1878, is compiled from *SB*, III, ii (1878), vol. III, *Anlagen;* they include measures to provide that ballots in Reichstag elections be cast in sealed envelopes (No. 66, p. 550), to insure the freedom of Reichstag deputies from arrest during sessions (No. 42, p. 521), to drop the exemption of certain military persons from

Social Democratic theoretical discussions reveal with equal clarity that they assumed the appropriateness of some kind of parliamentary system for a socialist society. The whole question of the best representative system was raised in a series of articles in the *Zukunft* in 1878, the contributors included Karl Luebeck, a German socialist who had lived in Zurich for many years; Max Kayser, a young Jewish Social Democrat from Breslau; and August Bebel. On the one hand, Luebeck launched a rather sweeping attack on the whole parliamentary conception because it did not allow for direct legislation by the people. On the other hand, Bebel developed a scheme for a proportional representation that would rest on highly centralized political parties. Finally, Max Kayser, disturbed by Bebel's plan for a representative system that would automatically strengthen the power of the party's central executive, tended to defend the electoral arrangement as it existed in Germany, at least against Bebel's ideas.[31]

The details of the political discussions are not so important as the spirit in which they were carried on. As a theoretical counterpart to the party's reform legislation in the Reichstag, they reveal that the Social Democrats perceived a direct connection between their democratic-political goals and their parliamentary tactics. Although antiparliamentarian sentiments, aroused by recognition that the Reichstag had only limited powers, sporadically affected the personal attitudes of some, such feelings were not strong enough to compel a major shift in tactics.

It should not be assumed that the parliamentary tactics of the Social Democrats calmed the fears of their enemies or encouraged the dominant classes in Germany to approach them in a more generous spirit. Quite the contrary, for although universal suffrage opened the way for a greater political integration of the Social Democrats into the system, neither the bourgeois liberals nor the feudal aristocrats had the slightest intention of encouraging such a development. Ludwig Bamberger, one of the most talented of the Progressives, complained bitterly against

municipal taxes (No. 50, p. 534), to reapportion the Reichstag seats according to the last census (No. 67, p. 551), to provide for the prosecution of persons who used threats during the elections (No. 68, p. 551), to alter the rules regulating the order of business in the Reichstag (No. 69, p. 551), to repeal all laws that required police approval for organizations and assemblies (No. 103, p. 851), and to provide full freedom in the choice of residence (No. 104, p. 851).

[31] C. Luebeck, "Die Proportional-Vertretung," *Die Zukunft*, I (1877/78), pp. 145–48, 153–65, 190–98; A. B., "Zur Wahlreform," *ibid.*, pp. 507–11; Max Kayser, "Gegen die Proportional-Vertretung," *ibid.*, pp. 624–26.

universal suffrage precisely because it offered a chance for the Social Democrats to become part of the system. In 1878, Bamberger did not assume that their parliamentary tactics made the Social Democrats any less dangerous to his bourgeois society. At the same time, Adolf Held, one of Germany's leading academic social reformers, believed that the socialist-economic ideas of the Social Democrats posed no special threat, but that the "political-revolutionary" aspects of their program were "genuinely dangerous" to German society. Held had carefully studied the development of the socialist movement, for he himself wanted effective social reforms to ameliorate the harshness of the capitalist system, but that did not diminish his hostility to the political goals of the Social Democrats.[32] Thus, the pursuit of parliamentary tactics by the Social Democrats in no case diminished the fear and bitterness of the other classes of society.

The Quest for Certainty in Economic Thought

Following the Social Democrats' adoption of a Marxist program at Erfurt in 1891, the common historical interpretation stated that in the late seventies the party was confused and eclectic about socialist principles. Karl Kautsky propounded this view with a certain degree of self-satisfaction it seems, because it highlighted the influence of his own theoretical writings and the significant role of the *Neue Zeit*, which he edited from its founding in 1883. This interpretation could be accepted today, if it did not itself create some confusions. It is true that the Social Democrats lacked a thorough knowledge of socialist principles, and of Marxism in particular. But some distinctions are necessary. What they lacked was a systematic knowledge of economic thought. This gap in their theoretical preparation reflected itself in two ways, in their uncertainty about how to treat practical economic issues as they arose and in their quest for a guide to the economic principles of a socialist movement. They did not, however, lack ideological clarity or personal commitment with respect to the principles of political democracy, and it was these principles, and not economic ideas about socialization, that guided much of their practice in the late seventies.

Uncertainty and disagreements about socialist-economic principles

[32] Ludwig Bamberger, *Deutschland und der Socialismus* (2nd ed.; Leipzig, 1878), pp. 29–35; Adolf Held, *Sozialismus, Sozialdemokratie und Sozialpolitik* (Leipzig, 1878), p. 32.

plagued the Social Democrats whenever they confronted a practical issue touching these matters. They could promote protective legislation for labor because of its clear benefits for the working class, but they foundered on issues such as Imperial monopolization and free trade. Both of these issues confronted them in 1876 when Bismarck initiated a program for an Imperial railroad monopoly and many industrial and agrarian interests wanted Germany to shift from free trade to protectionism. At the party congress in August 1876 the delegates addressed themselves to these issues, but without reaching satisfactory resolutions on either. Although they condemned private ownership of the railroads as an "unjustifiable monopoly," they also feared that nationalization by the Reich would advance the "interests of *the class* and militarist state." Thus, to endorse nationalization and at the same time reject Bismarck's program, they encouraged the individual states (*Bundesstaaten*) to move toward a public ownership of the lines within their own borders.[33] In this case, the Social Democrats clearly believed that they had followed the prescriptions of their democratic principles, although it is difficult to understand how they could have believed that nationalization of the railroads within the state of Prussia would not also advance the "interest of the class and militarist state."

The delegates exhibited even greater perplexity on the question of free trade versus protectionism. Some such as Auer, Fritzsche, and Kayser favored protectionism, but others believed in the free trade doctrines of the liberals. When agreement could not be achieved, the delegates found a sectarian solution to their quandary, simply declaring that the "socialists of Germany have no part in the fight between free trade and protection which has arisen within the ranks of the propertied classes." Had they followed the logic of that resolution, they should have avoided taking positions on almost all economic issues, but that would have been ludicrous. Strangely enough, in the same resolution, they added that the existing "trade treaties are unfavorable to German industry" and therefore ought to be altered to the latter's advantage! [34] In the following years, the ambiguity of this resolution opened the doors to all sorts of disputes within the party. It all stemmed from the fact that they lacked guidelines to economic problems which were as clear and convincing as the democratic principles that directed them on political issues.

[33] Quoted in Wilhelm Schroeder, *Handbuch der sozialdemokratischen Parteitage von 1863 bis 1909* (Munich, 1910), p. 127.
[34] *Ibid.*, p. 571.

Everything indicates that in the seventies the Social Democrats longed for theoretical assistance on the question of what economic policies were appropriate to a socialist movement, both for the present and the future. As they scanned the landscape of economic thought, numerous alternatives appeared, and they dabbled with one and the other for many years. On the one hand the Lassallean economic conceptions were losing their persuasiveness and gradually faded out of vision. On the other hand, although a few Social Democrats understood aspects of Marx's economic thought, the whole of the Marxist system had not yet made a popular impact. In the intervening years, the Social Democrats grasped at several passing theoretical figures in the hope of receiving instruction on the economics of socialism.

The most spectacular, but not necessarily the most significant of the theoreticians who attracted the interest of some Social Democrats was Eugen Duehring, a *Privatdozent* at the University of Berlin. Himself a rather rambling eclectic, Duehring nonetheless made an impact because his thought had broad socialistic tendencies and because his personal battles with the university authorities made him a *cause célèbre* with a group of young Social Democratic intellectuals in Berlin. The curious story of Duehring's momentary reputation among the Social Democrats and of his apparent threat to the influence of Marxism has been told in several places and needs no repetition here. The fact is that Duehring exerted no lasting influence on any of the Social Democrats, not even on Bernstein, who had been one of his original and most enthusiastic backers. It is doubtful that in the seventies the Social Democrats understood his system of thought—set forth in many tomes of involved verbiage—even as well as they understood Marxism.[35]

Duehring made his lasting contribution to Social Democracy in a negative way, by so arousing the fear and wrath of Engels that the latter felt compelled to write a thorough refutation of the "socialitary system" in 1877–1878. Probably no other single volume played such a decisive role in disseminating the Marxist system as Engels' *Herr Eugen Duehring's Revolution in Science*. For the young intellectuals of the eighties, of whom Bernstein and Kautsky were the most eminent, it served as a Marxist handbook, comprehensive, lucid, and convincing. When three chapters from the *Anti-Duehring* were published independently, first in French (1880) and then in German (1883) as

[35] Gay, *The Dilemma of Democratic Socialism*, pp. 94–103; Eduard Bernstein, *Sozialdemokratische Lehrjahre* (Berlin, 1928), pp. 52–59; Mayer, *Friedrich Engels*, II, pp. 282–95.

Socialism: Utopian and Scientific, its influence spread even to the rank-and-file Social Democrats. That impact was not felt, however, until the middle eighties.[36]

If Duehring's notoriety has far exceeded his significance, the historians of Social Democracy have often overlooked the less obvious influence of those thinkers who were closely associated with the emergent theories of State Socialism. In the seventies and eighties Germany was alive with social theorists, many of whom severely criticized the capitalist system and propounded a kind of conservative socialist system that could be developed by the existing monarchical authoritarian state. Conservative social thought had many sources and took a variety of forms. Years before, in the early forties, the Pomeranian economist Johann Karl Rodbertus had begun to publish social-economic studies that leaned toward a form of State Socialism. In 1872, a group of German academicians founded the *Verein fuer Sozialpolitik* (Society for Social Politics), an association devoted to the study of the social and economic problems created by industrial capitalism. Although this society represented no single theoretical program, a great many of its members advocated strong reform measures by the existing state and for that they were popularly dubbed *Kathedersozialisten* (Socialists of the Chair).[37] A few of these academicians sought to systematize their thought into an explicit theory of State Socialism which would solve the "social question" in economic terms without conceding the democratization of the German Reich as demanded by the Social Democrats. No doubt Adolf Wagner made the greatest effort to elaborate such a theory of State Socialism, but the same tendencies appeared in Hermann Wagener, Rudolf Meyer, and Albert Schaeffle.[38]

[36] More than any other Social Democratic leader, Liebknecht was responsible for arousing Engels to write the answer to Duehring. According to Mayer, *Friedrich Engels*, II, pp. 283–84, Liebknecht wrote several letters to Engels in 1875 urging the latter to refute Duehring. Unfortunately, these letters were apparently not available to Georg Eckert when he edited, Wilhelm Liebknecht, *Briefwechsel mit Karl Marx und Friedrich Engels* (The Hague, 1963).

[37] Surveys of these developments in Walter Vogel, *Bismarcks Arbeiterversicherung. Ihre Entstehung im Kraeftespiel der Zeit* (Brunswick, 1951), pp. 67–92; Heinrich Herkner, *Die Arbeiterfrage* (6th ed.; Berlin, 1916), II, pp. 149–56, 195–202. Also, Abraham Ascher, "Professors as Propagandists: The Politics of the Kathedersozialisten," *Journal of Central European Affairs*, XIII (Oct. 1963), pp. 282–302.

[38] Adolf Wagner developed a specific theory of State Socialism as a kind of middle ground between the principles of "individualism" and "socialism" (the latter taken as total collectivization), in *Grundlegung der Politischen Oekonomie* (3rd ed.; Leipzig, 1892), I, pp. 58–61. On Wagner, see also William H. Dawson,

On the surface, most Social Democrats exhibited the greatest contempt for the ideas of the conservative socialists and the bourgeois economists in the Society for Social Politics. But that is only part of the reality. The writings of these thinkers could not be dismissed if they offered ideas which seemed appropriate to the needs of Social Democracy. Thus, Carl August Schramm (1830–1905), an official in a Berlin insurance company and one of the few Social Democrats who had a grasp of Marx's theory of value, harbored a deep sympathy for Rodbertus, a fact that led him into a bitter feud with Kautsky and Bernstein in the eighties. Although socialist historiography has almost entirely forgotten about Schramm—so complete was his disgrace in the eighties—the whole party recognized in the seventies that he was undoubtedly more knowledgeable in economic theory than any other member. He alone accounted for a great number of the articles on economic subjects that appeared in the *Zukunft* in 1877–1878, and if he did not openly embrace State Socialism at the time, he in no case rejected it.[39]

Although an interplay between State Socialism and Social Democracy is difficult to identify precisely, one instance at least stands out with clarity. In 1874 Albert Schaeffle wrote a series of articles on *Die Quintessenz des Sozialismus* (*The Quintessence of Socialism*) which was published shortly thereafter in book form. Seeking to counter the ignorance of what socialism involved, both among its antagonists and protagonists, Schaeffle suggested that he had based most of his brief exposition of socialist economics on the theories of Marx.[40] It is not sur-

Bismarck and State Socialism (London, 1891), pp. 3–13, and William O. Shanahan, *German Protestants Face the Social Question* (Notre Dame, Indiana, 1954), I, pp. 401–06, who discusses Wagner's efforts at the *Kirchentag* in October 1871 to interest the Evangelical Church in a social program. On Wagener, Wolfgang Saile, *Hermann Wagener und sein Verhaeltnis zu Bismarck* (Tuebingen, 1958), and Hans-Joachim Schoeps, "Hermann Wagener—Ein Konservativer Sozialist. Ein Beitrag zur Ideengeschichte des Sozialismus," *Zeitschrift fuer Religions—und Geistesgeschichte*, VIII (1956), pp. 193–217. Schaeffle's life and work is discussed in Ralph Bowen, *German Theories of the Corporative State* (New York, 1947), pp. 121–37.

[39] Bernstein, *Sozialdemokratische Lehrjahre*, pp. 56–57; Kautsky, *Erinnerungen und Eroerterungen*, pp. 443–44. Cf. the series of six articles by Schramm, entitled "Nationaloekonomie," in the *Volksstaat* between April 2 and July 16, 1875, and C. A. Schramm, "Die Werththeorie von Karl Marx," *Die Zukunft*, I (1877/78), pp. 127–34.

[40] Albert Schaeffle, *The Quintessence of Socialism* (2nd ed.; London, 1890), pp. 1–2. The English edition was translated from the 8th German edition, but Schaeffle made no substantive changes in the original text, although he did add a concluding chapter which does not affect the text used here.

prising that the booklet attracted the attention and admiration of many Social Democrats. Bebel endorsed it without reservation, advising the deputies in the Reichstag on April 18, 1877, that if they wished to understand the true meaning of socialism they should read Schaeffle. Likewise, Bernstein has testified that Schaeffle's booklet embodied as much as any Social Democrat understood about socialist economics at the end of the seventies. And late in 1878, Karl Hoechberg purchased 10,000 copies of the booklet for free distribution among the academicians and educated classes of Germany.[41] That Schaeffle's booklet was widely read by interested Social Democrats cannot be doubted, for it was admirably brief, clearly written, and easily available through the party's distribution system.

By concentrating solely upon economic theory, Schaeffle inadvertently emasculated Marxism of its political and truly revolutionary implications. He focused so narrowly on what he thought to be the economic organization of a future socialist society that he failed to include Marx's analysis of the state as the political instrument of the ruling classes and his predictions about the revolutionary role of the working class. These aspects of Marxism may have been omitted simply to abbreviate the length of the exposition, or they may have resulted from ignorance on Schaeffle's part—something he set out to eradicate! In any case, Marxism devoid of these aspects may easily appear to be a demand for the immediate nationalization of all industries by any and all states. Indeed, that was Schaeffle's thesis as he explained that "*The Alpha and Omega of socialism is the transformation of private and competing capitals into a united collective capital.*" [42] All trends toward capital concentration and political centralization, in fact, "everything which trains the masses as a whole, which centralizes, which brings about a public union of individual forces on the largest possible scale, is very closely allied to socialism." [43] True, Marx had predicted that the road to socialism would be marked by a greater and greater concentration of capital, but in itself this tendency did not create socialism. The contrast became much sharper when Schaeffle dis-

[41] Bebel in the Reichstag, *SB,* III, i (1877), vol. I, p. 570; Bernstein *Sozialdemokratische Lehrjahre,* pp. 70–72; Kautsky, *Erinnerungen und Eroerterungen,* p. 410. Schramm reviewed Schaeffle's book favorably, with some criticisms of the exposition of Marx's theory of value; cf. C. A. Schramm, "Die Quintessenz des Sozialismus," *Vorwaerts,* No. 61, May 27, and No. 62, May 30, 1877, and "Herr Professor Dr. Schaeffle," *Vorwaerts,* No. 128, Oct. 31, 1877.

[42] Schaeffle, *The Quintessence of Socialism,* p. 20.

[43] *Ibid.,* pp. 17–18.

cussed the state. "Economically considered," he observed, "it [socialism] is rather the universal application of the special principle of the State and the municipality, the extension over the whole range of social production of the idea of an official public service. The collectivist principle, whether realizable or not, is essentially a State-principle." [44]

Schaeffle did not say so explicitly, but, as he understood it, socialism —Marxist or any other style—meant essentially State Socialism. If unsuspecting and unknowing Social Democrats approached Schaeffle's booklet in the belief that it offered a comprehensive introduction to the meaning of socialism—as many of them apparently did—then they had fallen into a frightful pitfall. If Schaeffle's work contained the essentials of socialism, if the concentration of capital and the collectivist "state principle" embodied the fundamental principles of their movement, then no logical ground existed on which they could base a democratic political opposition to Bismarck's program of monopolization. Then Bismarck, and even a few Junkers, had equal claim as socialists.

Obviously the Social Democrats could not accept Schaeffle without some modifications. Nevertheless, some of them imbibed a sufficient dosage to set up a tension within the movement between the traditional democratic-political principles and what they took to be their socialist-economic principles as defined by Schaeffle. These tensions emerged rather clearly in a series of articles on the problems of nationalization and municipalization that appeared in the *Zukunft* in 1878. In some of these articles, it is quite evident that the authors reflected the theoretical understanding of socialism that Schaeffle summarized in his booklet. Others, notably August Bebel, held firmly to the proposition that nationalization, or even municipalization within the existing German political structure would retard rather than advance the cause of socialism because it would strengthen the forces of Junker reaction and bourgeois capitalism that still controlled the Reich.[45]

[44] *Ibid.*, pp. 50–51. Adolf Held, one of the leading academicians in the Society for Social Politics, called attention to the fact that in his interest in the "economic-socialist ideas of Social Democracy," Schaeffle forgot to evaluate the "revolutionary purposes" of the movement. Held, *Sozialismus, Sozialdemokratie und Sozialpolitik*, pp. 45–46.

[45] One author, identified merely as "—s," complained that the party's opposition to the Imperial railroad monopoly was based too much on political grounds, i.e. democratic criticism of the Reich; "Zur Reichseisenbahn-Project," *Die Zukunft*, I (1877/78), pp. 75–80. Another, probably Schramm but identified only as "—m," agreed with "—s," but also suggested that municipal ownership of industrial operations and utilities would bring socialization without the risk of increasing the powers of the militarist state; "Ueber den Gewerbebetrieb der Communen,"

At this point it is possible to leave the Social Democratic quest for certainty in economic thought. Although several theories were tried, as of 1878, none had been found which completely corresponded to the needs of the Social Democrats. An unintegrated mixture of Lassallean and State Socialist ideas nevertheless directed most of their thinking about specific socialist-economic principles. When catastrophe struck in 1878, the Social Democrats were not much better founded in economic thought than they had been several years earlier. But their search was on, and with some of them in the most vigorous manner. In restrospect, it appears almost inevitable that Marxism should have supplied the needs of the Social Democrats in economic theory. Only time to absorb the complexities seemed necessary. It seems equally certain that the experience of twelve years of police harassment and official legal suppression contributed enormously to the prestige of the whole Marxist system by 1890. Before launching into that story, it is necessary to summarize some of the salient aspects of the relationship of the Social Democrats to the whole German society on eve of the Socialist Law.

On the Eve of Castastrophe: Social Democrats and German Society

On the surface, it seems that both the parliamentary tactics of the Social Democrats and their willingness to trust a State Socialist such as Schaeffle to instruct them in socialist economics would suggest that reformist tendencies outweighed revolutionary inclinations. But a danger lurks in such a generalization, for it superimposes the polemical framework of later decades on the realities of the seventies. The reality of the Social Democrats can only be penetrated by remembering their strained and hostile relationship to all the major aspects of German society. Although it is not the intention of this book to elaborate on the social and cultural isolation of the Social Democratic movement, distortions and misapprehensions might easily arise if the total context were not characterized briefly.

ibid., pp. 241–49, and "Ueber den Zusammenhang des wirthschaftlichen und des politischen Princips im demokratischen Socialismus," *ibid.*, pp. 296–98. On the other hand, August Bebel argued essentially that both municipalization and nationalization would hinder rather than promote the democratic political objectives of Social Democracy; "Der Gewerbebetriebe durch den Staat und die Commune," *ibid.*, pp. 465–74.

The notoriety and the dangers of Social Democracy in the view of the non-socialists stemmed not merely from their radical democratic political commitments but also from the fact that they seemed to challenge all the cherished beliefs and values of German society. In comparison with other Germans, who gloried in the new Reich, the Social Democrats were unpatriotic, although it is obvious that they too were proud of being Germans and often believed that their ideals represented a true patriotism. The majority of Germans never forgot the hostility of the Social Democrats to the annexation of Alsace-Lorraine, their thundering endorsements of the Commune, and their avowed internationalist outlook. The Social Democrats simply could not embrace the nationalist values of most Germans.[46]

Equally significant, the militant atheism of the leading Social Democrats aroused deep resentment among those Germans who still cherished the Christian faith. The bitter Social Democratic vituperations against the churches were more frequent in the seventies than they had been in the sixties. Christians and Social Democrats alike assumed that their respective philosophies were totally incompatible, that they had to confront each other as dedicated enemies. "Religion," wrote Albert Dulk in *Vorwaerts*, "is thus the most powerful enemy of socialism. . . . In one word, religion is the main bastion of anti-socialism, of reaction, the breeding ground of all social evil." [47] On numerous occasions in the seventies, Bebel launched vigorous onslaughts against both Christian doctrines and institutions. Johann Most, for whom violent rhetoric was the norm, fired his invectives against Christianity and sponsored a special *Kirchenaustrittsbewegung* (literally, "departure-from-the-churches-movement") among the working classes. Others, such as Joseph Dietzgen, contributed essays on a more theoretical level that provided the rationale for abandoning Christianity and embracing socialism.[48] It is safe to say that the socialists' militant atheism at-

[46] Cf. Roth, *The Social Democrats in Imperial Germany*, pp. 96–101.

[47] A. Dulk, "Religion," *Vorwaerts*, No. 58, May 19, 1878.

[48] See the following three items by Bebel: *Christenthum und Sozialismus* (Leipzig, 1874); *Glossen zu Yves Guyot und Sigismond Lacroix's Schrift: Die wahre Gestalt des Christenthums* (*Étude zur les doctrines sociales du christianisme*) (Leipzig, 1878); *Die Frau und der Sozialismus, passim.* Of Most's many vitriolic blasts against Christianity, see *Die Gottlosigkeit. Eine Kritik der Gottes Idee* (no publisher, no date, but 1877). Joseph Dietzgen, a tanner by trade, who won recognition for his philosophical knowledge, wrote a long series of articles for the *Volksstaat* in the early seventies on the topic, "Die Religion der Sozialdemokratie," reprinted in J. Dietzgen, *Kleinere philosophische Schriften* (Stuttgart, 1903), pp. 12–76.

tracted more attention and created more resentment than either their economic or political theories. It offered a clear instance of value confrontation, and illustrates strikingly how alienated the Social Democrats were from the beliefs and assumptions of the dominant classes.

The sentiments popularly associated with Social Democrats—lack of patriotism, sympathy for the Commune, militant atheism—probably played a more significant role in defining their "revolutionary" tendencies than the specific actions of the party which had remained within the bounds of legality. Without actually planning to go to the barricades, the Social Democrats projected an image of social rebellion, inciting the workers to class hatreds, vilifying the sacred faith of Christians, and heaping contempt on the revered achievements of Bismarck.

The sharp antagonisms between the Social Democrats and the values of the dominant classes and traditional institutions should not lead to the conclusion that no openings had appeared for a limited degree of reconciliation. Not all liberals and conservatives were unalterably opposed to the demands of the labor movement, even when they feared the increasing political significance of the Social Democrats. The existence of the so-called Hirsch-Duncker trade unions, the followers of the Progressive party, evidenced a commitment on the part of some liberals to advance the economic interests of labor. The establishment in 1872 of the *Verein fuer Sozialpolitik* (Society for Social Politics) revealed that a considerable number of liberal and conservative academicians addressed themselves energetically to the grievous social problems of German society. The members of the *Verein* had a considerable influence on the social thinking of the German educated classes and government circles, but this did not necessarily diminish the fear of a political working-class movement. Despite the good will of many liberals and conservatives toward the workers, this alone did not suffice to bridge the existing social gaps.[49]

Catholic social reformers, clerical and lay, also offered an opportunity for cooperation between workers and a traditional institution, but this too had limitations. In the seventies, the years of the *Kulturkampf*, many German Catholics also felt that they were aliens as they fought

[49] Roth, *The Social Democrats in Imperial Germany*, pp. 136–43, discusses the *Verein*, with special reference to Gustav Schmoller and Lujo Brentano, as one of the "counter-tendencies" to the class cleavage in German society. He observes, however, that despite the passage of Bismarck's social insurance program in the eighties "the class cleavage that the academic reformers wanted to diminish continued unabated because the antisocialist law of 1878 preceded the welfare legislation" (p. 142).

an agonizing struggle with the political spokesmen of the new Reich. The *Kulturkampf* thus precluded the possibility that Catholic social reformers might approach the working classes on behalf of the German political and economic system. Although the Catholic Center party and the Social Democrats both endured discriminations under the new Reich, their shared condition of distress could not counterbalance the enmity that separated them. The Social Democrats enthusiastically endorsed the struggle of modernism against the intellectual conservatism of the Church under Pius IX, and this conflict was most intense in the seventies when the social issue might have provided the basis for some communication between socialists and Catholics.[50]

Although a few currents in the seventies seemed to open the doors for the entrance of the Social Democrats into German society, others tended to bar the way, and the degree of socialist isolation increased rather than lessened in the late seventies and eighties. For this cleavage, the Social Democrats also bear some responsibility—they were sometimes bitter and intransigent when they might have been conciliatory—but the dominant classes of a society have the power to determine the possibilities of social and political integration, and in Germany these classes erected sturdy barriers against the workers who sympathized with the socialist movement. The erection of one of the highest barriers began in 1878.

[50] The Evangelical Church in Germany showed little concern for the working classes through the seventies: for its policies up to 1870, see Shanahan, *German Protestants Face the Social Question, passim.* Catholic and Protestant social movements are covered in August Erdmann, *Die Christliche Arbeiterbewegung in Deutschland* (2nd ed.; Stuttgart, 1909), and Karl Buchheim, *Geschichte der christlichen Parteien in Deutschland* (Munich, 1953). For a more detailed analysis of the socialists and the religious issue, see my article, "August Bebel and German Social Democracy's Relation to the Christian Churches," *Journal of the History of Ideas,* XXVII (April–June 1966), pp. 245–64.

CHAPTER III · DISINTEGRATION AND RECOVERY

The Castastrophe of 1878

On May 11, 1878, two shots were fired at Emperor Wilhelm I as he rode along *Unter den Linden* in an open carriage with his daughter. Fired from a faulty revolver by Max Hoedel, a deranged journeyman plumber, the shots went so far astray that not even the Emperor noticed that he was the target. On the same day, before Hoedel's act received a preliminary investigation, Bismarck telegraphed from Friedrichsruh that preparations should be made for measures against the Social Democrats. Bismarck anxiously sought to pin responsibility for the crime on the socialists, regardless of whether the evidence would support the charge. Within six days, the Prussian government presented the Bundesrat with a bill to outlaw the Social Democratic party.

The Social Democrats were understandably bewildered. Previous efforts by Bismarck to suppress their activities had failed, but the new attempt had numerous complicating factors. For one thing, the socialists in Leipzig did in fact know Hoedel because he had distributed their papers. But in April 1878 he had been expelled from the Leipzig organization for handling funds dishonestly. His expulsion from the party was announced in *Vorwaerts* on May 9, just two days before his attempt on the Kaiser's life. After his forced separation from the socialists in April, Hoedel had worked for the National Liberals in Leipzig and then for Stoecker's Christian Socials in Berlin. For their part, the Social Democrats believed this was sufficient to prove that they were in no way connected with Hoedel's criminal attempt.[1]

The German political situation in May 1878 was complicated for all the parties by the fact that Bismarck had multiple motives in promoting an "exceptional law" against the Social Democrats. One must recognize that given Bismarck's conservative *Weltanschauung* the Social Democratic movement appeared as a dangerous threat to his ideal of

[1] Bebel, *Aus meinem Leben,* II, pp. 405–06.

state and society. As Wolfgang Pack has suggested, there were four fundamental reasons for his desire to crush the Social Democrats: in constitutional-political outlook, they were republicans, and therefore a threat to the monarchy; in foreign affairs, they were internationalists, which implied to Bismarck that they would be the friends of Germany's enemies; in domestic affairs, they sought a fundamental transformation of the existing social and economic order, opposed to the Junker foundation of the society; and, in religious matters, they were atheists, and thus undermined the religious and moral norms of Christian society.[2]

For Bismarck's part, the political goals were the most dangerous aspect of the Social Democratic program, not the attack on the principles of capitalism or economic liberalism. The tactics of the Chancellor in the 1880's show that he assumed that he could suppress the political danger of Social Democracy without at the same time denying that the workers had legitimate complaints against the existing economic structure. The repression of a dangerous political movement was to be followed by ameliorative social legislation. In true Junker fashion, Bismarck chose to apply the whip before offering the carrot. But, because the whip was so indiscriminately applied against almost all workers' organizations, Bismarck's distinction between the political and economic goals was blurred, and the carrot could not achieve the purposes for which it was intended.

Bismarck stressed repeatedly the political danger of the Social Democrats as his chief motive for demanding legislation against them. His objectives, however, were not so simple. No doubt he wanted to crush the socialist movement, but he also aimed to weaken the liberal parties in the Reichstag to clear the path politically for a significant shift in economic policies. The economic crash of 1873 and the continuing slump in the subsequent years had created serious doubts among many Germans about the practicality of economic liberalism. New demands for greater state intervention in the economy came from various groups; industrialists, artisans, shopkeepers, and the large agriculturalists made a marked shift to protectionism. By the middle seventies, Bismarck gave evidence that he believed the Reich government ought to act to counter the economic depression. Pressured especially by the combined agitation of industrialists and agriculturalists, who also drew

[2] Wolfgang Pack, *Das parlamentarische Ringen um das Sozialistengesetz Bismarcks 1878–1890* (Duesseldorf, 1961), p. 8.

closer together politically, Bismarck had decided definitely by early 1878 to push for protective tariffs, a move that would be opposed vigorously by the free traders among the National Liberals and Progressives. It also happened that those liberals who were devoted to the principles of free trade would also be most opposed to the introduction of a special law discriminating against one party. Bismarck enjoyed an advantage here, for he could confront the free traders on an issue of patriotism and the defense of German society, while at the same time seeking to weaken them politically to clear the way for tariff legislation.[3]

Bismarck knew in May 1878 that he could not muster a Reichstag majority to accept an "exceptional law" designed to outlaw one political party, and also that the safety of German society did not demand such a measure. Had Bismarck desired nothing more than the means to give the established institutions added protection, he could have requested modifications in the existing legal code. Such a procedure would undoubtedly have received widespread support in the Reichstag, because all the parties were anxious to some degree about the expansion of Social Democracy. But Bismarck also wanted an issue to use against the liberal parties, and for that he had to exaggerate his demands against the Social Democrats. Even those close to him found his motives difficult to comprehend. Thus, his colleagues in the Prussian Ministry, sincerely wanting some means to fight Social Democracy, opposed an "exceptional law" because it had little chance of passing the Reichstag. In their sincerity, they did not grasp the thinking behind the Chancellor's moves.

The tactics Bismarck employed in May 1878 make it clear that he intended not only to combat socialism but also to provoke the majority in the Reichstag into rejecting the exaggerated measures he presented for that purpose. On the one hand, the government admitted that the Social Democrats were only indirectly responsible for Hoedel's act, thus conceding that the immediate cause for the law had no foundation. In this manner, Bismarck himself intimated indirectly that the opponents of the Socialist Law had legitimate reasons for rejecting it. On the other hand, the government and the conservative parties constantly

[3] On the relationship of the economic and political developments in the seventies, see Hans Rosenberg, "Political and Social Consequences of the Great Depression of 1873–1896 in Central Europe," *Economic History Review*, XIII (1943), pp. 58–68, and Lambi, *Free Trade and Protection in Germany 1868–1879*, pp. 113–90, the latter particularly for the activities of the industrialists and agriculturalists.

argued that those who opposed the "exceptional law" would be held responsible for permitting conditions which led to assassinations.[4] As Bismarck fully expected, the Reichstag rejected the first anti-socialist law with only the conservatives supporting it. What he did not expect, however, was that a second attempt on the Emperor's life would create new opportunities for him to exploit immediately.

On June 2, one week after the Reichstag rejected the first anti-socialist law, the strolling Emperor was seriously wounded by a shotgun blast fired by Dr. Karl Nobiling from a window on *Unter den Linden.* Bismarck immediately perceived his chance to dissolve the Reichstag, to pin Nobiling's act on the Social Democrats, and to blame the liberals because they had rejected the first anti-socialist bill. The next day the news bureaus reported that Nobiling had socialist convictions, a charge which was never substantiated because Nobiling died from wounds inflicted on himself by the same gun. His motives were never discovered, which in itself proved to be an advantage to the enemies of Social Democracy. Overriding the opposition in his own ministry and from some of the federal states, Bismarck pushed the Bundesrat into dissolving the Reichstag on June 11. The elections for the new Reichstag were set for July 30, while a torrent of abuse gushed over the Social Democrats. They faced an election under the worst possible conditions.[5]

Events had moved so rapidly that the Social Democrats entered the election campaign without sufficient preparation. A party congress which had been planned for June 15–18 in Gotha had to be postponed indefinitely when the authorities prohibited it. Everywhere the Social Democrats were on the defensive; it was nearly impossible to quiet the mass hysteria aroused by the charge that they were responsible for the attempts on the Emperor's life. Countless obstacles were thrown in the

[4] Cf. Pack, *Das parlamentarische Ringen*, pp. 30–35, for the thinking within the Prussian Ministry and the arguments of Bismarck and the conservatives.

[5] For material on Hoedel and Nobiling, see Ignaz Auer, *Nach zehn Jahren* (2nd ed.; Nuremberg, 1913), pp. 30–50, 53–64; Paul Kampffmeyer and Bruno Altmann, *Vor dem Sozialistengesetz. Krisenjahre des Obrigkeitsstaates* (Berlin, 1928), pp. 157–76. When Johann Most turned to anarchism in the 1880's, he praised the assassination attempts of Hoedel and Nobiling and maintained that the German anarchist August Reinsdorf was the inspiration for their acts. Reinsdorf had in fact met Hoedel in Leipzig, but Most's claim that these acts rested on an anarchist basis is without specific evidence. Cf. Johann Most, *August Reinsdorf und die Propaganda der That* (New York, 1890), pp. 21–22. For a Social Democratic description of the fanaticism aroused against the movement in the summer of 1878, see Bebel, *Aus meinem Leben,* II, pp. 414–17.

path of their campaign. The police searched their houses and placed many under arrest; socialist newspapers were confiscated, and meetings were dissolved for every imaginable reason. In Prussia, but particularly in Berlin, arrests and imprisonments for *lèse majesté* increased rapidly. According to Ignaz Auer, patriotic Germans would enter workers' meetings or beerhalls with a laboring clientele, and rise suddenly to toast the Emperor. Anyone in the hall who did not rise or remove his cap was accused of *lèse majesté*.[6] In this atmosphere, the party found it impossible to campaign as in previous elections. Tactically, the Social Democrats had to avoid provocative acts and speeches in order to dispel the fear and anxiety of the populace. For weeks the banner of the *Vorwaerts* admonished, "Party Comrades. Do not be provoked. The reaction needs an uproar in order to win the game."

Despite the enormous odds against them, the Social Democrats emerged from the election with only minor damage. They polled 437,158 votes, a loss of only 56,000 from their total of 1877; their mandate strength dropped to nine as against twelve in 1877, but they received nearly 8 percent of the total national vote. The large cities stood by the Social Democrats; in the city districts the Social Democrats actually increased their votes from 222,000 in 1877 to 240,000 in 1878. In Berlin alone, the socialist vote rose from 31,522 in 1877 to 56,147 in 1878.[7]

Although the persistence of Social Democratic strength annoyed Bismarck, he could look with some pleasure upon the other results of the campaign. In some respects, the election hurt the liberal parties more than the socialists. The government, the conservative parties, and Center party directed much of their campaign against the liberals with the charge, in one form or another, that the struggle against Social Democracy had to be linked with a fight against liberalism. The results indicated a marked shift to the political right. The mandates of the National Liberals dropped (from 127 to 99) as did the Progressives' (from 35 to 26), while seats increased for the Conservatives (from 40 to 59), the Free Conservatives (from 38 to 57), and the Center party (from 93 to 99). The opposition of the National Liberals to the "exceptional law" had also been broken, leaving little question but that the

[6] Auer, *Nach zehn Jahren*, pp. 66–67. On one day, June 8, 1878, according to Auer, a total of twenty-two years, six months' imprisonment was meted out to seven persons accused of *lèse majesté*.

[7] Adolf Neumann-Hofer, *Die Entwicklung der Sozialdemokratie bei den Wahlen zum Deutschen Reichstage 1871–1903* (3rd ed.; Berlin, 1903), p. 55.

new Reichstag would pass the repressive legislation. The new version of the anti-socialist legislation, under preparation by the Prussian Interior and Justice Ministries during the election campaign, was made public on August 14.[8]

The alignment of the parties on the Socialist Law was well defined when the new Reichstag met on September 9 to hear the oration from the throne. The two conservative parties were enthusiastic supporters, and the National Liberals once again, as in the sixties, abandoned the greatest principles of liberalism and stood solidly for the measure. The Progressives, on the other hand, although deeply hostile to the Social Democrats (especially on economic principles), refused to sanction a measure so violently inconsistent with their liberal principles. The Center party, except for a minority, held that one could not combat socialists through repressive legislation, but only by an active revitalization of the religious and moral foundations of the society. All of these positions were elaborated time and again after the house began to deliberate the bill on September 16.[9]

On the first day of debate, after several promoters of the bill had spoken, August Bebel took the rostrum and quickly launched a bitter and skillful attack on the Chancellor in conjunction with a defense of his own party. A classic rhetorical duel took place between Bebel, the most agile, brilliant, and determined Social Democrat, and Bismarck, the seasoned debater who knew the value of a sharp and witty tongue. The house could not fail to listen as Bebel justly demanded that the government substantiate its accusation that the Social Democrats had a responsibility for the assassination attempts. Tempering his wrath, Bebel carefully exposed the fraudulent reports of the Wolff news bureau which had announced that the assassins were socialists. He condemned the Reichstag deputies for their abysmal ignorance of the true nature of Social Democracy and for the irresponsible slanders which they had cast upon his party.[10] These contentions were defensive, but Bebel also intended to launch an offense.

He designed his offensive tactic to create suspicion about Bismarck's sincerity as a foe of socialism, and for that Bebel had hitherto unknown

[8] Pack, *Das parlamentarische Ringen*, pp. 63–73, 76–78.

[9] *Ibid.*, pp. 79ff. For the positions of the various parties on the Socialist Law, see also Gerhard Schuemer, *Die Entstehungsgeschichte des Sozialistengesetzes* (Goettingen, 1929); Ferdinand Toennies, *Der Kampf um das Sozialistengesetz 1878* (Berlin, 1929).

[10] *SB*, IV, i (1878), vol. I, pp. 38–39.

information to startle and disturb his audience. He revealed Bismarck's association with socialists in the early sixties climaxed by his secret conversations with Ferdinand Lassalle. At one time Bismarck had negotiated with socialists, but now he wanted to destroy them. Further, Bebel pointed out, Bismarck's right-hand man, Lothar Bucher, the one-time democrat of 1848, tried to engage Karl Marx to write for the *Preussischer Staatsanzeiger*. Details were added to build up the impact of this attack.[11]

Somewhat embarrassed by Bebel's exposures, Bismarck made a personal appearance in the Reichstag (unusual at that point in his career) to clear himself of the indictment that he had flirted with the socialists. Since he could not deny his talks with Lassalle, he tried to give them a completely non-political meaning, clearly distorting the record. The human and personal qualities of Lassalle had attracted him, Bismarck said, for the socialist leader had been "one of the wittiest and most amiable men" he had known. Lassalle had not been a republican, Bismarck continued, and certainly not a socialist like the current Social Democrats! With a sprinkling of his own wit, Bismarck observed that "Lassalle was ambitious in the grand style, and for him it was perhaps not certain whether the German Kaiserthum would be established with the Hohenzollern dynasty or with the Lassalle dynasty (great amusement [among the deputies]), but his conviction was monarchist through and through." To contrast Lassalle to the current Social Democrats, Bismarck focused on the Paris Commune. His whole understanding of socialism had changed, the Chancellor said, when either Liebknecht or Bebel (Bismarck could not remember who it had been) had praised the Commune as a "model for political institutions."[12] Once again Bismarck's memory erred, for in actual fact his determined opposition to the socialists began in 1870 when they refused to support the annexationist war against France. But it was more advantageous to exploit the fear of the Commune as a Red Terror. Throughout the debate, Bismarck and the conservatives constantly emphasized the revolutionary tradition in the socialist movement. In this way, it was their enemies who were most diligent in spreading the idea that the Social Democrats were willing to go to the barricades at any moment.

To make violent revolutionaries out of the Social Democrats Bismarck had to distort the record. In the debate on October 9, he

[11] *Ibid.*, pp. 41–43.
[12] *Ibid.*, pp. 68, 70.

claimed that the Social Democrats had never presented positive proposals for the improvement of the working class, that they had always maintained a position of "pure negation." [13] This was nonsense. What Bismarck meant was that the socialists had not made proposals with which he agreed. That had been the case with the Workmen's Protection Bill of 1877, the principle of which he never accepted. Bismarck adeptly overlooked the strong current of reformism in Social Democracy in order to accentuate the political dangers posed by the movement.

To counter the numerous charges against them, the Social Democrats, in turn, tended to exaggerate the peaceful reform nature of the party. Speaking calmly and judiciously for the most part, they presented themselves as the innocent victims of a vicious persecution. Perhaps it was fortunate that at the time of the debate Johann Most, equipped with a truly vitriolic tongue, was sitting in prison. But another socialist deputy, Wilhelm Hasselmann, was ready to hurl violent words at the Reichstag deputies. Using a full range of revolutionary rhetoric, Hasselmann spoke for two hours, defending the Commune and the revolutionary means and goals of socialism. He warned the government and the Reichstag majority that they would be responsible for "acts of violence" which might take place in the future and for the blood which would flow. Leaving the rostrum, he added with an apparent threat, that "Prince Bismarck might think a little about March 18, 1848." [14] Hasselmann's excited outburst seemed to validate what the advocates of the Socialist Law had always said, namely, that the moderation with which Bebel and others spoke was a disguise for their genuine violent intentions. Whatever tactic they used—calm or disruptive—the Social Democratic effort could not turn back the momentum which fear, hate, and ambition had generated for the repressive legislation.

On the nineteenth of October, by a vote of 221 to 149, the Reichstag passed the anti-socialist bill; two days later it became the law of the land. Softened slightly by the recommendations of the liberal parties and the Center party, the measure was not as severe as Bismarck, the Emperor, and the conservatives desired. In retrospect one can see that although harsh in many respects, the law was mild when compared to the ruthless techniques of repression employed in twentieth-century

[13] *Ibid.*, p. 125.
[14] *Ibid.*, pp. 145–57.

totalitarian systems. Nevertheless, it contained sweeping powers of suppression. It empowered the state and local governments to abolish societies with "social-democratic, socialistic, or communist" tendencies; to dissolve meetings where such tendencies were evident; and to prohibit the publication and distribution of Social Democratic newspapers, periodicals, and books. Fines and imprisonment were to be meted out to all who violated these decrees. For areas where Social Democratic tendencies were especially strong and threatened the "public safety," the authorities were empowered to impose a Minor State of Siege (*kleiner Belagerungszustand*) providing the means to expel the most dangerous persons. The law did not include one vital prohibition —the exclusion of avowed Social Democrats from running for public elective office. No doubt, in October 1878 most observers must have assumed that once the Socialist Law was implemented, abolishing all party organizations and publications, there would be little chance for Social Democrats to run for a Reichstag seat. They simply would not have the means to do so. Nevertheless, Bismarck objected to this loophole, and in the following year he sought energetically to close it, but to no avail. Indeed, elections offered the Social Democrats their most effective means for political self-preservation.[15]

Disintegration

The party's executive (the Central Election Committee) never made adequate preparations to counter the blows which hit the whole of the labor movement in the fall of 1878. The executive committee along with the Social Democratic Reichstag *Fraktion* and many other leaders of the party met in Hamburg on October 13, 1878, to plan for the immediate future. The voices of capitulation were stronger than the voices of resistance.

The five-member executive committee, composed of Hamburg Social Democrats, did not include the most dynamic leaders of the movement. August Geib and Ignaz Auer were its strongest personalities, but at the time Auer was living in Berlin and Geib, although young, was deathly ill. Of the others, Carl Derossi had been a functionary in the Lassallean organization for several years, while Georg W. Hartmann and H. Brasch were so disheartened that they shortly left the party.

In this situation, Geib's advice carried some weight, and he uncondi-

[15] For the complete text of the Socialist Law, see the appendix.

tionally advocated a total dissolution of the party organization in order to avoid prosecution under the new law. Some leaders were reluctant to submit to the Socialist Law so hastily, but they did not press their case. The party, hoping to emphasize its adherence to legality and, therefore, to avoid the worst repression, complied with the law with almost undue haste; on October 19 the executive committee voluntarily dissolved the whole party organization—two days before the Socialist Law became effective.[16] The same advice for compliance was given to the rank-and-file party members, repeatedly admonished not to provoke any further retaliation.

The Social Democrats built their tactic on two assumptions: First, they could not fashion any over-all policy until they knew in what manner the Socialist Law would be applied; and, second, they might encourage a mild execution of the law by proper and respectable actions themselves. By such compliance, they believed that the authorities would permit continued publication of their newspapers as long as no direct calls for the overthrow of the existing political and social structure were advocated. To make this approach quite explicit, Liebknecht and Hasenclever, the editors of the *Vorwaerts*, announced on October 21 that in the future they would "place themselves on the ground of the Exceptional Law" and cease to promote any of the ideas or actions prohibited by the Socialist Law.[17]

The initial optimism of the party leaders that avowed compliance would enable them to carry on a somewhat normal party life within the limits of the Socialist Law was soon dispelled. The Social Democrats had to wait only a short time to see how severely the police would implement the major points of the law. Within the first few days the three most important newspapers of the party, the *Vorwaerts*, the *Berliner Freie Presse*, and the *Hamburg-Altonaer Volksblatt* were suppressed by orders of the local police. This was a crushing blow, because these three newspapers alone employed many people; they had a value of several hundred thousand marks and a total subscription of about 45,000. In the months which followed, the police abolished all but two of the newspapers with a socialist tendency. By June 30, 1879,

[16] Bebel, *Aus meinem Leben*, III, pp. 17–19. The meeting of the Social Democratic leaders was immediately known to the Berlin Police Presidium through a report by a socialist editor, R. W. Wolff. The report, not entirely reliable because of its tendency to exaggerate the intentions of the Social Democrats to establish a secret organization, is summarized in Paul Kampffmeyer, *Unter dem Sozialistengesetz* (Berlin, 1928), pp. 136–38.

[17] "An die Leser des 'Vorwaerts'," *Vorwaerts*, No. 125, Oct. 21, 1878.

the toll was great; the police throughout Germany had suppressed 127 periodical publications (including newspapers) and 278 non-periodical publications. That was merely the beginning, but it was a hard reality.[18] The suppression of the newspapers not only destroyed the most effective voice of Social Democracy but it also created great economic problems within the party. Hundreds of party members had earned their living by working on these papers; in one stroke, editors, typesetters, and journalists were without any means of making money.

Many organizations with a slight Social Democratic connection hoped to be spared because the party had already dissolved itself. The hope was an illusion. Educational societies, glee clubs, entertainment clubs, mutual welfare societies, consumers' cooperatives—none was exempt from harassment if the police had the slightest suspicion of socialist affiliation. Considering the general ignorance of high government officials about the nature of Social Democracy, socialism, communism, and anarchism, it is not surprising that local police were poorly equipped to distinguish between persons truly connected with Social Democracy and others with only a devotion to the working class. The severe implementation of the Socialist Law immediately created the impression that it had been designed to destroy the entire labor movement, whatever the contentions of the government. Any workers' society not specifically identified with the Catholics, the liberals, or Stoecker's Christian Socials was immediately suspect to the ill-informed officers of public security.

The intense and indiscriminate manner in which the police implemented the Socialist Law is illustrated by the abolition of the trade unions. During the last months of 1878, the police abolished seventeen central committees of federated trade unions with all of their affiliates, and twenty-two other local unions.[19] A faint suspicion that Social Democrats were associated with a trade union was sufficient reason for its suppression.

During the seventies, the trade unions had made significant progress, stimulated in part by the fact that the Eisenachers were especially interested in them as an auxiliary to the party. As such, the trade unions had concerned themselves with politics only indirectly, focusing their attention on economic assistance for their members. For that purpose

[18] Auer, *Nach zehn Jahren*, p. 93; Mehring, *Geschichte der deutschen Sozialdemokratie*, IV, p. 156.
[19] Auer, *Nach zehn Jahren*, pp. 355–56.

they often had special funds for supporting workers in strikes, unemployment, sickness, incapacity to work, and burial. Now this whole structure was destroyed, sometimes not totally, since some groups were permitted to continue their welfare funds. Generally, however, they were totally abolished. Only the Hirsch-Duncker *Gewerkevereine* (Trade Associations) were unharmed because of their explicit adherence to the liberal parties.[20] The very fact that the police identified so many trade unions as allies of the Social Democrats backfired on the government. The workers had more reason than ever to view the socialists as their true defenders. Nothing did the cause of the government more harm than the arbitrary suppression of unions. The work of destruction was so complete that by the end of 1879 trade unions with Social Democratic sympathies no longer existed.

During the first months it seemed that the Socialist Law would certainly destroy the socialist movement. The enemies of Social Democracy were cheered. In the middle of November 1878, Schulthess's annual gleefully commented that "the execution of the Socialist Law is taking a completely satisfactory course"; all of those who had been threatened by the socialist movement were already beginning "to breathe easier. . . ."[21]

As their foes were encouraged, many of the Social Democrats lost heart. Everywhere there was evidence that they were despondent and weary. In the summer of 1878, Eduard Bernstein had left Berlin for Switzerland to serve as a private secretary to Karl Hoechberg. Now Bernstein was depressed, for the *Zukunft* had been prohibited in Germany, destroying the chief center of his work. But Paul Singer, the wealthy clothing producer from Berlin who had just fully attached himself to the party in the fall of 1878, assured Bernstein that although the party seemed to be shaken it would survive. Do not lose courage, Singer urged, for "out of the ruins will spring up a new life."[22]

New life did emerge, but not before the movement nearly disintegrated completely. The winter of 1878–1879 passed before Social Democrats could begin to find a new footing. The Prussian government had added new miseries for the socialists by imposing the Minor

[20] Josef Schmoele, *Die sozialdemokratischen Gewerkschaften in Deutschland seit dem Erlasse des Sozialistengesetzes* (Jena, 1896), I, pp. 64–75.

[21] H. Schulthess (ed.), *Europaeischer Geschichtskalender 1878* (Noerdlingen, 1879), p. 180 (hereafter cited as Schulthess with the year as title).

[22] Paul Singer to Eduard Bernstein, Nov. 22, 1878, in the Bernstein Archive, International Institute for Social History, Amsterdam, hereafter cited as IISH with references to the specific archival divisions.

State of Siege on Berlin on November 28, 1878. Henceforth, the Berlin police were empowered to expel persons who were considered "dangerous to public security and order." On the next day, sixty-seven of the best known Social Democrats, including Auer, Fritzsche, and Heinrich Rackow were ordered to leave Berlin. Confident that the socialist cause was just and good, those who were expelled from Berlin admonished their comrades against "acts of violence" and to "observe the law" because "in our legality our enemies must go to ruin." [23]

The New Role of Social Democratic Parliamentarism

Two fundamental conditions guided the development of the Social Democratic movement under the Socialist Law. First, by force of circumstances, the party's Reichstag *Fraktion* fell into a position of acting as the executive committee even before the *de facto* situation was officially endorsed by the Wyden congress in August 1880. These parliamentary leaders now held a unique position within the party as the only Social Democrats whose public activity was entirely legal. Second, it was equally clear that the movement could not base itself merely on the activities of its deputies in the Reichstag. Without some organization on the local level to hold the comrades together, the Reichstag leaders would be completely detached from the membership of the party. The severe implementation of the Socialist Law made it impossible to preserve a connection of Social Democrats without violating the law in some degree. Illegal activity, not necessarily conspiratorial, could not be avoided.

These two conditions created tensions within the movement throughout the twelve years of the Socialist Law. On the one hand, the Reichstag deputies were sometimes embarrassed when confronted by the greater radicalism of many party workers who were involved in the semi-underground activities on the grass roots level. On the other hand, the rank-and-file members were often frustrated when they wanted to exert direct pressure on their Reichstag deputies, especially when they sought to force the latter into paths of radicalism. Under these circumstances it was difficult to achieve a genuine integration of the public and private activities of the party, but, on balance, the public parliamentary activity, because it was a secure refuge, tended to take precedence.

[23] Auer, *Nach zehn Jahren,* pp. 97, 98–99.

There is considerable irony in this aspect of Social Democracy under the Socialist Law. Party tradition has always looked upon this as a great "heroic era," which indeed it was; but it was also the period when the parliamentary activity became the unavoidable focus for all discussion of socialist politics. Without exaggeration, one can say that neither before 1878 nor after 1890 was the role of the parliamentary leaders so significant for the internal development of the movement. In the other periods, the Social Democrats had numerous flourishing organizations, all of which were to some degree public spokesmen for the movement. The trade unions, for example, began to share leadership with the party leaders within a decade after the fall of the Socialist Law. Before and after the law, the party held annual congresses where policies were debated in the open and which attracted the attention of the German public.

Almost none of this holds true for the Socialist Law period. The trade unions reemerged by the middle eighties, but they had a limited political role because they could not avow Social Democratic ideas without the threat of dissolution. The three party congresses under the Socialist Law were secret and did not allow the great breadth of debate which characterized the congresses after 1890. The same holds true for Social Democratic newspapers. After 1883, when the authorities permitted the publication of the so-called "colorless" Social Democratic press, these papers were forced to be cautious and devoted much of their space to the speeches and actions of the parliamentary leaders. It could not be otherwise.

The personal composition and the policies of the Social Democratic Reichstag *Fraktion* were therefore of the greatest importance for the whole movement. When the Reichstag leaders were men of devotion, wit, and energy, the party's life was fairly well cared for; but when the *Fraktion* fell to those with frail hands and passive minds, or was decimated by arrests and imprisonments, the whole party suffered and the movement floundered in uncertainty. These weaknesses were especially apparent in 1879–1880, not merely because of the repressive conditions but also because many of the Reichstag leaders were not yet aware of the degree to which they had to use the parliament to address their followers scattered throughout Germany.

An examination of the Social Democratic *Fraktion* between 1878 and 1881 reveals that except for Liebknecht, Bebel, and Bracke its members were not especially talented men and that it suffered further from internal dissension. Sickness also plagued the group. The able and devoted Bracke was seriously ill and could not take part in Reichstag activity after 1878; he died in August 1880.[24] One other deputy, Klaus Peter Reinders, was also ill beyond recovery; he died in May 1879. Two of the oldest and most honored leaders of German socialism, Wilhelm Fritzsche and Julius Vahlteich—both had been at Lassalle's side in the sixties—were deeply discouraged by the difficult life under the Socialist Law. Although still active, they no longer exerted the influence of earlier years, and both emigrated to the United States shortly after the elections of October 1881. The youngest member of the *Fraktion,* Max Kayser, was just twenty-six years old in 1878; although his experience was limited, he had intelligence, a gymnasium education, and considerable confidence. Less able was Philip Wiemer, an original Eisenacher who had never succeeded to an influential role in the party.

Harmony within the *Fraktion* was especially disrupted by Wilhelm Hasselmann, one of the most colorful and flamboyant socialist agitators. A devoted Lassallean journalist, Hasselmann had never reconciled himself to the unification of 1875, in part because the central organ of the new party was published in Leipzig, the Eisenachers' stronghold. He was so hostile to the unification that he refused to become a coeditor of *Vorwaerts* with Liebknecht. Instead, he founded his own paper, *Die rothe Fahne,* and edited it from October 1876 until October 1878, when it was suppressed. He then brought out another, *Die deutsche Zeitung,* in which he carried on a special campaign of criticism against Auer, Bebel, and his old Lassallean comrade, Wilhelm Hasenclever. The tension between Hasselmann and the other socialist deputies ran high; already in April 1879 Bebel wrote to the ailing Bracke that the other deputies were prepared for a complete break with Hasselmann.[25]

As a group, this *Fraktion* was ill suited to give the Social Democratic movement unified and effective leadership in the first years under the Socialist Law. Even the stalwarts, Liekbnecht and Bebel, were not free to devote themselves wholly to party and parliamentary work. While

[24] On Bracke, see the lecture by Georg Eckert, *Wilhelm Bracke und die Anfaenge der Braunschweiger Arbeiterbewegung* (Brunswick, 1957), and Heinrich Leonard, *Wilhelm Bracke. Leben und Wirken. Gedenkschrift zum Funfzigsten Todestag am 22. April 1930* (Brunswick, 1930).

[25] Bebel to Bracke, April 13, 1879, quoted in Georg Eckert, *Aus den Anfaengen der Braunschweiger Arbeiterbewegung* (Brunswick, 1955), p. 64.

Bebel's personal livelihood was not seriously threatened by the Socialist Law—his woodturning shop continued to operate as usual—Liebknecht's chief income vanished when the Leipzig police abolished *Vorwaerts*. Forced to scramble for an income as a free-lance journalist, Liebknecht appealed to Engels for assistance in contacting English newspapers and periodicals which might be interested in articles. If that were not enough trouble for the "Old Soldier," he also had to sit in prison for three months following the middle of November 1878, and again for six months late in 1880.[26] Never very enthusiastic about parliamentary work, Liebknecht was in no position to devote his energies to it in 1879 and 1880. In view of all these troublesome circumstances, it is perhaps not surprising that the *Fraktion* did not make a spectacular showing in the 1879 session of the Reichstag.

The government made two efforts at the beginning of the Reichstag session in February 1879 to impose further restrictions on the parliamentary activities of the Social Democrats. Bismarck inspired both moves, revealing how deeply he felt about closing the loophole of parliamentary freedom for the Social Democrats. The first case involved Fritzsche and Hasselmann, who had been expelled from Berlin by the police when the Minor State of Siege was issued in November 1878. The question arose, therefore, whether their immunity from arrest, guaranteed to Reichstag deputies by Article 31 of the Imperial constitution, would be honored by the Berlin police when the session opened. It was doubtful that a majority in the Reichstag, although hostile to the Social Democrats, would stand by passively if the police interfered with immunity of deputies. At a meeting of the Prussian State Ministry on February 3, the Minister of Interior, Friedrich von Eulenburg, expressed the opinion that the parliamentary immunity could not infringe upon the power of the police to arrest Fritzsche and Hasselmann. He had to admit, nevertheless, that the Reichstag could insist on the right of all deputies to attend the sessions, in which case Fritzsche and Hasselmann would have to be arrested each time they left the Reichstag building and released again for each sitting! [27] When Fritzsche and Hasselmann arrived in Berlin to attend the session, the police arrested them immediately, and the Prussian State Prosecutor, Tessendorf, drew up charges. Bismarck, in turn, put pressure on the Reichs-

[26] For Liebknecht's difficulties, see the following letters which he wrote to Engels: June 8, 1878, and October 30, 1878; in Liebknecht, *Briefwechsel mit Karl Marx und Friedrich Engels*, pp. 256, 258. Also, Bebel, *Aus meinem Leben*, III, p. 162.

[27] Kampffmeyer, *Unter dem Sozialistengesetz*, pp. 166–67.

tag to approve the arrests and to declare that the immunity of the socialist deputies was null and void when it conflicted with an implementation of the Minor State of Siege.[28] The Reichstag deputies refused to follow the Chancellor's demands; on March 21, a majority approved a motion by Max Kayser, demanding that the case against the two socialists be dropped until the close of the session.[29] Momentarily defeated, Bismarck did not abandon his hopes of closing the Reichstag to the Social Democrats.

Bismarck also failed in a second attempt to restrict the Social Democrats. He introduced a measure in 1879 to empower the Reichstag to take punitive action against deputies who were "abusive" in the house. If accepted, the bill would have authorized the Reichstag to exclude some of its own members from its sessions for any length of time.[30] Although primarily directed against the Social Democrats, this bill could clearly have been used for the punishment of any minority group in the Reichstag. It certainly demonstrated—if that was necessary—Bismarck's utter disregard for the freedoms of the elected representatives of the people. Only the conservative parties were sufficiently callous to support it. In his attack on the bill, Bebel made an impassioned defense of the liberties fundamental to constitutional government.[31]

The tests with Bismarck settled in their favor, the Social Democrats could proceed to formulate their policies on forthcoming legislation and employ, when possible, their public positions to give direction to the distraught socialist movement. Trouble began immediately, however. On the one hand, the members of the *Fraktion* were not agreed among themselves on what approach to follow on forthcoming legislation—in particular, Bismarck's tariff bill of 1879. On the other hand, there was no coordination between the *Fraktion*, the rank-and-file Social Democrats, and the numerous party members who had left Germany and from abroad assumed the role of critics. Such disorder was no doubt inevitable. These complications almost destroyed the leadership role of the *Fraktion* before it was operative.

Bismarck's protective tariff legislation of 1879 led the *Fraktion* into a crisis from which it recovered only painfully. The Social Democratic party had no official position on protective tariffs; at the party con-

[28] *SB*, IV, ii (1879), vol. I, pp. 23–28.
[29] *Ibid.*, p. 536.
[30] The bill is in *ibid.*, vol. IV, *Anlagen*, No. 15, pp. 326–31.
[31] *Ibid.*, vol. I, pp. 290–96.

gress in 1876 the Social Democrats had passed a resolution which declared that the conflict between free trade and protection was purely a problem within the capitalist system, in no way touching the principles of socialism. In 1879, the question could not be disposed of so easily; it was now a practical question on which the socialist deputies had to make some decision. But within the socialist movement one could find supporters of both free trade and protectionism and the same dualism characterized the Social Democratic *Fraktion.*

The Social Democratic deputies met on April 12, 1879, to discuss the protective tariff bill and to agree, if possible, on a coordinated approach. The results of that meeting reveal the uncertainty and diversity among the delegates on the issue. All of those present—Bracke, Hasselmann, and Reinders were not there—agreed that the Social Democrats should support the restoration of the tariff on iron to its previous level. Some minor differences of opinion existed on the tariff for cotton yarn. However, Max Kayser wanted the Social Democrats to endorse the whole of Bismarck's new tariff program.[32]

Despite the fact that Kayser was the only member of the *Fraktion* in agreement with the whole tariff bill, his comrades selected him to speak for the party on this issue. Since the party had no official position, the socialist deputies were not particularly concerned, and there were many who agreed to a limited degree with Kayser's position. When Kayser spoke to the Reichstag on May 17, he explained that many of his comrades did not agree with his enthusiasm for protectionism.[33] Nevertheless, he broke one of the patterns which became a rule of Social Democratic agitation during the Socialist Law—namely, that a socialist could not agree with Bismarck in public even when he did so in private. Intransigent opposition had not been unusual among socialists, but after 1878 it was an unpardonable sin to suggest that Social Democrats were supporters of the Chancellor on any fundamental issue.

Kayser's tariff speech might have passed with little notice and no consequences under normal conditions, but in 1879 it created an uproar. Bitter invectives were cast at Kayser by two Social Democrats who from abroad published papers which were smuggled into Germany and read by the hard core of the rank-and-file. Karl Hirsch, who

[32] Bebel to Bracke, April 13, 1879, quoted in Eckert, *Aus den Anfaengen der Braunschweiger Arbeiterbewegung,* p. 64.
[33] *SB,* IV, ii (1879), vol. II, p. 1282.

had lived in Paris for several years, started the *Laterne* in December 1878. Now he used it for a vitriolic attack on Kayser, claiming that the tariff speech was a betrayal of Social Democracy and that the culprit should be read out of the party. Johann Most, who had just established the *Freiheit* in January 1879, charged that Kayser had violated the principles of the party by openly approving of Bismarck's tariff program.[34] Under normal conditions the criticism of two Social Democratic papers without official party standing would not have been too significant, but at a time when the rank-and-file had few socialist periodicals to read, the denunciations by Hirsch and Most made a striking impression. The indoctrinated socialist worker, who risked employer and police harassment by reading these papers, was in no mood to compromise with the Bismarckian system which had imposed such galling restrictions on his party.

For the members of the Reichstag *Fraktion*, the Kayser episode held numerous lessons which they could learn to their benefit as they struggled to keep their role as leaders of the whole movement. It was obvious, for one thing, that they needed their own newspaper to set up a systematic channel for communications with the membership at large. Only in that way could they be sure that the rank-and-file would understand their parliamentary role. The episode also indicated that some means was necessary to counter the super-radicalism into which numerous Social Democrats were drawn when they were abroad beyond the arm of the German police. The seasoned party leaders within Germany were not impressed by the super-radicalism of those who had fled persecution at home. As August Geib wrote to Karl Hoechberg, it was easy for socialists outside of Germany to denounce the role of Kayser in the Reichstag, but the weakness of the critics was "that from abroad one cannot organize and hold the party together." [35] Such distrust was certainly justified, but not sufficient to counter the potential influence of the radical critics from abroad. To obstruct such critics, the *Fraktion* had to make certain that its right to direct party policy was accepted without serious question, a predominance they would not achieve if the flounderings of 1879 were repeated frequently. The final lesson—possibly the most important—was that the *Fraktion* would endanger its popularity if its members failed to abide by the "rule of in-

[34] Cf. "Die Zolldebatte," *Die Laterne*, No. 21, May 25, 1879, p. 671; "Zur Kaiser'schen Rede und Abstimmung," *ibid.*, No. 23, June 8, 1879, pp. 735–37; *Die Freiheit*, No. 21, May 24, 1879, p. 1.

[35] August Geib to Karl Hoechberg, June 20, 1879, *Kleine Korrespondenz*, IISH.

transigent public opposition" to Bismarck's regime. It was not too long before the Social Democratic parliamentary leaders applied themselves to overcoming the weaknesses which were evident in the first half of 1879.

Steps toward Recovery: Der Sozialdemokrat *and "The Red Army Postal Service"*

It was apparent to the Social Democratic Reichstag deputies that the movement could not make a healthy recovery unless it had a newspaper loyal to the *de facto* executive committee. Obviously, such a journal had to be published where the German police could not interfere with its policies. The two papers which had already appeared—*Die Laterne* and *Die Freiheit*—were not suitable as "official" Social Democratic organs because the *Fraktion* could not control them. Furthermore, the *Laterne* collapsed at the end of June 1879, leaving the field to Johann Most, who already promoted a flamboyant super-radicalism. Long experience with their comrade Most taught the members of the *Fraktion* that they could not obligate him to agree with their tactics and policies if he had other views.

The two stalwarts in the *Fraktion,* Liebknecht and Bebel, were pursuing the possibility in mid-1879 of publishing a party paper abroad. Writing to Friedrich Engels about the plans in July 1879, Bebel suggested that they would give the editorship to either Karl Hirsch or Georg von Vollmar.[36] One of the key men, however, was still in the background. That was Karl Hoechberg, who, because of his wealth and publishing experience, would make the whole project possible. In his correspondence with Vollmar, Bebel indicated that Hoechberg, Bernstein, and Schramm—all had worked on the *Zukunft*—would play important roles in addition to the editor. Bebel also expected that Marx and Engels would support the paper and probably contribute to it.[37]

The plan for the paper ran into immediate trouble when Marx and Engels learned that Hoechberg and his assistant Bernstein had been enlisted as co-workers. The Londoners had a deep distrust of Hoechberg, aroused mainly by an article in the *Jahrbuch fuer Sozialwissenschaft und Sozialpolitik,* a journal Hoechberg founded after the *Zukunft* had been forbidden in Germany. The article, published anonymously, crit-

[36] Bebel to Engels, July 19, 1879, in Bebel, *Briefwechsel,* p. 43.
[37] Bebel to Vollmar, July 27, 1879, quoted in Bebel, *Aus meinem Leben,* III, p. 53.

icized the Social Democratic party for its unrelenting hostility to the middle classes.[38] Seeing in this a rejection of the fundamental principles of the *Communist Manifesto*, and certain that the continued influence of Hoechberg would mean more of the same, Marx and Engels wrote a long and angry letter, threatening to disavow their association with the German Social Democrats.[39] Other developments also aroused their suspicions. They had sponsored Karl Hirsch for the editorship of the new paper, but the Social Democrats in Germany naturally had reservations about the man who had attacked their parliamentary policies so vigorously in the *Laterne*. When Hirsch made certain demands which the Social Democratic leaders found unacceptable, negotiations broke down and they gave the editorship to Vollmar.[40] In the fall of 1879, therefore, the Social Democrats could not count on any support from the Londoners.

The party leaders, Bebel, Liebknecht, Bracke, and Auer, although disappointed that Marx and Engels had taken such an uncompromising position, proceeded with their plans. They were sure that the Londoners had condemned the party out of a misunderstanding, and some efforts were made immediately to repair the damage. Liebknecht and Fritzsche composed a joint letter to Marx and Engels, explaining that the untempered denunciations by Hirsch and Most had created the necessity for a party paper, that the editorial supervision would not be vested in the Zurich group around Hoechberg but would remain with the leaders in Germany, and finally that the *Jahrbuch* was unknown to them, but from what they knew they disapproved of it.[41] Some of the Social Democrats were not so patient. Ignaz Auer, with his usual disregard for the authority of theoretical leaders, wrote to Bracke that everything Marx and Engels had written about the negotiations with Hirsch was "nothing but stupidity." The party had not always acted correctly, Auer admitted, but, he wrote optimistically, "the matter

[38] "Rueckblicke auf die sozialistische Bewegung in Deutschland," *Jahrbuch fuer Sozialwissenschaft und Sozialpolitik*, I (1879), pp. 75–96. The article was originally drafted by a friend of Hoechberg, Dr. Karl Flesch, a member of the *Volkspartei* in Frankfurt am Main. Bernstein, Hoechberg, and Schramm revised it and published it with a three-star signature. Schramm was apparently responsible for most of the revisions. Cf. Bernstein, *Sozialdemokratische Lehrjahre*, pp. 77–80, and Kautsky, *Erinnerungen und Eroerterungen*, p. 414.

[39] Engels to Bebel, Liebknecht, and others, middle of Sept. 1879, in Bebel, *Briefwechsel*, pp. 48–63.

[40] Bebel, *Aus meinem Leben*, III, pp. 54–57.

[41] Fritzsche and Liebknecht to Engels, Oct. 21, 1879, in Liebknecht, *Briefwechsel mit Karl Marx und Friedrich Engels*, pp. 272–75.

will certainly straighten itself out." [42] It was a full year, however, before Marx and Engels were reconciled to the group around the *Sozialdemokrat.* As a consequence, they played no essential part in the establishment of the illegal socialist press in Germany.[43]

The first issue of the *Sozialdemokrat* came off the press in Zurich on September 28, 1879. Until January 1881 it was edited by Vollmar and following that by Bernstein until its final issues in September 1890. The control of the paper's policies did not rest with the Zurich group, but with an "Editorial Commission" composed of Bebel, Fritzsche, and Liebknecht.[44] The founders of the paper had no intention of permitting the control of their creation to slip into the hands of persons who were not actively leading the party within Germany. In the fall of 1879, they were specifically guarding against the chance that Hoechberg's group would dilute the revolutionary content, but they were equally alert to the danger that super-radicals such as Most might try to infiltrate the staff. In either case the leaders at home would be embarrassed or compromised.

For the most part, Bebel decided who would be on the staff. He had the allegiance of Vollmar and Bernstein, but even more important, he worked through Julius Motteler, a long-time friend from the sixties and a former Social Democratic Reichstag deputy (1874–1878), who served as the business manager and directed the smuggling of the paper into Germany. Completely loyal to Bebel, Motteler made frequent reports on staff affairs in Zurich. There were sometimes personal frictions between Motteler and the other staff members, for Motteler was a fussy, cantankerous person, who had, as Bebel wrote to Engels "a damned sensitive nose for everything suspicious. . . ." [45] Such a per-

[42] Auer to Bracke, Oct. 28, 1879, *Kleine Korrespondenz,* IISH.

[43] For more details on this whole episode, see Bebel, *Aus meinem Leben,* III, pp. 47–64; Bernstein, *Sozialdemokratische Lehrjahre,* pp. 87–91; Mehring, *Geschichte der deutschen Sozialdemokratie,* IV, pp. 166–68; Mayer, *Friedrich Engels,* II, pp. 333–39; Horst Bartel, *Marx und Engels im Kampf um ein revolutionaeres deutsches Parteiorgan 1879–1890* (Berlin-East, 1961), pp. 30–48. Bartel is the only one of these authors who tends to give Marx and Engels the greatest credit for the founding of the *Sozialdemokrat,* an interpretation which does not hold up in face of the evidence. It is true that their attack on the views of the group around Hoechberg may have forced the party leaders to limit the role of their benefactor, but not much more. Bartel accepts all of the judgments of Marx and Engels as necessarily true.

[44] The organization of the paper is described in the letter by Fritzsche and Liebknecht to Engels, Oct. 21, 1879, in Liebknecht, *Briefwechsel mit Karl Marx und Friedrich Engels,* p. 273–74.

[45] Bebel to Engels, May 12, 1888, in Bebel, *Briefwechsel,* p. 331.

son was extremely useful to Bebel as a source of reliable information on the activities of German socialists abroad. Liebknecht shared the supervision of the *Sozialdemokrat* with Bebel (Fritzsche had little influence even before he emigrated to the United States in 1881), but the "Old Soldier" never commanded an equal personal influence over the staff. As the only organ of the socialists for several years, the *Sozialdemokrat* greatly buttressed Bebel's accumulation of power within the party.

Bebel made sure that he never lost his influence over the staff of the *Sozialdemokrat*. When Vollmar asked to resign the editorial post at the end of 1880, Bebel moved quickly to guarantee that someone agreeable to him would be given the post. Bernstein and Kautsky were both considered, but Bebel obviously preferred "Ede." There were difficulties, for Bebel not only wanted Bernstein as editor but he also sought the support and encouragement of Marx and Engels. To them Bernstein's name implied the behind-the-scenes control of Hoechberg. Bebel had to reconcile opposites, and for that purpose he took Bernstein with him to London in December 1880—Bebel called it his "Road to Canossa"! —to enlist the endorsement of Marx and Engels.[46] The journey rewarded Bebel generously; after discussions with Bernstein, Engels became enthusiastic about him, smoothing the way for reestablished trust between the Londoners and the Social Democrats in the Bebel circle. The idea that Kautsky might be given the editorial post vanished by February 1881 because Bebel and Engels did not have complete confidence in him.[47] With Bernstein's appointment as editor, the policies

[46] Bebel, *Aus meinem Leben*, III, pp. 165–67.

[47] The process by which Bernstein was selected for the editorial post is extremely interesting for what it reveals about Bebel's evaluation of Kautsky in 1881. After Bebel had discussed many matters with Kautsky in January 1881, he wrote to Engels on February 11, commenting on the two candidates. Part of this letter appeared in volume three of *Aus meinem Leben*, pp. 169–70 (erroneously dated Feb. 2), published after Bebel's death in August 1913. Kautsky edited this last volume, although it is clear that Bebel had prepared the material before he died. The following is a section of Bebel's letter of February 11 that was omitted:

"I am naturally very pleased, as you have affirmed since the New Year that you are satisfied with the approach of the S[*ozial*]-*d*[*emokrat*]. So far as I know, the favorable opinion is widespread. I am completely of your view that B[ernstein] is better suited than K[autsk]y, who has all kinds of whims, which stem essentially from his conception and knowledge of Austrian conditions. K[autsky] was here recently and then I had a long discussion with him, and discovered that considerable differences of opinion between him and us could easily arise. Since K[autsky] is in no way established in the editorial post, much more he would only accept it provisionally, so I have written, just today, to B[ern]st[ein] as to whether he B[ern]st[ein] will definitely take the editorship. I hope that this happens, and then the problem would be solved." Bebel to Engels, Feb. 11, 1881, in Bebel, *Brief-*

and staff of the *Sozialdemokrat* were given definite form, held together by a chain of personal connections in which Bebel, and to some extent Liebknecht, was the vital link.

Founding the *Sozialdemokrat*, choosing the editor, securing the endorsement of Marx and Engels, defining the editorial policy—all of these sticky problems were more easily solved than setting up a distribution system, a matter routinely expedited by newspapers under normal conditions. Legally published in Zurich, the *Sozialdemokrat* could be distributed in Germany only by breaking the laws of the Reich. Despite the dangers and frustrations, the Social Democrats threw themselves into this task with the greatest enthusiasm. The result was an illegal distribution system which, considering the constant efforts of the police to destroy it, worked with amazing regularity and efficiency. Perhaps nothing in the twelve-year history under the Socialist Law highlighted the loyalty of the party members as much as the innumerable risks they took to distribute the *Sozialdemokrat*. Or, looked at from the other side, perhaps nothing demonstrates so vividly the incompetence and inefficiency of the police in Imperial Germany as their failure to do permanent damage to the smuggling system. For every barrier raised by the police against the distribution, the Social Democrats found ways and means to outflank the defenders of law and order.[48]

The success of the smuggling network depended upon the unflinching cooperation of hundreds of comrades, but the mastermind behind the operation was Julius Motteler, devoted, patient, and judicious in all that he undertook. A police informer disparagingly referred to him as the "Red Postmaster," but it was not long before Social Democrats used the title with the greatest admiration.[49] This somewhat fastidious

wechsel, p. 102. Kautsky's own account of this matter, *Erinnerungen und Eroerterungen*, pp. 467–70, makes it appear as if no question existed but that he would have been given the editorial post if he had wanted it.

[48] A rather comprehensive account of the police action against the labor movement for the whole period 1871–1898, built on the archival sources, has now been published by Dieter Fricke, *Bismarcks Praetorianer. Die Berliner politische Polizei im Kampf gegen die deutsche Arbeiterbewegung (1871–1898)* (Berlin-East, 1962). Other accounts, not as detailed as Fricke on the actual operations of the police, but also useful, include Kampffmeyer, *Unter dem Sozialistengesetz, passim;* Karl-Alexander Hellfaier, *Die deutsche Sozialdemokratie waehrend des Sozialistengesetzes 1878–1890* (Berlin-East, 1958), *passim;* and Ernst Engelberg, *Revolutionaere Politik und Rote Feldpost 1878–1890* (Berlin-East, 1959), *passim.*

[49] Franz Mehring, "Julius Motteler," *Aufsaetze zur Geschichte der Arbeiterbewegung* (Berlin-East, 1963), pp. 498–501, reprinted from the *Leipziger Volkszeitung*, No. 227, Sept. 30, 1907.

personality, a teetotaler among tankers such as Wilhelm Liebknecht and Friedrich Engels, easily distraught if his wife were not present to care for his needs, supervised a truly impressive illegal business. His apartment, on a hillside in Hottingen near Zurich, was known to the inner circle as "Olympus." From its height, Motteler peered out with a suspicious eye at all who approached.[50]

Motteler not only directed the "Red Postal Service," but he also managed a Social Democratic "Intelligence system" (*Sicherheitsdienst*), sifting and analyzing raw information to uncover informers and agents provocateur. Trustworthy Social Democrats passed to Motteler evidence on persons of doubtful loyalty; after each case had been examined carefully, the comrades were warned about suspicious followers by "The Iron Mask" in the *Sozialdemokrat*. Working quietly and persistently behind the scenes, never interrupting his Sunday afternoon strolls with his wife—known as "Auntie" to the staff—the "Red Postmaster" accomplished much for Social Democracy. If the public knew less about him than it did about parliamentary deputies such as Liebknecht, Bebel, and Vollmar, the German government wanted to know more; for ten years after the passing of the Socialist Law, Motteler was specifically prohibited from returning to Germany, a fate which never fell upon the parliamentary leaders.[51]

The smuggling system had to be adjusted to varying conditions, such as the degree of observation at border posts, the postal regulations, and the intensity of police surveillance in the areas of destination. In general, two methods were used for sending the *Sozialdemokrat:* By a letter envelope through the mail (directly or indirectly) and by large bundles smuggled over the border and distributed through the mails or by other means. Since an individual subscription to the *Sozialdemokrat* was not punishable by law, the direct mail delivery in letter envelopes was not too difficult; but it was too costly for most party members. Most of the papers were sent into Germany in larger quantities. For this the "Red Postmaster" used a variety of means, employing loyal members of the party at various intermediary points. In his apart-

[50] Eduard Bernstein, *My Years of Exile. Reminiscences of a Socialist*, translated by Bernard Miall (London, 1921), p. 106.

[51] On the *Sicherheitsdienst*, see Engelberg, *Revolutionaere Politik*, pp. 205–13, and Fricke, *Bismarcks Praetorianer, passim*. The smuggling system was actually begun, but not elaborated, by Joseph Belli, who worked with it throughout the eleven years. Motteler took full command in late 1879 or early 1880. Belli wrote one of the first accounts of the smuggling system, a delightful account with many amusing details: *Die rote Feldpost unterm Sozialistengesetz* (Stuttgart, 1912).

ment on "Olympus," Motteler would construct boxes and packages of every shape and size, always making sure that they were in no way conspicuous, while "Auntie" recruited everyone she knew to write addresses on envelopes and packages in a variety of handwritings.

The fastest method to get the bundles across the border was to pack them in a suitcase, or some usual form of traveling equipment, have a comrade in Zurich buy a ticket by fast train to a point across the border and deposit the suitcase as passenger luggage. Without boarding the train, the comrade in Zurich would enclose the baggage claim check and a set of directions in a envelope addressed to the agent at the other end of the line, and post it with the same train. With the claim check and the set of directions, the agent in Germany could pick up the innocent-looking baggage and expedite the delivery through the mails. Usually the papers had already been packaged in smaller bundles to appear as the merchandise of a respectable bourgeois business.[52]

Due to the police surveillance, numerous other means were needed to transport the illegal cargo over the border. The master of the border operation, Joseph Belli, had a contingent of workers on Lake Constance who smuggled the freight in boats. They used the Swiss-German border heavily, but many times the illegal paper was sent from Austria, France, Belgium, and Holland. Motteler had worked out a system of disguised messages so that the agents in Germany could telegraph him in Zurich on how the cargo arrived. If the shipment had arrived safely and was already re-shipped, the agent would report "Anna has departed." If part of the shipment had been lost or confiscated by the police, the report might read, "Uncle sick, letter follows." If everything had been lost, the agent would write, "Uncle extremely ill, recovery hopeless." When losses or confiscations were reported, Motteler and his co-workers would prepare another package and send it by an alternate route.[53]

At various times, the Social Democrats tried still another method of printing and distributing the paper. Instead of printing it in Zurich, the

[52] The above description is derived from a confidential report written by Motteler in 1895 for the benefit of the Italian socialists who were facing official suppression. The report, with the title "Bericht Julius Mottelers an italienische Genossen ueber die revolutionaere Anti-Geheimbundstaktik, die Rolle des 'Sozialdemokrat' und die Rote Feldpost," has been published for the first time by Engelberg in an appendix to *Revolutionaere Politik*, pp. 239–82. The information in my text is based on pp. 256–64, and from Belli, *Die rote Feldpost*, pp. 119–20. Hereafter this document will be cited with Motteler's name as "Bericht."

[53] Motteler, "Bericht," p. 265.

plates were sent to a Social Democratic printer in Germany where the paper would be run off and distributed. This method solved much of the smuggling problem from abroad, but it raised equally difficult problems. To insure secrecy, the printer was usually forced to print the paper at night with a limited number of trustworthy comrades. Likewise, the papers then had to be packed and mailed according to the local business techniques to avoid discovery. Despite these risks, the Social Democrats employed this system in emergencies and quite frequently after 1888, when the staff of the *Sozialdemokrat* was expelled from Switzerland; by this time there were numerous presses in the hands of Social Democrats and the police surveillance lost much of its effectiveness. The system was first used after the police had confiscated a whole shipment of the *Sozialdemokrat* going through the Basel route in April 1884. Since the police tightened the surveillance at all points, the plates for several of the following issues were sent to a printer in Stuttgart. For short periods after 1888, Social Democratic printers in Cologne, Altenburg, Burgstadt in Saxony, and Nuremberg ran off the paper. It was also printed in Hamburg, one of the most important entrepôts for the illegal distribution at all times. Whatever system the smugglers employed to distribute the *Sozialdemokrat*, it had to handle a considerable cargo. By 1884, some 9,000 copies of the paper were being sent into Germany; in the last two years of the Socialist Law, 11,000 copies were sent on the average.[54] The illegal distribution of such a quantity of newspapers every week ranks as a genuinely heroic achievement.

Although illegal, the smuggling operation was not reckless. Motteler and his associates took every precaution not to establish a system which, if broken by the police, could be interpreted legally as a "secret society" of the Social Democratic party. In each of the 110 localities to which packages of the paper were usually sent, Motteler corresponded with only one trusted party member for purposes of subscription, payment, and distribution. The whole system depended completely upon personal contact and trust, leaving a minimum of evidence that could be discovered by the police. Despite all the precautions, the police sometimes interrupted the operation, but they were never able to prove that it constituted an illegal reconstruction of the Social Demo-

[54] Engelberg, *Revolutionaere Politik,* pp. 183–85; Ernst Heilmann, *Geschichte der Arbeiterbewegung in Chemnitz und dem Erzgebirge* (Chemnitz [1912]), pp. 209–11; Hellfaier, *Die deutsche Sozialdemokratie,* pp. 175–78; Motteler, "Bericht," pp. 272–73.

cratic party organization dissolved in 1878.[55] Had the police succeeded, they would have had evidence for a successful prosecution of every Social Democrat involved in the distribution of the paper; that would have been a serious blow to the whole organization.

Steps toward Recovery: Early Organizational Developments

The establishment of the smuggling system for the *Sozialdemokrat* was made possible by the preservation of a considerable degree of local party activity and organization even during the years of the most severe repression. The organization of the Social Democrats is difficult to describe during these twelve years because it was informal, diffuse, and often transitory. A brief outline can be given, focusing first on the top levels and then on the pattern of local organizations.

When the Central Election Committee in Hamburg dissolved the national organization on October 19, 1878, the participants selected several members to preserve an unofficial and informal leadership. Liebknecht, Bebel, and Fritzsche were chosen—all were Reichstag deputies—and the informal headquarters of the party was transferred to Leipzig, where the three lived. In December of the same year, these three, along with Wilhelm Hasenclever and Bruno Geiser, founded a Committee of Assistance (*Unterstuetzungskomitee*) to collect funds for the support of the comrades who had been expelled from Berlin after the Minor State of Siege was imposed on November 28, 1878. Along with this innocent function, the Committee of Assistance provided a subsurface political leadership.[56] Since the rank-and-file party members also looked to the Social Democratic Reichstag *Fraktion* for leadership, the functions of these two groups merged. Together they offered the party the only leadership available on a national level.

The organizational issue could not be debated and resolved until the summer of 1880, when the Social Democrats held their first secret congress at the old Wyden Castle in Switzerland (August 21–23). Alternative organizational schemes were presented, but opinion was already

[55] Motteler discusses what he calls the "Anti-Geheimbundstaktik" as it applied not only to the distribution of the *Sozialdemokrat* but also to the whole scheme of Social Democratic organization. He emphasizes that the Social Democrats never built a national organization of a secret nature (the executive was openly held by the Reichstag deputies), although numerous activities of the party demanded a strict secrecy. "Bericht," pp. 246–55.

[56] Bebel, *Aus meinem Leben*, III, pp. 17–18, 25–28; Hellfaier, *Die deutsche Sozialdemokratie*, p. 55.

strongly in favor of recognizing the Reichstag *Fraktion* as the party's official executive committee. The delegates rejected a proposal for a "centralized tightly knit party organization" with an executive "supplied with comprehensive authority [*umfassenden Befugnisse*]." [57] Such an organization involved too much risk of being prosecuted as a "secret society" in violation of the Socialist Law. The plan, it should be noted, had been presented by the Berlin group, one of whom was in the pay of the Berlin Police President. It certainly would have played into the hands of the police. On the other hand, the delegates also rejected a plan which called for a committee of five—from the Reichstag *Fraktion*—whose only task would be to make preparations for the next party congress. This plan did not utilize the possibilities which could be exploited for leadership by the fact that the deputies to the Reichstag could operate legally and with parliamentary immunity.

The organizational plan finally adopted was presented by Ignaz Auer; one may safely assume that he had composed it in conjunction with Bebel and Liebknecht. It recognized the Reichstag *Fraktion* as the "party's official representative," set up a system for collecting contributions to the party, called for periodic congresses, and endorsed the *Sozialdemokrat* as the official party organ.[58] This plan outlines the structure on the top which remained throughout the period, except when, in 1886, the party severed its official connection with the *Sozialdemokrat* because that relationship had served as the basis for the conviction of several party members. It should be noted again that the organization at the top level continued to be an informal set of personal relationships; the traditional leaders of the movement always took part in party councils regardless of their elected position. Thus, although Bebel was not a member of the *Fraktion* between 1881 and 1883, and Liebknecht was absent between 1887 and 1889, no one questioned their right to participate in directing the party, but in fact expected it.

In their most radical move, the delegates at Wyden struck the word "legal" from the section of the Gotha program which stated that the party would work toward its goals with "all legal means." [59] On the

[57] The Social Democrats published a record of the Wyden congress, which omitted many of the subjects actually discussed. The organizational details were only briefly alluded to. The above comes from *Handschriftliches Protokoll des Wydener Kongresses 1880*, Sixth Session, August 23, 1880, in the Motteler Archive, IISH. The manuscript is not paginated.

[58] *Ibid.*

[59] *Protokoll des Kongresses der deutschen Sozialdemokratie. Abgehalten auf*

surface, that meant to the German public that the Social Democrats had been influenced by the super-radicalism of some of their comrades who demanded a completely illegal course. In reality, however, it merely meant that the Social Democrats recognized that they would have to engage in some illegal activity, chiefly the distribution of the *Sozialdemokrat*. It did not signal a turn to secret conspiratorial activity.

To facilitate communications between the German socialist societies abroad and the party at home, the delegates at Wyden accepted a suggestion by the "Zurich Comrades" for the establishment of a Communications Department (*Verkehrsstelle*).[60] Such a clearinghouse for information, reports, complaints, etc., could be highly useful, and it was natural that the editor of the *Sozialdemokrat*, Vollmar, should assume the task of directing it. In less than a month, however, the existence of the Communications Department created a false impression of a secret Social Democratic organization. Furthermore, Vollmar published a report of his own on the Wyden congress without clearing it with the *Fraktion*, releasing it to the public as though it were an official document of the congress. The document contained some outspoken language, and implied, among other things, that by striking the word "legal" from their program the Social Democrats were prepared to use any and all means to achieve their ends.[61]

Once again the issue was raised whether or not the leaders in Germany would be able to impose their unchallenged control over their comrades abroad who spoke in the name of German Social Democracy. In this case, Bebel wrote immediately to the Zurichers, warning them that the Communications Department had no authority to publish official documents on its own, and that its functions were merely to undertake the correspondence with foreign comrades, to release information under certain conditions, and to collect funds.[62] Bebel's concern was justified; the following March, Puttkamer read all of Vollmar's document to the Reichstag as evidence that the Social Democratic danger had increased.[63] By that time, however, nothing more was heard of the Communications Department in Zurich. It was simply

Schloss Wyden in der Schweiz vom 20. bis 23. August 1880 (Zurich, 1880), pp. 28–29.

[60] *Ibid.*, p. 47.

[61] Reinhard Jansen, *Georg von Vollmar. Eine politische Biographie* (Duesseldorf, 1958), p. 24.

[62] Bebel, *Aus meinem Leben*, III, pp. 154–55.

[63] *SB*, IV, iv (1881), vol. I, pp. 634–36.

dropped as a specific agency of Social Democracy, although the staff of the *Sozialdemokrat* continued to carry out the same functions without the title.

The decisions of the Wyden congress were significant not because they created an organization, but because they simply gave an official endorsement to the pattern which had emerged since early in 1879. Much of the discussion at the congress focused on the Most-Hasselmann issue (see next chapter), making these organizational matters peripheral. But the congress revived the morale of everyone associated with Social Democracy. The mere fact that the Social Democrats were able to hold a congress in secret, attended by some fifty-six delegates, proved that the initial blows of the Socialist Law had failed. Because almost all the delegates were agreed in their hatred of both the Bismarck government and the Most-Hasselmann clique, there was great camaraderie. The secretiveness, the romance of revolutionaries in an old castle, the sense that they were making history—all of this added glamour and excitement to their meeting.[64]

Turning from the top echelons of the party to the organizations on the local level, one finds a wide variety of forms serving the Social Democratic party. The leaders urged vigorously that comrades use whatever means possible to organize themselves, propagandize for the *Sozialdemokrat*, and collect funds for expelled persons in need. Local organizations did emerge, some already late in 1878, but the greatest steps were not made until 1880. The links between the local groups and the national leaders were personal, informal, and constantly shifting. Generally, however, the connection was made via a *Vertrauensmann* ("the man of trust"), a person whose reliability and loyalty was beyond question. The very choice of the word illustrates the highly personal and intimate character of these groupings. Seldom, if ever, did a *Vertrauensmann* receive any compensation for his services; his was a work of sacrifice.

In the early years, the party members gathered in various kinds of clubs, including choral societies, gymnastic groups, smoking clubs, and other innocent entertainment associations. These were permitted under the association laws of most of the federal states (*Bundesstaaten*) as long as no political purpose was detected. In Nuremberg, the socialists

[64] All the personal accounts of the Wyden congress by the participants reflect the tone of elation and good humor; this is especially true of the account by Belli, *Die rote Feldpost*, pp. 111–13. Cf. also Bernstein, *My Years of Exile, pp.* 129–33.

continued to assemble in a society known as the "Hocker," meeting each week in a different beerhall; in Bremen, they first banded together in "Workmen's Entertainment Clubs" and "Glee Clubs." The same pattern seems to have been duplicated wherever there were sufficient comrades.[65]

For a more effective local structure, the Social Democrats built election organizations which paralleled the electoral districts for the Reichstag or other representative bodies. Because the Socialist Law did not prohibit temporary associations for election purposes, individual Social Democrats could form "Societies for Municipal Elections," "Workers' Election Committees," etc. Depending on time and place, these election societies could call *Volksversammlungen* (popular assemblies), which, although not restricted to Social Democrats, could be dominated by party members. Behind all of this public activity, the Social Democrats had usually formed a semi-legal, or sometimes completely illegal, society to prepare for everything which would take place at public meetings when permitted. In some places, these organizations were highly refined. In Leipzig, for example, by 1881 the socialists had perfected an organization in which the two Reichstag districts were divided into nineteen subdistricts, each with a "Chairman" (*Obmann*); collectively the Chairmen formed a "Board" from which they chose an "Executive Committee" charged with directing all Social Democratic activity in Leipzig. The police destroyed this elaborate organization late in 1881, after the Minor State of Siege had been imposed on Leipzig; in a very short time, however, it was rebuilt and remained active throughout the eighties. Similar organizational patterns emerged in Barmen, Brunswick, and Breslau by the end of 1880, and it was not long before the same was true for every locale with numerous Social Democrats.[66]

The two largest cities of the north, Berlin and Hamburg, had especially active organizations, but Hamburg's was by far the most efficient. A brief outline will demonstrate that the German socialists did not lose their talent for organization even under the Socialist Law. The organization in Hamburg first emerged in the fall of 1879; by the mid-

[65] Georg Gaertner, *Die Nuernberger Arbeiterbewegung, 1868–1908* (Nuremberg [1908]), pp. 92–93; Ulrich Boettcher, *Anfaenge und Entwicklung der Arbeiterbewegung in Bremen* (Bremen, 1953), pp. 124–25; Wilhelm Schroeder, *Geschichte der sozialdemokratischen Parteiorganisation in Deutschland* (Dresden, 1912), pp. 33ff.

[66] Hellfaier, *Die deutsche Sozialdemokratie*, pp. 56–59.

dle of 1880, it was a fairly smooth-running machine. Here, too, the basic divisions paralleled the Reichstag electoral districts. For each election, a District Election Organization was set up, to be dissolved after the conclusion of the balloting. Behind the public organization, however, existed a parallel illegal structure with a continuous existence. Thus, in each of Hamburg's three electoral districts, the Social Democrats set up an Election Committee; collectively, these three committees formed a Central Election Committee, which, in turn, named an Executive Committee of four members for the whole of the Hamburg area, including one for Altona-Ottensen. For the whole organization, two different treasuries were established: A Parliamentary Election Fund to finance agitational brochures, leaflets, and election ballots, and an Assistance Fund for contributions to expelled persons and to cover legal costs. Various rooms in inns and beerhalls were used by the Executive Committee and the Central Election Committee for its sessions —all carried out in semi-secret. This same organization continued to operate in Hamburg throughout the Socialist Law, a considerable accomplishment in view of the fact that the Minor State of Siege was imposed on October 28, 1880, and that many leading socialists were expelled from Hamburg as a consequence. By the end of the eighties, no less than 5,000–6,000 socialists were part of the Hamburg organization.[67]

For the most part, the city organizations were the largest units established; that is, no structures were set up for a whole province or state. But even in this respect, the Social Democrats made some effort to build a centralized organization for larger geographical regions. Occasional regional meetings were held as early as 1880. Records of what transpired at these meetings are almost impossible to find, since the greatest secrecy was usually necessary. However, from the limited evidence it is safe to assume that many were called to dispatch matters in connection with elections. No particulars are available for a so-called *Landesversammlung* which took place at Mittweida, Saxony, at Whitsuntide 1880, except that it was an assembly for the Social Democrats in the whole area around Chemnitz. For the same area, further *Landesversammlungen* took place in 1883 (listed innocently as a meeting of a Stenographers' Club!) 1884, 1885, and 1886. In the Prussian province of Saxony (not to be confused with the Kingdom of

[67] *Ibid.*, pp. 115–22; Schroeder, *Parteiorganisation*, pp. 35ff.

Saxony), the first "*Provinzial- und Landeskonferenz*" took place in a garden restaurant near Halle on December 26, 1882; according to the police reports, eighteen delegates represented the towns in the surrounding area. The meeting, chaired by Wilhelm Hasenclever, discussed a wide range of subjects on party policy and drew up a plan for the organization of the Province of Saxony and the adjoining areas of the Arch-Duchy of Saxe-Weimar, the Duchy of Anhalt, and the Duchy of Saxe-Coburg-Gotha. Unless the police reports are grossly exaggerated, this certainly indicates a determined effort to organize Social Democrats on a regional basis. One more example may be added. According to the memoirs of Wilhelm Bock, the Social Democrats in the Thuringian region held no less than eight "*Parteitage*" during the Socialist Law. Attended by about thirty to forty delegates, these meetings were disguised under the names of glee clubs or gymnastic societies. It is apparent that there were numerous other regional conferences, but specific information is lacking. Various sources indicate that regional meetings took place in the Rhineland, Wuerttemberg, Silesia, Upper and Middle Baden, Schleswig-Holstein, Westphalia, and Hesse.[68] There is no evidence, except in the case of the Province of Saxony, that permanent regional organizations resulted from these conferences.

This summary of organizational developments for the political objectives of Social Democracy may be concluded with a brief mention of two types of groups with chiefly economic aims. Although the socialist trade unions had been destroyed by 1879, they began to reemerge around 1883 in the so-called period of the "mild practice." Known as *Fachvereine*, they were societies of craftsmen with a purely local organization. Some of these *Fachvereine* were influenced significantly by Social Democrats, but they had to avoid all mention of political matters in their statutes, meetings, and trade journals. In another connection, the passage of the Sickness Insurance in 1883 also offered the Social Democrats some organizational opportunities. The law allowed for the establishment of the so-called Independent Sickness Funds (*Freie Hilfskassen*) as part of the over-all insurance scheme. The Social Democrats immediately encouraged workers who were not members of some sickness program already absorbed by the Sickness

[68] Rudolph Strauss and Kurt Finsterbusch, *Die Chemnitzer Arbeiterbewegung unter dem Sozialistengesetz* (Berlin-East, 1954), pp. 41–42; Hellfaier, *Die deutsche Sozialdemokratie*, pp. 72–75; Wilhelm Bock, *Im Dienst der Freiheit. Freud und Leid aus sechs Jahrzehnten Kampf und Aufstieg* (Berlin, 1927), pp. 39–42.

Insurance to found such Independent Sickness Funds. With Social Democrats in command of an Independent Sickness Fund, it could serve as the legal front for political agitation.

Numerous owners of beerhalls, inns, and guest houses made possible much of the organizational activity of the Social Democrats. With no legal permission to establish their own headquarters, the local party members had to rely heavily on the willingness of innkeepers sympathetic to the socialist cause. In almost every locality there were a few safe beerhalls, either because the owners were silently affiliated with the movement, or because they could not afford to offend their working-class clientele. Someplace in Social Democratic literature there should be a poem of praise and gratitude to the bartenders who poured the grog as the angry men of Germany plotted their course!

Organization, Ideology, and Radical Temperament

The literature on German Social Democracy is replete with commentaries on the political and ideological consequences of the highly centralized party bureaucracy that developed after 1890. Since Robert Michels' classic study on the "iron law of oligarchy," no one has overlooked the fact that there is a definite relationship between the ideology and temperament of a movement and its organizational structure. The same considerations apply to the Social Democrats under the Socialist Law, but with consequences which differ greatly from the experience of later periods. Radically different conditions prevailed before and after 1890.

A functionary in the Social Democratic organization after 1890 no doubt had a measure of personal and economic security. In the years between 1878 and 1890, there were no functionaries as such, although some agitators, the Reichstag deputies, and many of the journalists received financial remuneration for their work from party funds. But these were the exceptions. Instead, an active role in party life offered only the assurance of personal and economic insecurity—one could easily face arrest or the loss of one's job. Such risks could not be taken lightly by a family man with several dependents; a father who devoted himself to Social Democracy had to be a daring person with a firm devotion to the socialist cause. For this reason, although precise data is lacking, it is generally safe to assume that the most active members on the local level were fairly young men.

The consequence of the above factors was that often, but not always, the local leaders appeared to be more radical than those leaders who held seats in the Reichstag. The local leaders had every reason to expect that their organizations might be destroyed at any time by police action. They sought to avoid this, but at the same time they learned that new structures could be erected with a little extra effort and time. Organizations appeared and disappeared, but their commitment to the movement and the ideal remained constant. One may conclude, therefore, that while organizational developments after 1890 gradually encouraged the growth of conservative sentiments, during the Socialist Law an involvement with organizational work required a radical temperament.

CHAPTER IV · INVITATION FROM THE LEFT: ANARCHISM AND SOCIAL DEMOCRACY

Alternatives for Social Democratic Action

DURING THE first years under the Socialist Law, the Social Democrats faced a great necessity not only to hold their numbers intact but, equally important, to formulate a policy of action which was appropriate both to the new conditions and to their principles of socialism and democracy. They did not have a great freedom of choice in this matter, but they did have some alternatives. Each had its appeals, each its weaknesses.

The first alternative, to which they had nearly succumbed, was to capitulate to Bismarck's demands, to abandon oppositional political activity as the representatives of the working classes, and to cooperate with the government's unfolding program of social welfare. The appeal of this alternative lay in its assurance that they would avoid persecution and imprisonment, but it clearly foretold the end of their independent political activity. Another possibility lay at the other extreme, to turn to an extreme radicalism, to the use of violence and the formation of an organization for conspiratorial purposes, abandoning completely the parliamentary rostrum. This course was soon demanded by Johann Most and a few others who gradually drifted into the anarchist movement. The third possibility was that the Social Democrats maintain themselves as an opposition party, pursue parliamentary work in the interest of the working class, and avoid both the use of violence and a capitulation to Bismarck. The Social Democrats chose this third course, and in view of their amazing growth by 1890 it is difficult to deny that for the most part they made the choice best suited to their cause.

Conditions under the Socialist Law created a certain appeal for the course of violent radicalism. In suppressing not only the Social Democratic party organization but also craft unions, workers' welfare funds, educational and entertainment societies, the government created deep fear and hostility among the workers with socialist inclinations. The circumstances forced the socialist worker to engage in some illegal activity, however limited it might be. Once the threshold of illegality had been passed, the pressing conditions could have thrust the Social Democrats into revolutionary violence directed by an underground, conspiratorial organization. The vindictive manner in which the authorities first implemented the Socialist Law created many of the objective conditions for such a development, while the conspiratorial activities of the "People's Will" in Russia provided a current model. The anarchist movement in western Europe, greatly influenced by the conspiratorial dreams of Bakunin, offered an equally significant stimulant for a reorientation of socialist action toward complete illegality. Anarchism offered an alternative that should not be underestimated, although from the perspective of one hundred years of Social Democratic history it would have been inconsistent with the party's traditions.

In the tense atmosphere of the first years under the Socialist Law, elections proved to be the safety valve. Avowed Social Democrats were free to campaign, not only for Reichstag seats but also for positions in the state diets and the municipal councils. This one feature alone markedly differentiated their objective situation from that of the revolutionaries in Russia. The great majority of socialist leaders in Germany had no intention of abandoning parliament as long as it remained open to them. They recognized the Reichstag's ineffectiveness in most areas, and they denounced German parliamentarism as a fraud, but they clung to it as the only outlet for legal operations. But for those few Social Democrats—notably Johann Most and Wilhelm Hasselmann—whose impatience with German parliamentarism could no longer be contained after 1878, anarchism offered a welcome alternative.

As an alternative choice, anarchism had made no serious penetration before 1880. Although Johann Most is remembered chiefly as an anarchist, he did not identify himself as such until late in 1880, and even then his views were rejected by many anarchists as too authoritarian and his influence was greater in the United States than in Germany. He never ranked as a recognized thinker among anarchists; at best he was a noisy journalist and a flamboyant agitator.

Like the other leaders of workingmen in Germany, Most had little contact with anarchists in the sixties and seventies. The German members of the International Workingmen's Association, for example, were untouched by Bakunin's influence. The Lassalleans, due to their feuds with the Eisenachers, sometimes treated the anarchists with courtesy, but only for tactical reasons. In September 1874, the Lassalleans even sent two delegates to the international congress of anarchists at Brussels. The Lassalleans, however, joined a few other delegates to demand that the congress recognize parliamentary activity as an essential ingredient for the emancipation of the working class. Anarchists were completely opposed to such views. Then, as later, the parliamentary issue constituted a fundamental point of antagonism between anarchists and socialists. The sporadic contact between the two groups continued. After the Gotha unity congress of 1875, Julius Vahlteich attended the anarchist congress at Bern in October 1876, but only as a guest.[1] The final contact took place in September 1877, when Wilhelm Liebknecht attended the Universal Socialist Congress at Ghent, an abortive attempt to revive the First International. Although well represented, the anarchists did not dominate this congress, as demonstrated by its approval of socialist-oriented resolutions. Engels, who had been deeply suspicious of the whole congress, was assured by Liebknecht that it had gone better than expected, and he added, "But what babblers of nonsense, these 'anarchists'!" [2] Anarchists and socialists did not meet again at international congresses until the 1890's at the meetings of the Second International.

Only a handful of German radicals considered themselves anarchists prior to 1878, and even afterwards the number increased only slightly. What influence existed was channeled through Switzerland from the Romance countries. The Jura Federation of French-speaking anarchists had desired in 1874 to penetrate Germany, but the first attempts failed completely. In the following years, Bern functioned as a center for contact between French- and German-speaking anarchists. A circle of anarchists met in the "Social Democratic Society of Bern," which included the French Communard Paul Brousse and the Germans Emil Werner and Otto Rinke. Under Brousse's leadership, they founded in

[1] Max Nettlau, *Anarchisten und sozialrevolutionaere. Die historische Entwicklung des Anarchismus in den Jahren 1880–1886* (Berlin, 1931), p. 122; George Woodcock, *Anarchism. A History of Libertarian Ideas and Movements* (Cleveland and New York, 1962), pp. 250–53.

[2] Liebknecht to Engels, Sept. 17, 1877, in Liebknecht, *Briefwechsel mit Karl Marx und Friedrich Engels*, p. 240. Cf. Woodcock, *Anarchism*, pp. 254–56.

July 1876 the *Arbeiterzeitung* as an organ for the spread of anarchism into German-speaking areas, but it collapsed in October 1877 after publishing thirty-three issues. In the same year, they founded a "German-speaking Anarchist-Communist party," but still had little success in penetrating Germany proper. One of the close associates of the group was August Reinsdorf (1849–1885), no doubt the most fervid and devoted German anarchist of this period. Reinsdorf and Werner toured Germany in 1876 and 1877 seeking to drum up sympathy for anarchism among the most radical Social Democrats. In 1876 Reinsdorf met Most, but the latter exhibited no inclination for anarchism at that time. At the time, Werner talked with Max Hoedel in Leipzig; but it was only a superficial contact, although Most later claimed that Reinsdorf had been the inspiration for Hoedel's attempt on the Kaiser's life. It is doubtful whether any anarchist groups were organized in Germany, although Max Nettlau has claimed—on the evidence from Prince Kropotkin's papers—that groups in Leipzig and Munich sent delegates to the anarchist congress at Verviers in September 1877. In April 1877, Kropotkin spoke optimistically about the possibilities of founding an anarchist party in Germany. However, apart from Reinsdorf, Rinke, Werner, and a few scattered associates, there was no anarchist movement in Germany.[3]

The passage of the Socialist Law thus enhanced the possibilities for anarchism in Germany. Almost inevitably, Social Democrats who grew impatient with a predominantly legal and parliamentary course sought allies among the anarchists. Anarchism recruited followers by default, not by an intrinsic attraction to its theory—by the revulsion against the restrained Social Democratic practice and an intense urge to flaunt a clenched fist in the face of Prince Bismarck. The new recruits to anarchism were often comparatively ignorant of its theory and ideals, looking upon it simply as a more radical version of socialism which sanctioned the conspiratorial activism from which the Social Democrats recoiled. This was certainly the case with both Johann Most and Wilhelm Hasselmann, the two men who gave anarchism in Germany its new impetus under the Socialist Law.

[3] Nettlau, *Anarchisten und Sozialrevolutionaere*, pp. 130–35; Max Nettlau, *Bibliographie de l'Anarchie* (Brussels, 1897), p. 157; Johann Most, *August Reinsdorf und die Propaganda der That*, pp. 21–22; Rudolf Rocker, *Johann Most. Das Leben eines Rebellen* (Berlin, 1924), pp. 97–112.

Most's Super-radicalism in Conflict with the Parliamentary Socialists

When Most began the publication of the *Freiheit* in January 1879, his outlook did not differ essentially from that of the Social Democratic leaders residing in Germany. Initially the party had been encouraged by the appearance of his paper, and Engels, putting aside some reservations about Most, hoped that he would have "good success." [4] But Most's mood soon began to change; no longer in the Reichstag as in earlier days, he began to downgrade it as an arena for socialist combat. On the anniversary of the uprising of March 1848, he proclaimed that the social question could be solved only by means of a violent revolution. The following month, the *Communistischer Arbeiterbildungsverein,* the London club which Most had joined and which assisted in the publication of the *Freiheit,* issued an aggressive "memorandum" against all socialist participation in the Reichstag. Reformist endeavors could no longer avail; illegal agitation, flamboyant propaganda, and violent revolution offered the only hope for the working class. In the following months, Most intensified his campaign for a radicalization of party activity; by the fall of 1879, the leaders in Germany already scrutinized his fulminations with great uneasiness.[5] They had cause for worry, because the network which had been established for smuggling the *Freiheit* into the Reich, with its center at Hamburg, operated quite successfully; all the evidence indicates that the *Freiheit* was read widely, especially in the larger cities.[6] The disciples attracted to Most through the *Freiheit* provided him with an important leverage as he sought to force the leaders at home along a more radical path.

[4] Engels to Liebknecht, March 1, 1879, in Liebknecht, *Briefwechsel mit Karl Marx und Friedrich Engels,* p. 264.

[5] "Denkschrift an die deutschen Socialisten," *Freiheit,* No. 17, April 26, 1879. Cf. also a three-part article, "Ist die Socialdemokratie eine Revolutionspartei?" *Freiheit,* Nos. 18, 19, and 20, May 3, 10 and 17, 1879.

[6] Cf. H. Laufenberg, *Geschichte der Arbeiterbewegung in Hamburg, Altona und Umgegend* (Hamburg, 1931), II, pp. 105ff.; Strauss and Finsterbusch, *Die Chemnitzer Arbeiterbewegung,* p. 44. However, by the middle of 1881, in his semi-annual report on the activities of the Social Democrats, Berlin Police President Madai indicated that due to severe financial difficulties only about 500 copies of each issue of the *Freiheit* had been printed in the first half of the year; Berlin Police President Madai's report for June 15, 1881, quoted in Reinhard Hoehn, *Die vaterlandslosen Gesellen. Der Sozialismus im Licht der Geheimberichte der preussischen Polizei 1878–1914* (Cologne and Opladen, 1964), I, p. 82.

The growing antagonism between Most and the parliamentary leaders of the party created new trouble and disunity at a time of serious crisis. At first, the fundamental reasons for the mutual hostility were hidden in a mass of verbiage. The young Karl Kautsky, still living in Austria, where he had associated with the radical wing of the Austrian socialist party under Andreas Scheu, sought to discover the true meaning of the conflict. In 1879, Scheu cooperated with the *Freiheit,* and Kautsky supported the revolutionary stand of Most. Kautsky looked upon the opposition of the German leaders to Most as a potential rejection of their revolutionary tradition. "I hope, however," he wrote to Vollmar in September 1879, "that the party [in Germany] is still a revolutionary and not a reform party, that Most is opposed for personal, perhaps also for tactical reasons, but not because of his revolutionary position." [7]

The problem, however, could not be reduced to these simple terms. Although Most came to espouse a completely anti-parliamentarian position, it would be inaccurate to conclude that by committing themselves to parliamentary practice the leaders in Germany thereby denied their revolutionary position. If socialists entered the Reichstag, Most would not be satisfied with anything short of a totally negative and intransigent opposition marked by the use of violent and provocative language.

The leaders in Germany could not understand why their moderate parliamentary approach should be taken as a denial of socialist principles. They sought to be realistic about all possibilities. Most talked much about revolution, but what were the chances of revolutionary action in 1879? In their public report to the party on the Reichstag session of 1879, the socialist deputies minimized the chances for successful revolution at the time. No doubt they were correct as they concluded that the government could easily thwart an insurrection, and that as a consequence the socialist movement would be set back at least a decade. Rather than irresponsible mouthings about revolution, the leaders wanted to reassure the German populace of their peaceful intentions in order "to give the reaction no possibility of using Social Democracy as a Red Terror." For that, a calm and moderate posture was necessary. They already perceived an "upsurge of public opinion" in their favor as a consequence of their adherence to legality.[8] All of this put a high

[7] Karl Kautsky to Georg von Vollmar, Sept. 18, 1879, Kautsky Archive, IISH.
[8] "Rechenschaftsbericht der sozialdemokratischen Mitglieder des deutschen Reichstages," Part 3, *SD,* No. 4, Oct. 26, 1879.

premium on respectability as a means to decrease popular fear of the socialists. For respectability, Most had even less patience than for parliamentarism.

Bebel was the chief defender, if not also the architect, of a peaceful and legal tactic to calm the popular fear of Social Democracy. Although Bebel rejected a charge by Engels that the party had made concessions to the "Beer Philistines," he admitted that the leaders desired to reassure the "petty bourgeoisie" and the "peasants" who had voted for the socialists in increasing numbers in recent years. In fact, Bebel conceded, these elements stood by the party in the election of 1878 when many wage workers did not, out of fear of losing their jobs. The petty bourgeoisie demanded respectability and moderation, and Bebel confidently argued that Social Democracy would gain most by projecting an image of prudence and legality.[9] He sought to find a balanced course by which Social Democracy would preserve its revolutionary principles without destroying its electoral base.

The balance could not easily be achieved, as illustrated by the advice Bebel gave to Vollmar, when he was first editor of the *Sozialdemokrat*. After Vollmar had written the first issues of the paper with considerable caution, Bebel urged him to use a "most decisive tone," since the mood of the socialists in Germany was gravitating more and more to the left. But no sooner did Vollmar follow this advice than Bebel warned him that some people now believed that the *Sozialdemokrat* had surpassed the *Freiheit* in the use of violent language. Now Bebel cautioned the editor not to print things that could be used against the socialists in Germany since there were rumors in Berlin that the Socialist Law, which was about to be renewed, would be made even more repressive.[10] The same advice held for the socialist deputies in the Reichstag; they had to avoid all unnecessary provocations without appearing to lack courage and the will to fight against the Socialist Law. As the parliamentary leaders carried on in the Reichstag with a moderate but oppositional policy, Johann Most—living safely in London—grew increasingly aggravated.

Pressed from the left by the radicalism of Most, and wishing to assure the German populace of their peaceful intentions, the Social Democrats entered the 1880 Reichstag session in a fighting but calculating mood. For them the chief feature of the session would be the

[9] Bebel to Engels, Nov. 18, 1879, in *Aus meinem Leben*, III, pp. 77–78.
[10] Bebel to Vollmar, Nov. 30, 1879, and Jan. 5, 1880, in *ibid.*, pp. 86–88.

debate on the first renewal of the Socialist Law.[11] Reflecting the assumption that legality was their strength, they came prepared to give specific information that local authorities executed the law illegally. To do this they introduced amendments to repeal almost all the points of the law; this would normally have given them the procedural right to take the floor as each point was discussed during the second reading. Although the tactic was not entirely successful, Wiemer, Bebel, Hasenclever, Fritzsche, and Kayser all brought extensive and detailed accusations against the authorities for illegal implementation of the Socialist Law.[12]

From the beginning, this tactic infuriated Johann Most. To Most, it seemed a demonstration of weakness, rather than strength, to argue that the authorities were guilty of illegalities in the implementation of the law while the socialist maintained their righteousness. A revolutionary party had no need to be so concerned about its legality.[13] As the Reichstag session continued through the spring of 1880, Most hurled more and more abusive language at his socialist colleagues. They could scarcely find a policy to satisfy the belligerent Most; he decried their stand on nearly every issue.

The hostility became especially bitter at the time of the Reichstag debate on Bismarck's seven-year military bill (the *Septennat*) in March 1880. The Social Democrats were traditionally opposed to the standing army, and yet they did not wish to give the impression that they would leave the German nation defenseless. They had always demanded that the standing army should be replaced with a national militia. In the debate on the military bill, Bebel reiterated this position which called for universal military training of short duration "until in truth all of the people are soldiers. . . ." [14] In addition, however, he had sensed a need to assure the Reichstag that socialists and workers were truly patriotic. "Should it happen," he said, "that some power desires to conquer German territory, the Social Democrats will make just as good a front against this enemy as any other party." [15] Naturally,

[11] The original Socialist Law was to expire on March 31, 1881. The law was renewed four times: In May 1880, effective until Sept. 30, 1884; in May 1884, effective until Sept. 30, 1886; in April 1886, effective until Sept. 30, 1888; and finally in February 1888, effective until Sept. 30, 1890.

[12] The Social Democratic amendments are in *SB*, IV, iii (1880), vol. IV, *Anlagen*, No. 113, p. 754; for their speeches, *ibid.*, vol. II, pp. 756ff.

[13] *Freiheit*, No. 11, March 13, 1880, p. 4.

[14] *SB*, IV, iii (1880), vol. I, p. 215.

[15] *Ibid.*, p. 211.

Bebel had limited this guarantee of socialist readiness to fight for Germany to a defensive war and, remembering his opposition to the Franco-Prussian War, no one could justifiably accuse him of surrendering to militarism. But for those who searched for evidence to charge the Social Democrats with capitulation, Bebel's speech offered ammunition.

Emotions flared, and Bebel was forced on the defensive when an anonymous socialist from south Germany declared in the *Sozialdemokrat* that the suppressed and enslaved worker had no Fatherland, only a place of birth. Let those who benefit from the Reich defend it.[16] Obligated to defend himself, Bebel explained that he gave his Reichstag speech to combat the mistaken view that the Social Democrats were "unpatriotic [*Vaterlandslos*]" because they were internationalists. The Social Democrats could only denounce patriotism, he argued, when rulers used it to feed national hatreds and turn the minds of the people from their own misery to the distractions of war. But that patriotism, Bebel reflected, which consists of the love of one's native land, of the "mores" and "speech" of one's birth, could be used beneficially to build a better society in the future. Socialists had an interest in the defense of their country, he continued, because Germany's defeat in war would not contribute to the liberation of the masses. The Tsarist power in the east haunted him as he concluded that it was certainly possible that the enemies of Social Democracy would view a Russian army in Berlin with pleasure.[17]

Bebel's explanations did not conciliate Most and his followers. They ridiculed Bebel's stand and poured out contempt for all talk of the Fatherland. "What is the Fatherland?" queried the *Freiheit*. "Is it the sod on which I was born and which I tilled in my childhood, which the Jew later took away because my father could no longer afford the tax burden? Is it the province which a despot [*Gewaltherr*] arbitrarily robbed because he was stronger? Is it Prussia, which the Hohenzollern would make a Great Power [*Grosstaat*] through robbery and plunder?" No! The enemy within must first be destroyed: "let us not think about a Fatherland until we can warm ourselves for it next to a fire made from the king's throne." [18] Such an uncompromising condemnation of

[16] "Sozialpolitische Rundschau," *SD*, No. 12, March 21, 1880.

[17] Open letter by Bebel, dated April 10, 1880, in "Erwiderung," *SD*, No. 16, April 18, 1880.

[18] W—r, "Unser Vaterland," *Freiheit*, No. 18, May 1, 1880. The author may have been Emil Werner, who had been an active anarchist for several years. The

Bebel's comments on patriotism polarized the hostile groups beyond reconciliation in May 1880.

The moderate tendencies of the Social Democrats in the 1880 session (Feb. 12–May 10) not only stimulated the embittered criticisms of Most but also intensified old frictions between Wilhelm Hasselmann and his comrades. Although a member of the socialist Reichstag delegation, Hasselmann frequently approved of Most's fulminations because he had never reconciled himself to the influence in the party won by Liebknecht and Bebel after unification in 1875. Under the conditions of the Socialist Law, Hasselmann's propensities for the use of radical and colorful language grew stronger; since 1878, he had been more and more influenced by the ideas of Blanqui and even the Russian anarchists. He had no clear idea of a revolutionary program, but he did have an overwhelming impulse to condemn Bismarck's system with bitter and impassioned language. The restraints of his colleagues could no longer contain his wrath; he prepared to disavow them and to proclaim his allegiance to a totally revolutionary course.[19]

On May 4, as the Reichstag was about to renew the Socialist Law and then adjourn the 1880 session, Hasselmann took the rostrum to call the socialists of Germany to deeds rather than words. An able speaker as well as journalist, the former Lassallean brought the house to attention and aroused some laughter as he declared with great bravado that he was a "revolutionary socialist." Under conditions created by the Socialist Law, he said, the working class had nothing to gain from a dozen deputies in the Reichstag who could speak occasionally about the suffering of the masses. "I think that the matter is much more serious. The starving people want bread! The workers of Germany want liberty."[20] How could people believe, he queried, that the workers would be satisfied with a few impotent deputies in the Reichstag?

> No, they [the workers], when free from their illusions will say: in our power and our courage alone is there still salvation.
>
> So, as we see that in Russia the Anarchists now act, so, as we see that the French workers sacrifice themselves—so, Gentlemen, the German workers will also act!
>
> (Oh oh! from the right. Great unrest)

Berlin police arrested him early in 1880, but it is not certain how long he was in detention. Cf. Rocker, *Johann Most*, p. 113.

[19] Mehring, *Geschichte der deutschen Sozialdemokratie*, IV, pp. 180ff., 199–200.

[20] *SB*, IV, iii (1880), vol. II, p. 1167.

(The President's bell rings)

Vice-President Freiherr zu Franckenstein: calls Hasselmann to order. . . .

Deputy Hasselmann: I have told you my conviction.

(Laughing)

Moreover you shall see that the people shall be their own judge. . . . I regret that from this tribune, from the side of several socialists, the Russian anarchists have been placed apart, as a party which stands estranged from us.

(Hear! hear!)

I for my person accept this association [with the Russian anarchists]. For my colleagues I cannot speak in this matter.

But the idea is driven deep into the consciousness of the people that the time of parliamentary chatter is past and the time for deeds begins.

(Hear! hear! Laughing) [21]

With that declaration Hasselmann hurriedly left the Reichstag—and Germany. He went first to Belgium, then to England, where he associated with Most on the *Freiheit*, and finally on to the United States, where he participated in the anarchist movement. For a few months he still had some influence in Germany.[22]

Together, Most and Hasselmann presented the party with its first serious internal crisis of the Socialist Law period. In the spring and summer of 1880, however, they did not have the strength for a truly effective challenge to the parliamentary leaders. Neither had yet worked through to an anarchist theory, although both drifted in that direction. As a matter of practical politics, their influence was weakened by living abroad; the parliamentary leaders were in direct contact with the party workers on the local level. Nevertheless, the parliamen-

[21] *Ibid.*, p. 1168.

[22] Hasselmann's existence in New York was filled with hardship. Hermann Schlueter, a member of the staff of the *Sozialdemokrat* who moved to the United States in 1889 and played a role in the socialist movement, wrote this description of Hasselmann. "I visited him [Hasselmann] in the café which he runs, without disclosing my identity. It must go very badly for him, and his café can in no case pay for itself. His wife works, and certainly, to cover the [café's] deficit. As we, my wife and I, entered, he was busy in the kitchen cooking soup. With a very dirty child on his arm, he finally came to bring us a glass of beer. Everything was covered with the dirt of Hasselmann and the fellow's appearance was disgusting. I almost felt sorry, although he really deserves his fate." Hermann Schlueter to Bebel, April 24, 1889, Bebel Archive, IISH.

tary leaders could not take the threat lightly, if only because their honor and prestige within the movement had been held up to abuse.

The Purge of Most and Hasselmann

Obviously the parliamentary leadership could not control Most and Hasselmann, but it was equally clear that the two rebels had no intention of abandoning their role in the party. With the *Freiheit,* still widely read among socialists, despite the increasing circulation of the *Sozialdemokrat,* Most and Hasselmann had an organ to rally their faithful. Early in 1880, Most had called for the formation of small cells of socialist revolutionaries; some cells were formed so that now he could count upon pockets of partisanship for his cause in various parts of Germany. At the same time, however, his unrestrained personal attacks on so many of the respected leaders of Social Democracy confused the issues. Had Most and Hasselmann developed a consistent and well-reasoned statement for a rejection of parliamentary participation by Social Democrats, they might have been more convincing. By mixing their anti-parliamentarism with abuse against such honored persons as Liebknecht and Bebel, they brought suspicion on their own case and, not least of all, encouraged the leaders at home to counterattack with equal vehemence and vindictiveness.

Early in the spring of 1880, the Social Democrats laid plans for a secret party congress to take place in May at Rorschach, Switzerland. Preparations were made for a confrontation, to deal decisively with the dissident voices of the super-radicals. But not surprisingly, Most and Hasselmann also had potential strength for the confrontation. Several local socialist groups demonstrated their disapproval of the parliamentary leaders by electing Most and Hasselmann to represent them at the congress. The Berliners chose both Most and Hasselmann along with Rudolf Tiedt, a tailor, to advance the cause of radicalism at the congress. In addition, Crimmitschau also chose Most, and his biographer asserts, perhaps with exaggeration, that he received no less than twelve mandates from locals in Saxony. In any case, their mandate strength certainly showed that Most and Hasselmann would have some popular support for their cause at Rorschach.[23]

[23] Mehring, *Geschichte der deutschen Sozialdemokratie,* IV, p. 182; Hellfaier, *Die deutsche Sozialdemokratie,* p. 180; Kampffmeyer, *Unter dem Sozialistengesetz,* p. 210; Rocker, *Johann Most,* p. 74.

At that point, however, a normally unfortunate event turned out to be fortuitous for the parliamentary leaders. They learned that the Berlin Police President had discovered the particulars of the forthcoming congress from one of his spies. This forced the socialists to postpone the conference, but it also gave them an opportunity to marshal their forces for a more effective counterattack against Most and Hasselmann.[24] It also gave the German Social Democrats living in Zurich, including Eduard Bernstein, a chance to discuss the issues of contention with Most, who had already arrived in Switzerland before the Rorschach congress was canceled. Although these meetings with Most were optimistically intended to probe the possibilities of reconciliation, they merely increased the misunderstanding and bitterness on both sides.[25]

When the leaders in Germany drew up plans for another secret congress, to be held at the old Wyden Castle near Ossingen in Switzerland, special precautions were taken to restrict the influence of Most and Hasselmann. For that reason the circular which secretly announced the congress emphasized that the meeting would be concerned only with the affairs of the party in Germany; therefore, it specified that the power of decision was to rest only with comrades who were active and "*living in Germany. . . .*" In order to assure that the congress would be an "expression of the collective will of the party," the announcement added that "*only delegates from groups* of party comrades can

[24] The postponement of the congress was announced in "An die deutschen Parteigenossen," *SD*, No. 20, May 16, 1880. According to Rocker, *Johann Most*, p. 76, the radicals sympathetic to Most were prepared to arrive at the congress with twenty-five to thirty delegates, and that for this reason Bebel and Liebknecht postponed the congress, using the story that it had been discovered by the police as an excuse. However, the records of the Berlin police leave no doubt that they were well-informed about the details of the congress plans. Cf. Fricke, *Bismarcks Praetorianer*, pp. 95–96. The Berlin police, interestingly, also knew about the new plans for the Wyden congress, but Social Democratic counter-intelligence did not discover this.

[25] Cf. Bernstein, *Sozialdemokratische Lehrjahre*, pp. 102–07; Kautsky, *Erinnerungen und Eroerterungen*, p. 457–58; Rocker, *Johann Most*, p. 79. The versions of the Zurich meetings are all filled with emotion. When Most returned to London, he published his own account of the meetings in Switzerland and repeated his charges against the party leaders. He denounced Liebknecht's oath to the King of Saxony, Kayser's support of protective tariffs, Bebel's speech on patriotism, and the "perverted policy with respect to parliamentarism." *Freiheit*, No. 22, May 29, 1880, p. 3. Several years later Julius Motteler wrote an unpublished account of the meeting, also filled with invectives against Most. "Vom vereitelten Congress zu Rorschach 1880 und H. Mosts Citation nach Zuerich," in Motteler Archive, IISH.

take part."[26] That meant that Most and Hasselmann could not receive mandates from their supporters in Germany. Although the parliamentary leaders had been willing in the early spring to arrange a direct confrontation with the two men, by the summer they had resolved to exclude them entirely. In order to be still better prepared, Bebel urged Motteler to make a careful collection of materials to support all charges against Most and Hasselmann. This would be necessary, he thought, because the Berliners would undoubtedly send delegates to represent the "spirit of Hasselmann." Finally, Bebel also planned to meet with his chief allies on the day before the congress convened to coordinate all aspects of the attack on Most and Hasselmann.[27]

It was a foregone conclusion that at the Wyden congress (August 21–23, 1880) Most and Hasselmann would be severely condemned, if not actually expelled from the party. They were not even present to defend themselves as they would have been at Rorschach. In all, there were not more than three delegates prepared to defend the rebels, and one of these, Heufelder (Berlin), was in fact in the pay of the Berlin Police President. Although the Social Democrats were suspicious of Heufelder, they could not prove his complicity at the time.[28] They had reason to be wary, because there was police involvement on behalf of the super-radicalism of Most and Hasselmann. Thus, the congress was presented with a "Protest of the Associated Berlin expellees from Hamburg and Vicinity," containing ten pages of charges against prominent members of the Social Democratic party. The delegates immediately became suspicious and assumed that it was the work of Koerner and Finn, two workers from Berlin who had seriously compromised themselves in 1878. In fact, recent work in the police files indicates that the "Protest" was written by the same spy who had reported confidential meetings of the Social Democrats to the police in late 1878.[29] Al-

[26] Circular of announcement, signed "Walther" [i.e. Vollmar], July 6, 1880, cited in Hellfaier, *Die deutsche Sozialdemokratie*, p. 181. Hellfaier found this copy in the archives of the Berlin Police President.

[27] Bebel to Julius Motteler, July 31, 1880, Bebel Archive, IISH.

[28] For recent research concerning Heufelder's role, see Fricke, *Bismarcks Praetorianer*, pp. 98–99, and Hellfaier, *Die deutsche Sozialdemokratie*, pp. 185–91, who quotes Heufelder's report to the police. Until the end of his life, Bebel was not aware that the police had received such detailed reports from inside the Wyden congress.

[29] *Protokoll des Kongresses der deutschen Sozialdemokratie. Abgehalten auf Schloss Wyden in der Schweiz vom 20. bis 23. August 1880* (Zurich, 1880), p. 14; Fricke, *Bismarcks Praetorianer*, pp. 94–95.

though the delegates did not know the full particulars, they were certainly justified in refusing to treat the "Protest" as a legitimate expression of rank-and-file feeling. The suspicion that efforts on behalf of Most and Hasselmann were instigated in part by stooges and agents provocateurs undermined the whole case for a radical anti-parliamentarism at the congress.

The greatest part of the discussion at Wyden focused on the feud with Most and Hasselmann, but it hardly deserves a detailed recounting. Matters of principle were much less central to the case against the rebels than the provocative manner in which those two had been intentionally disloyal to the party, slandered many respected leaders, and generally showed a total disregard for party discipline. Auer, Bebel, Fritzsche, Grillenberger, Frohme, Motteler, and Vahlteich, all spoke bitterly about the quarrelsome and disruptive role Hasselmann had played for several years. To no avail, Rudolf Tiedt, the one legitimate delegate from Berlin, sought to defend Hasselmann.[30] Most was the special target of Bebel, who recited a long list of items from the *Freiheit* which were anathema to the party. Bernstein, Vahlteich, Liebknecht, and Vollmar embellished the pattern outlined by Bebel. Hasselmann and Most were then officially expelled from the party; only three delegates voted against Hasselmann's expulsion and two on behalf of Most. With that vote, the parliamentary leaders had disposed of a threat, not merely to their leadership but to the principles of Social Democracy.[31]

The discontented Berliners refused to keep silent, despite their defeat on the Most-Hasselmann issue. Unhappy with the decision of the delegates at Wyden to transfer the official leadership of the party to the parliamentary *Fraktion*, the Berliners sought ways to restrict the independence of socialist Reichstag deputies. Tiedt demanded that a "Control Commission," consisting only of "workers," be empowered to supervise the work of the executive committee. He further specified that the "Berliners will have the term 'worker' construed so that 'party officials' are not included, and thus the latter will not be drawn into the control of the party leadership."[32] Tiedt's proposals predictably

[30] *Protokoll . . . Wyden*, pp. 31–37. The names of the speakers were not given in the published *Protokoll;* they come from the *Handschriftliches Protokoll des Wydener Kongresses 1880*, which parallels and expands the published account. In Motteler Archive, XII, IISH.

[31] *Protokoll . . . Wyden*, pp. 38–43.

[32] *Handschriftliches Protokoll des Wydener Kongresses 1880*, Sixth Session,

aroused much resentment. Vahlteich insisted that steps be taken to see that reasonable people would finally get control in Berlin. The same distrust of the Berliners was expressed by Carl Hillmann, trade unionist, typesetter, and sometime editor, who opposed the Berliners' interpretation of "worker" because such views would drive an unfortunate wedge between the party members. To prove this point, Hillmann recalled the "manipulations" of Schweitzer and concluded with a condemnation of the radicals in the Reich's capital.[33] The Berlin radicals lost on every issue at Wyden, but they were not turned from their role as critics on the left; throughout the period of the Socialist Law, the Berliners persisted as the most articulate foes of Social Democratic parliamentarism.

The action taken by the Social Democrats at Wyden precipitated Most's final swing to anarchism. Denounced vehemently by his former comrades and severed officially from all association with the party, nothing could hold him back. Henceforth, Most associated almost exclusively with anarchists, although he assimilated the thought of anarchism slowly, unsurely, and incompletely. For some time, he directed his energies toward the creation of an anarchist movement in Germany by appealing for the allegiance of the radical elements in Social Democracy, thereby seeking to undermine the strength of those former comrades who had disavowed him so completely. It was extremely difficult, however, to bring to life an anarchist movement of any consequence in Germany.

The Abortive Challenge of Anarchism to German Social Democracy

The intensified cleavage after 1878 between the German government and its radical foes, combined with the defection of two leading socialists to anarchism, created conditions more favorable to the endeavors of anarchists than had existed previously in Germany. The fact that the repression had disrupted the Social Democratic organization also led to fragmentation and confusion. For those with the temperament, the anarchists offered an alternative for continued revolutionary work.

The advantages for anarchism certainly existed, but a balanced view

August 23, 1880, Motteler Archive, IISH. The pages of the manuscript are not numbered.

[33] *Ibid.*

must concede that the disadvantages were more numerous in Germany in the early eighties. In Germany, the ideological influence on the workers and middle-class radicals did not favor anarchism, especially with respect to attitudes toward the state. Lassalle had encouraged the German workers to appeal for "state-help" as a means to achieve economic emancipation, and for their political weapon he recommended universal suffrage. These were still appealing slogans among socialists and workers in 1880, and both ideas were incompatible with the dominant themes of anarchist thought. Insofar as Marxism had some influence by 1880, it too contributed to an ideological resistance to anarchism. Although Marxism may certainly be taken as a socialist theory rejecting the state, particularly because of the doctrine of the "withering away of the state," at that time it was more often interpreted as a system in which the central functions were taken over by the state.[34] As a barrier against the penetration of anarchism, however, Marxism was probably more significant because the Eisenachers had personally sided with Marx and Engels against Bakunin in the First International.

The weakness of German anarchism also resulted from factors in the social and economic development. Anarchism tended to be strongest in those areas of Europe which were least advanced industrially and in societies characterized broadly by a minimum of group discipline. The German context contrasted to both of these features. The German workingman had matured in a society which emphasized group discipline as a virtue, and he worked in a rapidly industrializing economy. To that extent, the social-economic conditions militated against the influence of anarchism. Even with no theoretical study, the German workingman could perceive that the complex system in which he lived could not be revolutionized by the violent action of individuals or small groups.

The meager prospects of anarchism in Germany must also be related to the fact that international cooperation among anarchists had declined, especially after the passing of the fiery Bakunin in 1876. Five international anarchist congresses had taken place between 1872 and 1877, but it was 1881 before another convened and for the remainder

[34] See the discussion of Schaeffle's influence in Chapter II, above. Anarchists almost always referred to Marxists as authoritarian socialists. Much later than our period, the Dutch anarchist Domela Nieuwenhuis analyzed Marxism as a form of State Socialism; "Der staatssozialistische Charakter der Sozialdemokratie, " *Archiv fuer Sozialwissenschaft und Sozialpolitik*, XXVIII (1909), pp. 101–45.

of the eighties there were no conclaves of any size or consequence.[35] Despite the public fear of anarchism as an international danger—aroused in great part by the violent deeds of some Russian Populists—the movement was floundering and leaderless. Such a movement on the international level could do little or nothing to strengthen the frail body of anarchism within Germany.

It was also unfortunate that in the early eighties anarchists were abandoning the idea of a mass working-class movement in favor of direct action by individuals or secret conspiratorial groups. This tendency was officially encouraged by the anarchists at their London congress in July 1881.[36] Such a course was ill suited to assist and enliven the emergent anarchist movement in Germany, which needed a way to appeal to the workingman. Nevertheless, anarchism came to mean simply the advocacy of individual acts of violence, popularly propagated in the slogan "Propaganda by Deed." This became the favored catch phrase of Most and the other German anarchists in the eighties. Had they restricted themselves to a consistent anti-parliamentarism along with a defense of the workingman's interests, the anarchists might have challenged Social Democracy more seriously; but when they promoted individual acts of violence they undermined their own appeal to the mass of German workers.

An accurate picture of the German anarchist movement in the eighties is hardly attainable. Most and Hasselmann had outlined a plan for a network of cells (*Gruppen*) consisting of about five members each, with one liaison for contacts with the other cells. Aside from this, the members were to know only their immediate comrades. Although the *Freiheit* reported optimistically at Christmas 1880 that anarchist cells were being established in many cities, the network was never widespread or effectively organized. In all, only a few dozen cells existed with perhaps two hundred members; the chief centers were Berlin, Hamburg, Magdeburg, Hannover, Leipzig, Chemnitz, Cologne, Mainz, and some cities in southern Germany. In actuality, the anarchist organization consisted chiefly of the informal personal contacts among the recognized leaders, mainly August Reinsdorf, Otto Rinke, Viktor Dave, and Theodor Eisenhauer. But they were so often on the move or in hiding that they could not contribute to a durable

[35] There is a concise treatment of the international congresses in Woodcock, *Anarchism*, pp. 239ff.

[36] *Ibid.*, pp. 258–60.

organization. What anarchist groupings did exist probably reached their peak by 1881–1882; certainly after 1883 they declined steadily even though they had sufficient cohesion to distribute a few copies of the *Freiheit* for several years.[37]

The German contribution to anarchist thought in the eighties was also extremely meager. Its ideology lacked the qualities of rigorous thought which were necessary to challenge the lead of Social Democracy. The Mostian ideas of an ideal anarchist society served to confuse rather than to clarify the ideological goals of the anarchist movement in Germany. Most conceived of an anarchist society that was much too centralized for many of his comrades. Although anarchists recognized that he failed as an anarchist in theory, they did not refuse to work with him. Viktor Dave, a disciple of Proudhon and Bakunin, commented on Most's views at a trial of anarchists in October 1881. Most's conception, Dave said, was really an expression of "dictatorial socialism," to which genuine anarchists were completely opposed.[38] Max Nettlau is no doubt correct, therefore, when he says that one could hardly expect anarchism to make advances in Germany when Most himself was so ill prepared and unconcerned about understanding its fundamental principles.[39] The simple anarchism of "Propaganda by Deed" was a poor doctrine to compete with the Marxism which the young intellectuals, Bernstein and Kautsky, studied systematically and popularized energetically.

Organizationally and theoretically weak, the German anarchists achieved very little, either by way of attracting followers or by acts of violence and terrorism. The movement was seriously damaged by its inability to guard itself against police infiltration; arrests, imprisonment, expulsions, and executions almost completely depleted the anarchist leadership in Germany by 1885. Police action was much more effective against anarchism than it was against Social Democracy, no doubt because the former failed to arouse a mass following. New anarchist leaders did not spring up when their leaders were put under lock and key as was the case with Social Democracy.

The record of the German anarchists was filled with failure and undisciplined violence. The anarchists in the Frankfurt-Darmstadt area,

[37] Georg Adler, "Anarchismus," *Handwoerterbuch der Staatswissenschaften* (2nd ed.), I, pp. 311–12; Rocker, *Johann Most*, pp. 86, 89–90; Nettlau, *Anarchisten und Sozialrevolutionaere*, p. 153.

[38] Quoted in Rocker, *Johann Most*, p. 93.

[39] Nettlau, *Anarchisten und Sozialrevolutionaere*, p. 317.

for example, had been infiltrated by an agent of Police Chief Rumpf, leading to numerous arrests early in December 1880. Many of those arrested were tried and sentenced for treason by the German Supreme Court in Leipzig, October 1881.[40] The anarchists sought to get revenge against Rumpf, first by an unsuccessful attempt to dynamite the Police Building in Frankfurt (October 29, 1883). Then on January 13, 1885, Rumpf was found dead from the deep slash of a dagger. A young anarchist, Julius Lieske, was tried and executed for the crime, although he insisted on his innocence.[41] Whatever the truth of the charge against Lieske, the whole affair in Frankfurt was based on simple hate and revenge, not on any principles which could bring credit and honor to anarchism.

The futility of the anarchist "Propaganda by Deed" is best illustrated by the tragic career of August Reinsdorf, no doubt the greatest "hero" of German anarchism in the eighties. He laid the plot to dynamite a train carrying the Kaiser, the Crown Prince Friedrich, Prince Wilhelm, Bismarck, and many German notables to the dedication of the Niederwald Germania Monument near Rudesheim on September 28, 1883. Poorly planned and incompetently executed by two of Reinsdorf's comrades, the attempt failed miserably. The tragedy of the whole affair is heightened by the suspicion not only that the Berlin police were aware of the plot but also that Reinsdorf and his comrades may have received some financial help through an agent provocateur. In any case, the chief government witness, the weaver Rudolf Palm, who had approved of the attempt, had close connections with the Berlin police.[42] Despite its failure, the attempt was the most adventuresome "deed" by German anarchists, and Reinsdorf paid for it with his life on February 7, 1885.

At his trial, Reinsdorf proudly took responsibility for the Niederwald conspiracy and used the opportunity to explain the meaning of

[40] Rocker, *Johann Most*, pp. 89–90; Nettlau, *Anarchisten und Sozialrevolutionaere*, p. 162. For more details on the agents provocateurs among anarchists, see Richard Lipinski, *Die Sozialdemokratie von ihren Anfaengen bis zur Gegenwart* (Berlin, 1927–1928) II, pp. 98–100.

[41] Nettlau, *Anarchisten und Sozialrevolutionaere*, pp. 331–32; J. Langhard, *Die anarchistische Bewegung in der Schweiz* (2nd ed.; Bern, 1909), pp. 279–86. The Social Democrats also accepted the version that Lieske was innocent, but reiterated that the whole course of anarchism had been discredited. See "Der Prozess Lieske," *SD*, No. 28, July 9, 1885.

[42] According to Fricke, *Bismarck's Praetorianer*, p. 160, the evidence does not prove that the police inspired the attempt, but he does assert that their "*aktive* Mitwisserschaft" is "unzweifelhaft." Richard Lipinski, *Die Sozialdemokratie*, II, p. 100, asserts that through Palm the police did contribute 40 Marks to the attempt.

anarchism and its need to use violence. The exposition led him to a denunciation of Social Democracy, its principles and tactics. The Social Democratic party, founded to work for the emancipation of the workers, had betrayed them by becoming a "bourgeois party," willing to limit the struggle for emancipation to the election arena.[43] He lashed out bitterly against Social Democratic parliamentarism, which distinguished it sharply from the anarchist commitment to direct action. To the court, Reinsdorf proclaimed, "We [anarchists] will not wait until on the basis of historical development conditions get better, while simultaneously the reaction strives as far as possible to inhibit the efforts for the improvement of the situation. Therefore, an anarchist party has been formed in Germany, which will move from words to action. . . . For a long time the Social Democrats have limited their agitation thereon, that a number of men come to the Reichstag and that their [the workers'] stomachs are provided for through work. But the great mass of workers sees no prospect for the improvement of their condition in parliamentarism, in the battle with the ballot." [44]

Such statements by Reinsdorf and others did much to clarify the differences between anarchism and Social Democracy to the workers who were aware of these radical movements. The benefit, however, did not fall to the anarchists, as Reinsdorf predicted it would, but to the Social Democrats.

The threat of losing working-class support to anarchism did not worry the Social Democrats nearly so much as the danger of being held responsible by the public and the government for acts of violence and terror. On this issue, the Social Democrats were on the defensive for a long time, because the German public did not have a clear conception of the principles and tactics which differentiated anarchists from socialists. The confusion was natural. Anarchist leaders—notably Most and Hasselmann—had previously been Reichstag deputies of the Social Democratic party. Furthermore, the anarchists were wont to refer to themselves as socialists and defenders of the working class. And, the public knew that many Social Democrats had subscribed to the *Freiheit* and that even after the Wyden congress it was still read by Social Democrats. Likewise, the government always tied the anarchists to the Social Democrats in its public defense of the Socialist Law. Every two years, in the debates on the renewal of the Socialist Law,

[43] From a transcript of the trial, quoted in Hugo Friedlander, *Interessante Kriminal-Prozesse von Kulturhistorischer Bedeutung* (Berlin, 1912), p. 202.
[44] *Ibid.*, pp. 202–03.

the government charged that anarchism was merely a slightly more radical and violent version of Social Democracy.

The Social Democrats themselves sometimes contributed to the confusion. Thus, writing in the *Sozialdemokrat* on March 20, 1881, Bernstein greeted the news of Tsar Alexander II's assassination "with a feeling of inner satisfaction." [45] A month later the *Sozialdemokrat* carried an article of sympathy for the goals of the assassins of Tsar Alexander II. "The fighting methods which they [the Tsar's assassins] employed," the article explained, "are not our methods, but certainly their goals are the same as ours." For that reason, "Social Democracy in all countries holds their memory in honor; therefore, their names are indelibly engraved in our hearts." [46] Obviously, the distinctions between the methods used by Social Democrats and anarchists were not significant to non-socialists, and the Social Democrats in the Reichstag had much explaining to do in order to make them clear. Ignaz Auer spoke at some length on March 30 to clarify the differences, declaring that Bernstein's first statement merely supported all people who fought for freedom. He reiterated that the Social Democrats did not endorse violence, and that they had absolutely no connections with the Mostian anarchists.[47] On the following day, Puttkamer contested all of this, claiming in fact that Most's faction was the most influential element within Social Democracy. To substantiate this, Puttkamer recited a long list of articles from the *Sozialdemokrat* which he claimed represented a wild radicalism like that of Most.[48] Pushed into the corner, Bebel resorted to the tendency to disavow the radicalism of Social Democrats living abroad. In so doing he disavowed nearly every article in the *Sozialdemokrat* that had been written in flamboyant language![49] Incidents like this made it amply clear to the leaders in Germany that they had to educate their followers and the German public to the distinctions between Social Democracy and anarchism.

The distinction between the anarchists and the Social Democrats

[45] Leo, "Das Ende Alexander des Zweitens," *SD*, No. 12, March 20, 1881.

[46] "In Memoriam," *SD*, No. 17, April 24, 1881. A few months later, Karl Kautsky argued that the Russian anarchists would desist from assassinations when given the suffrage and that therefore the assassins stood "on the same ground with the voting German Social Democracy." To Kautsky, therefore, the goals were the same, only the tactics different. But he concluded that both voting and assassins were of no help for solving the social question. Cf. Symmachos [pseudonym for Kautsky], "Wahlen und Attentate," *SD*, No. 23, June 5, 1881.

[47] *SB*, IV, iv (1881), vol. 1, pp. 616–17.

[48] *Ibid.*, pp. 632–37.

[49] *Ibid.*, pp. 658–59.

sharpened in the minds of the public and the police as years passed. By 1884 at the latest, the government knew that the Social Democrats were quite justified in their repeated claims that they were distinct from the anarchists. The records show that by this year the Berlin police office recognized the genuine distinction, although in its public pronouncements and policies it proceeded as if no difference existed.[50] Nonetheless, the public could not fail to comprehend the distinction. Not merely the declarations of mutual distrust and rejection hurled back and forth between anarchists and Social Democrats, but all the actions of the two groups left no doubt about an irreconcilable cleavage. On the one hand, the anarchists not only rejected parliamentary participation but avowed and practiced "Propaganda by Deed." On the other hand, the Social Democrats deepened their commitment to a parliamentary course with each passing year under the Socialist Law.[51]

Although the anarchist challenge failed, the very fact of its existence had considerable significance for the course followed by Social Democracy. In their efforts to clear themselves of responsibility for anarchist deeds, the Social Democrats seemed obligated to emphasize their allegiance to peaceful parliamentarism. As a consequence, attitudes toward parliamentarism became significant as a key to the reliability and trustworthiness of individual party members. A Social Democrat who voiced anti-parliamentarian views might easily be suspected of sympathy for anarchism. By the late eighties, Social Democratic leaders undermined the prestige of anti-parliamentarians by accusing them of being anarchists. In this negative way, the anarchist movement contributed to the determination of the Social Democrats to hold firmly to parliamentary practice.

[50] Fricke, *Bismarcks Praetorianer*, pp. 155–56.

[51] As part of his campaign against all participation in the Reichstag, Most called upon his followers in Germany to desert the Social Democrats in the elections. Cf. his "Offener Brief an die Waehler des V. Berliner Reichstagswahlkreis," *Freiheit*, No. 20, May 15, 1880. It has been argued that Most's anti-election campaign had an effect in Berlin, where the Social Democratic vote in 1881 dropped by 40 percent from 1878. The argument is given by Ernst Drahn, *Johann Most: eine Bio-bibliographie* (Berlin, 1925), p. 15, n. 15. Reasons for rejecting Drahn's interpretation are given below in Chapter VI.

CHAPTER V · RADICALS AND MODERATES: TWO VIEWS OF SOCIAL DEMOCRATIC POLITICS

The Emergence of New Internal Divisions

UNTIL THE fall of 1880, the socialist movement appeared to be divided between the Most-Hasselmann group and the larger following which remained loyal to the leadership of the Reichstag *Fraktion*. In fact, however, Most and Hasselmann had represented only a small fringe, to be trimmed off with no detrimental consequences. These tribulations of the party, whether originating with Bismarck or Most, had created a degree of unity hitherto unknown to German socialism. The succeeding ten years of persecution cemented that unity in terms of organization, but ideologically and temperamentally serious divisions emerged immediately.

When the enemies on the extreme left—Most and Hasselmann—had been lopped off, the intraparty dialogue between "radicals" and "moderates" did not cease; but now the labels applied to different groups and had new meanings. Henceforth, the radical wing of the party consisted of those who were personally and ideologically attached to Marx and Engels; their chief spokesman within Germany was Bebel, supported usually, but not always, by Liebknecht, Vollmar, and later Paul Singer. In Zurich, they controlled the *Sozialdemokrat*, for all the leading staff members—Bernstein, Motteler, Hermann Schlueter—fell naturally into radical roles as the directors of an illegal publication; moreover, the Zurichers almost always regarded Bebel's judgment more highly than that of any other leader. Much of the strength and the ability of the radicals to work effectively within the party rested on the fact that they shared the conviction that Marxism should define the principles and tactics of the movement. Although they were hardly Marxists in any precise sense, they considered themselves such, because they were constantly encouraged and admonished by Engels, with whom most of them had a close personal relationship.

The moderates had no unified ideological guide to party principles and tactics apart from the diffuse traditions of the party. Although there were Lassalleans among them, especially Hasenclever and Frohme, Lassalleanism was no longer an up-to-date guide for the politics of a working-class party in the eighties and it provided only a limited degree of inspiration for the moderates. Ideologically they were eclectic, although that, too, is somewhat misleading because a number of them preferred not to include any of the fundamental Marxist ideas in their creed. The moderates also included some of the older Eisenachers, such as Auer and Blos, and more than once Liebknecht was found in agreement with them. Their strength within the party was derived from the fact that they included a majority of the Reichstag *Fraktion* during the middle eighties, but even with that they were never able to dominate completely the parliamentary policy of the party.

The differences between the radicals and moderates were sometimes sharp and clearly defined, but just as often the lines were not distinctly drawn. The antagonists seldom delineated the idological issues with care, for differences in temperament were often as important as disputes on matters of principle, and the oppressive conditions in Germany obstructed the course of open debate. Hemmed in by the Socialist Law, both groups realized that open fights would only harm the Social Democrats and give encouragement to their enemies. But even with this awareness, the disputes could not always be hidden from public view. With every threat of a split, Liebknecht used his personal influence, often to the disgust of Bebel and Engels, to diminish the significance of the differences and thereby to preserve the party unity for which he had worked so energetically in 1875.

Numerous issues divided radicals from moderates, including not only contrasting opinions about Marxism but also their attitudes on the possibility and desirability of revolution, the significance of parliamentarism for the principles and tactics of the party, the tone and content of the *Sozialdemokrat*, and the relation of their party to the left liberals in the Reichstag. One of the great issues, the proper Social Democratic response to Bismarck's welfare program, will be discussed at length in the following chapter because of its fundamental importance for the over-all policy of the party and for what it reveals about their own reform proposals. This chapter will outline the general differences on principles and tactics insofar as these can be identified and delineated. It focuses on the internal life of the party in terms of these topics, with only a secondary interest in giving a chronological account of the party history between approximately 1880 and 1884.

The Struggle for Control of Der Sozialdemokrat

No one could fail to recognize the key position of the *Sozialdemokrat* for the party's image in Germany and for the political direction of the movement. In 1879, everyone rejoiced that the party had its own organ, but it was not long before the editors of the *Sozialdemokrat* were severely criticized by various moderates within the party. Throughout the early eighties, they protested repeatedly against the use of violent language in the *Sozialdemokrat.* These protests resembled the criticisms the party leaders at home raised against the flamboyant language of Most in the *Freiheit.* Reflecting party sentiment, Vahlteich disclaimed all responsibility for Most's writings late in March 1880.[1] But then, only a few months later, Vahlteich privately criticized the "laughable revolutionary phrases" which Vollmar scattered throughout the pages of the *Sozialdemokrat.* Vahlteich could see no reason for entering into competition with Most in the use of abusive language.[2] The same criticism grew increasingly more intense after Bernstein became editor early in 1881, and the reasons were usually identical with the objections which had been raised against Most, namely, that the socialists living in Germany were reluctant to accept responsibility for what was written in a paper published abroad, where the editor felt less restraint.

As the discontent of the moderates increased by the fall of 1881, one of their number, Louis Viereck, sought to exert pressure on the *Sozialdemokrat* through Engels, with whom he was on good terms at the time. Viereck first suggested in September that the paper should not be written with such "sharpness." [3] He later complained about the "abusive language, lèse majesté, and direct appeals to acts of violence" found in the paper and contended that "only a fraction of the party is in agreement with this behavior. . . ." If the tone of the paper were milder, Viereck thought, the police would probably be less severe, for in south Germany most of the house searches, arrests, and trials in-

[1] *SB*, IV, iii (1880), vol. 1, p. 305.
[2] Vahlteich to Bernstein, July 17, 1880, Bernstein Archive, IISH.
[3] Louis Viereck to Engels, Sept. 8, 1881, Marx/Engels Archive, IISH.

volved people who read the *Sozialdemokrat*. Finally, with eyes obviously focused on the educated and liberal groups in German society, he said that the propaganda value of the paper amounted to nothing because so few issues were fit to give to "non-party members." [4] Engels naturally turned down the appeals for moderation, as he wrote to Bebel, "in all friendliness, but very decisively," and then heard nothing more from Viereck on the subject.[5]

The moderates were unwilling to keep their complaints private as the government cited inflammatory articles from the *Sozialdemokrat* late in 1881 to buttress its repressive measures against the socialists. Hoping to undercut the government's case, Blos and Hasenclever publicly disavowed all responsibility for the socialist papers published abroad during a Reichstag discussion of the Minor State of Siege on December 10, 1881. The socialists who went abroad and propagandized with words of abuse had no feeling for the situation in Germany, Hasenclever said, and from within the Reich there was no way to control them. Blos went even further. He argued—again with ideas reminiscent of the disavowals of Most—that there were actually two German socialist parties: a foreign party and a domestic party. The foreign party had its paper, the domestic party had none. The government, Blos claimed, unjustly held the domestic party responsible for the words and deeds of the foreign party.[6]

This public denunciation of the *Sozialdemokrat* could not pass unanswered, and Bernstein sharply condemned the "cult of expediency" embraced by Blos and Hasenclever. "Our deputies," he admonished, "are sent to the Reichstag to raise the voice of the proletariat, the voice of the suffering, the persecuted, and the oppressed. They are not to moan and complain, they are to protest; they should adhere to the position within the parliament which they take outside the parliament; they are the representatives of the disinherited and the outlawed." [7]

The confident language hid Bernstein's private worries. With some justification, he suspected that conspirators connived to oust him from the *Sozialdemokrat*. Happily, in the Reichstag he could count on Liebknecht, Grillenberger, Kraecker, and Vollmar (Bebel was not a deputy between 1881 and 1883) to stand resolutely behind him. But Liebknecht's son-in-law, Bruno Geiser, used his influence to coalesce the

[4] Viereck to Engels, Dec. 21, 1881, Marx/Engels Archive, IISH.
[5] Engels to Bebel, May 16, 1882, in Bebel, *Briefwechsel*, p. 122.
[6] *SB*, v, i (1881/82), vol. 1, pp. 299, 316.
[7] Leo [a Bernstein pseudonym], "Entweder—Oder!" *SD*, No. 51, Dec. 15, 1881.

group which Bernstein feared plotted against him.[8] In fact, Bernstein knew that Max Neisser, a close friend of Blos', had apparently suggested to Hoechberg that together they found a weekly journal of economics and politics, which by implication would compete with the *Sozialdemokrat.* The new journal Neisser thought, would complement the *Neue Welt,* the socialist literary magazine edited by Bruno Geiser. Although Hoechberg disapproved of Bernstein's Marxist leanings, he hesitated to sponsor such a project because he did not know to what extent he agreed with Blos. Even in disagreement, Hoechberg so cherished his friendship with Bernstein that he could never engage in secret schemes or open agitation against him.[9]

The efforts to start a new socialist weekly in 1882 fell through, but the campaign against Bernstein continued, even reaching the pages of the *Sozialdemokrat.* When Ernst Breuel, a Social Democrat who had campaigned unsuccessfully for a Reichstag seat in 1881, demanded that the paper be more "objective," Bernstein blistered him with the reminder that "we are not only the party of scientific socialism, but we are as such the party of the modern class conflict between capital and labor, a conflict which cannot be fought out with academic discussions." [10] When Breuel persisted, Bernstein published letters from comrades in Germany who fully approved of the tone and content of the *Sozialdemokrat.*[11] "The language of the party organ," wrote the party comrades from Hannover, "in view of the countless vile tricks of the government and the filthiness of the police, *cannot be made sharp enough.* . . . Therefore, be damned with all that so-called 'objectivity'." [12] And Bernstein, aware that many party comrades harbored a fervent class consciousness, continued to demand that the deputies in the Reichstag "show their colors." [13]

Moderates and radicals gave different meanings to their disputes about the *Sozialdemokrat,* and each in its own way had some justification. For their part, the moderates emphasized the issue of organiza-

[8] Bernstein to Engels, Feb. 17, 1882, and April 27, 1882, Marx/Engels Archive, IISH.

[9] Hoechberg to Bernstein, March 13, 1882, and Oct. 19, 1884, Bernstein Archive, IISH.

[10] "Der 'Sozialdemokrat' auf der Anklagebank," *SD,* No. 4, Jan. 19, 1882.

[11] "Noch einmal Herr Breuel," *SD,* No. 9, Feb. 23, 1882. The letters were printed in several issues, under the title "Wie die Parteigenossen urtheilen," *SD,* No. 9, Feb. 23; No. 10, March 2; and No. 15, April 6, 1882.

[12] "Korrespondenzen," *SD,* No. 20, May 11, 1882.

[13] "Bekennt Farbe," *SD,* No. 16, April 13, 1882.

tional responsibility. If they were to answer in the Reichstag for what Bernstein wrote in the *Sozialdemokrat,* then they should have control over the contents, or, lacking control, they should not be forced to endorse publicly what they had not yet read. The argument was presented succinctly by Julius Vahlteich, who, although no longer living in Germany, sympathized with the moderates' dilemma. "To elect deputies at home and preach revolution from abroad is nonsense," he told the Red Postmaster, "therefore, when founding the '*Soz. Dem.,*' we concluded that it should follow the tactic which our papers had maintained before the decree of the Exceptional Law." In itself, Vahlteich did not believe that the content of the paper was too "radical," but to demand that the deputies declare their agreement was "plainly foolish." [14]

On the other side, the radicals discovered an essentially ideological meaning in the dispute. It appeared to Bebel that the moderates intended to deny the class conflict and the "whole conception of the movement as a class movement," which had no place for compromises with the "ruling society." This interpretation also had an element of truth, for many of the moderates had little taste for making the class struggle a basic assumption of the socialist movement, but would have preferred an outlook that stressed the possibilities of cooperation with liberal-minded or even conservative reform groups in Germany. Bebel believed that truly fundamental issues divided the leaders and that a meeting of all concerned was essential to fight out the differences. At the same time he suspected that the moderates would not stand firmly by their convictions when engaged in a full debate on the ideological issues.[15] They were likely to give ground to the radicals on the surface without changing their genuine convictions. In this respect, Bebel erred somewhat, for when the party leaders held a secret conference in August 1882—for which, however, no public record was to be published—the moderates expressed their views with considerable frankness and determination.

[14] Vahlteich to Julius Motteler, March 23, 1882, *Kleine Korrespondenz,* IISH. Living in New York, Vahlteich wrote to his old friend to explain the reasonableness of the moderate position, and with the hope, no doubt, that Motteler would use his influence on the paper to persuade the other staff members that they should subordinate themselves willingly to the directives of the *Fraktion.*

[15] Bebel to Auer, Jan. 4, 1882, in Bebel, *Aus meinem Leben,* III, pp. 226–27. See also, —ml— [i.e., Miles, a Liebknecht pseudonym], "Die Impotenz des Klassenstaates," *SD,* No. 2, Jan. 5, 1882.

The Confrontation at Zurich, August 19–21, 1882

The widespread dissension among the top leaders of the party made it imperative that they meet for discussions to see if the various parts of the organization could be refitted for smooth operation. More than a few hours were necessary for such a confrontation between the staff of the *Sozialdemokrat* and the moderates, and, since the meeting could not be held in Germany, arrangements were made in Zurich. The conference included the staff members of the *Sozialdemokrat*, the Reichstag deputies, and three who did not hold seats at the time, Auer, Bebel, and Viereck. The chief order of business concerned the control and policy of the paper, but many other subjects were touched on during the three days in Zurich.

Despite the abbreviated record of this conference, it is clear that a majority of those present agreed with many of the moderates' criticisms. But even here the moderates lacked the decisive leadership necessary for a complete victory. Blos challenged Bebel's view that the *Sozialdemokrat* should be a "combat paper" (*Kampfblatt*) and argued that it should give much more attention to instruction in economics. The paper, Blos insisted, should be subordinate to the direction of the Reichstag deputies, the official executive of the party. Many supported Blos' presentation, including Auer, Grillenberger, Frohme, Hasenclever, Kraecker, Kayser, Geiser, and Viereck. Leave the "bloodthirstiness" (*Blutduerstigkeit*) to the *Freiheit*, Auer pleaded, and the "instruction" to the *Sozialdemokrat*. It was nothing less than "rebellion," Hasenclever complained, when editor Bernstein said that he could not work under the direction of the Reichstag deputies. Kraecker believed that censorship of the *Sozialdemokrat* was necessary due to the "uncouth manner of writing" which had been employed, and Kayser added that the "rude tone" (*rohe Ton*) should be eliminated and the socialists should work "positively" to show the workers that they were intent upon making improvements. While Grillenberger was not "troubled" by the "rude expressions," he was irritated by the youthful Bernstein's aggressive confidence and paternally admonished the editor not to get on his "high horse" (*hohe Ross*) and not "to play the school master" (*schulmeistern*).[16] Ede certainly re-

[16] From the *Zuericher Protokoll*, pp. 4, 6–8, a handwritten copy of minutes for the conference of August 19–21, 1882, in the Motteler Archive, IISH.

ceived his knocks, but he was also there to fight, and so were his supporters.

The moderates, under Blos' leadership, originally pressed for the adoption of a resolution sharply censuring the staff of the *Sozialdemokrat.* But Bernstein's friends, Bebel, Liebknecht, Motteler, Stolle, and Vollmar, blocked this move and then cooperated with Auer, who sought compromise and harmony, to get Blos' resolution revised. The compromise resolution specified that in questions of principles and tactics the *Sozialdemokrat* was subordinate to the conclusions of the party congresses and the "directives of the party officials" which in turn had to be consistent with the decisions of the congresses. Furthermore, striking at a particularly sensitive point, articles and letters received by the editor which contained "slanderous attacks" were not to be published until they had been approved by the "party executive," that is, the Reichstag *Fraktion.*[17] In effect, the compromise gave the moderates a victory on the principle of control without destroying the practical ability of the radicals to direct the ideological policy of the paper. It solved the problem temporarily.

The few references to ideological matters in the minutes of the Zurich conference, although not recorded in full, give some valuable clues to the differences between radicals and moderates, especially in view of the fact that such inside evidence is often lacking for the period of the Socialist Law. The discussions touched on Bismarck's State Socialism (see the following chapter) and the possibility or desirability of a revolution in Germany. Some of the radicals had an unshakable confidence that the revolutionary upheaval was not far off, while the moderates, not denying that a revolution might take place, were nevertheless not so encouraged by the prospect. Bebel saw the need for more economic education among the socialists, because, as he predicted, "at the moment our economic conditions lead rapidly to a catastrophe in old Europe." Liebknecht urged that more attention be given to organization, so that, if a situation like 1848 repeated itself, the socialists would be prepared, although no one could foresee with certainty whether or when such a revolution would come. Hasenclever assured his comrades, "the revolution will come," but whether within two years as some had predicted he doubted. He suggested that the only significant difference of opinion among Social Democrats on the

[17] The text of this resolution was not found in the Motteler Archive, but is taken from Kampffmeyer, *Unter dem Sozialistengesetz,* p. 213. Kampffmeyer used the *Zuericher Protokoll,* but he gives only a brief summary of the contents.

revolution concerned their expectations about when it would break out. Echoing such sentiments, Grillenberger believed that the revolution would not come "as soon" as some believed, but when it did, he assured his comrades, "you will find us at [our] posts." [18]

Not all the conferees were so willing to embrace revolution. For his part, Blos found so much talk about a revolution distasteful, and an "insurrection," which the *Sozialdemokrat* had seemed to prognosticate, was impossible. And Geiser, one of the most conservative of the moderates, could not see a revolution in the "foreseeable future" and further maintained that because "the evolution of culture also moves on without revolution, therefore, one should not always play up revolution as the last means for the realization of our goals." [19] Thus, Blos and Geiser, in contrast to the other moderates, could not accept revolution willingly, while the radicals, if they followed Bebel, not only saw it as desirable but as standing immediately before them.

Although the socialists at Zurich frequently mentioned the possibility of a party split, neither Bebel nor Vollmar—the most outspoken radicals at the time—sought to provoke a deep division. Bebel believed that the two "currents" could exist in the same party, and Vollmar suggested that the cause of the differences was in lesser tactical matters, not in principles. Although both radicals and moderates believed that the majority of the rank-and-file endorsed their particular views, neither side could overlook the great advantage to be gained by the enemies of socialism if the movement were divided. Auer warned the radicals that if a split did come, very few in the party would stand behind them. That contrasted sharply to Bebel's confident assertions that the great mass of the party rejected the opinions of the moderates and endorsed fully the tone and policies of Bernstein and the *Sozialdemokrat*.[20]

Despite the troubled background and the heated confrontation, the Zurich conference succeeded notably, for it revived something of the spirit of harmony and unity among the leaders that had taken hold of the party at the time of the Wyden congress. After the conference, Bernstein continued to be very disturbed about the attacks against him (and also by the evidence of sympathy for Bismarck's State Socialism), but he wrote that a "spirit of solidarity, of discipline" prevailed in the

[18] *Zuericher Protokoll*, pp. 4, 6, 8.
[19] *Ibid.*, pp. 4, 7.
[20] *Ibid.*, pp. 4, 7, 8.

party, and that the meeting had ended in "general harmony."[21] In truth, the first phase of the intraparty conflict between the moderates and radicals reached its peak with the Zurich conference and tapered off in the following half-year, but a second phase, even more intense, began in 1885 and very nearly split the party. Between the peaks of intraparty conflict, the radical-moderate grouping tended to hold its permanence, and for that reason it is important to explore in even more detail the ideological and tactical outlooks of these two groups.

Ideological Currents: The Moderates as Social Democratic Traditionalists

Although the moderates lacked an integrated outlook, they retained in one way or another two of the original ideological stimulants to the workers' movement in Germany, Lassalleanism and radical political democracy. In this respect, they may be called the ideological traditionalists of German Social Democracy, even though that term seems somewhat inappropriate for a movement which was only twenty years old in the 1880's.

It applies, nevertheless, because the Marxism of the radicals carried the implication that both of those original ideas should be rejected or greatly modified by the socialist movement. In the case of Lassalleanism, there is no question but that the radicals wanted to displace it completely. In the case of the radical political democracy—taken over from the bourgeois liberals—the radicals were not so certain. They had reached political maturity in devotion to that concept of democracy and they were not yet familiar with Marx's *Critique of the Gotha Program,* which contained some of his clearest criticism of bourgeois political democracy. Nevertheless, the Marxist influence on the radicals did turn them away from the idea of the "People's state," which had been the fundamental political idea of the Eisenachers.

In contrast, many of the moderates retained, although somewhat vaguely, the conceptions essential to the "People's state," and they rightly believed that these ideas had always been part of the Social Democratic ideology. As a preliminary, therefore, one observes that the moderate group included members whose ideas went in two directions, in themselves, somewhat conflicting. On the one hand, some of them (e.g., Blos and Rittinghausen) adhered fundamentally to radical

[21] Bernstein to Engels, Sept. 1, 1882, Marx/Engels Archive, IISH.

bourgeois democracy, while, on the other hand, several of them were still essentially Lassalleans (e.g., Frohme and Hasenclever). Given these two strains, it is obvious that the moderates could not develop an integrated ideology, but had to rely simply on the fact that both of these tendencies were found in the Gotha program and in the traditions of the party.

The influence of Lassalleanism with a great proportion of the socialists in Germany in the eighties, rested on the continued personal popularity of Ferdinand Lassalle. His very name evoked a cluster of vibrant memories of that romantic and brilliant person who had accomplished much for the German workingman. "With the masses of our party," Bernstein testified privately to Engels in 1882, "it is the popular author Lassalle, whom they esteem so highly. . . ."[22] Deeply concerned about the manner in which Lassalle's prestige contributed to the inclination of some Social Democrats to look on Bismarck's State Socialism with sympathy, Bernstein would have liked to have seen a comprehensive and destructive criticism of Lassalleanism. But he confessed that "any vigorous attack on him would awaken fanaticism, and to be sure, not only with the old Lassalleans. The people have too long looked upon Lassalle as their champion and would take it hard if one should suddenly contest his services."[23] As late as 1891, when Marx's *Critique of the Gotha Program* was first published, Bebel—certainly no friend of Lassalle—would have preferred that the "passionate invectives" against Lassalle in the *Critique* had been eliminated because even the socialists in Germany believed that the attacks stemmed from "personal hatred and jealousy. . . ."[24] But if many honored the name of Lassalle, few articulated a completely Lassallean program, and, ideologically, only the statist aspects of the original program exerted much influence.

Deeply ingrained Lassalleanism characterized the thinking of Karl Frohme, a man "enormously loved" in the Maingau, according to Bernstein. Admittedly a talented man, Frohme took so much pride in his learning and speaking that his socialist colleagues in the Reichstag faintly praised him with the nickname "Cicero."[25] But despite his talent and his popularity, Frohme failed to develop new avenues of

[22] Bernstein to Engels, Oct. 26, 1882, Marx/Engels Archive, IISH.
[23] *Ibid.*
[24] Bebel to Engels, March 30, 1891, in Bebel, *Briefwechsel,* pp. 408–09.
[25] Bernstein to Engels, June 12, 1881, and April 7, 1884, Marx/Engels Archive, IISH.

thought from Lassalleanism. Without hedging, Frohme wished to avoid a revolutionary upheaval through a peaceful solution of the social problems in capitalism. He saw the one means for that achievement in an application of the power of the existing state. The practical measure advocated by Frohme in 1883 was taken directly from Lassalle's original program, the extension of credit by the state for the establishment of producers' associations which would gradually transform capitalism into a "system of cooperative labor. . . ." [26] Nothing is more obvious, Frohme wrote two years later, "than the recognition that it is the State—that means, the ever-enlarging union of individuals which encompasses all particularized strength in an ethical Whole—which has the function of bringing about the evolution of humanity to freedom and well-being." [27] As a consequence of his desire for a peaceful solution of the social question by means of the existing state, Frohme relegated the democratic political demands of Social Democracy to a secondary status. Insofar as he believed in a "democratic socialism," Frohme assumed that it would be achieved through the social changes brought about by the state's support of cooperatives. [28] Acquisition of political power by the socialists in order to democratize and then socialize the society had little place in Frohme's thinking. The state was already an ethical institution, requiring only a solution of the social-economic problems created by capitalism to complete its mission.

Similar ideas are contained in the speeches of Max Kayser, the confident young Reichstag deputy from Breslau. Kayser not only looked upon the state as an ethical institution but also expressed strong sympathy for the nationalization program presented by Bismarck. And he constantly "promoted social reform" among his comrades, as Bebel said.[29] But his economic and political ideas did not undermine his fervid devotion to the working class. Kayser's life in the eighties illustrates that some moderates could be nearly as class conscious as the radicals. He was harassed so much by the police, and expelled from so many places, that at times he was forced to sleep overnight in railroad cars! Bernstein, one of the sharpest critics of Kayser's ideas, nevertheless gave a sympathetic picture of his personal role: "He is a poor devil, who has been ill-treated by the police. . . . He stands, however, thoroughly on

[26] Karl Frohme, *Die Entwicklung der Eigentums-Verhaeltnisse* (Bockenheim, 1883), p. 339.

[27] Karl Frohme, *Friedliche Entwicklung oder Gewaltsamer Umsturz? Ein Mahnwort an alle Gesellschaftsklassen* (Nuremberg, 1885), p. 13.

[28] Karl Frohme, *Demagogie und Sozialdemokratie* (Nuremberg, 1885), pp. 12–13. Cf. Also his pamphlet, *Aus Nacht zum Licht!* (Nuremberg, 1884).

[29] Bebel to Engels, Nov. 1, 1883, in Bebel, *Briefwechsel*, p. 168.

the standpoint of the class conflict, and if he abandoned his nationalization, he would accomplish more than he does now. With him, as with so many of our people, one must not forget that they have never gotten out of the atmosphere of the German Reich [*deutschen Reichsathmosphaere*]. At least Kayser is tolerant of the left. . . ." [30] Kayser's life offered fairly clear proof that the radicals were not always justified when they charged that sympathy for Bismarck's social and economic program implied a personal betrayal of the working class.

Turning from those who were influenced to some degree by Lassalleanism, one could find among the moderates representatives of a kind of liberal humanitarian and ethical socialism, repelled by constant talk about a class struggle and a revolutionary upheaval and lured by the vision of social harmony and a benevolent human progress. For men such as Karl Hoechberg and Bruno Geiser, socialism served its principles if it contributed to the achievement of what was good and beautiful for all humanity. In the seventies, Geiser's conception of socialism's goals essentially repeated the happiness principle of English Utilitarianism, a happiness to be achieved through the "harmonious evolution of the spiritual faculties of individuals." [31] He later based his exposition of socialism on thinkers from the German Enlightenment, Herder, Lessing, and Schiller, with only one mention of Marx, Engels, and Lassalle.[32] Geiser's writings indicate that socialism had no primary concern with the particular needs and demands of the working class. He insisted that socialism represented the "totality of humanity," and that it was the "highest duty" of the state and every "human association" to contribute to the achievement of happiness through the "harmonious development" of the physical and spiritual attributes of man.[33] So certain was his belief in a harmonious progress that he could comment without qualification that cultural history teaches "that with a rising culture, war and discord gradually decrease, and strife of every kind, even the competition for the goods of life, appears more and more in nobler and still less crude forms." [34] Geiser not only expounded these traditional liberal ideas of harmonious progress but he also liked to live

[30] Bernstein to Engels, Feb. 24, 1883, Marx/Engels Archives, IISH. Cf. Theodor Mueller, *45 Fuehrer aus den Anfaengen und dem Heldenzeitalter der Breslauer Sozialdemokratie* (Breslau, 1925), p. 69.

[31] Bruno Geiser, *Die Forderungen des Sozialismus an Zukunft und Gegenwart* (2nd ed.; Brunswick, 1876), p. 6.

[32] Bruno Geiser, *Unter welchen Bedingungen kann die Sozialdemokratie zum Siege Gelangen?* (Leipzig, 1880), pp. 1, 10–20, 52.

[33] *Ibid.*, pp. 7, 52.

[34] Bruno Geiser, *Die Ueberwindung des Kriegs durch Entwicklung des Voelkerrechts* (Stuttgart, 1886), p. 44.

in a luxurious bourgeois manner, something which obstructed a feeling for the working class and which Bebel found intolerable.[35] By contrast with Geiser, it is easy to see that those with Lassallean preferences—Kayser, Frohme, Hasenclever—had a much more immediate sense of working-class sentiments.

Many of the sentiments expressed by Geiser, and also by Frohme, can be found in Wilhelm Blos, with the difference that Blos retained a much closer relationship—personally and ideologically—to the radical democrats from south Germany with whom he had worked before joining the Eisenachers in 1872. He preserved a close friendship with several members of the *Volkspartei* and usually advocated close Social Democratic cooperation with reform-minded liberals if the latter made it possible, a position which the radicals never encouraged although they seldom condemned it explicitly. Like so many other Social Democratic leaders, radical or moderate, Blos made his living as a journalist, helping to edit the *Volksstaat* in 1872–1874, while Liebknecht was in prison, struggling for a position with numerous journals during the difficult early years of the Socialist Law, writing historical books and novels, and contributing substantially to the development of a moderate socialist press in the middle eighties. Through this kind of activity, Blos' views reached a fairly wide audience.[36]

Although of radical democratic convictions, Blos had no desire to be an active revolutionary, nor to use the class struggle as a fundamental concept for socialist policy. In Germany, the future belonged to democracy without the need of a revolution to introduce it. "We Germans," he reflected in a book on the French Revolution, "turn away with shudders from bloody catastrophes, from the murder of the defenseless, which does not correspond to our nature." [37] Revolutions of the old style, with bloodshed, mobs, and barricades, had come to an end in 1848, Blos concluded, because revolution in the new style "revolutionizes the minds, in the awareness that knowledge is power." [38] Such slogans from the treasury of liberal optimism were common with

[35] Bebel often doubted Geiser's reliability in handling the finances of the *Neue Welt*, due to his "style of living." Bebel to Derossi, Sept. 23, 1879, Bebel Archive, IISH. In the summer of 1886, Geiser rented quarters in a very comfortable pension in Heidelberg and lived a luxurious life. At the same time, he had financial troubles with a group in Hamburg. All of this led Bebel to demand that Liebknecht, Geiser's father-in-law, take some action to remedy these scandals. Bebel to Liebknecht, Nov. 1, 1886, Liebknecht Archive, IISH.

[36] Wilhelm Blos, *Denkwuerdigkeiten eines Sozialdemokraten* (Munich, 1914, 1919), II, pp. 17–19, 69, 109–10.

[37] Wilhelm Blos, *Die franzoesische Revolution* (Stuttgart [1888]) p. 613.

[38] Wilhelm Blos, *Die deutsche Revolution* (Stuttgart [1891]), p. 4.

Blos, and Bernstein's judgment that men like him were "aesthetic or academic socialists" was quite appropriate, despite the unjust implication that they had little to contribute to the cause of socialism. They preferred nonetheless to avoid a purely working-class socialism by appealing to all reform-minded citizens, whether they be proletarian, bourgeois, or even landed aristocrats.

Some of the moderates saw a definite possibility for the Social Democrats to cooperate with the radical liberals after the elections of October 1881, when the Progressives and the Secessionists (a split from the National Liberals) together won 109 seats in the Reichstag. In the same election, the *Volkspartei* increased its representation from three to eight Reichstag deputies. The prospects of a unified democratic bloc were considered by Blos already in February 1881, and he made the following suggestion to Engels: "We shall seek to form a new party, to which we draw all democratic elements with a new program so that we can push other persons forward. The program must include the usual democratic demands, the normal working day and something on the taking over of the mortgage system by the state." [39] Louis Viereck, another moderate, pursued the same idea before and after the October election, again in letters to Engels. In May, Viereck thought that if it "were possible to come out in a pure political opposition" the Social Democrats would have "extraordinary success." [40] After the election, in which the Social Democrats maintained most of their strength, Viereck observed that the government could not "think of mastering the bourgeois opposition without our [Social Democratic] 'help'." That meant of course that the bourgeois opposition would also have to make "extensive concessions" to the Social Democrats, which Viereck counted on because he had no intention at that time of suggesting that his party support the government.[41] Viereck believed that a new democratic left could be formed because the Progressives, like the National Liberals, would have their own "secession." "We would then have three groups in the Reichstag: a protective tariff, agrarian-clerical Right, with white blouses; a Manchester phalanx with liberal allies; and a reorganized democracy, as I have believed possible for a long time, and the realization of which appears to me to get nearer all the time." [42]

[39] Wilhelm Blos to Engels, Feb. 4, 1881, as quoted in Ernst Engelberg, *Revolutionaere Politik*, p. 43, n. 15.
[40] Viereck to Engels, May 6, 1881, Marx/Engels Archive, IISH.
[41] Viereck to Engels, Nov. 16, 1881, Marx/Engels Archive, IISH.
[42] Viereck to Engels, Dec. 2, 1881, Marx/Engels Archive, IISH.

The idea of a democratic bloc made no headway, in part because Engels and the radicals never encouraged it, and in part because the Progressives and Secessionists were not interested in tying themselves to socialists whose economic principles were far removed from theirs. In one sense, however, the radicals should have shown some interest in the scheme for a democratic bloc. Although Viereck did not profess to be a Marxist, the idea of a democratic bloc in opposition to the conservative rule of Bismarck harmonized to some degree with the Marxist theory of the stages of development leading to a social revolution. As long as the center of power in Germany rested in the hands of the landowners, the military, and a few great industrialists, some cooperation between the democratic parties was certainly in line with Marxist thought. To this extent, Viereck and Blos never accepted the Lassallean slogan—also included in the Gotha program—that in contrast to the proletariat "all other classes make up one reactionary mass." But at the same time, a Marxist could not accept Viereck's suggestion because it was intended to diminish both the class consciousness of the German workers and the proletarian orientation of Social Democracy.

The idea of a democratic bloc had no appeal to Bebel, who believed that the German bourgeoisie was no longer a dynamic class capable of standing in the way of the Social Democrats. In September 1881, Bebel predicted that the "victory" of the Social Democratic cause, "despite all Exceptional Laws and possible setbacks in the elections," could be expected in a "relatively short span of time." [43] A few years later, he concluded that the economic development in Germany had proceeded so far that Germany would in fact skip over the stage of bourgeois democracy.[44] Thus, Bebel did not oppose cooperation with the bourgeois democrats in itself, but simply found it unnecessary because they were becoming politically insignificant.

The moderates made some attempts to cooperate with the radical liberals and the *Volkspartei* in the Reichstag between November 1881 and March 1884. While Viereck's idea of a democratic bloc could not be realized, cooperation was possible on specific points. Thus, when

[43] Bebel to Engels, Sept. 20, 1881, in Bebel, *Briefwechsel,* p. 118. In this same letter, Bebel mentions that he had just visited Viereck in Munich, but he does not indicate whether they discussed the idea of a democratic bloc or not. It is quite likely that they discussed related topics at least, for Viereck was on good terms with both Bebel and Engels and was eager to have an important role in party affairs.

[44] Bebel to Engels, Nov. 24, 1884, in *ibid.*, pp. 198–99.

the Social Democrats introduced a bill to increase the number of Reichstag deputies according to the census of 1880, they were supported by seven members of the *Volkspartei*.[45] The chief socialist sponsor of the bill, Rittinghausen, believed that the German representative system could be improved. "We stand, gentlemen," he declared in the Reichstag, "at the beginning of magnificent social reforms, the importance of which is not yet known, but which in any case will be very significant. Once this course is begun, neither the Reichstag nor the government can draw back. We must move forward, although the goals cannot be indicated with complete clarity." [46]

The *Volkspartei* would not refuse to cooperate with the Social Democrats, as indicated by one of its leaders, Mayer. He praised Rittinghausen as a "scholar, thinker, and author on the question of legislative organization. . . ." Mayer admitted that reapportionment would enhance Social Democratic strength in the cities, but advised, "I believe that we have to accommodate ourselves to that; in any case, it is better for the Reich if the Social Democrats are concerning themselves with elections than with other things." [47]

The moderates agreed completely that Social Democrats ought to concern themselves with elections and parliament rather than with talk about revolution. They accepted parliamentarism without reservations, assuming that the Reichstag should be used not only for propaganda but for positive legislation and that a socialist society would employ similar parliamentary institutions. They were never uneasy about their parliamentary roles, in contrast to the radicals, who at times manifested a sense of guilt about their participation in a "bourgeois" institution. As far as the moderates were concerned, a socialist went to the Reichstag to bring about legislation, even if that demanded cooperation and compromise with non-socialists, liberal or conservative.

Briefly, as the ideological traditionalists of the Social Democratic party, the moderates encompassed strains of Lassalleanism and radical bourgeois democracy, seeking to make socialism a movement with a broad appeal to all reform-minded elements in the society. With strong humanitarian and ethical sentiments, many of them found the idea of the class struggle a detriment to Social Democracy, preferring to stress the possibilities of a peaceful and harmonious road to the good society.

[45] The bill is in *SB*, v, i (1881/82), vol. II, *Anlagen*, No. 39, pp. 112–13.
[46] *Ibid.*, vol. I, p. 526.
[47] *Ibid.*, pp. 527–28.

The Emergence of a Moderate Socialist Press

Distraught as the moderates were by the radicalism of the *Sozialdemokrat*, they welcomed the opportunity to establish newspapers within Germany through which they could disseminate their viewpoints. Not until the authorities relaxed the rigid implementation of the Socialist Law in 1883—the so-called "mild practice"—could the moderates proceed with considerable success. It was then possible in most areas of Germany to publish papers with some socialist tendency if dangerous political topics were avoided. That is, the papers had to be "colorless." The moderates were not disturbed by the pressure to remain "colorless" because it gave them a sound practical justification for avoiding the advocacy of a militant class consciousness and political revolution. If charged by radicals with being "opportunists," the editors of the "colorless" papers could always answer that they had no alternative if suppression were to be avoided.[48]

The most energetic and successful promoter of moderate papers was Louis Viereck. He founded no less than sixteen newspapers between 1882 and 1889, many of which, however, existed for only short periods of time.[49] Moving to Munich in 1881, he gained control of the *Sueddeutsche Post* by November 1882, a paper which had been closely associated with the Munich *Volkspartei*. Although Viereck's complaints against the *Sozialdemokrat* had been unfavorably received by Engels, he tried to win an endorsement from Engels with the assurance that, although there were differences between them, "the best intentions have at least guided me." [50] But no encouragement was forth-

[48] It should be noted that already in 1878 two Social Democratic papers had avoided suppression by changing their names and adopting a "colorless" policy. The *Nuernberg-Fuerther Sozialdemokrat*, published by Carl Grillenberger, was changed to the *Fraenkische Tagespost* on Sept. 30, 1878. The authorities in Nuremberg were obviously more liberal than most in their implementation of the Socialist Law; according to the list of literature and periodicals forbidden during 1878–1888 given by Auer in *Nach zehn Jahren*, pp. 334–37, not one item was suppressed by the Nuremberg authorities. Cf. also Gaertner, *Nuernberger Arbeiterbewegung*, pp. 87, 125. The other paper which lasted after 1878, the *Neue Offenbacher Tageszeitung*, edited by Carl Ulrich, was changed to *Offenbacher Tageblatt*, but it, too, was suppressed in 1886. Cf. Carl Ulrich, *Erinnerungen des ersten hessischen Staatspraesidenten*, edited by Ludwig Bergstraesser (Offenbach a. M., 1953), pp. 30–32, 73.

[49] A complete list of his papers and his Social Democratic career is given by Ulrich Hess, "Louis Viereck und seine Muenchner Blaetter fuer Arbeiter 1882–1889," in *Dortmunder Beitraege zur Zeitungsforschung*, VI (1961), pp. 1–50.

[50] Louis Viereck to Engels, no date, but sometime late in 1882. Viereck's wife,

coming from London, and the reason is understandable. According to one advertisement, the *Sueddeutsche Post* not only fought "for the principles of political freedom and the realization of the State of Law [*Rechtsstaat*], but it also promotes social reform with equal decisiveness. Thereby its guiding principle is '*no genuine freedom with the existing pauperism!* No social reform without the self-government of the people'." [51] These were still the slogans of a reform-minded bourgeois democracy for which Engels had little enthusiasm. In his most successful paper, *Das Recht auf Arbeit,* founded in May 1884, Viereck explicitly endorsed the social welfare program of Bismarck, arguing that the "great current" of social reform could succeed only if the working world cooperated with the state.[52]

Viereck's role in the socialist movement continued to grow as he won a Reichstag seat in the fall of 1884 and founded several new papers, including the *Harzer Post,* the *Thueringer Wald-Post,* the *Koenigsberger Volksblatt,* and the *Deutsches Wochenblatt.* With such a widespread enterprise, Viereck employed several Social Democrats with journalistic experience, among them two young and very talented writers, Max Kegel and Dr. Bruno Schoenlank. For a short time, Ignaz Auer also worked with Viereck. As it expanded, the enterprise also prospered financially, netting Viereck an annual income of about six to seven thousand marks, according to reports in early 1886.[53] Bebel observed that, with his "very industrious vein," Viereck had exploited the great need for reading material among the socialists with "undeniable skill." He was helped by the fact that the *Sozialdemokrat* arrived in

Laura, also wrote to Engels (July 5, 1882) about the newspaper undertaking, reporting that her husband was working extremely hard. Both letters are in the Marx/Engels Archive, IISH.

[51] From an advertisement in *Der Weber-Strike zu Crimmitschau,* Heft 1, of *Sozialpolitische Zeit- und Streitfragen* (Munich, 1883), p. 24. This was the first of a series of pamphlets published by Viereck on various social issues.

[52] *Das Recht auf Arbeit,* No. 1, May 28, 1884, p. 1. The statement reads: "This weekly owes the impulse for its establishment to no less a person than the Imperial Chancellor, Prince Bismarck, who, in the Reichstag sitting on the ninth of this month, directed the following memorable request to the German legislature: 'Give the worker the right to work as long as he is healthy; provide care for him when he is sick; provide security for him when he is old'."

[53] Hess, "Louis Viereck und seine Muenchner Blaetter fuer Arbeiter 1882–1889," pp. 18–25. Although Auer worked for Viereck, he was not personally attached to him; like many others, Auer found Viereck's sense of his own importance overbearing. Auer commented: "He [Viereck] lives continually with the naïve view that the whole world is only there for him." Auer to Schlueter, Nov. 11, 1887, *Kleine Korrespondenz,* IISH. The estimate of Viereck's income comes from Bebel to Motteler, March 7, 1886, Bebel Archive, IISH.

Germany too late for party members to rely on it for current news. Bebel suggested that party members supported Viereck's papers for that reason, and confidently concluded that they were not "led astray" by his moderate views.[54] It hardly seems possible, however, that Viereck's endeavors did not have some impact, at least until 1887, when he was expelled from the party for not publicly signing the announcement of the congress at St. Gall.

In Berlin, the moderates established the *Berliner Volksblatt* in 1884 with the financial assistance of Paul Singer; the paper was under the initial direction of Blos, assisted by Hasenclever. Although Bebel trusted Singer, he had misgivings about the others around the paper, and noted later that R. Cronheim, the editor after July 1884, privately admitted to being an anti-semite.[55] The *Volksblatt* expressed no well-defined ideological position, although it repeated the Lassallean formula for state-help and showed a detailed concern for the facts on working hours, wages, social insurance, and the affairs of the trade unions. The influence of the *Volksblatt* cannot be judged precisely, but by the last years of the eighties its distribution far exceeded that of the *Sozialdemokrat*, and since it appeared six times weekly the socialists in Berlin and vicinity relied on it for current news, party information, and some ideological guidance.[56]

In addition to the publications discussed so far, numerous other "colorless" papers appeared, as well as the trade union journals. The views of the radicals were not necessarily excluded from any of these papers, if only because the speeches of Social Democratic Reichstag deputies, especially Bebel and Liebknecht, were often printed. Likewise, these papers frequently carried educational articles on social and economic subjects, including expositions of Marxist theory as well as purely reformist and Lassallean ideas. But both by force of circumstances and by preference the "colorless" press buttressed the position of the moderates, and Bebel observed in 1884 that even the trade union journals were often more radical in outlook than the papers edited by party members.[57] Although the moderates reached a wide audience through

[54] Bebel to Engels, April 23, 1886, in Bebel, *Briefwechsel*, pp. 272–73.

[55] Bebel to Engels, Dec. 7, 1885, in Bebel, *Briefwechsel*, p. 250.

[56] The following are the best figures available for the circulation of the *Berliner Volksblatt:* 1884, 2,400; 1885, 4,000; 1888, 11,000; 1890, 25,000. Blos, *Denkwuerdigkeiten*, II, p. 110; Paul Kampffmeyer, *Zur Geschichte des Sozialistengesetzes. Artikel und Dokumente* (no place, 1928), p. 33. This is a printed manuscript which was never published; copy in IISH.

[57] Bebel to Engels, April 18, 1884, in Bebel, *Briefwechsel*, pp. 175–76. Unfortu-

these publications, the quantity did not fully compensate for the fact that they lacked the ideological consistency and temperamental determination of the radicals.

Ideological Currents: The Radicals as a Marxist Avant-garde *and Ambivalent Parliamentarians*

The radicals considered themselves the disciples of Marx and Engels, and this fact in itself ought to suffice as an outline of their ideological position; but it does not. The fact is that although they had become far more explicit about their socialist theory than the moderates, the radicals were often uncertain about how to relate Marxism to their practical problems as socialist political leaders. Because the ideological and practical contributions of the radicals are central to most of this study, the present section attempts only to outline the direction of radical thinking on some crucial topics: political democracy, parliamentarism, and the future socialist society.

Previous parts of this study noted that the concept of the "People's state" embodied the Eisenacher commitment to a radical form of bourgeois political democracy and that both Marx and Engels subjected this concept to severe criticism in 1875. At the time, Engels suggested privately to Bebel that socialists should completely drop the term "People's state" to express their political goal, replacing it with *Kommune* or *Gemeinwesen.* Either of these terms, Engels argued, should be used to distinguish the goals of proletarian socialism from the traditions of bourgeois democracy. To some degree Bebel followed Engels' advice by ceasing to use the idea of "People's state" in his speeches and writing, and in the eighties his fellow radicals imitated the same pattern. Even the moderates, it should be noted, made less use of "People's state," although this is partially explained by the fact that the Lassalleans had never used the term. With the concept of the "People's state" fading into the background, it is important to discover what direction the political thinking of the radicals was taking.

The radicals tried to clarify their own ideas about democracy through criticisms of bourgeois political liberalism, based in some

nately it has been impossible to obtain copies of most of these papers for investigation, but some information on them is available in the local histories of Social Democracy and in Kampffmeyer, *Zur Geschichte des Sozialistengesetzes*, pp. 33–34. For a bibliography of the trade union press, see "Gewerkschafts-Organe," in *Handbuch des Vereins Arbeiterpresse* (Berlin, 1914), III, pp. 128–47

measure on such tenets of Marxism as the class struggle. The consequence of this approach reveals at times a muddled groping for answers, combining simple logic with a rigid application of the class struggle.

The young Karl Kautsky, fast becoming the chief radical theoretician, implied from the class struggle that the bourgeoisie had become a "reactionary class" and, therefore, that nothing in liberalism could be appropriated by proletarian socialism. In his mind there was an inflexible identity between liberalism and the bourgeoisie. Stressing an absolute cleavage between bourgeois liberalism, with its emphasis on individual liberty, and his proletarian socialism, Kautsky concluded that "the necessary consequence of democracy is not Social Democracy, but anarchism." Kautsky endorsed the concept of "liberty" only when used negatively, to mean the "destruction of the hitherto domination by a class or a person," but he completely rejected the ideal of "absolute individual liberty." The mission of the proletariat, Kautsky reasoned, was not to achieve individual liberty, but "to destroy this individual liberty of the capitalists and landlords, and in place of this unbearable compulsion of individuals over the whole, set the compulsion of the whole over the individuals, a compulsion which is grounded in the nature of man and will therefore be borne gladly by everyone. . . ." [58]

After being rebuked for his narrow economic interpretation of liberalism in which he had never mentioned liberty of thought, speech, the press, assembly, and so forth,[59] Kautsky explained that when the "whole is understood as an 'association of equal men'," then "the individual has no rights against the whole, but merely duties." Now he had pinned everything on the achievement of equality, as he queried, "Is not rational and moral liberty already embodied in equality?" [60] He carried this principle over to the practical activity of the proletariat—a class of equals—in the Social Democratic party. In Kautsky's view, the party represented the whole of the proletariat, and thus the worker had only to be moved by the "communist instinct, that feeling of duty, which tells us that the disinherited class has a demand upon our whole

[58] Symmachos, "Freiheit," *SD*, No. 28, July 7, 1881.

[59] A. B. C., "Sozialismus, individuelle Freiheit und Gleichheit," *SD*, No. 36, Sept. 1, 1881. The author of the article was Robert Seidel, a Swiss Social Democrat. Cf. Eduard Bernstein, "Kautskys erstes Wirken in der deutschen Sozialdemokratie," *Die Gesellschaft. Ein Sonderheft zu Karl Kautskys 70. Geburtstag* (1924), p. 72.

[60] Symmachos, "Freiheit. Antwort an den Genossen A. B. C.," *SD*, No. 37, Sept. 8, 1881.

person, not just upon a small part of it, the limits for which are individual liberty. We are obligated to give all for the party; the party, contrariwise, does not have to give us the slightest thing." [61] The totalitarian elements in Kautsky's view are obvious, mitigated only by his expectation that equality would exclude the possibility of serious injustices.

Similar condemnations of bourgeois liberalism and democracy, whatever particular arguments they might include, were not unusual among the radicals. How much progress did they make in the elaboration of a political goal which was appropriate for proletarian socialism? Not very much, one must answer, although they did use the Marxist class analysis of the state. More than anyone, Engels was directly responsible for the gradual but uneven acceptance among the radicals of the view that socialist thought had no place for a concept of the state, not even a democratic state. He had explained that view in the *Anti-Duehring*, and its influence can be traced in Bebel, Bernstein, and Kautsky. In the first edition of *Die Frau und der Sozialismus* (1879), Bebel already said that in the socialist society the "existing state organization" would become superfluous, but he still spoke of the socialist ideal as the *Volkstaat*, and he listed the usual democratic demands as components of it.[62] In the second revised edition (1883), after quoting directly from the *Anti-Duehring*, Bebel predicted not only the collapse of the existing state but also the disappearance of all political power. "With the state, its representatives also vanish: Ministers, parliaments, standing army, police and gendarmes, courts, lawyers, and state attornies, prison systems, tax and tariff administration, the whole political apparatus." [63] Since all forms of political power appeared only with the rule of class, politics as such would vanish with the abolition of class rule. When the anarchists cited Bebel's exposition as proof that they had always been correct in their total rejection of the state, Bernstein, quoting Engels almost word for word, answered that anarchy would also disappear along with the political rule by class.[64]

Bebel and Bernstein had obviously made progress in Marxism by making a class analysis of the state, but they failed to take the further

[61] Symmachos, "Klassenkampf und Sozialismus," *SD*, No. 40, Sept. 29, 1881.

[62] Bebel, *Die Frau und der Sozialismus* (Zurich-Hottingen, 1879), pp. 105–06.

[63] Bebel, *Die Frau in der Vergangenheit, Gegenwart und Zukunft* (Zurich, 1883), p. 178.

[64] Leo, "Sozialismus und Anarchismus," *SD*, No. 4, Jan. 18, 1883; and also, Leo, "Der Sozialismus und der Staat," *SD*, No. 52, Dec. 20, 1883.

suggestion of Engels that socialists elaborate their ideal of society around concepts such as *Kommune* or *Gemeinwesen.* They could expose the weaknesses of pure political democracy and predict the disappearance of all the forms of the political state, but these remained essentially negative contributions. The positive statement of how socialism would in practice achieve a society far more just than any under political democracy was never presented with any clarity, and certainly not on the basis of the Commune, as desired by Marx and Engels. Although the radicals commemorated the Commune every March, none of their essays made any effort to show the socialist rank-and-file how it could be viewed as even a vague outline for a socialist society. On the contrary, these articles often stressed the failure of the Commune as a socialist endeavor, leaving very little reason for the reader to believe that for a Marxist the Commune was anything more than a glorious and tragic episode in the history of the class struggle.[65]

In sum, the radicals were rapidly undermining the confidence of their followers in political democracy without replacing it with a more convincing concept. Or, if they presented a picture of the future socialist society, as Bebel did in *Die Frau und der Sozialismus*, they stressed the non-political nature of that society. If politics did not apply, then neither did the concepts of traditional democracy, and as far as the future socialist society was concerned the radicals could forget about political theorizing and turn their attention to social and economic problems. If the radicals had been mere theorists about the goals of Social Democracy, these tendencies would not have created a problem, although their ideas at the time would not have met a rigid Marxist standard. The radicals, however, were also German politicians with a need for unity in theory and practice.

This unity was difficult to achieve. On the one hand, the conception of a future society without politics reenforced their estrangement from the political institutions of liberalism, especially the parliaments. And, since the radicals most often denied that the socialist society could be achieved through parliamentary means, they were also in-

[65] The articles commemorating the beginning of the Commune on March 18, 1871, were always combined with a memorial for the revolution of 1848, which had of course broken out in Berlin on March 18, 1848. In no case was an effort made to explore the Commune for its lessons relative to a future socialist society. Cf. the following: "Ein Gedenktag der Revolution. 1848. 1871," *SD,* No. 12, March 21, 1880; "Gedenktage des Proletariats," *SD,* No. 11, March 13, 1881; "Gedenktage des Proletariats," *SD,* No. 12, March 16, 1882; "Zum 18. Maerz," *SD,* No. 12, March 15, 1883; and "Zum Gedenktage der Maerzkaempfe," *SD,* No. 11, March 13, 1884. Such commemorative articles appeared in each subsequent year, but apart from them no other essays appeared on the Commune.

clined to deprecate the significance of parliamentarism for their immediate goals. On the other hand, the radicals continued to be parliamentarians in practice, and in fact the leading radical, Bebel, was also the party's leading parliamentarian! Given their theoretical and emotional objections to parliamentarism, this could not fail to create conflicts within them about their current political behavior. Their only consistent explanation was that they participated in parliament for purely agitational purposes.[66] But this broke down as the years under the Socialist Law passed because the radicals became involved in promoting positive reform legislation, especially after 1884.

As a consequence of these cross-pressures, the radicals became highly ambivalent about parliamentarism. They could neither reject nor accept it completely. This contrasted significantly with the moderates, who were willing to accept parliamentarism in theory and practice, and criticized only its imperfections as they were evident in the German Reichstag. To the radicals that was "opportunism."

The ambivalent parliamentarism stands out clearly in a statement prepared by several radicals to preface the published minutes of the Copenhagen congress of March 1883. The statement is significant in this respect, but also because for the first time it identifies the Social Democrats exclusively with Marx. The radicals wrote,

> "We are not a parliamentary party—we do not send our deputies to the various representative bodies to parley—but also we are not makers of revolutions [*Revolutionsmacher*]. German Social Democracy is proud that its attitude is always to follow the principles of its great master Marx, who would have nothing either of parliamentarism or of the making of revolutions [*Revolutionsmacherei*]. We are a revolutionary party, our aim is a revolutionary one, and we permit ourselves no illusions about its accomplishment by parliamentary means. But we also know that the manner in which it will be achieved, depends not upon us, that we cannot make the conditions under which we fight, but that we have to study those conditions and we know that our task in conjunction with this knowledge consists simply in acting according to what we know." [67]

[66] The theme that parliamentary participation was only for agitational purposes was often repeated. Cf. Selim [Liebknecht's pseudonym, Miles, reversed], "Der Parlamentarismus," *SD*, No. 24, June 12, 1881; and "Der Parlamentarismus begraben," *SD*, No. 26, June 21, 1883.

[67] *Protokoll ueber den Kongress der deutschen Sozialdemokratie in Kopen-*

The statement summarizes the weakness and the strength of the radicals. They scornfully rejected parliamentarism, but patiently perfected an organization for the election of parliamentary deputies. They talked confidently about revolutionary goals, but carefully cast aside any consideration of revolutionary means. They triumphantly proclaimed their Marxism, but cautiously interpreted that to mean intensified study of economic conditions. They were ambiguous and ambivalent, not for a lack of Marxism, but because they could not bring their theory together with their practice. Despite that, they continued to win the trust of the German workingman, because they had immense moral strength and a deep devotion to their cause.

The question of parliamentarism continued to haunt the radicals throughout the eighties. In many respects it was the most significant theoretical and practical problem which confronted them during the Socialist Law. Everything seemed to tie in with it, especially the question of whether they were revolutionary socialists and what they expected the revolution would be like. With each year that passed under the Socialist Law, the tactical use of the parliamentary institutions began to soften the theoretical objections to parliamentarism of several of the radicals. Throughout most of the eighties, however, their general attitudes are best summarized in the phrase "ambivalent parliamentarism."

The broad differences separating radicals from moderates tended to hold throughout the period of the Socialist Law. On the chief issues facing the party, the leaders of Social Democracy usually divided into these two groups, although the lines were sometimes obscured. Most of the time the antagonism was not intense because internal divisions were overshadowed by a hatred of the common enemy. Nonetheless, the intraparty frictions reached a peak in 1885 and threatened to split the movement.

The next three chapters take up the various problems which the party faced in the context of German society. Throughout, it is clear that the separation between radicals and moderates played an important role in determining the over-all policy of the party. To deal with the first problem—the challenge presented by State Socialism—it is necessary to return to the early eighties.

hagen. Abegehalten vom 29. Maerz bis 2. April 1883 (Hottingen-Zurich, 1883), p. 4.

CHAPTER VI · INVITATION FROM THE RIGHT: STATE SOCIALISM AND SOCIAL DEMOCRACY

Social Democratic Uncertainty in Response to State Socialism

IT HAS BEEN necessary to postpone a detailed discussion of the Social Democratic response to Bismarck's legislative program of monopolies and social insurance until the pattern of ideological disagreements within the party could be examined. The differing views about Social Democratic politics, as described in the last chapter, played a major role in fashioning party policy for many years. Although both moderates and radicals agreed in denouncing the super-radicalism of Most and Hasselmann, such unanimity did not emerge when it became necessary to formulate a policy on Bismarck's program. Thus, the Social Democratic response to Bismarck's program reflected the fundamental differences on the party's principles and tactics.

Although the question of how Social Democrats ought to treat the projects of monopolization had already arisen in 1876, it became more and more pressing after 1880. Thus, just at that point when the leadership of the party had seemingly resolved the problem of super-radicalism on the far left, the question of how to relate to State Socialism came into focus. This proved to be a difficult problem to resolve, because State Socialism presented both a more consistent theoretical challenge and a more practical program than anarchism did.

It is not surprising that the Social Democrats encountered numerous difficulties in trying to define their relationship to State Socialism. The difficulties were complicated by the fact that State Socialism posed a major ideological challenge at a time when the Social Democrats had no opportunity to subject the issues to a full and open debate. During the early eighties, the authorities throughout Germany implemented the Socialist Law with relentless severity, making it impossible for the

Social Democrats to assemble in an atmosphere that permitted unrestrained debate.

A second difficulty stemmed from numerous confusions about the meaning of State Socialism itself. Since the Social Democrats themselves were still in search of certainty in economic theory, they were not always clear about what was involved in their theoretical confrontation with State Socialism. Likewise, although the phrase "State Socialism" had become part of common parlance in Germany by 1880, it had no precise meaning, even to those academicians who were knowledgeable in all the relevant literature. *Laissez-faire* economists often used the term in polemical literature in a pejorative sense, to designate any program that advocated a degree of state regulation in the economy. On the other hand, the founders of the *Zentralverein fuer Sozialreform auf religioeser und konstitutionell-monarchischer Grundlage,* Rudolf Meyer, Adolf Wagner, and Rudolf Todt, used the term positively and called their official newspaper the *Staatssozialist.*[1]

Despite the difficulties in arriving at a clear definition of State Socialism, some broad characteristics can be identified as they applied at the time. First, State Socialism recognized an obligation of the existing state to undertake measures for the improvement of the working classes. The specific measures set forth varied with the various promoters of State Socialism. Second, it advocated some level of nationalization or monopolization, also varying in degree with different writers. Usually the German State Socialists looked to the Reich and not to the individual states (*Bundesstaaten*) or the municipalities for the implementation of their program. Third, State Socialism was loyal to the monarchical state and the values of the established churches and generally aimed to attract the working classes to the existing system. With some State Socialists, such as Todt and the Court Chaplain, Adolf Stoecker, the chief motivation was to restore working-class loyalty to Protestant Christianity. Political reform was not an aim of the State Socialists, for most of them were deeply conservative.

The difficulties of the Social Democrats in confronting State Socialism on a theoretical level stemmed from the fact that they themselves had absorbed so much of its thought in the late seventies. As already noted, the booklet by Albert Schaeffle, *Die Quintessenz des Sozialis-*

[1] Cf. Paul Goehre, *Die evangelisch-soziale Bewegung, ihre Geschichte und ihre Ziele* (Leipzig, 1896), pp. 10ff.; Walter Frank, *Hofprediger Adolf Stoecker und die christlichsoziale Bewegung* (2nd ed.; Hamburg, 1935), pp. 38ff.

mus, had become a handbook of socialist economics for the Social Democrats (see above, Chapter II). Equally important, the Lassallean glorification of the state opened the door for Social Democrats to view State Socialism with favor, although Lassalle's emphasis on universal suffrage also tended to close the door. Ultimately Marxism offered the most impressive theoretical system for a consistent Social Democratic rebuttal of State Socialism. In fact, the influence of State Socialism among Social Democrats offered Karl Kautsky and Eduard Bernstein their first significant opportunity to employ Marxism in a major ideological struggle.

Bismarck's program of monopolization and social welfare confronted the Social Democrats with the practical challenge of State Socialism. Although Bismarck made no pretense of being a theoretical spokesman for State Socialism, his program corresponded with its general tenets. Observers of the German scene commonly referred to his measures as examples of State Socialism, and the Social Democrats approached his projects with the same assumption. Thus, as the Social Democratic Reichstag deputies fashioned their response to Bismarck's program, they were also presenting the outlines of their own answer to the larger challenge of State Socialism as a theory.

The initial uncertainty of the Social Democrats about how to respond to the Bismarck program of monopolization and social welfare is apparent from many sources. The conflicting positions presented in the *Zukunft* discussions (see Chapter II) on nationalization foreshadowed the ambiguity that characterized the Social Democratic response when confronted with a fuller version of Bismarck's State Socialism after 1880. Numerous party leaders expressed agreement with much of Bismarck's program, arising no doubt from their belief that nationalization necessarily meant a step toward socialism. Thus, in April 1878, Wilhelm Bracke told Engels that he approved of the Imperial nationalization of the railroads; he even thought that the projected tobacco monopoly was "not unacceptable." He added hastily that he would nevertheless oppose any public Social Democratic support for Bismarck's economic program.[2]

Other sources indicate that some Social Democrats thought of the monopolization program as a genuinely socialist measure. In the sum-

[2] Wilhelm Bracke to Engels, April 26, 1878, quoted in Karl Marx and Friedrich Engels, *Briefe an A. Bebel, W. Liebknecht, K. Kautsky und Andere.* Teil I, *1870–1886*, edited by W. Adoratski (Moscow-Leningrad, 1933), p. 175.

mer of 1880, two lead articles in the *Sozialdemokrat* unconditionally endorsed the tobacco monopoly. Georg von Vollmar, notorious for his radicalism in the early eighties, edited the paper at that time. One is justified in assuming that if Vollmar did not write the articles, he must at least have given his editorial approval. The writer called upon the Social Democrats to campaign for the tobacco monopoly because of its threat to the bourgeoisie. "For the monopoly," went the second installment, "because it brings harm to the bourgeoisie; for the monopoly, because it improves the situation of the workers; for the monopoly, because it smooths out the road economically and morally for Social Democracy; for the monopoly, in one word, because it is a part of the overthrow of the existing social order, which we have inscribed upon our Banner!" [3] The State Socialists could not have disagreed with much of that, although they did not view the tobacco monopoly as "part of the overthrow of the existing social order." Some Social Democrats did disagree and said so, demonstrating the cleavage of opinion within the party.[4]

The confrontation with Bismarck's State Socialism posed a fundamental challenge to the party's democratic political principles. If Bismarck's program of monopolization and social welfare had to be recognized as genuine socialist measures, then the Social Democrats had no grounds on which to oppose a socialism instituted by the authoritarian Reich. This posed a question of priorities for the Social Democrats. Could nationalization by Bismarck bring about socialism without a democratization of the German government? For those who viewed the democratic political principles of Social Democracy as its chief goals, the answer was "no." For others, democratization could wait. Thus a fundamental tension emerged between the traditional democratic-political principles of the party and what they took to be their socialist-economic ideas. This was the underlying problem posed by Bismarck's State Socialism.

The Confrontation with Bismarck's State Socialism in 1881

The full impact of the challenge of Bismarck's State Socialism did not hit the Social Democrats until 1881. On November 17, 1881, the

[3] "Neue Taktik, II," *SD*, No. 24, June 13, 1880.

[4] H. Rackow, "Gegen das Tabaksmonopol," *SD*, No. 27, July 4, 1880; and two articles signed "Dbsch" (identity not known), "Gegen die 'neue Taktik'," *SD*, No. 28, July 11, and No. 29, July 18, 1880.

well-known social message of the Kaiser was presented to the Reichstag, outlining the over-all scheme for Accident, Sickness, and Invalid Insurance. Deliberations on these measures occupied much of the Reichstag's time through 1884. Combined with the tobacco monopoly, which came before the Reichstag in 1882, these measures forced themselves into the center of Social Democratic discussions. It is no exaggeration to say that Bismarck's State Socialism created a serious crisis in the Social Democratic party—a crisis which was largely hidden from public view.

The Imperial social welfare program posed a painful dilemma for the Social Democrats. In economics they had been tutored to think along the lines of State Socialism, and a number of the leaders were sufficiently impressed by the insurance scheme to be tempted to approve it openly. This included many of the moderates, Frohme, Grillenberger, Rittinghausen, Kayser, and Hasenclever. It was impossible, however, for Social Democrats simply to accept the Imperial insurance program without undermining their political opposition to the Iron Chancellor. However, it was equally impossible for the Social Democrats, who actively demanded improvements for the working class, simply to reject a program of social welfare because of their political opposition to Bismarck. The radicals were especially determined to avoid the danger of undermining their political opposition by a too sympathetic response to the social welfare program.

Social Democrats—especially the radicals—had to find a course by which they could both accept and reject the insurance program. The course was found. In the spring of 1881, when a draft for the Accident Insurance was first debated in the Reichstag, the Social Democrats introduced a series of amendments to the bill. In essence the Social Democratic changes fully agreed with the principles of Bismarck's bill, but in detail they greatly extended the benefits for workingmen. Simply put, the Social Democrats affirmed that the Chancellor was moving in the right direction, but they complained that he was not prepared to move far enough.[5]

Explaining the "official" stand of the Social Democrats on April 4, 1881, Bebel admitted that his party was happy to see the bill for Accident Insurance, but hastily added that the measure would be a genuine reform only if the amendments of his party were incorporated.[6] Some

[5] For the Social Democratic amendments, see *SB,* IV, iv (1881), vol. IV, *Anlagen,* No. 201, pp. 1050–52.

[6] *Ibid.*, vol. I, pp. 746, 748, 755.

weeks later, Liebknecht revealed the party's view of the issue when he commented in the Reichstag, "Now then, Gentlemen, Prince Bismarck may move further toward our goals—on this course we march together, and we do not hang on his coat-tails." [7] Some of the moderate deputies expressed a much deeper approval of the path taken by the Chancellor. Georg Hartmann, a long-time Lassallean, lashed out at those Liberal parties in the Reichstag which intended to hinder Bismarck's further pursuance of the "socialist principle," while Ignaz Auer and Wilhelm Hasenclever mixed criticism of specific points in the Chancellor's draft with a conciliatory and sympathetic commentary on the over-all goals.[8]

The Social Democrats had found the ideal tactic for responding to the welfare aspects of Bismarck's State Socialism. Thereafter, they followed the same practice of introducing amendments or parallel bills, giving themselves the opportunity to accept the principle of Bismarck's legislation and also specific reasons for voting against it. Since their amendments were never incorporated into the final bills, they could always vote against the welfare legislation on the ground that it was wholly inadequate and therefore fraudulent.

The public rejection of the Accident and Sickness Insurance Bills, beginning in the spring of 1881, merely camouflaged the fact that, within the party, Bismarck's State Socialism continued to exert a seductive appeal. Therefore, a constant discussion of State Socialism went on behind the scenes. In great part, the radicals lined up against the moderates on this issue, although the lines were often blurred.

The debate on State Socialism was stimulated by the events around the election of October 1881, for the campaign focused on the issues raised by Bismarck's program for monopolization and social welfare. Bismarck hoped to reduce the strength of all parties which objected to this economic program and to gain a Reichstag built on the conservative parties with assistance from the National Liberals and the Centrists. He likewise expected that the promise of social welfare would undermine the strength of the Social Democrats with the working classes. State Socialism thus became a direct political challenge to the Social Democrats in the election.[9]

The election of October 1881 thus combined two serious disad-

[7] *Ibid.*, vol. II, p. 1455.
[8] *Ibid.*, pp. 1517, 1529, 1757–58.
[9] Ziekursch, *Politische Geschichte*, II, pp. 355–56.

vantages for the Social Democrats: a new ideological challenge at a time when the police were suppressing party agitation with great severity. Although the party had been reorganized with amazing skill, it faced almost overwhelming obstacles. The Minor State of Siege, imposed on Berlin late in 1878, had been extended to Hamburg and vicinity in 1880 and to Leipzig in June 1881. The chief agitators of the party were expelled from all of these cities, creating considerable hindrances to campaigning. Throughout Germany, policemen, most often rather poorly disguised plainclothesmen, haunted the paths of the notorious Social Democratic leaders. After Bebel had visited the Viereck in Munich in July 1881, Laura Viereck wrote to Engels with some amusement that "while Bebel was here we had a quite respectable guard; a police commissar went daily back and forth in front of our house, even after B [ebel] had gone." [10] (Bebel enjoyed the close presence of the defenders of law and order throughout the duration of the Socialist Law. A policeman awaited him nearly every day as he left the majestic halls of the Reichstag!) Even in Glauchau-Meerane, one of the old strongholds of the Eisenachers, two uniformed policemen traced Auer's every step throughout the campaign.[11]

In addition to the difficulties created by the constant police harassment and the underlying appeal of Bismarck's unfolding welfare program, the Social Democrats had to contend with a political challenge from the camp of Adolf Stoecker and the Christian Social party. Although Stoecker's initial plan of January 1878 to found a working-class party that would be loyal to Protestant Christianity and the Hohenzollern monarchy had already disintegrated, his movement still posed a threat to the Social Democrats. He attracted a small following, including some workingmen, by exploiting anti-semitic sentiments and endorsing the State Socialist plans of Bismarck. In matters of social reform, Stoecker was far more radical than the Chancellor. Insofar as State Socialism had a spokesman who could speak to the masses, the Court Chaplain filled the bill. The fact that Stoecker had concentrated his efforts in Berlin also made his movement a significant threat to Social Democracy.[12]

The election posed two special tasks for the radicals in the Social

[10] Laura Viereck to Engels, July 5, 1881, Marx/Engels Archive, IISH.

[11] Auer, *Nach zehn Jahren,* p. 111; Mehring, *Geschichte der deutschen Sozialdemokratie,* IV, pp. 193–94.

[12] Frank, *Hofprediger Adolf Stoecker,* pp. 43–50; Dietrich von Oertzen, *Adolf Stoecker. Lebensbild und Zeitgeschichte* (Berlin, 1910), I, pp. 138–46.

Democratic party. First, they had to rally all Social Democrats to present a united front in the campaign in order to make a respectable showing at the polls. That called for the kind of campaign that would reconcile intraparty differences in the face of a common foe. But second, they had to launch an exposé of Bismarck's program in order to undermine its appeal to the rank-and-file Social Democrats. This task necessitated a clarification of the broad issues raised by Bismarck's State Socialism, and it is worth some special attention.

Eduard Bernstein and Karl Kautsky wrote some of their most stinging criticisms of State Socialism at the time of the 1881 election. From the time that Bernstein became editor of the *Sozialdemokrat* early in 1881, he used that post to counter the threat of State Socialism. Both he and Kautsky sought to apply their first serious studies of Marxist theory to clarify the thinking of the Social Democrats on their political relationship to State Socialism. Already in the first part of the year, Bernstein had warned the readers of the party paper not to be led astray by the Chancellor's apparent altruism. Later, Kautsky analyzed State Socialism as a program to buttress the power of the "Militarist Monarchy" by giving the people "bread without freedom." During the campaign itself, Bernstein wrote a rebuttal of State Socialism which he based on Marx's class analysis of the state. In December, after the election, he warned the Social Democrats that by their unrestrained attacks on the economic views of the liberals they would fall into the traps set by the State Socialists.[13]

The total Social Democratic vote in the election of 1881 dropped from what it had been in July of 1878, but it is difficult to determine whether this resulted from the challenge of State Socialism or simply from the restraints imposed by the severe police repression. While it appears that the repression was most responsible, the evidence also shows that in those few districts where representatives of the State Socialists campaigned energetically the Social Democratic vote dropped markedly.

[13] Leo [pseudonym for Bernstein], "Staatshuelfe!?," *SD*, No. 2, Jan. 9, 1881; Leo, "Staatssozialismus und Klassenstaat," *SD*, No. 41, Oct. 6, 1881; Leo, "Manchesterthum, Sozialdemokratie und 'soziale Reform'," *SD*, No. 49, Dec. 1, 1881; Symmachos [pseudonym for Kautsky], "Der Staatssozialismus und die Sozialdemokratie," *SD*, No. 10, March 6, 1881. Many of the articles from the *Sozialdemokrat* on the whole State Socialist debate are reprinted in Horst Bartel, "Zur Politik und zum Kampf der deutschen Sozialdemokratie gegen die Bismarcksche Sozialpolitik und gegen den Rechtsopportunismus in den Jahren 1881/84," *Zeitschrift fuer Geschichtswissenschaft*, VI (1958) pp. 1089–1106.

The testing ground centered in Berlin. There, Social Democratic percentages dropped seriously in all districts where advocates of Bismarck's State Socialism campaigned. Thus in Berlin's second district, where Stoecker himself campaigned, the Social Democratic percentage dropped from 26.3 in 1878 to 9.5 in 1881. It should be noted that the Social Democrats did not concentrate on this district in 1881, merely placing Louis Viereck's name in contention as a kind of test candidate. Nevertheless, the loss of votes was noticeable. The fourth and the sixth districts had always been Social Democratic strongholds, but there too they lost ground. In the fourth, Bebel was matched against the Progressive Traeger and Adolf Wagner, who ran as a "Social Conservative," and the Social Democratic percentage dropped from almost 50 in 1878 to 32 in 1881. In the sixth district, the Social Democratic percentage dropped from 41 in 1878 to 27 in 1881. In all of Berlin, the Social Democrats received only 20,168 votes in 1881, against their 56,147 of July 1878. In contrast, the combined vote of Stoeckers' Christian Socials and the Social Conservatives reached 46,228.[14]

There is every reason to believe that the drop in the Social Democratic vote in Berlin stemmed from the challenge of the Stoecker-State Socialist movement. No other explanation is very convincing.[15] Louis Viereck, the inactive test candidate in the second district made this same analysis. "I do not doubt in the least," Viereck wrote to Engels shortly after the election, "that the bulk of the 47,000 anti-semitic ballots were recruited from our earlier voters. . . ." Two weeks later, he added, "A third of our former voters, holding us for dead, have thus, on the first ballot, experimented with State Socialism." [16]

It appears from this that State Socialism posed something of a popular threat to the Social Democrats. It proved, however, to be a transitory threat. The reasons for this may not be too difficult to fathom. For one thing, few State Socialists were also interested in becoming the popular leaders of working-class masses. Stoecker was unique in that respect, and so was Adolf Wagner, who, however, never ventured to

[14] Neumann-Hofer, *Die Entwicklung der Sozialdemokratie*, p. 30; Eduard Bernstein, *Die Geschichte der Berliner Arbeiterbewegung* (Berlin, 1907), II, p. 75.

[15] The suggestion by Ernst Drahn that Most's anti-parliamentarian campaign in the *Freiheit* caused the loss of Social Democratic votes is not very convincing. Most himself received 42 votes in the fifth district, indicating that not all anti-parliamentarians stayed away from the polls. See Drahn, *Johann Most: eine Bio-bibliographie*, p. 15, n. 15.

[16] Louis Viereck to Engels, Nov. 2, 1881, and Nov. 16, 1881, Marx/Engels Archive, IISH.

harangue the masses as Stoecker did. For another thing, once the Accident and Sickness Insurance programs were passed by 1884, the Social Democrats could argue convincingly that these measures had not solved the problems of the workingman.

Although a set-back for the Social Democrats, the election of 1881 did not permanently damage the electoral possibilities of the party. Viewed from the position of the radicals, Bebel's failure to win a seat, and not the mere loss of votes, proved to be the greatest disaster. The most able spokesman for the radical wing of the party had been eliminated from the Reichstag *Fraktion*, and thus from the official leadership. Of the twelve Social Democratic deputies elected in 1881, only Liebknecht and Vollmar could be counted with certainty among the radicals.[17] But Liebknecht, although a fighter for Social Democracy and a hater of Bismarck, often played a conciliatory role within the party, intent upon avoiding internal feuds in a time of troubles. And Vollmar, although overflowing with radical rhetoric, had absorbed a large dose of State Socialist thinking. The moderates could therefore dominate the *Fraktion* with little difficulty, a fact of the greatest importance at a time when the Reichstag would be debating the Iron Chancellor's social welfare legislation. In this situation, the radicals had to apply great pressure on the *Fraktion* through the *Sozialdemokrat* and the personal influence of Bebel. That pressure created an intensification of the internal frictions and led to a considerable behind-the-scenes debate on all issues, especially State Socialism.

Social Democratic Discussions of State Socialism: The Internal Struggle

Internal tensions within the Social Democratic party built up rapidly in the first half of 1882. The moderates, angered and sometimes embarrassed by Bernstein's revolutionary rhetoric in the *Sozialdemokrat*, tried to impose their will through the *Fraktion*, the accepted executive committee of the party. The radicals, outnumbered in the Reichstag, and more and more devoted to Marxism, feared that the

[17] The following won seats in the election: Blos (Reuss old Line), Dietz (Hamburg II), Frohme (Hanau), Bruno Geiser (Chemnitz), Grillenberger (Nuremberg), Hasenclever (Breslau-East), Kayser (Freiberg in Saxony), Kraecker (Breslau-West), Liebknecht (Offenbach), Rittinghausen (Solingen), Carl Stolle (Zwickau), and Vollmar (Mittweida). Neumann-Hofer, *Die Entwicklung der Sozialdemokratie*, pp. 46, 55.

moderates would compromise the party's principles at almost any moment.

The dangers of the inclination of some Social Democrats to flirt with State Socialism were quite apparent to Friedrich Engels in London. Although Marx's pace had slowed, Engels remained in close touch with Bebel and Liebknecht in Germany and Bernstein in Zurich. Kautsky had been living in London off and on, and on occasion other German Social Democrats would drift into London to spend a pleasant hour with Engels over a pitcher of grog. Thus, Paul Singer, a Berlin clothing producer and a member of the party since the late seventies, frequently visited Engels on business trips to London. From talks with Singer, Engels could detect how State Socialistic assumptions had become commonplace with Social Democrats. "He [Singer] belongs to those," Engels wrote to Bebel in May 1882, "who see in the nationalization of something a halfway or in any case a preparatory measure [toward a socialist economy] and are therefore enthusiastic for protective tariffs, tobacco monopoly, railroad nationalization, etc." The reason for these "fibs," Engels observed, was the "one-sidedly exaggerated struggle against Manchesterism." [18] Engels tried to set straight the thinking of Singer, but it took some time.

In the summer of 1882, in conjunction with the controversy between the moderates and Bernstein over control of the *Sozialdemokrat*, the debate on State Socialism also reached a boiling point. When the leaders of the party met in secret conference at Zurich in August 1882, State Socialism was one of the central themes of the discussion. The debates were often "very heated," with Bernstein in the midst of the controversy.[19] He believed that the continued influence of Lassalle explained the inclination of Social Democrats to approve of Bismarck's program. He therefore vigorously opposed a suggestion that the party reprint Lassalle's brochures for agitational literature on the basis that many of the Lassallean writings could be supported by every State Socialist. Manchesterism, he declared, was much less dangerous to the Social Democrats than State Socialism. For agitational literature, he proposed that a new brochure be made of Engels' "Socialism: Utopian and Scientific." [20]

Bernstein received very little support. Ignaz Auer argued that

[18] Engels to Bebel, May 16, 1882, in Bebel, *Briefwechsel*, p. 123.

[19] Blos, *Denkwuerdigkeiten*, II, p. 48.

[20] *Zuericher Protokoll* (conference of August 19–21, 1882), p. 2, Motteler Archive, IISH.

Lassalle's writings were not harmful, but necessary, especially since nothing "significant" had been written since 1878. Liebknecht admitted that Lassalle's writings supported State Socialism, as Bernstein understood it, but saw no danger or harm in using them. Not even Bebel raised objections to Lassalle's writings, or at least the record does not indicate that he did. Finally, Max Kayser completely opposed Bernstein's view that State Socialism posed greater dangers for Social Democracy than Manchesterism. Far from perceiving a threat, Kayser concluded that "Bismarck's State Socialism makes much too much allowance to Manchesterism." [21]

After his anxious warnings went unheeded at the Zurich conference in August, Bernstein grew more and more worried. On September 1, 1882, he communicated his anxiety to Engels. There were many people in the party, Bernstein observed, who were of the opinion that "from the socialist side something must always 'happen'." They were not people to make revolutions or plan assassinations, but they were no longer permitted to agitate in the manner which had been customary before the Socialist Law. Therefore, they looked toward legislative activity. "But now since one cannot constantly or simply present Workmen's Protection Laws, [and since] in Germany, thanks to the Lassallean agitation, a colossal State Cult haunts our ranks, so the danger is always present that these elements will fall for an agreeable but completely unsocialist project, if only the word 'state' plays a role in it, and if the whole matter is presented as directed against big capital or is actually directed against the so-called mobile capital." [22] The sin was found not only among the former Lassalleans, Bernstein noted in a later letter, but also "many Eisenachers are still very attached to Lassalle." [23] Thus, Bernstein believed that, except for Lassalle's influence, State Socialism would never have had the appeal among the Social Democrats that was so evident in 1882. Whatever the cause, he wanted to let Engels know that the movement faced trouble.

Bernstein's alarm aroused Engels to consider writing a criticism of the State Socialists and Bismarck's socialism which could be printed in the *Sozialdemokrat*, much as the *Anti-Duehring* had been run in the *Vorwaerts*. One part of that criticism, Engels added, could be devoted to an exposé of Lassalle's errors.[24] Engels dropped the idea by early

[21] *Ibid.*, pp. 2–3.
[22] Bernstein to Engels, Sept. 1, 1882, Marx/Engels Archive, IISH.
[23] Bernstein to Engels, Sept. 15, 1882, Marx/Engels Archive, IISH.
[24] Engels to Bernstein, Sept. 13, 1882, in Friedrich Engels, *Die Briefe von*

1883, however, believing that the inclination among Social Democrats to support Bismarck's State Socialism had waned. As evidence, Engels reported that he had talked once again with Paul Singer, who previously had supported all nationalization, but had now freed himself of such ideas and was of "regular revolutionary" convictions.[25] Engels had made a small sampling, not sufficient to give him a very accurate picture of the sentiments within the Reichstag *Fraktion.*

The Reichstag was scheduled to return to the sickness and accident programs in the spring of 1883. Before it convened, the Social Democrats held their second secret congress, at Copenhagen in March, where they first formulated the party's official statement on Bismarck's social reforms. The resolution, which was "unanimously" adopted, declared that the party believed neither in the "honorable intentions" of the government nor in the "ability of the ruling classes" to carry out a reform. The party affirmed its conviction "that the so-called social reforms will only be used as a tactical means to divert the worker from the correct path." Finally, the resolution called upon the socialist deputies to protect the interests of the working class in all proposals which touched on the "economic condition of the people." [26]

Opinion at the Copenhagen congress was not as "unanimous" on Bismarck's social reform as the published record indicated. Those moderates who sympathized with Bismarck's program lacked courage to speak out, especially against the forceful criticism and skillful leadership of Bebel. The sympathizers kept their true feelings private. There were rumors, however, about the compromising attitude of many leaders which Bebel reported to Engels. Bruno Geiser was reported to have said that the class conflict was an "invention" of Marx; Wilhelm Blos expressed himself in a "hateful manner" at a memorial service for Marx in Stuttgart; Wilhelm Hasenclever was "enchanted" over the "politeness" with which some Junkers treated Social Democrats in the Reichstag; and Moritz Rittinghausen had spoken openly about an approaching "era of great social reforms." Max Kayser and Rittinghausen, Bebel had heard, were intent upon voting for the sickness insur-

Friedrich Engels an Eduard Bernstein. Mit Briefen von Karl Kautsky an Ebendenselben, edited by Eduard Bernstein (Berlin, 1925), pp. 78–79.

[25] Engels to Bernstein, Feb. 8, 1883, in *ibid.*, p. 109. Nearly three years earlier Engels had published in French a short analysis of Bismarck's socialism, limited to a discussion of the protective tariff and the Imperial railroad monopoly. The article, in two parts, did not appear in German. "Le Socialisme de M. Bismarck," in l'*Égalité*, March 2, 1880, p. 6; and March 24, 1880, p. 4.

[26] *Protokoll . . . Kopenhagen*, pp. 29–30.

ance, but he could not confirm this.[27] Clearly, the resolution rejecting Bismarck's reforms was a façade of unity, approved not out of full agreement, but out of the moderates' fear of being discredited by Bebel before the whole party.

In public, nevertheless, the Social Democrats preserved the appearance of complete party unity. When the Reichstag first debated the Sickness Insurance Bill in April 1883, they returned to the tactic initiated in the spring of 1881. They presented a bill of amendments designed to increase the compensation to sick workers and to extend the insurance to categories of workers not included in the government bill.[28] Once again the Social Democrats challenged the particulars of Bismarck's social welfare, but not its general principles. Grillenberger warned the Reichstag not to assume that the Social Democratic amendments represented a true socialist plan because they had been adapted to existing conditions.[29] But Rittinghausen assured the house that he would not make reproaches merely because the sickness insurance had weaknesses in particulars. With obvious conciliatory intent, Rittinghausen assured his listeners: "It goes without saying that when one enters a new terrain for the first time, one cannot proceed with the certainty which is necessary to create a truly good thing; in such matters it is also necessary to pay a high cost for learning." [30] But because the sickness insurance did not incorporate their amendments, the Social Democrats voted against it. The same held true for the accident insurance when it was debated and passed in the spring of 1884. In the debates, Vollmar accused the government of betraying its own "high flying State Socialist plans" in the face of bourgeois demands.[31] Wilhelm Blos later added further reprimands for the manner in which the government had conceded points to the propertied classes.[32] With that, the Social Democrats once again cast negative votes.

The direct confrontation between Social Democracy and Bismarck's State Socialism had passed, but its significance needs further comment. No doubt, as Bernstein maintained at the time, the Lassallean "State Cult" encouraged many Social Democrats to interpret Bismarck's program as a form of socialism that their party ought to accept. But even

[27] Bebel to Engels, May 2, 1883, in Bebel, *Briefwechsel*, p. 155.
[28] Social Democratic amendments in *SB*, v, ii (1882/83), vol. vi, *Anlagen*, No. 251, pp. 950–55.
[29] *Ibid.*, vol. iii, p. 1995.
[30] *Ibid.*, vol. iv, p. 2469.
[31] *SB*, v, iv (1884), vol. i, p. 36.
[32] *Ibid.*, vol. ii, pp. 1112–13.

apart from Lassalle's statism, the Social Democrats had been instructed to think along the lines of State Socialism from the middle seventies. The writings of men such as Schaeffle had exerted influence at a time when the Social Democrats searched eagerly for thinkers who could unravel the intricacies of socialist economic theory.

Bernstein had alluded to another reason for the appeal of State Socialism in his letter to Engels. Many Social Democratic leaders, he noted, wanted to see improvements in the conditions of the working class immediately, and they were usually the same people who had little expectation of a nearing social and political revolution in Germany. They would have preferred to have the Reichstag accept their own legislative suggestions, but their influence was too meager to bring results. Therefore, when Bismarck opened the path for such reform, they were genuinely eager to follow his lead. They were pessimistic about the possibilities of a revolution in the near future and were not at all convinced that it would solve the social question if it did come.

Thus, contrasting optimistic and pessimistic views about the possibilities of revolution in Germany shared in shaping attitudes toward State Socialism. At the Zurich conference, a sharp line had divided August Bebel, who constantly expected a revolution momentarily, and the moderates, most of whom left the idea of revolution for the distant future. Others even looked upon revolution as undesirable. Bebel found the moderates' pessimism about revolution detrimental to the policies of Social Democracy; it undermined the political independence of the party. As he explained in a letter of October 1882, some people in the party "do not believe in the level of the present revolutionary development and therefore dream more or less of a social reform in alliance with other elements." [33] Since Bebel believed firmly in an approaching revolution, partial reforms were of minor importance to him. The total solution of the labor question would come shortly with the revolution.

For the moderates, revolution in the future did not offer a satisfactory solution for intolerable conditions in the present. Only fragmentary evidence remains about the thinking of the moderates who, in the interest of reform, privately endorsed Bismarck's social program. Therefore, a few unpublished letters from the pen of Karl Hoechberg are exceptionally valuable. Although Hoechberg had helped financially to launch the careers of Bernstein and Kautsky, he regretted their

[33] Bebel to Comrades in New York, Oct. 9, 1882, quoted in Heinrich Gemkow, *Friedrich Engels' Hilfe beim Sieg der deutschen Sozialdemokratie ueber das Sozialistengesetz* (Berlin-East, 1957), p. 79.

commitment to Marxism. He therefore encouraged them to embrace Bismarck's program. "One must force the government on this path [of reform]," he wrote to Bernstein in June 1884, "in order to prepare for the socialist state, to make it easier; otherwise one fine day we may stand before a sticky problem, which we may not solve—*because the time is lacking for us*." [34] In his reply, which is not extant, Bernstein must have assured Hoechberg that in time the economic development within capitalism would lead to the complete transformation of society. "It is noteworthy," Hoechberg answered, "that you always answer everything by time, a consequence of the Marxist theory of history; and still more noteworthy, that you are absolutely in no hurry. *I am in a hurry*. . . ." [35] In his haste for social reform, Hoechberg was willing to put aside democratic political demands. He admitted gladly that if the welfare of the people were improved, it did not concern him whether it was accomplished through a monarchy or a republic.[36]

Although Hoechberg spoke only for himself, scattered evidence indicates that the other Social Democratic sympathizers with Bismarck's program agreed with the general tenor of his arguments. The fact that they did not openly vote for the Chancellor's legislation merely hid their inner inclinations. The crucial point is that Bismarck himself had made it politically impossible for even the moderate Social Democrats to vote for his legislation. In the context of the repressive Socialist Law, no self-respecting Social Democrat could openly endorse the Chancellor's program without implicit treason to his own cause.

By June 1884, when the Reichstag passed the Accident Insurance Bill, the Social Democrats had confronted the crisis created by Bismarck's State Socialism without suffering an open fissure in the party. For the official position of the party, the principle of democratic-political opposition had triumphed over the attraction for economic expediency.

The rejection of the Bismarck legislation did not in itself solve the larger problem of the Social Democratic theoretical approach to State Socialism. Throughout the period, Bernstein had continued to publish exposés of Bismarck's social program in hopes that the theoretical foundation for a rejection would be thoroughly understood in the

[34] Karl Hoechberg to Bernstein, June 8, 1884, Bernstein Archive, IISH.
[35] Hoechberg to Bernstein, June 21, 1884, Bernstein Archive, IISH.
[36] Hoechberg to Bernstein, Oct. 28, 1884, Bernstein Archive, IISH.

party.[37] Bernstein and Kautsky, themselves so recently initiated into Marxism, believed that the Social Democrats suffered from an insufficient theoretical knowledge of Marxist economics. Thus, in the years of the State Socialist debate, a concerted effort was launched, signaled especially by the founding of the *Neue Zeit* (1883), to disseminate Marxism and make it the undisputed master of Social Democratic thought. As these young intellectuals studied and wrote, always under the benevolent and approving gaze of Engels in London, Marxism gradually displaced the reliance of the party on other economic theorists. The last word, however, had not been heard from the advocates of State Socialism within Social Democracy.

Lingering State Socialism: The Marxists against the Rodbertus Enthusiasts

During the years that the party debated Bismarck's program, a few Social Democrats joined in a new flourish of partisan interest in the works of Rodbertus, the conservative socialist. After Rodbertus died in 1875, Adolf Wagner edited Lassalle's letters to Rodbertus (1878) and subsequently supervised the publication of the unpublished writings. In 1882, Rudolf Meyer published the letters he had received from Rodbertus.[38] In the universities, professors and students turned more attention to the theory of the Pomeranian economist. A Rodbertus movement emerged on the German stage, with Wagner and Meyer coaching at either wing. Among its number could be found a few Social Democrats and some intellectuals who occasionally flirted with Social Democracy: Moritz Wirth, Georg Adler, Max Quarck, Conrad Schmidt, Hermann Bahr, Max Schippel, and Carl August Schramm.[39] Most of them contributed to the growing bibliography on Rodbertus as a social and economic thinker. Of these, only Schramm had been

[37] Cf. the following in the *Sozialdemokrat:* "Die Impotenz des Klassenstaates," No. 2, Jan. 5, 1882; "Das Maerchen vom 'sozialen Koenigthum'," No. 10, March 1, 1883; Leo, "Der Sozialismus und der Staat," No. 52, Dec. 20, 1883; "Klassengesetzgebung," No. 20, May 10, 1883; "Klassenkampf und soziale Reform," No. 30, July 24, 1884.

[38] Adolf Wagner (ed.), *Briefe von Ferdinand Lassalle an Carl Rodbertus-Jagetzow* (Berlin, 1878); Dr. Rodbertus-Jagetzow, *Briefe und socialpolitische Aufsaetze*, edited by Rudolf Meyer (Berlin, n. d. but 1882).

[39] Robert Michels, "Rodbertus und sein Kreis," in Carl Rodbertus-Jagetzow, *Neue Briefe ueber Grundrente, Rentenprinzip und Soziale Frage an Schumacher*, edited by Robert Michels and Ernst Ackermann (Karlsruhe, 1926), p. 48.

a Social Democratic party member for many years; Quarck, Schmidt, and Schippel soon became active Social Democrats. In the seventies, Schramm had been recognized as one of the best informed Social Democrats on economic theory. Like many others, he was expelled from Berlin late in 1878 and then became one of Karl Hoechberg's closest coworkers in Switzerland. Schramm shared Hoechberg's dislike of revolution and longed for a socialist movement which would work in harmony with all groups favorable to social reform. With these credentials, Schramm was the person best suited to promote the cause of Rodbertus among the Social Democrats.[40]

For those other bourgeois intellectuals who were troubled by the social question, Rodbertus held a natural attraction. Such bourgeois intellectuals were subject to conflicting cross-currents: Their natural loyalty to Bismarck's Reich was increased with the passage of the social reforms, but they were simultaneously drawn toward the Social Democrats as the representatives of the workers. Typifying such an ambiguous outlook was Hermann Bahr, who waxed enthusiastic for all of Bismarck's achievements and fraternized with Social Democratic leaders at the same time.[41] In Rodbertus' theory, these intellectuals found their solution—a socialism which combined severe criticism of capitalism with the possibility of unquestioned loyalty to the Bismarckian Reich.

It is clear that the Rodbertus movement had dangerous implications for the Social Democratic party. His economic theory apart, Rodbertus had been an unrelenting antagonist of liberalism and democracy, and an equally devoted protagonist of German monarchism. If the Rodbertus movement now succeeded, the Social Democrats would have to take him as a founder for the theory and practice of their party. The principles of democracy and internationalism would suffer, as would the emphasis on the class struggle and the proletarian orientation of Social Democracy. All that was revolutionary in Marx would be in jeopardy. While this tendency would have increased the party's attractiveness in the eyes of numerous intellectuals who feared social and political revolution from below, it would have subverted the party's role as a defender of the democratic principle in German soci-

[40] For more detail on the Rodbertus bibliography see my article, "German Social Democracy and German State Socialism, 1876–1884," *International Review of Social History*, IX (1964), p. 221.

[41] Hermann Bahr, *Selbstbildnis* (Berlin, 1923), pp. 171–72, 176, 187–89.

ety. Equally important, just as the prestige of Rodbertus increased in the eyes of many Social Democrats because of his connection with Lassalle, so the Lassallean current would be reenforced by the inclusion of Rodbertus as one of the recognized sources for socialist theory. Therefore, it was all important to the Marxists in the party to demolish completely Rodbertus' appeal. For Engels, Kautsky, and Bernstein, the leaders in the work of demolition, the crucial task was to demonstrate that Rodbertus had failed as a social-economic scientist. If they could refute the arguments of those who claimed that Rodbertus was one of the founders of "scientific socialism," then the rest of his appeal was also undermined.

The issue, therefore, was fought out on the battlefield of economic theory. More specifically, a large part of the battle raged around the claim, first made by Rodbertus himself, that Marx had plundered an early work of his, *Zur Erkenntnis unsrer staatswirtschaftlichen Zustaende* (1842), for basic ideas. Both Engels and Kautsky were aroused to these issues early in 1884 when a new work, *Das Kapital*, by Rodbertus was published posthumously with an introduction in which the plundering charge against Marx was repeated.[42] Kautsky had just begun his study of Rodbertus, as he assured Engels, "in order to fight him" and with the intent to write a critical article in which recent publications on and by Rodbertus would be reviewed.[43] Such work was necessary, Kautsky wrote later, because "he [Rodbertus] has a great number of enthusiastic followers in our own ranks. A genuine hatred against Marx and Marxism dominates our educated people, and they eagerly grasp after every non-Marxist socialist, from Louis Blanc to Rodbertus, to play them up against Marx. . . ." [44] The awareness of this hostility to Marx alerted Kautsky to the need for a completely sound Marxist critique of Rodbertus, and so he turned to Engels for advice. Engels obliged, giving careful counsel. Kautsky queried, Engels answered; Kautsky sent drafts of his article, and Engels returned them with tutorial revisions. Rodbertus haunted nearly every letter.[45] Kautsky's critique appeared in the *Neue Zeit* in the late summer,

[42] Carl Rodbertus-Jagetzow, *Das Kapital. Vierter sozialer Brief an von Kirchmann*, edited by Theophil Kozak (2nd ed.; Berlin, 1913), p. xii, from "Einleitung" to the 1st edition of 1884.

[43] Kautsky to Engels, Feb. 14, 1884, in Benedikt Kautsky (ed.), *Friedrich Engels' Briefwechsel mit Karl Kautsky* (Vienna, 1955), p. 98.

[44] Kautsky to Engels, May 29, 1884, in *ibid.*, p. 118.

[45] See the exchange of letters between Feb. 16 and Oct. 22, 1884, in *ibid.*, pp. 100–153.

1884.[46] At the same time, Engels was preparing a German edition of Marx's *Poverty of Philosophy;* Engels' introduction was devoted almost entirely to a criticism of Rodbertus and to a demonstration that Marx could not have derived fundamental ideas from the Pomeranian economist. As it also appeared late in 1884, the attack on Rodbertus was in full swing.

The controversy which ensued between Schramm, defending Rodbertus, and Kautsky, promoting Marx, need not be followed in detail. Although Schramm wrote a stinging reply to Kautsky, published in the *Neue Zeit*, the Marxists were in control of the theoretical journal as well as the party newspaper and used both to further the attack on Rodbertus.[47] Frustrated and angry, Schramm demanded that a committee of university professors be called in to arbitrate the dispute between him and Kautsky. Failing in that, Schramm wrote a booklet, *Rodbertus, Marx, Lassalle,* which the Social Democratic press in Zurich refused to publish but which came out late in 1885 under the auspices of Louis Viereck, a Social Democratic Reichstag deputy who was enticed by Bismarck's program.[48] Schramm frankly admitted that the revolutionary doctrines of Marx repelled him, and he asserted confidently that the great majority of the party agreed with him. He couched his pro-Rodbertus inclination in a glorification of Lassalle: "Rodbertus, Marx, Lassalle, they are the great founders of a world-historical movement, but Lassalle is the greatest of the three." [49] Schramm may or may not have been correct about the majority's reluctance to embrace revolutionary doctrines, but he certainly failed in

[46] Karl Kautsky, "Das 'Kapital' von Rodbertus," *Neue Zeit,* II (1884), pp. 337–50, 385–402.

[47] On the debate, see C. A. S[chramm], "K. Kautsky und Rodbertus," *Neue Zeit,* II (1884), pp. 481–93, and an immediate rejoinder by Kautsky, "Eine Replik," pp. 494–505; Karl Kautsky, "Schlusswort," *Neue Zeit,* III (1885); pp. 224–32; Karl Kautsky, "Aus dem Nachlass von Rodbertus," *Neue Zeit,* IV (1886), pp. 258–63; "Materialistische Geschichtsauffassung," *SD,* No. 7, Feb. 12, 1886; "Staatssozialismus," (by "s"), *SD,* No. 12, March 18, 1886.

[48] Carl A. Schramm to Hermann Schlueter, (Business Director of the *Sozialdemokrat*), May 9, 1885, in *Kleine Korrespondenz,* IISH; Schlueter wrote to Kautsky that he had never read such a "masterpiece of perfidy" as Schramm's booklet. May 16, 1885, Kautsky Archive, IISH.

[49] C. A. Schramm, *Rodbertus, Marx, Lassalle. Sozialwissenschaftliche Studie* (Munich [1885]), p. 75. With the appearance of this booklet, Bernstein issued an extensive denunciation in serial form: "Ein moralischer Kritiker und seine kritische Moral," *SD,* No. 4, Jan. 21; No. 5, Jan. 28; No. 6, Feb. 5; and No. 7, Feb. 12, 1886. In reply, Schramm complained bitterly that a "clique" in the party no longer represented the program but blindly "believes in the possibility of achieving the goal of the movement through a violent revolution. . . ." "Polemik," *SD,* No. 9, Feb. 26, 1886.

his drive to make Rodbertus equal to Marx for Social Democracy. In 1886 he left the party and the other members of the Rodbertus group either separated completely from the Social Democracy or modified their views considerably. Late in 1886, Engels observed that the Rodbertus threat had been "smashed," although, he reflected, it had been serious at the time.[50]

The differences of opinion among Social Democrats on how to approach Bismarck's State Socialism had remained below the surface for the most part. Only the theoretical debate about the significance of Rodbertus for Social Democracy broke into the open in 1884. In some measure, the pressures of the Socialist Law had forced the Social Democrats to make a united front against the government. The Social Democratic tactic on the social welfare measures had been formed in that atmosphere.

While the debate on State Socialism was going on, other developments were taking place which created a new situation for the Social Democrats by late 1884. Around 1883–1884, the authorities softened their implementation of the Socialist Law, permitting greater freedom of discussion within the party. At the same time, Bismarck's expectation that he could kill socialism with kindness went unrealized, and the Social Democratic movement demonstrated a new dynamism. The partial lifting of the repressive lid, combined with the revitalization of the labor movement, created the conditions for a new crisis in Social Democracy, for the underlying cleavage between moderates and radicals had not yet been resolved.

[50] Engels to Laura Lafargue, Nov. 2, 1886, in Frederick Engels, Paul and Laura Lafargue, *Correspondence* (Moscow, 1959), I, p. 394.

CHAPTER VII · GROWTH OF SOCIAL DEMOCRACY CREATES A MAJOR CRISIS FOR THE PARTY

By 1884 the whole of the German labor movement was making a healthy recovery from the destructive storm that had hit it in 1878. Everywhere there were unmistakable signs that the labor movement was once again on its feet: Electoral success within all representative bodies was becoming common with the Social Democrats; socialist-oriented newspapers were appearing in increasing numbers; and local craft unions once again were organizing workers and pressuring employers for higher wages and better working hours.

The expansion of Social Democracy encouraged every party member, but it also harbored unseen dangers. As the party increased its representation in the Reichstag, some socialist deputies still wanted to explore the possibilities of cooperation with the government of Bismarck. The antagonisms between moderates and radicals intensified, and a major crisis hit the party as a result of its growth.

Elements of Social Democratic Expansion: Urbanization, Trade Unions, Local Elections

After several years of severe repression, the government and the local authorities sensed that police measures were not always appropriate for countering the appeal of socialism to the workers. In conjunction with the passage of the insurance programs, the authorities had shifted therefore to a policy of "mild practice" around 1883, hoping in that way to offer more assurances to the workers that the government was their true friend. To a degree this shift in policy was an implicit admission that the Socialist Law was a practical and moral failure as a means to combat the "evils" of Social Democracy, a comment that appeared frequently in the newspapers of many parties by 1883.[1] It

[1] Cf. the convenient collection of newspaper opinion in Friedrich Apitzsch, *Die*

could thus be interpreted as the government's confession that the Social Democrats had always been correct when they warned that persecution would benefit their "spiritual" movement just as it had benefited early Christianity, by creating martyrs and heroic legends.

But the policy of a "mild practice" failed to draw the German workers away from the Social Democratic movement. Ironically, many workers probably gave the Social Democrats as much credit as they gave the government for the welfare measures, because party agitators often quoted Bismarck's admission that except for the existence of the socialist movement the program would not have been initiated.[2] The heightened concern about the social question in government and academic circles was also an obvious recognition that the Social Democrats had raised genuine issues, and this too could not fail to improve the party's reputation in the eyes of many workers. In a sense, it appeared that no matter which course the government followed, repressive or progressive, the Social Democrats would receive the rewards.[3]

Along with Bismarck's social welfare program, the general progress of German industrialization also created new opportunities for the growth of Social Democracy. Although economic historians sometimes interpret the years from 1873 to 1896 as a depression period, this in itself is misleading. Although the period had deflationary features, all indices indicate that German industrial production, except for a few minor dips, rose steadily during the whole epoch, especially in the eighties. At the same time, these decades were also characterized by the customary shorter periods of business expansion and contraction, the longest contraction coming between 1873 and 1878.[4] The upturns and downturns in general business prosperity tended to be reflected, sometimes with lags, in the wages and costs of living for the workers. Although it is not possible to demonstrate that the political fortunes of the Social Democrats necessarily depended on the good or bad condi-

deutsche Tagespresse unter dem Einfluss des Sozialistengesetzes, published dissertation, Leipzig (1928) *passim.*

[2] Bismarck in the Reichstag on November 26, 1884, *SB*, VI, i (1884/85), vol. I, p. 25.

[3] The German authorities were especially distraught by the ability of the Social Democrats to exploit the government's reform legislation for their own purposes. Police President Madai covered this frustrating development in two confidential reports on the Social Democrats on March 4, 1884, and November 4, 1884, in Hoehn, *Die vaterlandslosen Gesellen*, I, pp. 191–94, 217–18.

[4] Joseph A. Schumpeter, *Business Cycles* (New York and London, 1939), II, p. 467; Bry, *Wages in Germany*, pp. 19, 325.

tions of the workers, some general observations are possible for the recovery of the party in the eighties. It is generally true, other things being equal, that the Social Democratic party tended to flourish as the demand for labor increased and wage rates rose. This correlation would be difficult to demonstrate for the seventies, however, since several other variables affected the fortunes of the movement. During the expansionist *Gründerjahre*, 1871–1873, the two socialist movements faced the intense hostility of nationalist Germans and their own internal difficulties, and thus their growth may have been limited by these factors. The growth of the party between 1876 and 1878 may have been the result of unification and better organization, so that the prevailing economic tendencies were of only peripheral significance. For the eighties, the picture is clearer.

Although the years between 1878 and 1881 were expansionist for German business, wage rates did not reflect this rise until the following years. Taking an index number of 100 for 1913, statistics of weekly earnings (real wages) for all industries show that after reaching a high of 84 in 1875, earnings dropped to a low of 70 during 1880 and 1881, and then rose again to 75 in 1882–1883, 80 in 1884, 83 in 1885, 85 in 1886, and 87 in 1887.[5] One may also assume, although specific statistical data on unemployment is almost entirely lacking for Germany before 1890, that employment opportunities also rose with the general improvement in the economy. According to a report of the Berlin Police President, the number of employed persons in Berlin shops and factories had dropped to 29,292 in 1878 from 66,892 in 1875 and then rose again to 73,652 by 1881.[6] These figures give no indication of unemployment percentages since the total labor force available in Berlin is not known for these years, but they definitely suggest a marked rise in the demand for labor in the early eighties. Despite the lack of specific data, there is no reason to doubt that there was an increased demand for labor after 1881–1882. This in turn created the objective economic conditions which were more favorable for a revival of trade unions, a development also made possible by the government's shift to a "mild practice," as we shall see shortly.

The gradual rise in real wages after 1882 can not be interpreted to mean that henceforth the German worker was freed from social

[5] Bry, *Wages in Germany*, p. 361.

[6] Cited in Kuczynski, *Die Geschichte der Lage der Arbeiter unter dem Kapitalismus*, III, p. 256. On the lack of unemployment data, see Schumpeter, *Business Cycles*, II, p. 509.

misery. On the contrary, little or nothing was done during the eighties to improve the conditions of work in shops and factories or to reduce the length of the working day. Equally important, the housing situation showed no improvement. As German industrialization proceeded at a steady pace, the population movement to the cities grew to large proportions in the 1880's; between 1880 and 1890, the number of cities with a population over one hundred thousand increased from fifteen to twenty-six. At the same time, the rural population continued to decline, not only in relation to the urban population but in absolute numbers as well.[7] There is no doubt that housing for farm laborers had often been deplorable, but in the eighties Germany faced an acute crisis in urban housing. Contemporary observers and scholars testified to the overcrowded and unsanitary living conditions of the German workers in towns and cities; in 1886 the *Verein fuer Sozialpolitik* published a two-volume study describing in detail the wretched housing facilities in numerous cities.[8] It was not unusual for whole families to live in one room, while beds in cellars and attics were often rented to workers in shifts. One researcher discovered that in Dresden 55 percent of all living quarters consisted of only one room, while in Breslau it was 62 percent, and in Chemnitz it rose even to 70 percent.[9] With miserable living quarters, rising rents, and uncertain employment, the new city worker found an opportunity for both friendship and social protest in the Social Democratic party. The large-city vote of the party grew substantially in the eighties; by 1887, the Social Democrats polled almost 37 percent of the vote in city districts.[10] These were developments which the anti-socialist parties found impossible to curb.

Was it not possible, however, that the high rate of German emigration, which reached its peak in the early eighties, would offset the gains made by the Social Democrats through urbanization? Some German economists in fact believed that emigration was carrying off the political discontents from the lower classes. The pattern of emigration, however, does not bear this out, for emigration tended to be

[7] Ludwig Elster, "Bevoelkerungswesen," *Handwoerterbuch der Staatswissenschaften* (4th edition), II, p. 695.

[8] *Die Wohnungsnoth der aermeren Klassen in deutschen Grossstaedten und Vorschlaege zu deren Abhuelfe*, in *Schriften des Vereins fuer Sozialpolitik*, XXX and XXXI (Leipzig, 1886).

[9] H. Peus, *Der Wohnungsjammer des Proletariats* (Dessau, 1894), pp. 3ff., as cited in Kuczynski, *Die Geschichte der Lage der Arbeiter unter dem Kapitalismus*, III, p. 398.

[10] Max Schippel (ed.), *Die Sozialdemokratie und der deutsche Reichstag*, in the *Berliner Arbeiterbibliothek*, No. 10 (Berlin, 1889), p. 21.

highest in rural areas among peasants, farm laborers, petty traders, and handicraftsmen and not among the working classes in the large urban areas. In 1885, Karl Kautsky drew up some statistical tables which in fact showed that in almost all cases emigration was lowest from those districts with a high Social Democratic vote. The districts in which the conservative parties were strongest, it turned out, suffered the greatest loss of population through emigration abroad.[11]

Some Social Democratic workers emigrated to be sure, but the party discouraged it, and only those who were expelled from their homes or who wished to avoid imprisonment because of their intense political activity resorted to it as a last measure. During the period of the Socialist Law, the party lost very few of its experienced leaders through emigration, and some of those who did leave, such as Most and Hasselmann, were bid farewell with no regrets. Many of the socialist agitators who left Germany went no further than London or Zurich and from those places remained in close contact with the party at home. There is no evidence to indicate that the growth potential of the socialist movement was hampered to any degree by emigration.

In addition to the general benefits the Social Democrats gained from urbanization, the improving economic condition of the workers after 1882 also contributed a new thrust for the formation of trade unions. Workers whose unions had been dissolved by the authorities in 1878–1879 were naturally eager to reestablish their organizations as soon as the chance offered itself. Fortunately for them, the rising demand for labor coincided with the government's shift to the policy of "mild practice," reducing slightly the legal restrictions against the formation of trade unions. Ironically, when the social welfare legislation was debated, government officials expressed the belief that, if given more freedom to organize, the workers would henceforth show more trust in Bismarck's government and less in the Social Democrats. As the police relaxed their repression, local associations of skilled craftsmen, known as *Fachvereine*, appeared in considerable numbers in 1883 and following; a few *Fachvereine* had already appeared in the previous years. Since the earliest *Fachvereine* had no connections with the So-

[11] A. Sartorius von Waltershausen, "Auswanderung," *Handwoerterbuch der Staatswissenschaften* (4th edition), II, p. 96; "Die deutsche Auswanderung," *Neue Zeit*, III (1885), pp. 253–57. The article is not signed, but it is ascribed to Kautsky by Werner Blumenberg, *Karl Kautskys Literarisches Werk* (The Hague, 1960), p. 36. The above observations are also supported by Mack Walker's recent study, *Germany and the Emigration 1816–1885* (Cambridge, Mass., 1964), pp. 184–88.

cial Democrats, it seemed for a time that the government's hope for a politically neutral trade union movement was not beyond realization.[12]

In a few years, however, everyone recognized that although the *Fachvereine* disavowed all political associations, most organized workers drifted toward the Social Democrats. For example, in 1882 a Berlin gilder, Ferdinand Ewald, won the endorsement of the Christian Socials, some National Liberals and Conservatives for a plan to have a central committee of *Fachvereine* send a petition of workingmen's demands to the government. Such a petition was in the tradition of the downtrodden worker who looked upon the Monarch as a beneficent defender of the poor against the rich. The Social Democrats in Berlin were understandably suspicious of Ewald, but their members attended his meetings, and Ewald soon learned that if he wished to attract a mass following for his plan he could not pursue his middle-of-the-road policy. By February 1883, Ewald was moving toward the Social Democrats, and in 1884 he became one of the party's first elected deputies to the Berlin *Stadtverordnetenversammlung* (Municipal Council).[13]

The experience of the Ewald movement made it clear that a viable trade union movement could not exist in explicit opposition to Social Democracy, although an open political allegiance was equally impossible. The government authorities by their earlier indiscriminate use of the Socialist Law to abolish trade unions, had made it easy for the Social Democrats to identify their cause with the cause of all workingmen.

Increasing rapidly, the number of *Fachvereine* rose to 1,021 in 1885 with a collective membership of about 58,000. In some crafts the leaders looked beyond the local organization to national affiliations; by the end of 1884, the Berlin police noted that thirteen central associations of trade unions existed. Apart from occasional strikes for higher wages or lower working hours, both the local and national organizations directed much of their energy toward the establishment of mutual assistance funds, some of which affiliated with the national sickness insurance. In the summer of 1886, the Berlin police recorded that there were thirty-four central sickness and burial funds with 2,764 local affiliates and a total membership of 263,684. Realizing that such funds were especially dangerous, since they also served indirectly as instruments for the political purposes of the Social Democrats, the govern-

[12] Schmoele, *Gewerkschaften*, I, pp. 81–82.

[13] *Ibid.*, pp. 81–90; Bernstein, *Berliner Arbeiterbewegung*, II, pp. 90–92, 97–102.

ment had already tightened the regulations in 1884. At that time, the Social Democrats sought to counter these government moves, but without success.[14] Even during the period of "mild practice" the police kept a sharp eye on the activities of all trade union organizations.

Under the circumstances, the trade union movement was fragmentized and localized, with none of the centralization and tendency toward uniformity which developed after 1890. Each *Fachvereine* had to adjust its activity to local conditions, legal as well as economic, and they formed policies independent of each other. Social Democratic influence, therefore, varied in degree from craft to craft and locale to locale because the relationship between party and the *Fachvereine* had to be vague and tenuous. In contrast with the party, there was a break in the composition of the trade union leadership before and after 1878. The new group of trade union leaders was generally separated by a full generation from the older Social Democratic leaders.[15] The two groups had matured in entirely different political and economic environments, the party's leaders in the pre-1871 era and the new trade union leaders within the Bismarckian Reich. The new trade union leadership thus achieved its position in the years when Bismarck was sponsoring the welfare legislation, and this could not help but influence its social and political outlook to some degree. Despite all these variations and differences, and the fact that the trade unions could not openly offer the party organizational assistance, their emergence gave an undeniable impetus to the spread of Social Democratic tendencies among workingmen.

The growth of the Social Democratic movement was equally evident from the results of elections, not only for the Reichstag but also for the state diets and the municipal councils. One can hardly overestimate the significance of the fact that in the middle years of the Socialist Law the Social Democrats first achieved sufficient electoral strength to place a meaningful number of deputies in the Saxon Diet and in several municipal councils.

In the home territory of the Eisenachers, Saxony, the Social Demo-

[14] Statistics from Franz Rohleder's "Bureau für Arbeitsstatistik" (Munich), reprinted in Hellfaier, *Die deutsche Sozialdemokratie*, pp. 235–36, and from police reports in Fricke, *Bismarcks Praetorianer*, pp. 148–49 n. 256, and p. 202.

[15] The significance of this difference has been noted by Gerhard A. Ritter, *Die Arbeiterbewegung im Wilhelminischen Reich* (Berlin-Dahlem, 1959), p. 109.

crats continued to make a respectable showing in the elections to the state diet. After the first Social Democrat, Otto Freytag, won election to the diet in 1877, the party increased its delegation in nearly every subsequent biennial election. In 1879, both Liebknecht and Puttrich won seats, and in July 1881 Bebel received his first mandate for the Saxon Diet, and the party as a whole won slightly over 7 percent of the total vote. This gave them four deputies in the diet, a small number (the assembly had ninety-one deputies), but they were very active and vocal. In 1883, they did not add in number of deputies, although Vollmar replaced Freytag. But in 1885 they once again added one member, now totaling five.[16]

The Social Democrats had strength not only in the large industrial cities of Leipzig, Chemnitz, and Dresden but also in the smaller towns which had important industrial traditions, Glauchau-Meerane (an old Eisenacher stronghold), Zwickau (an important mining region), and Crimmitschau. However, due to the minimum tax requirement for voter qualification, the Social Democrats could not hope to pull the votes of the poor industrial worker. But Saxony still had a large artisan population which had supported the Saxon *Volkspartei* and the Eisenachers in the previous two decades, and much of the Social Democratic strength still rested with this stratum.

For the grass roots revival of the Social Democrats, election campaigns for seats on municipal councils were also significant. These campaigns did not have much national propaganda value because the candidates were attuned almost exclusively to local issues rather than the great principles of the party. Although it is almost impossible to ascertain the exact number of municipal councils on which the Social Democrats had representatives, notable progress was also made during the Socialist Law. According to various sources, by 1881 the Social Democrats had elected deputies to the municipal councils in Brunswick, Bremen, Esslingen, Glauchau-Meerane, Lambrecht (Palatinate), and Mannheim.[17] But the big breakthrough came in 1883–1884, when they elected four more to the council in Bremen, and for the first time

[16] Cf. Schulthess, *1879*, p. 320, and *1881*, p. 220. "Brief vom Kriegsschauplatz," *SD*, No. 30, July 21, 1881; "Sozialpolitische Rundschau," *SD*, No. 39, Sept. 24, 1885.

[17] Mehring, *Geschichte der deutschen Sozialdemokratie*, IV, p. 172; Georg Eckert, *Die Braunschweiger Arbeiterbewegung unter dem Sozialistengesetz*. I. Teil (*1878–1884*) (Brunswick, 1961), pp. 66ff.; Boettcher, *Anfänge und Entwicklung der Arbeiterbewegung in Bremen*, pp. 124ff.; Hoehn, *Die vaterlandslosen Gesellen*, I, p. 11, citing a report by Police President Madai.

won no less than four seats on the Berlin council. That marked the beginning of an extremely active socialist participation in the local government of the Reich's capital city.[18]

The success of the Social Democrats in elections to the municipal councils, although admittedly rather limited, offers some suggestions about the composition of the Social Democratic electorate. In the first place, universal suffrage did not apply in any of these elections, and we must assume therefore that industrial workers could have made up only a segment of the total Social Democratic vote. Small towns, such as Esslingen and Lambrecht, had very limited industrial operations, and Social Democrats could win elections only by appealing to other strata of society. A recent local history of the Socialist movement in Brunswick makes it quite clear that in the early eighties the party leaders appealed directly for the support of the lower-middle class, the *Mittelstand*.[19] If Brunswick was at all typical, and there is every reason to believe that it was, then in the towns the German Social Democrats worked in close cooperation with the "petty bourgeoisie," especially if the latter had a democratic political tradition. Even in the case of Berlin, the center of the most radical and intransigent socialist leaders, the party could hardly have won seats on the council without very significant assistance from the "petty bourgeoisie."

In the municipal councils, the Social Democrats had no choice but to work on a purely reformist basis, within the system of local government, not against it. The evidence all indicates, although it is admittedly spotty, that in the councils the Social Democrats applied themselves to detailed and limited reform measures. In the case of Berlin, the Social Democrats frequently advocated programs of municipalization, and except for the fact that they were also members of an outlawed party which called itself revolutionary one might easily mistake them for British Fabians.[20] This may not be surprising, but it may also be far more significant for the origins of reformism and revisionism than scholars have hitherto realized.

[18] Paul Hirsch, *25 Jahre sozialdemokratischer Arbeit in der Gemeinde* (Berlin, 1908), p. 2.

[19] Eckert, *Die Braunschweiger Arbeiterbewegung*, pp. 30–31, 101–03.

[20] Hirsch, *25 Jahre sozialdemokratischer Arbeit in der Gemeinde, passim.* That the Social Democrats were naturally drawn into "responsible cooperation" in the municipal councils has also been noted by Hermann Heidigger, *Die deutsche Sozialdemokratie und der nationale Staat 1870–1920* (Goettingen, 1956), p. 52.

Election Success in 1884: A Prelude to Crisis

The Reichstag elections in the fall of 1884 provided the most striking evidence of Social Democratic growth and government failure. When the balloting ended, the party had captured twenty-four Reichstag mandates, a popular vote of 549,990, and 9.71 percent of the total. It certainly marked a decisive turning point in the fortunes of the Social Democrats under the Socialist Law, for the setback of the 1881 election was completely reversed. Henceforth, the party showed steady increases at the polls.

The election stands as a turning point, not only for election increases, but also for the policies of the party in a deeper sense. The quantitative changes implied some qualitative changes. For the first time in the twenty-year life of the political labor movement, the party's deputies were in a position where they could possibly affect the outcome of Reichstag voting. This was true, not merely because of their twenty-four seats, but because the parties on which Bismarck could rely had again failed to achieve an absolute majority. The possibility emerged therefore that the Social Democrats could become a factor in the parliamentary bargaining for votes, especially when Bismarck's opposition needed support on close issues. In addition, with twenty-four deputies, the party leaders sensed a responsibility to their own electorate, to consider to what extent they were obligated to pursue a positive policy in the Reichstag rather than their usual intransigent opposition.

Social Democracy was thus going through the first stage of the metamorphosis from a largely protest movement—a sect—to a political party in the modern parliamentary sense, involving the possibilities of swapping votes in elections, parliamentary maneuverings, and compromises on legislation. To be sure, this was only the first stage, in some ways not much more than a hint that such a transformation of the party was possible, and the change was certainly not effected before 1890. Still, the essential factors for the transformation existed, and they led directly to the great crisis that threatened to split the party in 1885. The moderates joyfully embraced the chance to become a full-fledged modern parliamentary party, while the radicals, sporadically lured by the possibility, were more often troubled and angered by the "opportunism" encouraged by the new situation.

The election itself created opportunities for "politiking" by the Social Democrats. Bismarck was faced with a threat of increased strength by the liberal left. After a group of loyal Manchesterians (Secessionists) split from the National Liberals in 1881, they merged with the Progressives in March 1884, forming the new *Deutsch-Freisinnige Partei* (literally, German Free Thought party), dubbed the "Crown Prince's Party" because of its clear preference for the "liberal" views of Crown Prince Friedrich and his princess, Victoria, the daughter of the English Queen. Driven by the fear that, upon the death of Wilhelm I, he would be left to face a new Emperor with strong Reichstag support, Bismarck was more intent on destroying the *Freisinnige* party than the Social Democrats in 1884. On the national level, therefore, the campaign focused on the bitter antagonism between Bismarck and the *Freisinnige* party. In that situation, the conservative parties, and also the National Liberals, did not play up their hostility against the Social Democrats, but sometimes gave the impression that the socialists were a lesser evil than the *Freisinnige*.[21] The ramifications of this did not emerge until the run-off balloting in November, when the chance of election deals became quite apparent.

The conditions under which the Social Democrats campaigned in 1884 were thus much less onerous than at any time since 1877. Still, they did not enjoy complete freedom. But many local conferences were called to nominate candidates, and in Saxony, for example, all the districts had chosen their candidates by July.[22] The party's Reichstag *Fraktion*, meeting at Borsdorf near Leipzig on August 29–30, 1884, authorized a Central Election Committee of Auer, Bebel, Grillenberger, Hasenclever, and Liebknecht "to draw up a plan of battle" for the election campaign.[23] They drew up an *Aufruf der sozialdemokratischen Fraktion* (obviously written in great part by Bebel) and distributed it widely. Designed to appeal to as broad a spectrum of opinion as possible, the program was a mosaic intermingling the various ideas of the whole movement, Lassallean, Marxist, and democratic. The campaign literature in general is a strong reminder of the

[21] Eyck, *Bismarck*, III, pp. 377ff.; Nipperdey, *Die Organisation der deutschen Parteien vor 1918*, pp. 206ff.

[22] *Berliner Volksblatt*, No. 87, July 16, 1884, p. 2. In his summary account of Social Democratic activity during 1884, Police President Madai reported about meetings which had taken place in the "open air," but he does not provide any exact numbers and mentions only a few specific places. In Hoehn, *Die vaterlandslosen Gesellen*, I, pp. 220ff.

[23] Bebel to Motteler, August 31, 1884, Bebel Archive, IISH.

strength of the traditional socialist ideas even with the increased penetration of Marxism. Throughout Germany, the Social Democrats campaigned with exuberance. "The election campaign is glorious," Liebknecht wrote to Kautsky: "But work, work, work! In the last six days I had nine meetings, one conference, and twenty-five hours of railroad and stage-coach travel." [24]

No serious possibility for making election deals between Social Democrats and other parties emerged for the first ballot on October 28, in which the party picked up nine Reichstag seats. But, given the big Bismarck push against the *Freisinnige* party, there was even a chance that when running against *Freisinnige* candidates Social Democrats would attract conservative votes in the run-off balloting. On the other side, because the anti-Bismarckian liberals were pressed to find support, they too might look to the Social Democrats for help. Aware of these possibilities, the Central Election Committee immediately issued directives that, in districts where no Social Democrat was in the run-off, support should only be given to those other candidates who declared that they were against the extension of the Socialist Law, the sharpening of the penal code, new restrictions on universal suffrage, the lengthening of the legislative periods, the introduction of "Labor Books," and new taxes on the necessities of life.[25]

The declaration laid the ground rules for the run-offs, but it did not eliminate the possibility that individual party members would become involved in deals. The conservative parties, following Bismarck's line, wanted to receive working-class support in return for endorsing Social Democratic candidates who were in contests with radical liberals. All of this created some embarrassment for the Social Democrats. Thus, when conservatives in Frankfurt am Main inquired of the Chancellor how they should vote in the run-off between the Social Democrat Sabor and the *Volkspartei* candidate Sonnemann, the word came back, "The Prince wants Sabor." [26] When Sabor won the seat, the Social

[24] *Aufruf der sozialdemokratischen Fraktion zur zweiten Reichstagswahl unter dem Sozialistengesetz,* in August Bebel (ed.), *Die Sozialdemokratie im deutschen Reichstag. Taetigkeitsberichte und Wahlaufrufe aus den Jahren 1871 bis 1893* (Berlin, 1909), pp. 218–47. Wilhelm Liebknecht to Karl Kautsky, Oct. 10, 1884, Kautsky Archive, IISH.

[25] Declaration by the Zentral-Wahlleitung, Oct. 30, 1884, quoted in Auer, *Nach zehn Jahren,* p. 135.

[26] There is considerable doubt that the contents of the telegram were specified by Bismarck himself, as indicated by H. Ritter von Poschinger, *Fuerst Bismarck und die Parlamentarier* (Breslau, 1896), III, p. 147. But there is no question that such a telegram was sent and that it created considerable discussion. The story is

Democrats could not easily free themselves of the charge that it was a gift of the reactionaries!

Franz Mehring has even admitted that here and there the Social Democrats may have won through unsolicited conservative support. But Mehring seems to be in error when he asserts that the Social Democrats never "flirted" with the reactionaries. Bebel in fact learned that in Breslau an arrangement had been made so that the Free Conservative Prince Carolath would receive socialist support in one district in return for swinging his voters to Hasenclever in another district. Although Carolath had agreed to the first three conditions in the declaration of the Central Election Committee, Hasenclever was actually trading votes, a tactic which had never been endorsed. This deeply angered Bebel, but in the interest of the party, he kept it quiet.[27] Reviving old images of alleged Lassallean corruption, Bebel wrote to Liebknecht on November 15, that "the *Schweitzerei* is still deep in Hasenclever, he out-schweitzers [*ueberschweitzert*] even Schw[eitzer]." And a few days later Bebel added that Hasenclever was completely controlled, "in heart and mind," by the "Spirit of Schweitzer." [28] Such bargains seemed to give credence to the frequent charge by radical liberals that Social Democrats and state-interventionist conservatives were really brothers, despite all appearances to the contrary.

Although furious about compromises with conservatives, Bebel could see the necessity for offering Social Democratic support to the anti-Bismarckian Liberals. During the campaign, he observed in a letter to Engels that the parties to the right of the socialists no longer formed "one reactionary mass" as previously, a situation certainly favorable to his party.[29] Therefore, the Social Democrats commonly supported the candidates of the *Freisinnige* party in most run-off votes. But Bebel grew somewhat suspicious about an agreement in Munich by which Vollmar traded votes with the National Liberals who were willing to support Social Democrats rather than the party of the Catholic Church. This arrangement made Vollmar's victory possible, and thus the Social Democrats won their first mandate from the Bavarian capital after several previous attempts. Few realized it at the time, but this

repeated by numerous authors; Cf. Bebel, *Aus meinem Leben*, III, p. 12; Rein, *Die Revolution in der Politik Bismarcks*, p. 289.

[27] Mehring, *Geschichte der deutschen Sozialdemokratie*, IV, p. 249. Bebel to Liebknecht, Nov. 10, 1884, Liebknecht Archive, IISH.

[28] Bebel to Liebknecht, Nov. 15, and Nov. 17, 1884, Liebknecht Archive, IISH.

[29] Bebel to Engels, Oct. 3, 1884, in Bebel, *Briefwechsel*, p. 185.

also marked the beginning of Vollmar's shift away from his radicalism of the early eighties.[30]

No city was so important for intraparty developments as Berlin, and here too Bebel fell into conflicts with the influence of the old Lassalleans. Hasenclever campaigned for a seat not only in Breslau but also in Berlin's sixth district, where he also won because it was one of the strongholds of the Social Democrats. Determined to exclude as many of his intraparty foes as possible from Berlin, Bebel demanded privately that Hasenclever take the seat from Breslau. As Hasenclever related to Auer, Bebel threatened to have the party executive call a congress to deal with the whole matter. "Such threats," Hasenclever remarked with apparent humor, "leave *me* completely cold. . . ."[31] Auer likewise expressed unhappiness that Bebel treated Hasenclever so harshly. With his typically easy-going manner, Auer quickly overlooked the weaknesses in his comrades when they showed bad judgment as he believed Hasenclever had. He complained to Liebknecht that "in Bebel there is not a drop of diplomatic blood and therefore he must curb his desire to play the Party Diviner [*Parteivorsehung spielen*]."[32] But in such matters Bebel had little patience or kindness, and Hasenclever dutifully took the Breslau seat. One bothersome person at least would find his influence diminished in Berlin. But Bebel's problem remained, for he had few completely trustworthy associates in Berlin. "With the exception of Singer," Bebel wrote to Liebknecht, "I trust *no one in Berlin*, and Singer is weak; he believes in the honor of people and permits himself to be misused."[33] Of course, the residue of Lassallean influence in Berlin bothered Bebel, and he wanted to destroy it completely.

The returns in the run-offs, during the middle of November, added fifteen seats to the nine won on the first ballot of October 28, giving

[30] Bebel to Liebknecht, Nov. 15, and Nov. 17, 1884, Liebknecht Archive, IISH. Cf. Mehring, *Geschichte der deutschen Sozialdemokratie*, IV, pp. 248–49; Jansen, *Georg von Vollmar*, p. 32.

[31] Hasenclever to Auer, Nov. 13, 1884, Liebknecht Archive, IISH.

[32] Auer to Liebknecht, Nov. 15, 1884, Liebknecht Archive, IISH. Bebel had already rebuked Auer personally for taking such a light-hearted approach to the Hasenclever affair. Bebel to Auer, Nov. 14, 1884, Liebknecht Archive, IISH.

[33] Bebel to Liebknecht, Nov. 17, 1884, Liebknecht Archive, IISH. Bebel maintained that Hasenclever was in large part responsible for the choice of Social Democratic candidates in Berlin and for the position which the "highly questionable Ewald" had on the business staff of the *Berliner Volksblatt*. Bebel to Liebknecht, Nov. 10, 1884, Liebknecht Archive, IISH. Bebel also complained to Motteler about Hasenclever's influence in Berlin. Bebel to Motteler, Nov. 17, 1884, Bebel Archive, IISH.

the Social Democrats a total of twenty-four deputies. Although this victory rested on some support from non-socialists, most party members received it with great joy and high expectations. But not all the radicals were so pleased. Of the twenty-four deputies, no less than eighteen leaned heavily toward the moderate view of Social Democratic politics. Many of the moderates were in an optimistic mood, because with the relaxed police pressures they had a hope of influencing legislation. The maneuverings of the campaign were therefore only a prelude to what followed.[34]

The strength of the moderates in the new *Fraktion* troubled Bebel, Bernstein, and Engels. During the campaign, Bernstein had surveyed the party's candidates and concluded that in some cases defeat rather than victory would benefit Social Democracy. He had misgivings about Viereck, as he told Engels, ". . . I spoke yesterday with an expelled worker from Leipzig, an excellent comrade, concerning the election in Leipzig-Land. As I mentioned to him that Viereck was campaigning there, he was much upset and was of the opinion that he [Viereck] would not come through for he is too unpopular with the comrades. You are wrong, I told him, the comrades themselves chose him; I fear, he will win." Bernstein's fear was justified, Viereck did win. But even when he looked at others, Bernstein saw no reason to be encouraged. "Viereck, Heine, Singer—" he continued in the same letter, "that is no improvement. Singer is certainly a thoroughly good fellow, but a frightful philistine. The only good thing is that he personally puts much value on Bebel." [35] Engels too felt discouraged, but he believed immediately after the initial ballot on October 28 that since the "worst" Social Democrats had already been elected the run-offs would improve the quality of the *Fraktion*.[36] But that proved to be an illusion, the representation of the radicals on the *Fraktion* was only slightly strengthened in the run-offs. With a *Fraktion* of this nature,

[34] The elected Social Democrats were: Auer (Glauchau), Bebel (Hamburg I), Blos (Brunswick), Bock (Gotha), Dietz (Hamburg II), Frohme (Altona), Geiser (Chemnitz), Grillenberger (Nuremberg), Harm (Elberfeld), Hasenclever (Breslau-East), Heine (Magdeburg), Kayser (Auerbach), Kraecker (Breslau-West), Liebknecht (Offenbach), Meister (Hannover), Pfannkuch (Berlin VI), Roediger (Reuss, younger Line), Sabor (Frankfurt am M.), Schumacher (Solingen), Singer (Berlin IV), Stolle (Zwickau), Viereck (Leipzig-Land), Vollmar (Munich II), Wiemer (Reuss, older Line). In 1886, Geyer won a seat in Stollberg which increased the *Fraktion* to twenty-five. Neumann-Hofer, *Die Entwicklung der Sozialdemokratie*, p. 46.

[35] Bernstein to Engels, Oct. 24, 1884, Marx/Engels Archive, IISH.

[36] Engels to Bernstein, Nov. 11, 1884, in Engels, *Briefe an Eduard Bernstein*, p. 159.

everything depended on Bebel's ability to hold them in line if, in the minds of the radicals, the principles of Social Democracy were not to be compromised.

The Radicals View a Positive Parliamentary Role for the Party

The election results impelled the radicals to reexamine their conception of the parliamentary role of the party. They recognized that with twenty-four deputies the party had new possibilities, and some new dangers. As the new Reichstag was about to convene on November 20, Bebel, Bernstein, and Engels were all giving careful consideration to the new circumstances. They had to recognize that the Social Democrats now were numerous enough to enjoy all the privileges of an independent *Fraktion,* giving them the opportunity to place their deputies on the legislative committees. Since committee work was done quietly, the long hours it consumed did not have the direct agitational benefits that one could expect from speaking in the plenary sessions of the Reichstag. Routine committee work required patience, knowledge, and parliamentary skill; it assumed that the members were engaged in a process of positive legislative activity. In addition to participation on the committees, the socialists were also able to put one of their members, Hasenclever, on the Reichstag's Council of Senior Members (*Seniorenkonvent*), which made decisions on the legislative agenda and other matters concerning parliamentary procedure. With members on the committees and the Council of Senior Members, the Social Democrats had an obligation to probe the possibilities of a more positive approach to parliamentary work.[37]

Taking the first steps toward becoming a modern parliamentary party was tortuous for a radical such as Bebel, although he, like Bernstein and Engels, agreed that it would be necessary to concentrate on a "positive" policy. The three men concluded that the Social Democrats would have to introduce legislation that was both fitted to existing circumstances and consistent with their principles. Bernstein thus publicly proclaimed, "We will not be so lacking in taste as to bother the

[37] The chief socialist committee members were the following in the 1884/85 session: Liebknecht and Vollmar on the election review committee; Kayser and Viereck on the committee for petitions; Kayser on the accident and sickness insurance committee; Stolle on the postal savings committee; Singer on the committee on tariffs; Sabor and Vollmar on a committee on court constitutions; and Bebel and Dietz on the committee for the steamship subsidy. Cf. *SB,* VI, i (1884/85), vol. VI, *Anlagen, passim.*

Reichstag with measures which are unfeasible under present circumstances; certainly not . . . ; rather we will proceed with complete political realism [*ganz realpolitisch vorgehen*], as *realpolitisch* as one can scarcely desire." [38] At the same time Engels privately suggested numerous practical reforms which could be introduced by the Social Democrats, including the "normal working day (ten hours, gradually dropping to around eight), domestic and international factory legislation (whereby the domestic can go further than the international), radical transformation of the liability obligation, accident and sickness legislation, workman's disability, etc. . . ." [39]

Since Engels agreed with them, Bernstein and Bebel were perplexed when liberals in Germany interpreted Bernstein's public statement as a decisive turn in Social Democratic thinking toward reformism, as a "Damascus." As Bebel saw it, Bernstein had merely made explicit what had always been understood. The legislative proposals of the party would all follow directly from their principles, and Bebel even wrote optimistically that legislation for a normal working day might be passed since the Center party had already made such proposals. On the whole, however, Bebel did not expect that any socialist proposals would be accepted and he had no regrets if the parliamentary role of the party should remain chiefly educational.[40]

The moderates were willing to interpret a positive parliamentary policy in a much broader sense, accepting minor reforms or benefits for the workers and society at large which had been presented by other parties. If some legislation promised to improve working conditions or create jobs in areas of unemployment, they were always tempted to give their approval. In this they contrasted to the conception of Bebel.

Bernstein's reflections on a proper parliamentary policy reveal some of his doubts about the radical position. He agreed that protective labor legislation should be introduced, but this covered only a small portion of the reform possibilities which arose in the Reichstag. In a letter of November 15, 1884, he showed an acute perception of the complexities involved in a responsible parliamentary policy.

[38] "Was aus unserem Wahlsieg folgt," *SD,* No. 46, Nov. 14, 1884. Cf. "Was Nun?" *SD,* No. 47, Nov. 21, 1884.

[39] Engels to Bernstein, Nov. 11, 1884, in Engels, *Briefe an Eduard Bernstein,* p. 159.

[40] Bebel to Engels, Nov. 24, 1884, in Bebel, *Briefwechsel,* pp. 196–98.

> The actual economic question bothers me less than the *political.* According to my view, our negative position can not be followed in many of these questions, since twenty-two or twenty-three votes can often be of importance [*in's Gewicht fallen*]. Take, for example, the military question. It is certainly good to declare that we are opponents of standing armies and therefore to vote against the military budget. But that in itself does not get us around the necessity to take a stand on important particular questions, even though we have relinquished the right to put forward independent proposals aiming at the abolition of especially oppressive practices. I would very much like to hear your view on this, for our customary authority on military questions—Liebknecht—seems to me on this matter to be inadequate. In the election campaign, for some time, our people have diverged from the program so far as to be satisfied with a "reduction of the length of service." [41]

Bernstein had touched upon a fundamental question for the radicals. Was it not implicit in a positive approach that the party's *Fraktion* commit itself to encourage numerous minor reforms in systems which they opposed in principle? Could the party take the blame for the failure of a piece of reform legislation in the Reichstag if their votes could swing the balance? This question had not arisen, at least not seriously, when the few Social Democratic votes could make no difference. In effect, Bernstein was asking, although he might not have recognized it at the time: Are not the moderates justified when they suggest that the Social Democrats should endorse reforms, regardless of who introduces them? Bernstein showed an awareness that the party was going through a change, that it was necessarily becoming a modern parliamentary party which could not avoid involvement in all aspects of the legislative process.

Steamship Subsidy Crisis

The difficulties of a positive parliamentary approach became apparent to the Social Democrats almost immediately after the new Reichstag convened on November 20, 1884. All the members of the *Fraktion* agreed that protective labor legislation should be introduced, and dur-

[41] Bernstein to Engels, Nov. 15, 1884, Marx/Engels Archive, IISH.

ing the Christmas holidays Bebel drafted a Workmen's Protection Bill which the Reichstag debated in 1885. In such matters, the Social Democratic deputies reached agreement readily. But to the majority of the deputies a positive policy also implied a willingness to support non-socialist legislation if it gave some promise of rewards for the German workingmen. In these matters there was no easy agreement, and the difficulties raised in 1885 nearly split the party.

The crisis that rocked the party in 1885 was actually a fundamental conflict that had been building up for some time. Essentially, it was once again a struggle between the moderates and the radicals, but with features that distinguished it from earlier quarrels. For one thing, the earlier disputes took place at a time when the Social Democrats were hard pressed by the police, necessitating party solidarity even when fundamental differences existed. In 1885, however, the intraparty antagonists felt fewer restraints and were willing to push their points of view with more vigor, even at the risk of revealing serious dissension publicly. For another thing, the moderates were proportionately stronger in 1885 than in earlier years, and they were confident of widespread support from the rank-and-file. They were thus encouraged to enter into the spirit of parliamentarizing, even when accused of opportunism.

An aspect of Germany's budding colonialism in 1884 sparked the crisis in German Social Democracy and revealed the complex difficulties in defining the limits of a positive parliamentary policy. Although the colonial question had never been debated at a party congress, Social Democrats generally agreed that they were opposed to such expansion in principle. The authors of the campaign *Aufruf* of 1884 gave the problem only a passing comment, declaring that the party was not "unfriendly" to efforts to increase Germany's export trade, but that "modern over-production" could not be relieved by a "palliative means" that sought an export trade in colonies. The Social Democrats did not support the argument that colonialism could serve the purposes of social and economic reform. Using Marx's *Capital*, the *Sozialdemokrat* attacked such a defense by analyzing colonialism as merely another form for the accumulation of capital. Even the *Berliner Volksblatt*, although controlled by the moderates, demolished the argument that colonialism would provide markets for German production.[42]

[42] Cf. *Aufruf* (1884), in Bebel (ed.), *Die Sozialdemokratie im deutschen Reich-*

Only one associate of the Social Democrats, Karl Hoechberg, argued privately for the advantages of colonialism. But even he focused more on the benefits for Germany as a great power than on possible social and economic gains. He saw no less than "*1000* reasons for colonies," [43] and outstanding among these was the chance that German colonies would be a means to fight the "English world power." [44] As he admitted to Bernstein, he also presented his arguments to Auer, who would pass them on to Singer, in an effort to encourage pro-colonial views among the Social Democrats. Hoechberg failed, however, for he was already too far removed from the mainstream of the party to exert any great influence.

The party crisis was precipitated by the question of whether or not a subsidy for steamship lines, proposed by Bismarck, was to be considered as an integral part of German colonialism. On April 23, 1884, one day before he declared the protectorate over Southwest Africa, Bismarck sent the Bundesrat a scheme for the establishment of German postal steamship lines with an Imperial subsidy of not over four million marks. The measure, which reached the Reichstag in May, called for two main lines connecting Hamburg and Bremerhaven with ports in the Far East and Australia. The *Freisinnige* party so vigorously opposed the whole steamship project that Bismarck felt obligated to attend a meeting of the committee, an unusual step for the Chancellor. He stressed that there were no necessary connections between the steamship lines and the new colonial policy. Then, before any further progress could be made on the bill, the Reichstag session closed on June 28, and the measure had to be introduced again after the new Reichstag met on November 20, 1884. The social Democrats had not entered into any phase of the debate on the steamship subsidy in the session that closed in June.[45]

The new steamship bill, debated first on December 1, 1884, added an African line to Bismarck's original scheme and raised the subsidy from 4,000,000 to 5,400,000 marks annually. The addition of the African line certainly hinted at a connection with colonialism. In other respects the plan was the same.[46]

stag, p. 243; "Marx ueber das Kolonialsystem," *SD*, No. 28, July 10, 1884; *Berliner Volksblatt*, No. 111, August 13, 1884, p. 1.

[43] Hoechberg to Bernstein, June 21, 1884, Bernstein Archive, IISH.

[44] Hoechberg to Bernstein, Oct. 28, 1884, Bernstein Archive, IISH.

[45] *SB*, v, iv (1884), vol. IV, *Anlagen*, No. 111, pp. 826–30; Schulthess, *1884*, pp. 71–74.

[46] *SB*, VI, i (1884/85), vol. v, *Anlagen*, No. 16, pp. 70–73.

The Social Democrats still maintained their public silence in November, but behind the scenes a serious dispute had developed within the party's Reichstag delegation. A number of the deputies, conscious of the unemployment in German shipyards, believed that the creation of the steamship lines would provide new jobs. In addition, to defend their sympathy for a measure of the hated Chancellor, they accepted Bismarck's explanation of a clear distinction between the establishment of the postal lines and colonialism.[47]

Within the Social Democratic *Fraktion*, no unity could be achieved on the steamship subsidy. In their first public statement, which appeared on December 11, 1884, the deputies declared that many of them considered the steamship issue merely a "question of practicality and not of principle. . . ." Therefore, the question of how the *Fraktion* would vote was left open. But they also implied that if the government could show that the steamship lines would promote industry and trade and would be under the control of the Reichstag, then they might vote for the measure.[48] This statement merely side-stepped the real issue and postponed the final decision for a later date.

In the middle of December, the Social Democratic deputies were involved in heated debates among themselves on the steamship subsidy. For three days, Bebel wrote on December 15, they had been fighting without getting near an agreement. The moderates were pushing hard for approval. Auer, Dietz, Grillenberger, Hasenclever, and Viereck were the most vocal advocates of the subsidy in the *Fraktion*. On the other side, Bebel carried the burden, although he had support from Liebknecht and Vollmar. "Auer gave a speech," Bebel wrote in disgust, "which one would have believed to be by a fanatical Nat[ional] Lib[eral]." [49] In this fight, Bebel's best tactic was to prove that the steamship subsidy was an integral part of Bismarck's colonial policy. To do this he needed assistance, and so he urged Motteler in Zurich to make sure that the *Sozialdemokrat* would explain the direct relationship between colonialism and the steamship subsidy.[50]

When the differences between the supporters and opponents of the steamship subsidy could not be resolved, the Social Democrats concluded before the end of December that each deputy should vote ac-

[47] Blos, *Denkwuerdigkeiten*, II, p. 126.
[48] "Sozialpolitische Rundschau," *SD*, No. 50, Dec. 11, 1884.
[49] Bebel to Schlueter, Dec. 15, 1884, Bebel Archive, IISH.
[50] Bebel to Motteler, Dec. 21, 1884, Bebel Archive, IISH.

cording to his own view. However, in order to avoid a public display of the dispute, they also agreed that no one would speak in the Reichstag on the issue. That was at least a tactical victory for the radicals, who were in the minority. Of the twenty-four deputies, only Bebel, Liebknecht, Harm, Roediger, Stolle, and Vollmar were definitely opposed to the subsidy.[51] Not even Paul Singer, for whom Bebel had considerable admiration, could be drawn away from support for the subsidy.

Bebel complained that the whole matter could not be cleared up because the Socialist Law prohibited a widespread socialist press attack on the steamship subsidy. "The *S[ozial] D[emokrat]* is not sufficient," he admitted dejectedly.[52] The comment would have been more accurate had Bebel noted that the moderate socialist press had no interest in making much of an attack on the subsidy. But the absence of press criticism of the subsidy posed only one problem for the radicals. Equally disturbing, the Social Democrats had two representatives on the Reichstag committee which deliberated the steamship subsidy, one was Bebel, the other Dietz, one of the most outspoken socialist supporters of the subsidy. Consequently, had Bebel chosen to present a full critique of the subsidy in committee, he might well have been contradicted by Dietz on numerous points. Dietz would have been supported by the other socialist deputies.[53]

Pressure on the moderates had to be applied from outside the *Fraktion*, thereby enlarging the dispute to the party as a whole. To assert such pressure, only one instrument was available to the radicals, the *Sozialdemokrat*. In an effort to bring popular socialist opinion against the moderates, Bernstein printed numerous letters from rank-and-file Social Democrats opposed to the subsidy. Many of these critical letters came from socialists living abroad, in Zurich, Paris, London, and Brussels, but some were also from within Germany, Munich, Koenigsberg, Rostock, and several other places. They were unanimous in condemning the stand of the moderate deputies. Although this kind of

[51] Bebel to Engels, Dec. 28, 1884, in Bebel, *Briefwechsel*, p. 207. The text mentions a "Heim," apparently a printing error, since no such name existed and Blumenberg's footnote refers to Harm.

[52] *Ibid.*, p. 207.

[53] Unfortunately the reports of the committee hearings do not identify the speakers; it is therefore impossible to determine whether disagreements between Dietz and Bebel were heard in committee. For the committee report, see *SB*, VI, i (1884/85), vol. VI, *Anlagen*, No. 208, pp. 803–30.

pressure might be effective, it also fired the wrath of the moderates who believed that they should be free from such blatant criticism in the party organ over which they had technical control.[54]

In their defense, the moderates spelled out ideas that reveal the spirit in which they approached parliamentary politics. Seeking to calm the troubled waters, Auer explained in a long letter in the *Sozialdemokrat* that the steamship subsidy had no relationship with colonialism and that it would benefit German workingmen. "I harbor a sympathy for the steamship subsidy," he explained, "because in this I see a means to promote the exchange of goods among the peoples of the various parts of the world, to increase trade and thereby to strengthen the work of peace." In addition to economic gains for German workers, the new lines would make cultural and humanitarian contributions for the whole world. Auer viewed the steamship lines as "transmitters of culture [*Kulturtraeger*]," and the Social Democrats had every reason to endorse these progressive steps.[55]

Auer also had some pertinent comments on the nature of the Social Democratic party. He could not understand why some Social Democrats insisted that the party should always take a unified and intransigent opposition to the government. Nor could he comprehend why intraparty differences were always considered harmful by some comrades when such disputes were obviously the sign of a healthy movement. Clinching his argument, he added significantly, "The Socialist Workers party is not a sect in which the members are sworn to the letter, but a political party in which there is room, as there must be, for different opinions on subordinate points." [56]

That touched the fundamental issue of the whole crisis, involving more than the steamship subsidy itself. Were the Social Democrats willing to recognize the full implications of the fact that their movement was changing from a single-minded protest movement to a modern parliamentary political party? Auer and the other moderates were

[54] These letters were reprinted under the heading "Sprechsaal" in numerous issues of the *SD*, in 1885; see, No. 4, Jan. 22; No. 5, Jan. 29; No. 6, Feb. 5; No. 7, Feb. 12; No. 8, Feb. 19; and No. 21, March 12. In addition, ten other protests which were not published in the *Sozialdemokrat* have been edited by Rudolf Rothe, in "Zum Streit um die Dampfersubvention," *Archiv fuer Sozialgeschichte*, I (1961), pp. 109–18.

[55] "In Sachen der Dampfersubvention," *SD*, No. 5, Jan. 29, 1885. Auer's letter is published as part of the article.

[56] *Ibid.* This whole crisis was one of the most disturbing episodes of Auer's party life, according to Eduard Bernstein, *Ignaz Auer. Eine Gedenkschrift* (Berlin, 1907), p. 49.

prepared to follow these implications. For the radicals, however, it was a painful transformation, because they could not overcome their ambivalent attitude toward parliamentarism.

In London, Engels fretted about the deep cleavage of opinion within the socialist Reichstag *Fraktion* which threatened to split the party. Hoping to avoid such a disaster, Engels decided to give his associates in Germany some advice. The result was a curious proposal that ultimately left Engels in a rather compromising position in the eyes of Bernstein and Bebel. Although essentially opposed to socialist support for the steamship subsidy, Engels sought a tactic by which the majority could be persuaded not to vote for the subsidy without at the same time forcing them to back down in disgrace. He thus accepted the view that the subsidy question did not involve matters of principle, but could be treated tactically. Bebel, however, did not agree; to him it was clearly a matter of principle. But, significantly, working through Liebknecht, not Bebel, Engels suggested that the Social Democrats present Bismarck with a kind of give-and-take proposition.[57]

Liebknecht followed Engels' suggestion to the letter. Writing in the *Sozialdemokrat* on January 8, 1885, Liebknecht said that he had received a plan from a friend living abroad, without actually identifying Engels. Liebknecht then suggested that the Social Democrats should approach the government with the following proposition: "If you [the government] give us four to five million [Marks] annually for workers' cooperatives (not loans, but donations, as for the ship owners), then we will talk it over. If you give us guarantees that the domains in Prussia, instead of going to the large lease-holders or the farmers who are unable to exist without day wage-labor, shall be leased out to workers' cooperatives, that public works shall be contracted to workers' cooperatives instead of to capitalists, good, we will act differently."[58] The proposition came word for word from Engels' letter to Liebknecht.

Knowing that Bebel's approval was essential if the suggestion were to be followed, Engels immediately wrote him a letter of explanation. Engels recognized, as he told Bebel, that the government would never accept a proposal whereby the domain could be leased out to workers' cooperatives. Therefore, if the moderates made this a prerequisite to

[57] Engels to Liebknecht, Dec. 29, 1884, in Liebknecht, *Briefwechsel mit Karl Marx und Friedrich Engels*, pp. 284–85. This is a fragment of the whole letter, but it contains the complete statement of Engels' proposal.

[58] W. L., "Zur Dampfersubvention," *SD*, No. 2, Jan. 8, 1885.

their support of the steamship subsidy, they would have a way, "with respectability and without compulsion" to vote against the subsidy plan.[59]

Engels then spelled out his plan in more detail, revealing that he believed that it also embodied sound socialist principles for the socialization of society. Workers' cooperatives would be set up with state-help in factories in which work had stopped during a period of crisis. The crisis-ridden factories would be purchased and reorganized on a cooperative basis. Domains or estates would be taken in lease and built upon the cooperative principle. It would be necessary, Engels continued, to demand that the cooperatives be given preference over the capitalists in all matters of public contract. In addition, the socialists should demand freedom for the trade unions with recognized rights as jurisdictional persons. With the guarantee of trade union rights and the establishment of the cooperative system as he suggested it, Engels believed that this would "lead gradually to a transition of the total production into cooperative [production]." [60]

It is impossible to avoid the observation that this was indeed a curious proposal for Engels to make. It seemed to suggest two ways in which Engels stood closer to the moderates than to the radicals. First, he was willing to bargain with Bismarck, something which Bebel found personally repulsive and tactically detrimental for the cause. In effect, it was Engels' own way of saying that Social Democracy was no longer a sect but a political party. Second, Engels' suggestion seemed to have certain Lassallean ideas about how the capitalist society could be transformed—and, note, "gradually"—into a cooperative system of production. Although he had not suggested that this would mean the achievement of a truly socialist society, he had committed himself to the idea that it indicated a sound road toward a socialist society.

Engels found no sympathizers for his proposal among the radicals, except for Liebknecht, whose judgment he himself always questioned! Eduard Bernstein was perplexed and disturbed, and he did not keep this a secret from Engels. The moderates and compromisers, he wrote to Engels on January 15, 1885, would receive encouragement from the proposal. The steamship subsidy, Bernstein argued, had become a test case for the political stand of the party, "hence, [I] am not in agreement with the settlement proposal which is ascribed to you and which

[59] Engels to Bebel, Dec. 30, 1884, in Bebel, *Briefwechsel*, p. 210.
[60] *Ibid.*, pp. 211–12.

Liebknecht made in the previous number [of the *Sozialdemokrat*]. Our people must once and for all avow their principles [*Farbe bekennen*]. . . ." The slightest willingness to support the steamship subsidy, Bernstein believed, would imply some kind of approval of colonialism, since the two could no longer be isolated from each other. Bernstein preferred to see the socialist deputies vote against the subsidy; but he would be satisfied if they abstained from voting, if in doing so they also made a "blunt rejection" of colonialism.[61]

Bernstein built his uncompromising rejection of the subsidy on political grounds, whereas Engels offered his "settlement proposal" with specific attention to a possible economic gain. Later, Engels in fact said to Bebel, "You are above all an economic party," and then chided the Social Democrats for an inability to handle economic questions to their advantage.[62] Obviously, Engels thought his proposal would teach the Social Democrats how to approach an economic problem to their benefit. But the danger of Engels' position, Bernstein believed, was that it threatened to sacrifice the political effectiveness of the Social Democrats without the countervailing assurance that real economic gains would be made. In fact, as Engels himself admitted to Bebel, no one could anticipate that the government would even consider the bargain.

Bebel was no less unhappy than Bernstein with Engels' "settlement proposal," but he waited until December 1885 before he laid out his objections. First, Bebel said, the Empire had nothing to do with domain lands which were controlled by the individual states. Therefore, the proposal for agricultural cooperatives would have to be presented to a state like Prussia, rather than to the Empire. Second, Bebel thought it would be "wrongheaded" (*verkehrt*) for the Social Democrats to take a "kind of trading or chess player's standpoint in politics. . . ." To pursue such tactics served only to "obscure" the "standpoint on principle. . . ." Then he concluded that

> We can only present demands, which, with a good conscience, we can say may be realized if one wants them. With this kind of subsidization of agricultural cooperatives—at one time believed a possible [means to bring] the collapse of bourgeois society—we would arrive at the most unhappy experiment. These cooperatives would collapse as those founded on Schulze's Self-Help. And then with

[61] Bernstein to Engels, Jan. 15, 1885, Marx/Engels Archive, IISH.
[62] Engels to Bebel, Dec. 30, 1884, in Bebel, *Briefwechsel*, p. 211.

this proposal you make a regrettable concession to Lassalleanism. On principle I was against the subsidy, because it means bourgeois subsidization and because with State-Help we cannot artifically lengthen the life of bankrupt bourgeois society.[63]

Certainly Bebel and Bernstein were on solid ground when they argued that Engels' proposal involved measures which were impractical and therefore could not bring real economic benefits. When they objected, however, that Social Democrats would be tarnished if they bargained with Bismarck, they merely revealed their reluctance to enter into the spirit of the parliamentary political system. The fear that socialist principles would be betrayed by such bargaining never crossed Engels' mind, and for that he was a political realist, recognizing that the Social Democrats had achieved sufficient strength to exploit all parliamentary possibilities without seriously endangering their ultimate principles. But in their relations with Bismarck's Reich, the radicals preferred to shun all bargaining, seeing in this only a replay of the unprincipled machinations of Lassalle and the much hated Schweitzer.

It is clear that no one, not even Liebknecht, tried to pursue the suggestion that Engels had given the party. The *Sozialdemokrat* even received letters expressing scorn for the whole idea. Heinrich Rackow, a German Social Democrat living in London, said that he "was rather perplexed to hear such proposals presented in seriousness by a comrade." [64] How much more bewildered might he have been had he known that the suggestion came from his London neighbor, Engels! The "settlement proposal" died almost before it had been presented.[65]

The Social Democratic *Fraktion* arrived at its own set of conditions

[63] Bebel to Engels, Dec. 7, 1885, in *ibid.*, p. 248.

[64] H. R., "Kolonialpolitik und Dampfersubvention," *SD*, No. 7, Feb. 12, 1885.

[65] Social Democratic historiography has never made much out of this dispute with Engels, although it was taken to be extremely important in 1885. None of the radicals agreed with Engels, but they did not emphasize this in their later writings, apparently to shield Engels from criticism. In his own memoirs, Bernstein mentioned Engels' proposal on cooperatives, but failed to point out that he had severely criticized the whole idea. *Sozialdemokratische Lehrjahre*, p. 158. Likewise, in his biography of *Friedrich Engels*, II, pp. 367–68, Gustav Mayer gives the proposal as Engels presented it, but without any mention of the criticisms of Bebel and Bernstein. Mayer had access to these letters by Bebel and Bernstein. Mehring, *Geschichte der deutschen Sozialdemokratie*, IV, pp. 266–73, does not say anything about Engels' proposal in connection with his discussion of the steamship subsidy. But even more interesting, a recent author who actually cites Bernstein's letter of January 15, 1885, in another connection, completely overlooks the fact that Engels was criticized. Cf. Engelberg, *Revolutionaere Politik*, pp. 97–99. One might safely conclude that Engels has had his protectors.

which they presented as prerequisites for their approval of the steamship subsidy. The chief condition was that all ships for the new lines were to be new and built in German shipyards, a direct reflection of their interest in the unemployment problem. In addition, to disassociate themselves from colonialism, they were unwilling to endorse the African line and a Samoan branch line, the two which made the connections with Germany's new empire. These conditions were embodied in a Social Democratic bill of amendments which also reduced the amount of the steamship subsidy from the government's 5,400,000 to 3,700,000 marks in accordance with the reduction in the number of lines. Their bill also specified that provisions were to be made so that the ships would be built by German labor.[66]

To a limited degree, therefore, the radicals had also recognized that it was in the interest of the party's unity to present a kind of bargain to the government. Their bargain, however, differed from Engels' proposal in two significant respects. First, it presented conditions that were sufficiently practical to appeal directly to unemployed workingmen in German shipyards, whereas Engels' proposal had shifted much of the emphasis to depressed agricultural areas. Second, the radicals in no way implied, as Engels did, that acceptance of their conditions would mean a step toward socialism. The radicals were also sure that the Reichstag majority would not accept their conditions, and therefore the whole *Fraktion* would be obligated to vote against the steamship subsidy. In the debate on the steamship subsidy (March 12 and 16, 1885), Dietz explained that the socialists hoped that the measure would reduce the high unemployment in German shipyards. For that reason they insisted that all ships for the lines had to be new and built by German labor. In commenting on the Social Democratic amendment, Bismarck agreed that any new ships should be built in German shipyards by German labor, but he could not accept the condition that the lines be outfitted exclusively with all new ships. Such a condition, the Chancellor argued, would put an unreasonable limitation on the whole plan.[67]

The conditions laid down by the Social Democrats were of course unacceptable to a majority in the Reichstag, and the whole *Fraktion* voted against the steamship subsidy in March. With that, the dispute on the subsidy issue itself ended, but the fundamental issues it had raised for party tactics and principles persisted. The steamship quarrel

[66] "Sozialpolitische Rundschau," *SD*, No. 9, Feb. 26, 1885; *SB*, VI, i (1884/85), vol. VI, *Anlagen*, No. 244, pp. 1093–94.

[67] *SB*, VI, i (1884/85), vol. III, pp. 1773–74, 1778, 1846.

had opened up a wide range of problems on which moderates and radicals held differing points of view.

The Persistent Crisis: Control of Der Sozialdemokrat

The party crisis actually deepened in the early spring of 1885 just as the initial cause of friction, the steamship subsidy issue, was being resolved. The struggle now shifted to the policy and control of the *Sozialdemokrat*, and it was fought with all the more bitterness because personal feelings and ambitions were involved as well as matters of party tactics.

The memory of their previous unpleasant confrontation with Bernstein still haunting them, the moderates once again were incensed that the editor used the party organ to incite opposition to their stand on the subsidy issue. They could not forgive Motteler, an old comrade to many of them, for enclosing a special denunciation of the subsidy supporters with an issue of the *Sozialdemokrat* late in January or early in February. They could not overlook the insult when Bernstein stubbornly refused to print a "declaration" in which they had reprimanded the staff and asserted that as the party's executive they alone had the authority to determine the policy of the paper. They were infuriated in the middle of March when Bernstein gave them an ultimatum: either they could send their "declaration" to the members of the party on their own, or he could publish it in the paper along with a strong statement announcing his resignation.[68] They knew that Bernstein would not resign without a fight and that Bebel and the other radicals would launch a vigorous campaign to discredit them in the eyes of the rank-and-file. Nevertheless, it was an unbearable embarrassment to have the party's executive openly chastised by the party paper, and the moderates were anxious to settle accounts with the recalcitrant Bernstein.

A heated conflict went on throughout the spring of 1885. On the one side, chiefly Bebel and Bernstein; on the other, Auer and the moderates; and in the middle, Liebknecht, who sought frantically to reconcile the warring factions. During the last week of March, Auer received Bernstein's "ultimatum." Obviously angered by Bernstein's show of independence, Auer wrote to Liebknecht on March 27, declaring that a "rebellion" had broken out in Zurich. He urged Lieb-

[68] Bernstein, *Sozialdemokratische Lehrjahre*, pp. 158–59.

knecht to go to Zurich along with one of the "Stuttgart deputies" (meaning apparently Dietz or Blos) to study and report on the situation so that the Reichstag *Fraktion* could decide what course to follow. "To be sure," Auer admitted, "the paper is first of all a party organ and as such is responsible to the party; but the party is permanent only so long as the congress meets, before and after this time the *Fraktion and its executive is to represent the party*." Auer was technically correct when he added that Bernstein's interpretation turned the matter "upside down." [69]

Liebknecht hurried off to Zurich late in March, obviously siding more with Auer's point of view than with Bernstein's. Years later, Bernstein still insisted that Liebknecht had assumed a "downright dictatorial tone" while in Zurich negotiating with the staff.[70] In any case, it seemed to all the other radicals that Liebknecht had abandoned them.

In Zurich, Liebknecht applied pressure to Bernstein and Motteler, ultimately compelling them to publish a slightly revised version of the "declaration" by the moderates. This revised version, drafted by Liebknecht on the spot, also failed to appease Bernstein and Motteler, but they published it in the April 2nd issue. It conceded that the editorial staff of the *Sozialdemokrat* had a right to independent criticism, but not if intended to discredit the party's Reichstag deputies. Such criticism, the "declaration" said, served only to jeopardize the party's ability to act decisively in times of stress. The crucial passage asserted that "it is not the paper which is to determine the policy of the *Fraktion*, but it is the *Fraktion* which has to control the policy of the paper." [71] This statement could be interpreted in only one way—as a defeat for Bernstein, Motteler, and the radicals.

Nothing in Bebel's nature allowed him to take setbacks cheerfully, and this was no exception. The moderates wanted a fight, fine, he would fight them, even if it threatened to split the party, because he was convinced that many of them were already a detriment to the cause of proletarian socialism. Addressing an angry epistle to the Reichstag *Fraktion* early in April, he accused them of seeking to prohibit all criticism of their actions and to set themselves up as "absolute rulers over the policy of the party organ. . . ." The dreadful consequence of their authoritarian action would be the abolition of "free-

[69] Auer to Liebknecht, March 27, 1885, Liebknecht Archive, IISH.
[70] Bernstein, *Sozialdemokratische Lehrjahre*, p. 160.
[71] "Erklaerung," *SD*, No. 14, April 2, 1885.

dom of press" within the party; the paper would become the organ of the Reichstag deputies, not the party. To their faces, he accused them of the "greatest cold-bloodedness" by contradicting the "freedom of opinion" within the party. Finally, pulling his trump card, he warned that if the moderates sought to suppress criticism in the party organ he would be forced "to appeal to the party." [72]

The moderates realized that Bebel was not bluffing, that he was ready for combat, and that he could give them a frightful drubbing in front of the party. His polemical talents could not be equaled by any two or three of the moderates, unless perhaps Liebknecht stood firmly by them. But although Liebknecht and Bebel might oppose each other behind the scenes, the moderates knew that it was most unlikely that they would tear each other apart in an open fight.

Confronted by Bebel's threatening wrath, the moderates began to back down. They agreed to join with the editors of the paper to draft a new compromise statement that would be essentially satisfactory to both sides. Thus, the *Fraktion* conceded in the new statement that "absolute freedom of criticism" was essential to the party, and the editors admitted that certain limitations on criticism were necessary in order not "to hamper the party leadership in the fulfillment of its duty." [73] This new clarification settled a few frictions, but the battle of 1885 was far from concluded.

The crisis had reached down to the grass roots membership of the party. In Frankfurt am Main, a wave of hostility against the moderates was evident. The same issue of the *Sozialdemokrat* (April 23, 1885) which carried the compromise statement between *Fraktion* and editor also included a long and bitter denunciation of the moderates by socialist comrades in Frankfurt. These Frankfurt critics denounced the moderates for sympathizing with the steamship subsidy, for trying to impose a "kind of exceptional law in our internal party life," for violating the "principle of equality," for denying revolutionary principles, and for leading the Social Democrats into the "swamps of parliamentarism." They contrasted the revolutionary will of the members with the opportunism of the *Fraktion*. "While the comrades in the whole of Germany . . . strive with an iron energy to create an army and organize the proletariat . . . our deputies appear to enter more and more into diplomatic undertakings with the representatives of the

[72] Bebel to the Social Democratic Reichstag *Fraktion*, April 5, 1885, Bebel Archive, IISH.

[73] Untitled entry, *SD*, No. 17, April 23, 1885, p. 4.

present system, and to reconcile themselves with those representatives." [74] This denunciation by the Frankfurt comrades led to increased hostilities, making it abundantly clear to the German public that the Social Democratic party was passing through a time of troubles.

The tempest in Frankfurt raged on in May and June with the authors of the above denunciation attacking the followers of Karl Frohme, one of the moderates' intellectual leaders. Frohme was still very influential in the Maingau, although he represented Altona in the Reichstag. With both sides screaming "foul," Frohme answered the Frankfurt denunciation in a public statement published in the *Frankfurter Zeitung*, claiming that the majority of the socialists in the area supported him. Bebel admonished Frohme severely for using a non-socialist newspaper to voice his claims.[75] A whole series of angry public exchanges took place which only reaffirmed the impression that the party was about to split wide open.[76]

In private, Liebknecht and Bebel disagreed sharply on the cause of the trouble in Frankfurt. Liebknecht flippantly observed to Kautsky that the original Frankfurt denunciation of the *Fraktion* was the work of "a dozen harmless bawlers," but Bebel accepted it as a legitimate expression of the popular sentiment in the party.[77]

It is clear that the disagreements between Liebknecht and Bebel served to perpetuate the crisis. Out of personal conviction, Liebknecht had tended to side with the moderate majority in the *Fraktion*, but his overriding goal was to reconcile the feuding factions. Still proud of the role he had played in helping to unify the German labor movement in 1875, he would have suffered great agony if ten years later it were destroyed by internal dissensions. Bebel did not seek to split the party, but at the same time he did not shy away from the possibility. He did see, nevertheless, that he could not overcome the moderates without some help from Liebknecht. For that reason, Bebel used a hard line, hoping to dissuade Liebknecht from offering moral support to the moderates.

After making a trip to Zurich late in April to get a first-hand ac-

[74] "Korrespondenzen," *SD*, No. 17, April 23, 1885.

[75] "Auch ein Protest," *SD*, No. 21, May 21, 1885. This article reprints Frohme's statement from the *Frankfurter Zeitung*.

[76] *Frankfurter Zeitung*, No. 150, May 30; No. 151, May 31; No. 175, June 24[?], 1885. Clippings filed under "Parteistreit 1885," in Vollmar Archive, IISH.

[77] Liebknecht to Kautsky, May 2, 1885, Kautsky Archive, IISH; Bebel to Liebknecht, May 9, 1885, Liebknecht Archive, IISH.

count from Bernstein and Motteler of everything that had occurred, Bebel felt certain that Liebknecht was in the wrong.[78] When convinced of his own rightness, neither friendship nor prudence restrained Bebel from waxing vindictive and abusive, or from using every means to win a battle. Now he turned on Liebknecht. He complained about the role of Geiser, and intimated that Liebknecht should put tight reins on his son-in-law.[79] He castigated Liebknecht for demanding that Bernstein should not publish criticisms of socialist comrades before he, Liebknecht, had reviewed them.[80] To Bernstein, Bebel reported that he had assailed Liebknecht for hushing up the "deep-going differences of opinion on matters of principle" which existed in the party.[81] Striking blow after blow, Bebel made a particularly abusive charge at the end of May: "It appears to me," he chided, "that the whole manner in which you [Liebknecht] now act against the Zurichers, *also against Ede* [Bernstein], who complains *most bitterly* about you in a letter to me, is intended *to crush and trample under* the Zurichers with fulminating attacks and charges, or to force them to resign their positions and then see docile tools in their places." [82] Three days after this excessive accusation, Bebel charged that no doubt existed about Liebknecht's ambition to install himself as the "absolute Lord of the paper. . . ." [83] These were incredibly abusive denunciations, all the more startling since Bebel, often severe and domineering in relations with his comrades, fired them against Liebknecht, renowned for being affable and conciliatory.

Did Bebel truly believe that Liebknecht could have such a lust for power? It is difficult to conclude that Bebel genuinely believed his own charges. It is more plausible to assume that Bebel had employed a tactic—somewhat cruel and insensitive—literally to compel Liebknecht to choose sides. Forced to that decision, Bebel could be almost certain that Liebknecht would choose to stand with the radicals. In effect, Bebel presented Liebknecht with that choice in a letter of May 27, when he warned that "if it comes to a smash-up [*Krach*] I stand, in the most decisive manner, on the side of the Zurichers, and Engels also. . . ." [84]

[78] Bebel to Liebknecht, April 28, 1885, Liebknecht Archive, IISH.
[79] Bebel to Liebknecht, May 9, 1885, and in a later letter, Nov. 1, 1886, Bebel pressed Liebknecht to do something about Geiser; Liebknecht Archive, IISH.
[80] Bebel to Liebknecht, May 23, 1885, Liebknecht Archive, IISH.
[81] Bebel to Bernstein, May 22, 1885, Bebel Archive, IISH.
[82] Bebel to Liebknecht, May 27, 1885, Liebknecht Archive, IISH.
[83] Bebel to Liebknecht, May 30, 1885, Liebknecht Archive, IISH.
[84] Bebel to Liebknecht, May 27, 1885, Liebknecht Archive, IISH.

No evidence exists to substantiate Bebel's accusation that Liebknecht had ambitions to become "absolute Lord" of the paper or that he wanted to expel Bernstein from the editorial post. There had never before been any personal animosity between Bernstein and Liebknecht, although they disagreed at times. To be sure, Bernstein himself complained directly to Liebknecht in May that as editor he intended to demand the rights of editorial control as long as he had to take public responsibility for the contents of the paper.[85] Liebknecht recognized fully the justice of Bernstein's demands. A few days after receiving the letters, Liebknecht in fact defended Bernstein in a meeting of the *Fraktion* when Wilhelm Blos and four other moderates proposed to depose Bernstein as editor. Bebel himself admitted that Liebknecht had helped decisively to preserve Bernstein in his position.[86]

Pressured by the constant bombardments of his friends, Liebknecht gradually shifted his position so that the moderates could no longer take encouragement from his action. His buoyancy and optimism were not easily crushed, however, and he confidently continued the work of reconciling the differences in the party. During June, he tried to think of ways to restore unity in the ranks. First, of course, the disagreements with Bebel, Motteler, and Bernstein had to be resolved. As Bebel told Engels on June 19, he and Liebknecht, after almost coming to a "break," once again understood each other, especially since Liebknecht's "eyes were opened" to the fact that there were fundamental antagonisms in the party.[87] But Liebknecht did not really believe that there were fundamental differences in principles, as he told Motteler in private letters. He believed that attitudes toward parliamentarism were at the heart of the crisis, but he was still optimistic that "there is certainly unity in *theory; in practice* with each individual question the best comrades can *diverge* from one another."[88] Consistent with this thinking, he undertook a personal mission to the Frankfurt area during the second week of July, traveling between Mainz and Offenbach, in an effort to reconcile the factions. Although Bebel believed that his "reconciliation effort" would not succeed, even Engels was pleased as he read a report of Liebknecht's speech at Offenbach on July 14 in which the "Old Soldier" had attempted to explain why the party had

[85] Bernstein to Liebknecht, May 2, 1885; May 9, 1885; and May 17, 1885, Liebknecht Archive, IISH.

[86] Bebel to Bernstein, May 22, 1885, Bebel Archive, IISH.

[87] Bebel to Engels, June 19, 1885, in Bebel, *Briefwechsel*, p. 224.

[88] Liebknecht to Motteler, July 10, 1885, Liebknecht Archive, IISH. One month earlier, June 12, he told Motteler that parliamentarism was the "burning question" before the party; in *ibid.*

no cause to split over the parliamentary issue.[89] Liebknecht's efforts toward restoring harmony helped at least to reduce tensions during the summer of 1885.

Harmony was never completely restored in 1885, and for that matter, the crisis left some deep wounds in the party that were remembered long after the Socialist Law itself had lapsed. But in June both radicals and moderates in the *Fraktion* feared the consequences of a party split. The chief foe was still outside the party, and it was only to the advantage of the enemy to prolong needlessly the hostilities. As the deputies drafted a "report" on the Reichstag session that had closed in the middle of May, they minimized the differences existing within their ranks. The radical members were even willing to write in a strong defense of all the work of the Social Democratic deputies, including their participation on Reichstag committees and the Council of Senior Members, both of which had been criticized by some anti-parliamentarians among the rank-and-file.[90] The *Fraktion* also agreed to postpone publication of the "report" until August, in order to let tempers cool and, no doubt, in order not to appear too ludicrous in the eyes of the German public which knew that the crisis had nearly split the party.[91]

The Unresolved Problem

At the end of 1885, several repercussions followed the major crisis. Personal animosities between leading radicals and moderates continued to haunt the inner peace of the party for many months to come. The feuding in Frankfurt boiled over again in the fall when Frohme spoke in highly nationalistic terms about Germany's "lofty mission!" The Reichstag *Fraktion* sought to arbitrate the dispute at a closed meeting on November 25, but it degenerated into long and bitter exchanges between Frohme and Bebel.[92] Frohme and Hasenclever were also behind a move to have Social Democrats run for seats in the Prussian Diet

[89] Bebel to Bernstein, July 17, 1885, Bebel Archive, IISH; Engels to Bebel, July 24, 1885, in Bebel, *Briefwechsel,* p. 232.

[90] "An die Genossen," printed separately, but sent out with the *Sozialdemokrat* in the issue of August 6, 1885. Working through Vollmar particularly, Bebel managed to have a dominant voice in the drafting of the "report." See, Bebel to Vollmar, June 14, and June 18, 1885, Bebel Archive, IISH.

[91] Auer to Liebknecht, June 2, 1885, Liebknecht Archive, IISH.

[92] "Deutschlands Beruf in der Oekonomie der weltgeschichtlichen Entwicklung," *Berliner Volksblatt,* No. 217, Sept. 17, 1885, *Beilage,* p. 1; Bebel to "Werther Genossen," Dec. 4, 1885, Bebel Archive, IISH.

which radicals such as Bebel vigorously opposed.[93] At the same time, a long discussion about the value of the normal working day as a panacea for the social question erupted. Moderates such as Auer, Grillenberger, and Viereck maintained that by setting legal maximums on working hours unemployment would be reduced significantly. Using Marx's *Capital*, Liebknecht argued that, although desirable, the normal working day could not solve unemployment because employers would intensify the work load and technological advances would make increased production possible without employing more workers.[94]

In all of these disputes, the personal rancor between the two groups created many unpleasantries. Grillenberger complained privately on November 23 that party members were obstructed from expressing opinions in the *Sozialdemokrat* unless they followed the "Borsdorf Pope," meaning Liebknecht. "The paper," he continued, "is then the organ of Misters Bebel, Liebknecht, and Ede [Bernstein], and *every* other opinion is tabooed therein." No one could speak in opposition, Grillenberger added a few days later, "for the Old Man [Liebknecht] is Allah, [he] is great and Ede is his Prophet." [95]

On the other side, Bebel and the radicals continued to look upon Viereck's activities with deep suspicions. Although Bebel assured Engels in December that the *Fraktion* had been brought in line, Viereck wanted to coalesce an opposition to the radicals around himself.[96] Bebel warned the staff of the *Sozialdemokrat* about Viereck's intrigues and prepared for an open battle.[97] At the same time, Auer grew impatient with Bebel's authoritarian inclinations and his special dislike of Viereck. "August wrote me," Auer informed Liebknecht in April 1886, "that he intends to pick a quarrel with [Viereck] in the 'S[ozial] D[emokrat]' and bring the case before the congress. I wrote back to him, [asking] whether he imagines that his statements are sacrosanct? To me, at least, nothing is known of his canonization and

[93] Bernstein, *Berliner Arbeiterbewegung*, II, p. 160; Bernstein, "Wie es im Jahre 1885 stand," *Neue Zeit*, XXXI, part I (1912/13), p. 432; "Die Frankfurter Sozialdemokratie und die Landtagswahl," *SD*, No. 45, Nov. 5, 1885.

[94] Viereck's article, "Zu frueh belobt," *Das Recht auf Arbeit*, No. 65, August 19, 1885; Liebknecht's first articles, "Ueber den Normalarbeitstag," *SD*, No. 43, Oct. 22, and No. 44, Oct. 29, 1885. Liebknecht wrote a longer series, answering all of his critics, "Ueber den Normalarbeitstag," *SD*, No. 45, Nov. 5; No. 46, Nov. 12; and No. 47, Nov. 19, 1885. See also Bernstein's criticism of the moderates, "Sind wir noch Sozialdemokraten?" *SD*, No. 45, Nov. 5, 1885.

[95] Grillenberger to Motteler, Nov. 23, and 26, 1885, *Kleine Korrespondenz*, IISH.

[96] Bebel to Engels, Dec. 7, 1885, in Bebel, *Briefwechsel*, p. 246; Bebel to Liebknecht, Jan. 8, 1886, Liebknecht Archive, IISH.

[97] Bebel to Hermann Schlueter, Jan. 8, and Jan. 19, 1886, Bebel Archive, IISH.

just as little do I believe in his infallibility. I wrote all of that to him—and to be sure, very bluntly." [98] Although Auer's admonitions did not deter Bebel, the showdown with Viereck did not come until the summer of 1887. At that time, Viereck lost out completely.

The persistent personal animosities aroused by the crisis of 1885 illustrate that the crucial issue had not been resolved. The conflict over the steamship subsidy was a symptom of an inner tension created not only by the long-standing differences between moderates and radicals but also by the fact that the growth of the Social Democrats gave them an opportunity to enter German parliamentary politics, not merely as an outside protest movement, but as a party within the German political system.

On the surface, the radicals resisted the invitation to Social Democracy to become a party within the German political system. In reality, however, they could not completely withstand the force of circumstances, as the following chapter will indicate. Parliamentarism offered opportunities for minor reforms which not even the radicals could disregard. At the same time, living under the Socialist Law, their sense of alienation from German society had been reenforced. As long as the dominant classes—aristocratic and bourgeois—wanted to repress the political movement that had grown up to represent the working class, the radicals reciprocated with equal exclusiveness. Faced with this cleavage in German society—imposed from above—the radicals made a virtue out of a necessity. The doctrine of the class struggle gave them a rationale for insisting on the spiritual and political isolation of Social Democracy from all bourgeois institutions as a prerequisite for a movement of proletarian socialism.

By contrast, the moderates would not make a virtue out of their isolation from the dominant German cultural and political system. They searched willingly—some of them even enthusiastically—for a way to integrate themselves into the system. Thus, when an opportunity seemed to offer itself, the moderates preferred to forget momentarily about the repression of the Socialist Law and to probe the possibilities of integration.

The activities of the Social Democrats in 1885–1886 must be examined in more detail to see to what extent the radicals were also influenced by the increased parliamentary strength of the party. Only part of the significance of these years has been indicated thus far.

[98] Auer to Liebknecht, April 27, 1886, Liebknecht Archive, IISH.

CHAPTER VIII · THE DEEPENED PARLIAMENTARY INVOLVEMENT: ITS RELATIONSHIP TO REVOLUTIONARY EXPECTATIONS AND POLITICAL DEMOCRACY

Social Democratic Parliamentary Activity at its Peak and the Unresolved Question of Parliamentarism

THE CRISIS of 1885 provides a rather clear picture of the internal tensions created by the growth of the party. The story of that turmoil itself does not, however, provide a full account of all the ramifications of the growth and the new situation in the middle eighties. To complete the picture, it is also essential to evaluate the parliamentary work which did not create any significant dissension within the party. This is all the more important because in 1885 and 1886 the parliamentary work of the Social Democrats was more intense than it had ever been.

It is not the intention of this chapter to recount all the parliamentary work of the Social Democrats, but simply to present a complementary side of the 1885 crisis. This should provide substance for the contention that in the middle eighties the Social Democrats took a few hesitant, but important, steps in the direction of becoming a parliamentary political party within the German system. Equally significant, we shall notice that in the Saxon Diet the radicals, under Bebel's leadership, pursued a parliamentary reformist policy that contrasted sharply to their intransigent posture in the Reichstag. The radicals were in complete control of Social Democratic activity in the Saxon Diet, and for this reason considerable importance is placed on what they did there. In effect, we may observe that in the Saxon Diet they dropped many of their sectarian trappings, if not quite all of them.

Finally, the parliamentary experience of the middle eighties obligated the radicals to pursue further the rethinking of their stand on parliamentarism. The rethinking was only partially accomplished, very little by Bebel, much more by Liebknecht. Liebknecht felt that he had to grapple with the issue of parliamentarism as he had in the late sixties. As a result of his renewed interest in this problem, he completely shifted from his earlier position. Rather suddenly, in the middle eighties, Liebknecht concluded that parliamentary institutions were useful not only for propaganda but also as essential instruments for the achievement of a socialist society.

Liebknecht thus reflected the changes that had taken place in the development of Social Democracy. In another way, his own efforts to harmonize revolutionary socialism with parliamentary reformism show that he embodied the several currents in Social Democracy. For that, he was naturally inconsistent, but his contradictions provide a mirror of party development.

Economic and Social Reforms in the Reichstag

The chief Social Democratic legislative initiative of the middle eighties was a Workmen's Protection Bill, drafted originally by Bebel and introduced in the Reichstag toward the end of January 1885.[1] In most respects, it resembled the bill which had been introduced in 1877, and also the measure which Schweitzer had presented to the North German Confederation in 1869. It will be remembered that in 1869 Liebknecht and Bebel both denounced Schweitzer's bill as a betrayal of the principles of socialism, by adding glory to Bismarck's political creation. Their attitude about such bills had changed, even if they continued to believe that in other ways Schweitzer had betrayed the German working class.

Two things are particularly interesting about the Workmen's Protection Bill of 1885. First, many non-socialists greeted it as a serious and legitimate contribution to labor legislation, not as an issue raised simply for agitational purposes. No doubt reflecting the sentiments of many Reichstag deputies, the Conservative Koeller expressed his satisfaction with the socialists' positive approach on January 31, 1885.[2] Finally, the fact that the Reichstag deputies sent the bill to a commit-

[1] The bill is in *SB*, VI, i (1884/85), vol. v, *Anlagen*, No. 144, pp. 519–24.
[2] *Ibid.*, vol. II, p. 1023. See also, comments in Schulthess, *1885*, pp. 25–27.

tee, which in turn debated it at length late in 1885, also demonstrates that it was accepted as a legitimate piece of legislation.

The second interesting feature is that, in addition to calling for legal regulations on working hours and conditions, the bill conceived of a whole range of Imperial agencies to carry out the new provisions. An Imperial Labor Office (*Reichsarbeitsamt*), seated in Berlin, was to be the central agency for the supervision of working conditions. It was to have subordinate Labor Offices (*Arbeitsaemter*) for each district with between two hundred thousand and four hundred thousand inhabitants. The Imperial Labor Office and the local Labor Offices would have the right to inspect all enterprises, whether owned privately or publicly. Each district Labor Office was also to establish an Employment Office, offering services without charge, and a Labor Board (*Arbeitskammer*), authorized to collect detailed information on social and economic conditions. Composed half of employers and half of employees, each Labor Board was also responsible for appointing four of its members to a Court of Arbitration (*Schiedsgericht*) for solving labor disputes. The Imperial Labor Office was obligated to arrange an annual conference on labor questions for all members of the Labor Boards. In all, it was an elaborate plan, which from a socialist standpoint, as Bebel admitted to Engels, had definite weaknesses. But since the opponents of the Social Democrats overlooked the deficiencies, Bebel was content with the draft.[3]

The bill must be taken as the prime illustration of what Bebel viewed as a positive parliamentary policy for the Social Democrats. When the Reichstag briefly debated the measure on March 11, 1885, both Bebel and Grillenberger concentrated on the practical aspects of the bill and the ease with which it would fit into the existing Industrial Code. As they said, it represented only their immediate goals as stated in the second half of the Gotha program, not the whole of the socialist program.[4] But the *Freisinnige* party nonetheless interpreted the Workmen's Protection Bill as an expression of the "radical revolutionary thinking" of the Social Democrats.[5] To a Manchesterite, it certainly was revolutionary, even Conservatives viewed it with less alarm, willing as they were to see state intervention in the economy.

The Workmen's Protection Bill was sent to a committee in the

[3] Bebel to Engels, Feb. 7, 1885, in Bebel, *Briefwechsel*, p. 217.

[4] *SB*, VI, i (1884/85), vol. III, pp. 1732–33, 1748–50.

[5] As reported in "Die erste gesetzgeberische Leistung der Sozialdemokratie," *Berliner Volksblatt*, No. 61, March 13, 1885.

spring of 1885, where it died when the Reichstag session ended in May. The Social Democrats were at a disadvantage at the time because they had no representatives on the committee, a deficiency which they remedied at the beginning of the next session, obtaining seats for both Auer and Pfannkuch.[6] In the new session, beginning in the fall of 1885, the bill received considerable attention. In a plenary session on December 2, Pfannkuch explained that the Social Democrats did not hope for the ruin of existing society but sought simply "to bridge over the chasm" that divided the classes of German society. Two days later, Auer gave another resumé of the practical objectives of the bill, and then it was sent to committee.[7]

The committees of the German Reichstag were not inclined to spend much time on bills which they viewed as peripheral, but this committee devoted nine serious sittings to the Social Democratic measure. The plan for an Imperial Labor Office and subordinate Labor Offices stimulated the greatest discussion, since these were vigorously opposed by the *Freisinnige* deputies. It is not surprising that the committee voted to reject the bill, since even the non-socialist members who sympathized with the plan preferred to endorse a bill presented by some other party.

The committee nevertheless made two recommendations to the Reichstag which were directly related to the contents of the bill. First, it recommended that the number of German factory inspectors be increased and that the size of each inspection district be reduced. Although the Social Democratic plan would have replaced the state factory inspectors with the Imperial system of regulation and control, the committee at least recognized the need for greater supervision. Second, the committee members asked that Industrial Courts (*Gewerbegerichte*) be established to supervise labor disputes. They also accepted the principle—included in the Social Democratic bill—that these courts should be composed equally of employers and employees.[8]

The Social Democrats expressed both disapproval and satisfaction with these minor recommendations. On the one hand, in the committee hearings, Auer and Pfannkuch had supported the demand for more factory inspectors, but on the other, Kayser told the Reichstag that his

[6] For the slightly revised version of the socialists' Workmen's Protection Bill, reintroduced in the fall of 1885, see *SB*, VI, ii (1885/86), vol. IV, *Anlagen*, No. 10, pp. 63–69.

[7] For Pfannkuch, *ibid.*, vol. I, p. 167; for Auer, *ibid.*, p. 212.

[8] *Ibid.*, vol. III, p. 1507.

party had no faith in a simple proposal for more inspectors. But Kayser also admitted that although the Social Democrats were unhappy that the committee had rejected their bill, they were nevertheless content that the committee had done its work adequately.[9]

When the Social Democrats could see clearly after the second plenary debate on their Workmen's Protection Bill (March 15, 17, and 24, 1886) that it had no prospects for acceptance, they focused on the single issue of factory inspection. They now aimed to transfer part of the responsibility of factory inspection from the individual states to the Imperial government. Thus, they asked that an Imperial law regulate "the position of factory inspection" by setting up national standards which each state would be obligated to follow.[10] They believed that a mere increase in the number of factory inspectors, as recommended by the committee, would not bring significant improvement in working conditions unless high standards were also enforced throughout the Reich. Although this measure was also rejected by the Reichstag, one must note that the speeches of Pfannkuch, Grillenberger, Kayser, and Vollmar demonstrated that the Social Democrats genuinely believed that their legislative efforts would bear some fruit.[11]

The Social Democrats did not limit themselves to bills for labor protection, but introduced other measures that seemed to reveal a willingness to reform aspects of the society they despised. Thus, one of their bills proposed a minor economic reform for the system of army reservists. Concerned about the welfare of the reservists' families, the Social Democrats sought legislation to provide subsidies for such families when in need. Their bill specified that the military budget should be increased so that special allocations could be made to subsidize reservists' families. To receive a subsidy for his family while on reserve duty, the serviceman was to make a request to the War Ministry. The amount of the subsidy would be set according to the size of the family and its financial need.[12]

Unfortunately there is no evidence as to how this army reform

[9] *Ibid.*, pp. 1511, 1514.

[10] *Ibid.*, vol. v, *Anlagen*, No. 198, p. 950.

[11] *Ibid.*, vol. III, pp. 1530–36, 1623ff. The demand for an Imperial system of factory inspection had previously been presented by Emil Kaler, "Die Fabrikinspektoren," *Neue Zeit*, II (1884), p. 322. In 1888, the number of factory inspectors in the major states was as follows: Prussia, 18; Bavaria, 4; Saxony, 7; Wuerttemberg, 1; Baden, 1. From F. Schuler, "Die Fabrikinspektion," *Archiv fuer Soziale Gesetzgebung und Statistik*, II (1889), p. 544.

[12] *SB*, VI, ii (1885/86), vol. IV, *Anlagen*, No. 59, p. 164.

measure originated in the Social Democratic *Fraktion.* It had no specific basis in the program of the party, unless it was thought to be connected with the demand for a National Militia. This is conceivable, but not very convincing. Possibly it reflected the thinking expressed by Bernstein in his letter of November 15, 1884, to Engels. At that time Bernstein remarked that while it was fine for the Social Democrats to oppose militarism, it was also advisable to take a position on minor reforms of the military system. In any case, this bill is one of the clearest bits of evidence that the Social Democrats were prepared to reform a system which they totally opposed in principle. There is no evidence that in 1885 anyone, including Bebel, had objections to the proposed subsidy for reservists' families.

The Army Reform Bill, first debated on December 15, 1885, had a measure of good fortune, but some of the other parties were amazed that Social Democrats were introducing such measures. Was it not strange, they wondered, that the loudest critics of the military system were now willing to help reform it and thereby make it less objectionable? Were the Social Democrats not giving some implicit recognition to the military system? Was it not peculiar, others queried, that a party which votes against the whole Imperial budget now proposes that the military budget should be increased?

Although the first Social Democratic speaker, Harm, avoided all these problems, the Conservative Koeller spotted the dilemma of the Social Democratic position. Questioning their sincerity, he pointed out that they were making budget recommendations but had refused hitherto to place one of their deputies on the budget committee, and, more incisively, that just a short time earlier they had declared that they would vote against the whole military budget. Now they were introducing a measure to add a substantial sum to that very budget! [13] Something was wrong, Eugen Richter, the leader of the old Progressives, agreed. It seemed to him that the Social Democrats had a choice: either they could reject the whole military budget—as they had in the past—or they could proceed as did every other party by evaluating and committing themselves on each particular item in the budget. Without questioning the sincerity of the Social Democrats, Richter offered the rather perceptive suggestion that possibly the Army Reform Bill indicated that the socialists were being led "more and more by parliamentary practice" and that henceforth they would follow the

[13] *Ibid.*, vol. 1, p. 391, 392–93.

course of other parties and examine each part of the budget on its merits.[14]

Richter had thus touched the issue which lay at the root of the crisis of 1885. The Social Democratic response shows that his interpretation had some validity. Auer and Harm, both moderates, were obviously somewhat embarrassed by the point that their party had no deputies on the budget committee, and they hastened to say that in the next session they would seek to have a socialist on the budget committee.[15] In fact, the Social Democrats hurried to make an agreement with the *Freisinnige* party whereby Hasenclever took Rickert's seat on the committee. Given the intransigent protest traditions of the party on all matters related to the military budget, this act amounted to a significant shift.

Auer also sought to explain away the apparent contradiction in the socialist parliamentary tactics which had been pointed out by Koeller. The explanation is extremely interesting for what it reveals about the moderates' conception of the party's parliamentary role. It clearly shows that Auer, the moderate, wanted to equate the parliamentary role of the Social Democrats to that of an opposition party in the British House of Commons. As he said,

> we [Social Democrats] make proposals where, in our opinion, it is necessary that new practices be instituted; we vote for individual items, reject others, according to whether we hold them useful or harmful. In the end, however, we follow the constitutional principle, that because we are not in agreement with the government, we decline to approve means for it. We would, if through our numbers we had the power, force the government to step down and make room for another. That is the secret of our position, and I do not find anything whatsoever in it which is contradictory.[16]

Auer thus explained how the Social Democrats could retain the spirit of the protest movement while simultaneously absorbing elements common to modern parliamentary parties. But his explanation lacked true contact with the realities of German parliamentary politics. The German government was appointed by the Emperor, not by a majority in the Reichstag. Auer would have his listeners believe that the Social Democrats were merely casting a "no-confidence vote" in Bismarck's

[14] *Ibid.*, p. 394.
[15] *Ibid.*, pp. 395–96.
[16] *Ibid.*, p. 396.

government, but in reality their negative votes on the budget meant something different in the German context. The negative vote on the total budget was a protest in principle against the whole German system, not merely against Bismarck's ministry. Therein lay the obscurity and the ambiguity in the socialists' position. The Social Democrats wanted to reform parts of the military system without admitting that they approved of any part of it. This same pattern appears in some of their other legislation. On the one hand preserving a sectarian mentality (reenforced by the conditions under the Socialist Law) they were impelled to repeat constantly their unqualified rejection of the whole system under which they lived. This was the rule of intransigent opposition, cherished especially by the radicals. But on the other hand, drawn by the practical political possibilities of an enlarged Reichstag *Fraktion* and aware of their potential strength at the polls, they could not entirely avoid some involvement with the system. Total opposition became impossible, but symbolic rejection was still possible. Thus, the Social Democratic rejection of the budget was pure symbolism, because they knew that their negative votes could not hinder its passage and that they could not force Bismarck to resign.

The Reich government greeted the socialist Army Reform Bill with amazing cordiality. The Minister of War, Bronsart von Schellendorf, had only one major objection to the bill: he thought it belonged in the regular domestic budget rather than in the military budget.[17] So the Social Democrats had hope of success. The prospects were even brighter when, Koeller declared in the committee meeting on January 28, 1886, that he agreed fully with the principle of the socialist proposal. Although the committee did not integrate the measure into the military budget, it nonetheless adopted a resolution requesting that "as soon as possible" the Reich government draft a similar bill as part of the domestic budget. The postponement was criticized by Hasenclever, but he also expressed his pleasure with the progress which had been made and his confidence that the Social Democrats would support the committee's resolution. The Social Democrats did in fact support the resolution when the Reichstag adopted it on February 12, 1886.[18]

The moderate socialist press hailed the progress on the army reservists' bill as a concrete success for the parliamentary activity of the Social Democrats.[19] If one probes the nature of that success, the pic-

[17] *Ibid.*, p. 392.

[18] *Ibid.*, vol. II, pp. 799–801, 1044.

[19] "Ein Erfolg der Sozialdemokraten im Reichstage," *Berliner Volksblatt*, No.

ture is not so clear. What principle had been won for socialism? No one made that clear, not even during the debates. What gain had been made for political democracy? No one could identify that. The bill had been intended simply as a piece of minor reform legislation to ameliorate the financial hardships suffered by reservists. The joy of the moderate Social Democratic press with such a minor victory reveals, if in a small measure, the manner in which parliamentarism offered the party a limited degree of integration into the German political system.

One other measure to which the Social Democrats lent their support illustrates the growing involvement of the *Fraktion* in the political system. In December 1885, the government presented the Reichstag with its plans for a canal from Kiel to the mouth of the lower Elbe, the North Sea Canal.[20] There was ready socialist support for this project, embarrassed only by the fact that the government emphasized the military advantages of the canal, giving the possible economic benefits only minor attention. Liebknecht wanted to find a tactic by which the party could endorse the plan without compromising the socialist stand against militarism. Discussing the problem in correspondence with Engels, Liebknecht proposed that the Social Democrats call for a shallow canal, which presumably could handle freighters, but not warships. Engels found this tactic unrealistic. A deep canal was necessary, he argued, because freighters were constantly increasing in size and a shallow canal would soon be useless for trade. It would be "madness," Engels wrote to Bebel, to reject the deep canal on the pretext of opposing its military use.[21]

The Social Democrats supported the North Sea Canal project without any publicly dissenting voices in the first debate on January 9, 1886. Speaking for the *Fraktion*, Blos reported his party's unhappiness that the government had stressed the canal's military advantages, for the Social Democrats preferred to stress its benefits for trade and as a measure which would create jobs for German workers. But, reflecting the traditional Russophobia of the Social Democrats, Blos admitted that his party also recognized that the canal would be "useful to a certain degree to weaken Russian influence."[22] In that case, the Social

24, Jan. 29, 1886. The same paper continued to follow the deliberations with much interest; see *ibid.*, No. 28, Feb. 3, 1886, *Beilage*, pp. 1–2.

[20] *SB*, VI, ii (1885/86), vol. IV, *Anlagen*, No. 63, pp. 167–68.

[21] Engels to Liebknecht, Jan. 7, 1886, in Liebknecht, *Briefwechsel mit Karl Marx und Friedrich Engels*, p. 292; Engels to Bebel, Jan. 20–[23], 1886, in Bebel, *Briefwechsel*, pp. 251–52.

[22] *SB*, VI, ii (1885/86), vol. I, p. 449.

Democrats themselves were counting on military benefits from the canal vis-à-vis Russia. It was one of the incidents which showed the Russophobia of the socialists to be a factor that weakened their opposition to militarism.

The above tactics made it increasingly difficult for the radicals to insist that they used parliamentarism only for agitational purposes. This is even clearer in the case of their work in the Saxon Diet.

Economic and Social Reforms in the Saxon Diet

The relationship of the Social Democrats to the Saxon Diet offers some of the best evidence about how even the radicals could seek integration with German political systems if the conditions were appropriate. The first significant indication came in 1879, when Liebknecht took the required oath of loyalty to the king of Saxony. Some Social Democrats were bewildered when they learned that Liebknecht was willing to take the oath. Some non-socialists were amused that the "Old Soldier" should find himself swearing fidelity to a monarch! The oath was not significant, Liebknecht's defenders said, because the king of Saxony was not a real power in the Reich. Furthermore, if the socialists refused to take the oath, they would be excluded from the diet, thereby forfeiting the gains for which they had worked so hard. In subsequent years, the socialist deputies to the diet took the oath as a matter of course, and nothing more was heard about it.

In the diet, the Social Democrats pursued a reformist policy from the beginning, and in fact expanded that policy during the middle years of the eighties. How was this possible in view of the fact that all the Socialist deputies to the Saxon Diet were radicals? In part it was possible because, although particularism had died as a practical issue in Germany, a particularist cast of mind hung on with many of the Social Democrats of the Eisenacher tradition. In the founding years of the sixties, Prussia had been the enemy, not the Saxon state, undesirable as the latter might have been in many respects. The Reichstag was the product of unification through Prussian arms, and therefore tainted by its evils. Hostile as the radicals might be to the ruling classes in Saxony, they were noticeably more comfortable in a parliament with Saxon reactionaries than with Prussian Junkers.

There is another aspect to the work of the radicals in the Saxon Diet.

As a local state parliament, the Saxon Diet had no competency to deal with the larger issues of the German Reich. Its legislative work was limited to local domestic problems, offering less opportunity as a forum for the dissemination of the party's broad principles. The Reichstag debated the great issues which required a clear statement of Social Democratic principles. Likewise, the German public and the rank-and-file of the party were less aware of what happened in each of the local state and provincial diets throughout the nation. But everyone focused attention on the Reichstag. A slight deviation from the avowed principles of the party, so carefully avoided by the radicals in the Reichstag, might pass with little or no notice if perpetrated in a state diet.

In the early eighties, when the Socialist Law was applied with severity, the Social Democrats in the Saxon Diet limited themselves to criticizing governmental practices.[23] Early in 1882, they introduced one of their first bills, a detailed revision of the Saxon Mining Law of June 16, 1868.[24] In the session of 1883–1884, they stepped up their legislative initiatives, introducing measures to reduce the slaughtering tax on swine, to have covered cabooses built for brakemen on the railways owned by the state of Saxony, and to reform the laws regulating the employment of domestic servants.[25] The bill for covered cabooses was intended as a protective measure for workmen, but as Vollmar admitted, it had nothing to do with socialism as such, nor did it call for anything new, for Saxony's neighbors had already provided such protection for their railway brakemen.[26] Nevertheless, the Social Democrats took it as a measure of their influence when the Saxon Minister of Finance, Koenneritz, announced several years later that cabooses had been added to the state railways.[27]

When elections for the Saxon Diet were called for September 15,

[23] In 1880, Liebknecht pressed the government to disclose whether persons receiving relief funds were stricken from the voting lists and to make a full report on a serious explosion in a mineshaft near Zwickau. Saxony, *Mittheilungen ueber die Verhandlungen des ordentlichen Landtags im Koenigreiche Sachsen waehrend der Jahre 1879/80*, vol. I, p. 619; vol. II, pp. 1104–13. Hereafter these proceedings will be cited as, Saxony, *LT. Mitt.*, with year and volume number. The document volumes will be cited as, Saxony, *LT. Acten,* with year, volume, and number of document. The *Acten* volumes are not paginated.

[24] *Ibid., LT. Acten* (1881/82), vol. II, No. 153.

[25] *Ibid., LT. Acten* (1883/84), vol. I, No. 18, No. 28, and No. 73.

[26] *Ibid., LT. Mitt.*, vol. I, pp. 217–18.

[27] Cf. Emil Nitzsche, *Saechsische Politik. Ein Handbuch fuer Saechsische Waehler* (Dresden, 1903), p. 142.

1885, the Social Democrats issued a campaign program which, in contrast to much of their campaign literature in connection with Reichstag elections, stressed immediate local needs rather than the general principles of the party. The program called for the introduction of universal suffrage in municipal and diet elections, a progressive income tax to replace all other taxes, the assumption of poor relief costs by the state of Saxony, a greater frugality in the Saxon domestic budget, better pay for lower ranking state officials and workers, reform of the educational system to provide free schooling with more opportunity for the children of the poor, and finally a reform of the "Law on Dissenters" to conform to the principle of "absolute freedom of conscience." [28]

The Social Democrats won three contests in 1885, increasing their delegation from four to five members. The delegation consisted of Bebel (elected in 1881), Vollmar (elected in 1883), Fritz Geyer, Carl Stolle, and Kaden (all elected for the first time in 1885). The impression of general success was damaged only by Liebknecht's defeat in all three of the districts in which he ran; his defeat by eighty votes in Leipzig-Land, the seat he had won in 1881, proved to be especially bitter. As Bebel told Engels, in Liebknecht's difficult financial situation, the 12 marks per diem allowance for all Saxon Diet deputies had always been an "acceptable supplement." [29]

Since the radicals had complete control of the Social Democratic delegation to the Saxon Diet, we must assume that the policies they followed met their standards of a revolutionary—and Marxist—parliamentary tactic. But our first glance at a piece of Social Democratic legislation in the Saxon Diet late in 1885 may disturb our picture of the radicals. They introduced a bill for the extension of Saxon state fire insurance to cover movable property.[30] It was apparently Vollmar's special project, but all the socialists supported it. With this measure, as with some of those presented by the socialists in the Reichstag, the opponents of Social Democracy expressed gratification for the new positive approach it demonstrated.[31] Speaking on the bill on December

[28] The campaign program is printed in "Sozialpolitische Rundschau," *SD*, No. 39, Sept. 24, 1885.

[29] "Sozialpolitische Rundschau," *SD*, No. 38, Sept. 18; No. 39, Sept. 24; and No. 40, Oct. 1, 1885. Bebel to Engels, Sept. 19, 1885, in Bebel, *Briefwechsel*, p. 236.

[30] Saxony, *LT. Acten* (1885/86), vol. 1, No. 16.

[31] *Ibid., LT. Mitt.*, vol. 1, pp. 182–83.

9, 1885, Vollmar presented it as an issue between the value of state insurance and private insurance.[32]

As Vollmar and Stolle presented their case, they sounded much more like State Socialists than revolutionary Social Democrats. When the Saxon Minister of State, Nostitz-Wallwitz, doubted that state insurance would be more beneficial than private insurance, Vollmar confessed that he had "much greater confidence in the state and its efficiency than did the Herr Minister." [33] He elaborated by arguing that with a compulsory system of fire insurance the question of profits would vanish, risks would diminish and the people would have confidence in it.[34] Adding to Vollmar's long discussion, Stolle answered a charge of the liberals that state insurance would restrict individual liberty with the assurance that the people were "very satisfied with the procedures of these [Saxon] officials." "Gentlemen," Stolle continued, "a person in need of insurance would joyfully see the approach of a state official; and no one sees in the state official an enemy, but a friend in whom he places his trust." "In the name of humanity we demand the protection of the state for the poor." [35] These were certainly generous words for the state of Saxony but they did not sway the majority in the diet. The resolution was dropped without further consideration.

One cannot avoid asking a question of the Social Democrats at this point. How different in principle was the Social Democratic measure for state fire insurance from Bismarck's insurance programs which the party had rejected? On examination, one must conclude that Bismarck's program was in principle much closer to the actual socialist program than the fire insurance. The state fire insurance involved only a piecemeal reform of a very limited measure, whereas Bismarck's program had broad implications. The state fire insurance had no direct relationship to the Social Democratic party program, whereas Bismarck's insurance certainly had a positive connection. In the Reichstag, the Social Democrats had rejected Bismarck's insurance program because in their judgment it was inadequate to solve the social problem, but in the Saxon Diet they themselves initiated reform measures that were completely insufficient as contributions toward a solution of the social

[32] *Ibid.*, pp. 174–75, 178–79.
[33] *Ibid.*, p. 180.
[34] *Ibid.*, pp. 180–81.
[35] *Ibid.*, p. 190.

question. In the Reichstag, they had occasionally expressed doubts about the sincerity of the government in promoting the insurance program, but in the Saxon Diet they assured a skeptical audience that the local state could improve conditions for workers, even when the state officials themselves made no pretense to be reformers.

Unfortunately, Bebel's role on the fire insurance bill is not clear. He did not speak on the subject, but there is no evidence that he had reservations about it. Had Bebel objected to the fire insurance bill, he could no doubt have obstructed it, for Vollmar still sided with the radicals, although it is also apparent that he became more moderate after 1884.[36] Stolle too had been one of Bebel's most faithful followers in the intraparty disputes and there is no evidence that they had fallen into disagreements.

In response to other measures in the Saxon Diet, the radicals also groped clumsily for a harmony between their own revolutionary principles and the urge to endorse minor social reforms with little relationship to socialism. One of the most revealing incidents arose when the Saxon government allotted 8,000 marks in its 1886–1887 budget for the establishment of a so-called labor colony on the Schneckengruen estate near Plauen in the Voigtland. Comparatively new in Germany, such labor colonies were designed to provide temporary work and shelter for Germany's increasing number of vagabonds. The original spirit behind the movement was the Protestant pastor, Friedrich von Bodelschwingh, whose social conscience had been disturbed in the late seventies by the fate of the unemployed wanderers. The first colony was established at Wilhelmsdorf near Bielefeld in March 1882 under Bodelschwingh's sponsorship. By 1886 there were fifteen similar labor colonies in Germany.[37]

The principle behind these labor colonies and the nature of their organization certainly had little in common with the principles of Social Democracy as expressed in the Gotha program, much less with

[36] Cf. Jansen, *Georg von Vollmar*, pp. 32ff.

[37] G. Berthold, "Arbeiterkolonieen," *Handwoerterbuch der Staatswissenschaften* (2nd ed.), I, pp. 463–64. Karl Kautsky related some interesting facts about the labor colonies in a review article of a book by G. Berthold, *Die Entwicklung der deutschen Arbeiter-Kolonien* (Leipzig, 1887), in *Neue Zeit*, v (1887), pp. 523–24. Kautsky noted that the following facts demonstrated that the labor colonies were not a great contribution to social reform: a great number of the inhabitants of the labor colonies had criminal records (up to 84 percent at the Friedrichswille Colony); it was impossible for the inhabitants to save money in such colonies; and that 54 percent of the inhabitants left the colony without any prospect of employment outside.

Marxism in general. But when the Schneckengruen project was discussed in the Saxon Diet on January 26, 1886, Bebel announced that the socialists would vote for it because they recognized that an "actual state of distress" existed as a consequence of the bourgeois system of society. To protect the market of local craftsmen in the Plauen area, he requested that the inhabitants of the Schneckengruen colony produce only items which would be of use to themselves. He noted that the basketmakers around Wilhelmsdorf, the site of the first labor colony, complained that they were forced to compete with cheap labor. Finally, Bebel explained that he viewed a labor colony only as a "palliative means" to ease the distress of unemployment and in no way a measure of socialist policy.[38] In that way he asked his audience to recognize that Social Democrats were willing to approach minor reforms in a positive mind, but he had also admitted that he would cooperate with an existing state in the interest of piecemeal reform.

The contrast between the approval of the Schneckengruen project by the radicals in the Saxon Diet and their consistent rejection of Bismarck's insurance programs in the Reichstag is almost overwhelming. On numerous occasions in the Reichstag, the Social Democrats had said, and were to say again in 1889 in the discussion of the Invalid Insurance, that they agreed with the principle of Bismarck's program, but rejected it because of its inadequacies. But in the Saxon Diet, Bebel himself could explain that the principle of the labor colonies was inadequate, that in addition it was only a "palliative means"—and yet he could vote for it. Even the moderate Louis Viereck, a friend of Bismarck's social program, refused to endorse the Schneckengruen project on the ground that the labor colonies were simply voluntary prisons.[39]

How was it possible for the radicals to endorse such a weak instrument of reform without undermining the principles which they so staunchly defended in the Reichstag? It was possible in great part precisely because the issue arose in the Saxon Diet and not in the Reichstag. In the more relaxed atmosphere of Dresden, even the radicals could lean in the direction of becoming a reformist parliamentary party. Obviously they felt much more a part of the system in Saxony than in the Reich as a whole. Here they could occasionally talk of the

[38] Saxony, *LT. Mitt.* (1885/86), vol. 1, pp. 484–85, 489.

[39] "Schneckengruen," *Das Recht auf Arbeit*, No. 94, March 10, 1886, pp. 1–2. At the St. Gall party congress in October 1887, Bebel had to answer sharp criticisms of his support for the Schneckengruen Labor Colony. See below, Chap. x.

broad principles of their protest movement, but that did not restrain them from taking up the tasks of parliamentary reform work in all seriousness.[40]

The Saxon Diet thus proved to be a more effective training ground for the radicals as parliamentarians than the Reichstag. They learned, for example, that a Social Democrat could support government social reforms without betraying the ultimate goals of his party. They also learned that intransigent opposition was not the only way to defend the interests of the working class. They happily found that they could abandon sectarianism without undermining their genuine devotion to socialist principles. All of this seemed to indicate that they were overcoming their ambivalent parliamentarism, at least when they worked in the Saxon Diet.

The actions of the radicals in the Saxon Diet demolishes completely the validity of the repeated slogan that Social Democrats used parliamentarism only as an agitational weapon. In fact, they could expect little direct propaganda value from their work in the Saxon Diet. That explains why they readily assumed a reformist attitude when they entered the diet. Otherwise their time would have been completely wasted. Activity in the Reichstag, however, had a direct propaganda value, and the radicals continued to use it for this purpose. The propaganda value of the Reichstag influenced the tactics of the Social Democrats, impelling them to pay greater attention to their broad principles and to follow the rule of intransigent opposition. However, even in the Reichstag, from late 1885 to early 1886, the radicals tended to approach parliamentary work with fewer agitational overtones and more serious legislative intentions.

Social Democrats in Defense of Political Liberalism

There are indications that in the middle eighties the Social Democrats were almost inadvertently assuming the responsibility of pushing forward the principles of liberalism while the liberal parties themselves had weakened in this task. Even the radicals, although they looked

[40] It should be noted that the Social Democrats also introduced a bill for educational reform, calling upon the state government of Saxony to subsidize local school districts, for a unified system of textbooks, and for guaranteed free elementary education. Although this bill made no progress in the 1885/86 session, the Social Democrats reintroduced it in the late eighties. For the bill, see Saxony, *LT. Acten* (1885/86), vol. 1, No. 48.

upon the parliamentary institution as a transitional bourgeois structure, showed definite signs that they felt a responsibility to push for the full realization of liberal principles.

The prospects were not good, however, for liberalizing Germany's political institutions in the middle eighties. Not only was Bismarck hostile to the Reichstag—he was angered especially by his failure to get a majority in 1884—but the liberals themselves had lost much of their dynamism years before. The eighties were stagnant years of conservative reaction, offering little impetus for a revitalization of German liberalism. The National Liberals, having first abandoned their genuine liberal principles in the sixties for Bismarck and national unity, did not return to those principles even when Bismarck wanted to discard them in the early eighties. The liberalism of the Progressive party, and the new *Freisinnige* party, was more genuine, but not much more effective.

None of the Social Democrats had confidence that the liberals would push Germany toward political democracy with genuine effectiveness, but Bebel in particular reflected on the meaning of this for the future prospects of Social Democracy. Some Germans seemed to think that the unification of the Progressives and Secessionists, forming the *Freisinnige* party early in 1884, would inspire a new era of liberalism. Bebel doubted this, concluding, quite correctly, that the move was designed chiefly to provide the Crown Prince Friedrich with a "governmental party [*regierungsfaehige Partei*]." Bebel's judgment seemed to be confirmed by the results of the election of 1884 when the *Freisinnige* party did not make a good showing. He could not avoid the conclusion, as he wrote to Engels, that "middle class radicalism" was "dead" in Germany.[41]

The political impotency of the German liberals had a long tradition, but to a socialist with a Marxist tendency it posed a special problem. What would take the place in Germany of the expected stage of liberal bourgeois political rule, the benefits of which would provide the levers by which the working class could gain education, experience, and increased political influence? Bebel reflected on this problem, although he did not attempt to translate the conclusions of his thinking into practical party policy. His speculation led him to the conclusion that

[41] Bebel to Engels, April 18, and Nov. 24, 1884, in Bebel, *Briefwechsel*, pp. 174, 198. In the latter letter, Bebel estimated that of the thirty-five seats won by the *Freisinnige* party in the run-offs, no less than two-thirds were due to crucial support from Social Democratic voters (p. 198).

for Germany it was impossible to expect a "radical bourgeois transitional stage," something which might hold for "petty-bourgeois France." [42] In Germany, Bebel thought, the economic development had so far outstripped the political development that it seemed possible to jump over the intermediate stage, going directly from the existing system into the first phases of socialist development. Consistent with that thinking, Bebel repeatedly told Engels and constantly warned his comrades that the collapse of capitalist society approached rapidly.

Bebel's private speculation that Germany would jump over the "radical bourgeois stage" did not harmonize completely with the proposals of the Social Democrats in the Reichstag or with some of his public speeches at the time. Had he held consistently to his expectation, there would have been no need for the Social Democrats to push for the perfection of "bourgeois" institutions. But in the fall of 1885 the Social Democrats in fact heeded a call to defend Germany's rather anemic parliamentary institution.

On November 19, the Conservatives introduced a measure to lengthen the Reichstag's legislative periods from three to five years, thus reducing the efficacy of universal suffrage. Immediately the Social Democrats retaliated by launching a counterattack for two-year legislative periods.[43] In speaking for the shortened legislative periods, Max Kayser and Bebel made it clear that in their minds parliamentarism was not the best system for popular representation, nor an ultimate goal of Social Democracy.[44] Nevertheless, Bebel said, the Social Democrats "strive for parliamentary rule and behind the parliamentary rule a popular rule. We desire that the Reichstag should be not merely an equal factor with the Bundesrat; we want to see it made into the decisive factor in the German Empire. And, so far as we can bring that about, at first only theoretically with our small minority, we will certainly do it. By the presentation of our bill, as I believe, we have done this in the clearest and most decisive manner." [45] In effect, Bebel had declared that the Social Democrats would have to take up the struggle for a liberal democracy where the liberals had dropped it.

With still other measures in the 1885–1886 session, the Social Democrats took up the fight for the principles of parliamentary govern-

[42] *Ibid.*, p. 199.

[43] *SB*, VI, ii (1885/86), vol. IV, *Anlagen*, No. 14 (the Conservative bill), p. 73; No. 18 (the Social Democratic bill), pp. 80–81.

[44] *Ibid.*, vol. I, pp. 244–45 (Kayser).

[45] *Ibid.*, p. 283.

ment as originally conceived by radical liberals. Completely on their own initiative, the socialists introduced a bill providing per diem and travel allowances for Reichstag deputies.[46] This same measure had been introduced by the *Freisinnige* party late in 1884, when the Reichstag had passed it but it had died in the Bundesrat. Speaking on the new bill on February 17, 1886, Hasenclever noted that a *Freisinnige* newspaper was greatly amused by the fact that now Social Democrats presented a bill taken "word for word" from an earlier proposal by the radical liberals. This only proved, Hasenclever said, that such a reform was absolutely necessary. Even the *Sozialdemokrat* agreed that the socialists had to fight for causes like this which the liberals had betrayed.[47] With the support of the *Freisinnige*, Center, and several minor parties, the Social Democratic per diem bill passed the Reichstag, but it was killed again in the Bundesrat.

The Social Democrats were indeed taking responsibility for advocating the measures they believed liberals should have implemented years before. But they could not always get the assistance of the radical liberals. Thus, their other measure, to reapportion the Reichstag districts and to increase the number of seats according to the most recent census, received no endorsement at all from the other parties.[48] The *Freisinnige* liberals perceived a threat to their own self-interest in reapportionment, as the Social Democratic vote was constantly rising in the cities.

The proposals of the Social Democrats in the cause of perfecting the parliamentary system were certainly consistent with the general development of their party in the context of German politics. The socialist movement had become a significant factor in German politics before the bourgeois liberals had completed the work they started decades before. It was natural, therefore, to strive to complete that work, especially if one believed, as most of the moderates did, that socialism would be and ought to be achieved through some peaceful and gradual process.[49] The promotion of these measures also harmonized with the party's program, which called for the realization of a democratic polit-

[46] *Ibid.*, vol. IV, *Anlagen*, No. 45, p. 138.

[47] *Ibid.*, vol. II, pp. 1093–94. "Sozialpolitische Rundschau," *SD*, No. 50, Dec. 10, 1885.

[48] For this bill, see *SB*, VI, ii (1885/86), vol. V, *Anlagen*, No. 152, p. 742.

[49] A lead article in one of the moderate papers predicted optimistically that in the future the "conclusions" of the Reichstag would be in agreement with the "views of the people." "Der deutsche Reichstag," *Berliner Volksblatt*, No. 261, Nov. 7, 1885.

ical structure. Nevertheless, the advocacy of these measures raised further questions for deliberation by the Social Democrats.

In the context of events within the Social Democratic party since the fall of 1884, the *Fraktion*'s program for a further democratization of the Reichstag highlighted the need for a more precise understanding of the relationship of parliamentarism to the goals of the socialist movement. Clearly, in view of the party's growth, the intense legislative activity of its deputies between 1884 and 1886, and its inherited obligation of pushing for principles betrayed by the liberals, the old slogan that Social Democrats used parliamentarism chiefly for propaganda purposes had become an anachronism. More rethinking was necessary, and even the radical Social Democrats realized it. The experience of the middle eighties stimulated a discussion about the proper place of parliamentarism in the tactics and principles of the party. The result, however, reveals only a groping for answers, never a solution that cleared away the obscurity and ambiguity which had characterized Social Democratic thought about parliamentarism for several years.

Bebel and Liebknecht on Parliamentarism and Revolutionary Expectations

The radicals had the greatest need to rethink the issue of parliamentarism for the tactics and principles of Social Democracy. The moderates, for the most part, were content to accept nearly all the implications of parliamentary work. For those moderates who shied away from a glorification of the class conflict and revolution, parliament offered the most desirable institution for the gradual move toward socialism. For them, no special problem existed; one used the parliamentary bodies for social and economic reforms, and one might also use a perfected Reichstag in a socialist society. They were willing to use the Reichstag for agitation, but unwilling to stop there. To be entirely fair to these moderates, one must say that many of them, although not all, would certainly have been on the barricades had a revolution broken out in Germany. It was not so much a matter of courage, but of preference, and they saw no reason to downgrade the importance of parliament, either as a means or as a goal.

The radicals were faced with a problem, and they realized it. The socialist society, radicals such as Liebknecht and Bebel had always maintained, would be achieved through some kind of revolution. In 1869, Liebknecht had opposed all socialist participation in the parliamentary institutions, minimizing even its agitational value. He had maintained that parliamentarism was both tactically insignificant for Social Democracy and contrary to its fundamental principles. That was too extreme for Bebel, who from his first participation in the political work of the labor movement believed that parliamentary participation offered significant tactical opportunities. But both had agreed that parliamentary work would not be the means for the achievement of socialism and that parliamentarism would not be part of the new society. However, the developments in the middle eighties forced some deeper consideration of the problem.

Bebel's reflections did not lead him to a new position; both hostile sentiments to the Reichstag and his revolutionary expectations deterred him from making a new approach. His heart longed for the collapse of existing society. "Every night," he wrote to Engels with almost childlike faith in 1885, "I go to sleep with the thought that the last hour of bourgeois society strikes soon." [50] From the beginning of the eighties, the expectation that a revolution was about to break was embedded deep in Bebel's whole person. In 1881, he intimated some bewilderment when Engels did not share all of his belief that the general collapse was so near.[51]

Bebel expressed these expectations periodically in the following years. On November 24, 1885, he assured Engels that in Germany they were moving toward the revolution with "giant strides," but he was disconcerted that his socialist comrades were still laughing at him for his assertions that the "crash" was about to come.[52] Again on April 23, 1886, he complained to Engels that for several years he had been "ridiculed" by the "greatest part of his party" for holding that the "catastrophe" would come in the eighties. "It is too bad," he reflected, "that Marx is dead; it would give him joy [to see] how rapidly the old world disintegrates and the seeds for the new sprout up." [53] He buttressed his expectations of a fast approaching revolutionary situation with a wide range of evidence—for example, rising unemployment, increased concentration in industrial organization, the decline in handicraft production, and discontent among the workers as indicated by strikes.

[50] Bebel to Engels, Dec. 7, 1885, in Bebel, *Briefwechsel,* p. 249.
[51] Bebel to Engels, Feb. 11, 1881, in *ibid.*, p. 103.
[52] Bebel to Engels, Nov. 24, 1884, in *ibid.*, p. 199.
[53] Bebel to Engels, April 23, 1886, in *ibid.*, pp. 274–75.

And, as noted above, he had concluded in the middle eighties that in Germany there would not be a transitional stage of radical bourgeois liberalism. The objective historical development of the political and economic system, he concluded, had reached a point where only a major crisis was needed to open the way for a rapid transition to the beginnings of a socialist society.[54] Given this mental framework, it is not difficult to see that for Bebel socialist parliamentary activity could be viewed as a temporary preoccupation without significant meaning for the achievement of socialism.

Added to Bebel's social analysis were personal feelings of disgust, distaste, and disenchantment with parliamentarizing. Late in December 1884, at the very time when he was drafting the Workmen's Protection Bill, he was so depressed by the manner in which "parliamentarism" was a shelter for "corruption" [*Versumpfung*] that he often thought of abandoning it completely.[55] In the middle of 1885, he complained bitterly that the majority in the *Fraktion* had been corrupted by parliament. Holding Reichstag seats, he said scornfully, "satisfies their ambition and their vanity; with great self-complacency they look upon themselves as among the 'chosen of the nation' and find immense pleasure in the parliamentary comedy; they take it *very* seriously."[56] It disgusted Bebel. By March 1886, after he himself had been so energetic in the parliamentary work of the previous eighteen months, he poured out his inner despondency and bitterness to his old friend Motteler: "I often have a deep loathing for all of this parliamentary chattering; after every speech I sense a kind of moody dejection [*Katzenjammer*], because I must say to myself that there upon that platform which is of such importance to people, and which is taken seriously by so many, [there], no destiny will be decided."[57] There is no reason to doubt the sincerity of Bebel's stated distaste for parliamentary "chattering." He had no cause to deceive his closest friends. But it is precisely this sincerity that raises questions.

If, on the basis of his analysis, Bebel could be so confident that revolution was imminent, and if he found parliamentary activity so repelling—yes, degrading—what purpose was served by his energetic

[54] References to these conditions and the expectations they aroused appear frequently in Bebel's letters; see, for example, his letters to Engels on June 19, 1885, and Sept. 19, 1885, in *ibid.*, pp. 226–27, 237–38.

[55] Bebel to Liebknecht, Dec. 28, 1884, Liebknecht Archive, IISH.

[56] Bebel to Liebknecht, July 26, 1885, Liebknecht Archive, IISH.

[57] Bebel to Motteler, March 13, 1886, Bebel Archive, IISH.

work in the Reichstag and the Saxon Diet? Would it not have been more in line with his analysis and more satisfying to his personal longings to have devoted his tremendous energies to the formation of an organization with specific revolutionary goals? By his own detailed attention to parliamentary matters, did he not also contribute—unintentionally, to be sure—to the corruption of principles which he unmercifully condemned in his fellow socialist deputies? If in truth, so much was to be feared, and so little to be gained from parliamentarism, wherein could he discover reasons for his own energetic involvement in electioneering politics?

These questions certainly highlight the dilemma not only of Bebel but of all the radicals. For Bebel's part, one may seek answers to the questions by reference to two factors: his conception of the nature of revolution and the hard realities of his party's existence under the Socialist Law. In brief, he believed that although the revolution might involve violence and great physical struggle, it would come to the socialists, they would not create it. Furthermore, Bebel could not know exactly what the revolution would be like, and he was therefore unable to conceive of what precisely the socialists had to do in order to prepare for an active role. On the one hand, Bebel believed that the socialists had to be prepared when the collapse came; on the other, he feared that they might act prematurely. Speculating on the nature of the revolution in 1881, he told Engels: "When things develop further, which is not to be doubted, I hold it possible that in a certain moment the ruling classes will find themselves in a kind of hypnotic state and will let everything take its course almost without opposition." [58] Indeed, he hoped that the revolution would require practically no socialist action to be successful.

This passive conception of revolution, combined with the realities of party life under the Socialist Law, make more understandable Bebel's continued activity in the parliaments. As a socialist he had to exploit whatever means were available for the preservation of the movement and the dissemination of its principles. But, more important, as a leader of Social Democracy it was almost impossible for Bebel to abandon the Reichstag without destroying his own power within the party. For these reasons, parliamentary work remained a practical necessity. But none of these reasons reduced the tension within him. On the contrary, they merely sustained his ambivalent parliamentarism.

[58] Bebel to Engels, March 28, 1881, in Bebel, *Briefwechsel,* p. 106.

A significant contrast emerged in the middle eighties between the approaches of Bebel and Liebknecht to the parliamentary issue. When one recalls that Liebknecht had proclaimed himself the uncompromising foe of all parliamentarism in 1869, it is astounding to find him groping his way toward a theoretical synthesis of revolutionary socialism and parliamentary reformism. That is, nonetheless, what he did. His shift is full of irony, for Liebknecht had never shown any of Bebel's patience with legislative tasks, although he took to speaking in plenary sessions with sheer delight. As the "Soldier of the Revolution," the personal appellation he most enjoyed, Liebknecht had vociferously denied that parliaments were useful to Social Democrats for anything but agitation. And he had often disputed even the agitational value of parliamentary participation. As late as 1881, he wrote: "We [Social Democrats] are not only convinced that legislatively nothing of importance can be achieved in the present Reichstag and under the ruling parliamentary regime, [but] we are also in principle opponents of modern parliamentarism and the existing form of popular representation." [59] A few years later his opinions were different.

Liebknecht's shift formed an integral part of his efforts to reconcile the clash between moderates and radicals in 1885. In June of that year he had decided that confusion about parliamentarism lay at the root of the trouble. He tried to find the arguments to prove that on this issue there were disagreements only on tactical matters, not on principles. But this led him into a contradiction with his earlier expositions. In the middle of July, he gave lectures on parliamentarism and, in one speech, apparently gave the impression that in 1885 he looked upon parliamentarism with much more favor than he had in 1869! For that, Bebel had some ready criticisms, although he had seen only a newspaper summary of Liebknecht's speech. So he reminded Liebknecht: "In 1869 you polemicized against parliamentarism *in itself* and *not* against the North German Confederation. In 1876 or '77 you printed *this* speech *anew.* I *disagree* with [the idea] that since then something in the situation has changed so that [our] views on the value of parliamentarism could change. At most, we have had experiences which speak even more *against* the *value* of parliamentarism and which impose on us a *much greater caution* in its use." Admitting that some of his criticism might not be justified because he had not seen an exact text of the

[59] Selim [Miles with reversed spelling, a Liebknecht pseudonym], "Der Parlamentarismus," *SD,* No. 24, June 12, 1881.

speech, Bebel nevertheless added contemptuously, "if, however, [it is true that] you see the changed situation in this, that you say that the North German Confederation was a quagmire, [and] in contrast the German Empire contains the embryo of a 'Free State!' so with this explanation I grabbed my head and questioned as to whether I was awake or in a dream. (And in 1877 the Empire existed already six years.)" [60]

Certainly, Liebknecht's thinking was in flux, creating the inconsistencies. Was he merely temporizing his usual intransigent anti-parliamentary statements in the interest of party harmony? Was he giving the moderates a little compensation for the embarrassment they suffered? Or was he genuinely shifting his outlook?

Liebknecht was truly altering his orientation, especially with respect to the means for achieving socialism. In several pamphlets from 1886 and 1887, he completed his synthesis between revolutionary socialism and parliamentary reformism. It should be noted, before we examine these pamphlets, that they were stimulated not merely by the growth and development of the party, but also by a need to answer the critics in Germany who claimed that the Social Democrats were insurrectionists not substantially different from the anarchists. In this polemical context, Liebknecht may have exaggerated his reformist statements. However, Liebknecht's writing had always been polemical, and we need not assume that he exaggerated any more in 1886–1887 than at other times.[61]

To present his case, Liebknecht first identified a qualitative change that had taken place in the nature of the Social Democratic movement. "Our party," he wrote, "gradually puts away childish things and emerges from its years of indiscretion [*Flegeljahren*]. Perhaps expressed more accurately: German Social Democracy developed from a sect into a party, and came more and more to a consciousness of its duties as a party." The clear implication of that change, he said, was a recognition that the party worked within limits imposed by reality for "practical goals." [62]

[60] Bebel to Liebknecht, August 9, 1885, Liebknecht Archive, IISH.

[61] Stepped-up agitation by the anarchists from their center in London revitalized the government's claim that Social Democrats were the allies of anarchism. Although the private reports of the police recognized the mutual hatred of anarchists and Social Democrats, it was nevertheless maintained that they were essentially the same since their goals were so similar. See, e.g. the reports of Police President Madai, July 6, 1885, and July 24, 1886, quoted in Hoehn, *Die vaterlandslosen Gesellen,* I, pp. 247ff., and pp. 272ff. See also below, Chap. x.

[62] Wilhelm Liebknecht, *Warum verfolgt man uns? Zur Naturgeschichte des Sozialistengesetzes* (Hottingen-Zurich, 1886), pp. 3–4.

The next step was Liebknecht's chief problem: to find the way by which his commitment to revolutionary socialism could be harmonized with the new realization that parliamentarism was also important. Much depended upon his concept of revolution. Like other Social Democrats, Liebknecht had often given a gradualist and evolutionary interpretation of revolution. He sometimes advanced it for tactical reasons, to persuade the people that Social Democrats were not violent conspirators and insurrectionists. At the same time, this interpretation of revolution was not inconsistent with Marxism. Marx himself had allowed that in some countries the actual transitional phase from capitalism to socialism could be slow and comparatively peaceful.[63] But Liebknecht would sometimes make revolution identical with all historical change. Thus, he wrote in 1871: "All of human history is a continuous revolution. History is the revolution in permanence—it is becomingness, growth, change, progress—perpetual transformation, because life is perpetual creation." [64] Such statements were not unusual, but prior to the mid-eighties Liebknecht had never used this interpretation of revolution to imply an endorsement of parliamentarism. He had always refused to believe that parliamentary activity could be a means toward socialism. Liebknecht was now prepared to abandon that opinion.

To illustrate his argument, Liebknecht described the revolution that had changed a "petty-bourgeois society" into a "bourgeois society." That revolution, he said, had occurred gradually, without anyone's being able to specify the exact time of the change. "Well, that was an economic revolution. And the transition from this bourgeois society to the socialist society will be realized just as organically, just as gradually, and just as irresistibly." [65]

Combining this interpretation of revolution with his view that Social Democracy had emerged from a sect into a party, Liebknecht could

[63] At a public meeting in Amsterdam, shortly after The Hague Congress of the First International (September 2–7, 1872), Marx declared, "We know that special regard must be paid to the institutions, customs, and traditions of various lands; and we do not deny that there are certain countries, such as the United States and England, in which the workers may hope to secure their ends by peaceful means." Quoted in G. M. Stekloff, *History of the First International* (New York, 1928), p. 240.

[64] Wilhelm Liebknecht, *Zu Trutz und Schutz* (5th ed.; Hottingen-Zurich, 1883), p. 18. This speech was first given on Oct. 22, 1871.

[65] Vetter Niemand [pseudonym for Wilhelm Liebknecht], *Umsturz und Parlamentarismus. Den Umstuerzlern und Parlamentarien gewidmet*, in Vetter Niemand, *Trutz-Eisenstirn*, Part 3 (London, 1890), p. 33. The preface is signed, "Summer, 1887."

easily embrace parliamentarism as a completely appropriate means toward socialism. True, he was not prepared to say that parliamentary reformism offered the only road to socialism. He posed the question: "Are the revolutionary goals of Social Democracy to be reached by the road of reform?" No absolute answer could be given, he said, but it was entirely conceivable that these goals could be reached through parliamentary reforms. "We can well imagine," he continued, "that in a country which has universal suffrage and in which the material development and the mental framework present no obstacles, the implementation of the social revolution will be accomplished by the path of reform." [66] Later he became more explicit: "The revolutionary demands—as we have already proved—can be achieved by way of reform." [67] With that, Liebknecht believed that he had satisfactorily demonstrated a harmony between revolutionary goals and parliamentary means.

What significance did Liebknecht's reorientation have? His change was not simply an isolated personal development, nor was it merely another voice added to the moderate chorus in praise of parliamentarism. It reflected the thinking of those who were aware that the party had reached a level where qualitative changes could take place. In his role as conciliator, Liebknecht sensed all of these changes and announced his willingness to follow some of the implications. In his role as a radical, he was telling the other radicals how they could overcome their ambivalent parliamentarism. And it was significant that none other than Liebknecht was willing to recognize these changes and take up the work of parliamentary reform to reach socialism. If the most vigorous opponent of parliamentarism could now embrace it, what was to keep the others from following suit?

The Persistence of Ambivalent Parliamentarism and its Meaning

The nature of Liebknecht's shift is ironic in that he made it at precisely the same time that the radicals were gaining control over the party after the crisis of 1885. Furthermore, he presented his new view at a time when the government returned to a policy of severe repression and the Social Democrats lost seats in the Reichstag election of February 1887. These new developments completely destroyed the

[66] *Ibid.*, p. 28.
[67] *Ibid.*, p. 30.

parliamentary possibilities which had existed immediately after 1884 for the Social Democrats. Thus, Liebknecht's pamphlets did not make the impression they might have made had they appeared early in 1885, when most surely, they would have given the moderates a theoretical defense for their position.

Liebknecht's pamphlets came a bit too late to have that impact. Instead, the radicals, as will be seen in the subsequent chapters, had gained control, and Bebel had the upper hand in defining party policy. As a consequence, it was not Liebknecht's new view that predominated, but the same ambivalent parliamentarism which Bebel had represented from the early years of the Socialist Law. Not until the Socialist Law fell in 1890, did Liebknecht's view once again gain ground. Nonetheless, Liebknecht's rethinking of the party's role and its policies offers a clear indication that the middle eighties had marked a truly important qualitative change in its development.

The persistence of ambivalent parliamentarism meant, however, that the Social Democrats could not unify their theory and their practice. Although the experience from late 1884 through early 1886 had increased the willingness of many Social Democrats to accept parliamentarism as both a means and a goal of the party, this was not true of August Bebel. In the following years, Bebel gained more and more control in the party, and as he did so, ambivalent parliamentarism characterized its approach. At the same time, the return of the authorities to a harsher implementation of the Socialist Law destroyed the parliamentary possibilities that the party had enjoyed in the middle eighties.

CHAPTER IX · SOCIAL DEMOCRATS AT BAY

A NEW WAVE of oppressive practices directed against the labor movement by the German authorities obstructed the enlarging parliamentary activity of the Social Democrats in 1886. Once again, as in the early years of the Socialist Law, the party had to concentrate on the fight for survival. Parliamentary activity remained essential, but less in the hope of influencing legislation than in the need to sustain the party's life. It was a serious struggle, for the Iron Chancellor wanted desperately to achieve the goal of the Socialist Law—the destruction of Social Democracy as a political force.

The German government's turn to a more severe oppression in 1886 was in part a response to labor's new restlessness. A slight economic upswing in the European economy during the preceding year created the conditions for an enlivened labor movement. In Germany that brought increased trade union activity and new efforts to organize the workers. Strikes and demonstrations increased.[1]

Not just in Germany, but throughout Europe the change was apparent at the beginning of 1886. For the British labor movement that was a decisive year. Gigantic rallies, such as the one in London's Trafalgar Square on "Mad Monday" (February 8, 1886), alerted the authorities in Germany to the international aspects of the new surge of labor activity. Belgium, too, gave evidence of a militant labor movement. The faction-ridden Belgian labor movement suddenly achieved unity in 1885 and formed the Belgian Labor party. Intense labor unrest hit Belgium, as strikes and riots spread throughout the country in March 1886. The German government watched all of these outbursts with exceptional interest and concern.[2]

[1] The increase in the number of strikes was watched closely by the police. Cf. Fricke, *Bismarcks Praetorianer*, pp. 195ff.

[2] G. D. H. Cole, *A History of Socialist Thought*. Vol. II: *Marxism and Anarchism* (London, 1954), pp. 406–08; "Der Aufstand in Belgien," *SD*, No. 14, April 1, 1886. Beginning with the Trafalgar Square rally on February 8, the German Embassy in London made special reports to the Foreign Ministry on the labor movement in England. In his report on the rally, the German Ambassador, Paul von Hatzfeldt, noted especially that such incidents had not taken place in London

Police Spies and the Renewal of the Socialist Law

The government indicated an intention to shift toward a severe repression of the Social Democrats during the debates on the Socialist Law (February–April 1886). The activities of the Social Democrats in the preceding years hardly warranted severe measures. The government even admitted that the Social Democrats had demonstrated a real interest in a peaceful legislative solution of social problems. Nevertheless, in 1886 Bismarck demanded the renewal of the Socialist Law for a five-year period on the ground that it was needed to hold revolutionary tendencies in check.[3] In particular, the Prussian government insisted that significant anarchist influence still penetrated the socialist movement. The evidence for this claim was meager, namely, the fact that a few anarchist papers circulated in small numbers in the larger cities.[4]

The debate on the Socialist Law began on February 18. On the same day, and before the government could develop its case, the Social Democrats used their weapons skillfully to undermine the confidence of the Reichstag in the Socialist Law and its execution. In a sensational speech, Paul Singer presented evidence to prove that the Berlin Police, who were subordinate to the Prussian Interior Ministry, had employed a man by the name of Ihring, alias Mahlow, to infiltrate a Berlin Social Democratic group as an agent provocateur. Ihring-Mahlow, Singer disclosed, was no ordinary spy. He had drawn together a small group of Social Democrats, intending to give them lessons in the use of dynamite. His extremism soon aroused suspicion; the socialists investigated and discovered his true identity.[5]

for many years. Hatzfeldt to the Foreign Ministry, Feb. 9, 1886, No. 38, in Germany, Foreign Ministry Archives, *Europa Generalia*, No. 82. University of California Microfilms, Series I, Reel 209, frames 389–91. Hereafter these archives will be cited as Germany, FM Archives, UC, I or II [for Series], R. [Reel] and frm. [frame]. There are also sources from the University of Michigan Microfilms which will be cited as Germany, FM Archives, UM, etc. All of the documents related to the Social Democrats are under the Foreign Ministry Archival division *Europa Generalia*, No. 82.

[3] The government's reasons for a renewal of the Socialist Law are in *SB*, VI, ii (1885/86), vol. V, *Anlagen*, No. 143, pp. 664–65.

[4] *Ibid.*, vol. IV, *Anlagen*, No. 17, pp. 76–80.

[5] *Ibid.*, vol. II, pp. 1120–21. Throughout the period of the Socialist Law, untrustworthy followers were exposed. In Zurich, Julius Motteler regularly received reports on persons who were suspected as spies or who were for other reasons

Faced with this evidence, Puttkamer, the Prussian Interior Minister, indignantly denied that his subordinates would have employed an agent provocateur. The next day, however, Puttkamer returned to admit that, in fact, Ihring-Mahlow was employed by the Berlin Police. But Ihring-Mahlow, Puttkamer asserted, was a fine reliable fellow, who only observed the activities of the Social Democrats from within and did not promote provocative deeds. Then Puttkamer turned his wrath on the Social Democrats, demanding that Paul Singer make known the names of those who were witnesses against Ihring-Mahlow. Singer knew that Puttkamer would bring charges against his socialist comrades, but he could not withhold all names without weakening his accusations against the Berlin Police. He therefore gave the names of the two leading witnesses, Franz Berndt, a cabinet maker, and Jens Christensen, a writer and tutor.[6]

With the exposure of Ihring-Mahlow, the Social Democrats struck a sharp, but not decisive blow against the renewal of the Socialist Law. Most of the deputies in the *Freisinnige* and Center parties opposed the law, but they were also aware that they could not muster a majority to repeal it. With this situation, Windthorst prompted the Center party to propose a compromise version of the Socialist Law which would eliminate its harshest aspects, especially the extraordinary power of the police authorized by the Minor State of Siege.[7]

Negotiations on the compromise involved the Social Democrats directly. Bebel covered the whole subject in a letter to Julius Motteler on March 13. He reported that the *Freisinnige* party had indicated its willingness to vote for Windthorst's compromise if the Social Democrats sanctioned it. With the assistance of the *Freisinnige* party, Windthorst had a possibility of getting a majority for his compromise. Then Bismarck would either have to accept the compromise version or dissolve the Reichstag.[8]

The attitude of the Social Democrats was crucial, but they were di-

untrustworthy. After investigation the comrades were warned through the *Sozialdemokrat*. On this "Security System" (*Sicherheitsdienst*), see Engelberg, *Revolutionaere Politik*, pp. 205–13.

[6] *SB*, VI, ii (1885/86), vol. II, p. 1123, 1142–43, 1165. On the testimony of Ihring-Mahlow, Berndt and Christensen were tried and sentenced to six months in prison for perjury. A higher court, however, reversed the decision on the grounds that Ihring-Mahlow's testimony was unreliable. Bernstein, *Berliner Arbeiterbewegung*, II, pp. 174–77; Eugen Ernst, *Polizeispitzeleien und Ausnahmegesetze, 1878–1910* (Berlin, 1911), pp. 61–64.

[7] Schulthess, *1886*, p. 81.

[8] Bebel to Motteler, March 13, 1886, Bebel Archive, IISH.

vided; several wished to give Windthorst their approval. According to Bebel: "Auer, who feels exceptionally well at backstage manuevers [*Coulissenschieben*] and scoffs at us as Philistines who judge matters from a limited horizon, defended the [Windthorst] plan with enthusiasm. . . ." [9] Auer, whom Bebel accused of a desire to play the role of a "diplomat," had the support of Grillenberger, Hasenclever, and Kayser. But Bebel completely opposed the compromise plan, even avoiding Windthorst so that he would not have to discuss the issue. Windthorst attempted to speak seriously with him on March 12, but Bebel would only exchange a few pleasantries. "From the short exchange of words," Bebel commented, "I noticed that W[indthorst] was in an exceptionally depressed mood; also, he has aged noticeably in recent times." [10] Bebel had no intention to cheer up Windthorst, because he did not believe that the Social Democrats would gain an advantage from the compromise version of the Socialist Law. Singer and Liebknecht agreed with Bebel. All of the Social Democratic deputies realized that on this issue they had to be united. Therefore, Auer, who never could overcome Bebel's opposition, dropped his plan.[11]

Windthorst's compromise failed, and the Socialist Law was renewed on April 2 for another two years (to September 30, 1888) by a vote of 173 to 146.[12]

The Suppression Increases: Puttkamer's Decrees

Once the Reichstag had renewed the Socialist Law, the German authorities increased the restrictions on the Social Democrats and the trade unions. Puttkamer commanded the new campaign against the labor movement.

Puttkamer's first target was labor's use of strikes for higher wages. Although the strike movement in Germany lacked the enormous vitality of its counterparts in England, the United States, and Belgium, a series of local strikes began in 1884. The revived trade unions faced a new situation in Germany. The Sickness and Accident Insurance pro-

[9] *Ibid.*
[10] *Ibid.*
[11] *Ibid.*
[12] The Reichstag committee which reviewed the Socialist Law had voted against its renewal. In the final voting in the plenary session, the whole of the *Freisinnige* party voted against it, but 27 of the 99 Center deputies under Hertling's leadership still supported the Socialist Law. *SB*, VI, ii (1885/86), vol. III, pp. 1850–51.

grams of the Reich government had largely preempted the function of the trade unions as insurance agencies for the workers. The trade unions still needed to set goals for the workers, and so, much more attention was turned to wages. Against this movement Puttkamer prepared to act.[13]

On April 11, just nine days after the renewal of the Socialist Law, Puttkamer issued a special Strike Decree. The decree expressed Puttkamer's conviction that the Social Democrats were directly responsible for the outbreak of strikes. It authorized the police to use the measures of the Socialist Law to prohibit strikes when "tendencies serving upheaval" were evident. The police were to be alert to Social Democratic influence in the wage movement, especially among the railroad workers. The most dangerous strike leaders were to be expelled from those areas where the Minor State of Siege was in force.[14] Puttkamer advanced the decree on the assumption that the strikes derived inspiration from, and served the purposes of the political goals of Social Democracy.

In actual fact, only an indirect link connected the strike movement and the goals of the Social Democrats. While the party fully endorsed the trade union movement, it publicly discouraged the use of strikes.[15] At the time of a large strike of masons in Berlin in the summer of 1885, the *Berliner Volksblatt* observed that strikes were valuable only as schools where the workers could learn the need for organization and unity.[16] The same paper warned that striking workers had no political interests. It noted that in England and the United States, where strikes were common, the working class had not organized politically. Therefore, it concluded, "socialism and strikes are things which have no connection." [17] The position of Social Democracy, Hasenclever explained

[13] Adolf Braun, *Die Gewerkschaften vor dem Kriege* (2nd ed.; Berlin, 1921), pp. 37–38. In 1884, weavers in Zeulenrode, glass workers in Dresden, factory workers in Crimmitschau, masons and carpenters in Leipzig, all struck for higher wages. Some 12,000 masons in Berlin struck during the summer of 1885; in March 1885 the workers in a Bielefeld sewing machine factory struck. Gemkow, *Friedrich Engels' Hilfe*, pp. 149–50; Bernstein, *Berliner Arbeiterbewegung*, II, pp. 158–60, 189–90; Schulthess, *1885*, p. 68.

[14] Schulthess, *1886*, p. 92. The railroad workers were to be watched especially because almost all the railroad lines in Prussia were state-owned by 1886. In Bavaria, Saxony, Baden, and Wuerttemberg the railroads were also state-owned.

[15] "Die Sozialdemokratie und die Gewerkschaften," *SD*, No. 42, Oct. 14, 1886.

[16] "Die Arbeitseinstellungen," *Berliner Volksblatt*, No. 192, Aug. 19, 1885.

[17] "Im Zeitalter der Streik," *Berliner Volksblatt*, No. 152, July 3, 1886.

in the Reichstag on May 21, 1886, maintained that strikes were insufficient to improve the social conditions; he looked rather to legislation designed to reduce hours and increase wages.[18]

Despite their spoken reservations on strikes, the Social Democrats were closely affiliated with most of the striking workers. The party fully endorsed the trade unions, and numerous Social Democrats were members of the striking unions. In that sense Puttkamer was correct, although the public policy of the Social Democratic party did not advocate strikes.

Further restrictive measures followed the Strike Decree. On May 11, the Prussian Interior Ministry directed that, for Berlin and vicinity, all meetings at which "public affairs" were to be discussed had to have police permission forty-eight hours in advance of the meeting time.[19] Previously it had been sufficient to get permission for such meetings twenty-four hours in advance. The new regulation rested on the extraordinary powers granted under the Minor State of Siege paragraph of the Socialist Law. Still further restrictions were implemented by an extension of the Minor State of Siege. On May 20, the Minor State of Siege was imposed over Spremberg and vicinity after workers had marched through the streets singing the workers' "Marseillaise" and creating an uproar on May 1. [20]

The Social Democrats could do little to challenge these new restrictions. Their best tactic was to demand that the Reichstag hold a full debate on the measures taken by the Prussian Interior Ministry. In an interpellation, the Social Democrats charged that the Strike Decree of April 11 violated Article 152 of the Industrial Code, which guaranteed workers the right of combination for the improvement of working conditions.[21]

The Reichstag discussed the Social Democratic interpellation concerning Puttkamer's Strike Decree on May 21, 1886. Since the majority of the delegates had little sympathy for the criticisms raised by the Social Democrats, there was scant hope of forcing Puttkamer to modify his repressive measures. Nevertheless, Hasenclever gave a well-reasoned exposition of how the Strike Decree violated the workers'

[18] *SB*, VI, ii (1885/86), vol. III, p. 2100. Hasenclever's explanation was seconded in "Die Interpellation im Reichstage," *Berliner Volksblatt*, No. 119, May 23, 1886.

[19] Schulthess, *1886*, p. 113. The area included Potsdam, Charlottenburg, Teltow, Niederbarnim, and Osthavelland.

[20] The Prussian report on the Spremberg Minor State of Siege is in *SB*, VI, ii (1885/86), vol. VI, *Anlagen*, No. 305, pp. 1629–30.

[21] *Ibid.*, No. 298, p. 1597.

right of combination. From the *Freisinnige* party, Ludwig Bamberger agreed that the Strike Decree would have a detrimental effect in the long run.[22] But Puttkamer showed that he had no patience for all that talk about the worker's right of combination. He made his classic statement about the insidiousness of all labor movements: "Behind every large labor movement, which at the present time calculates by means of force and agitation, namely through work stoppages, to bring about an increase in wages, and which draws many branch trades into the same misery, behind every such labor movement lurks the Hydra of violence and anarchy. (Oho! from the Social Democrats—absolutely correct! on the right)."[23] Despite Puttkamer's disregard for the workers' right of combination, the Reichstag made no recommendations against the Strike Decree.

One month later on the last day of the session, June 26, the Reichstag briefly discussed the imposition of the State of Siege on Spremberg and Puttkamer's decree of May 11, which required that police permission be secured forty-eight hours in advance of a meeting. Although the session was closing, the debate grew more animated with tempers aroused on both sides. The Social Democrats fired salvo after salvo at the Prussian government, and especially at Puttkamer. Their mood was excited, confident, and hostile. "We are armed and go to battle," Paul Singer shouted, "we shall see which is stronger: police paroxysm or German Social Democracy."[24] There was manifestly a new *esprit de corps* among the socialist deputies, created by the severe practices of the government. Singer and Hasenclever led a chorus of Social Democratic catcalls and hisses as the representatives of the government spoke. The most moderate Social Democrats joined in. Karl Frohme spoke eloquently of the party's determination not to go to its knees regardless of how "brutal" the "vengeance" of the government might be.[25] The speeches were powerful, but the results negligible. It was the last day of a Reichstag session. The deputies were leaving Berlin; no one had much time for the complaints of the Social Democrats.

Puttkamer and Bismarck had thus won the first round. During the month of May alone, the police closed down forty-seven meetings which were in progress in Berlin. More Social Democrats were expelled from Berlin. Paul Singer received orders on June 29 to depart

[22] *Ibid.*, vol. III, pp. 2099–2101, 2110–11.
[23] *Ibid.*, p. 2112.
[24] *Ibid.*, p. 2186.
[25] *Ibid.*, pp. 2186–89, 2193.

from Berlin by July 3.[26] The Prussian pattern of severity was imitated by the police in Saxony. But the Social Democrats fought back when possible. In the Reichstag on September 18, 1886, Vollmar and Viereck presented evidence to show that workingmen's meetings in Saxony were dissolved even before the police had any proof of Social Democratic influence. Their contention that the Socialist Law was employed unconstitutionally to restrict the worker's right of combination was staunchly supported by the *Freisinnige* deputy Stauffenberg.[27] The Reichstag, however, made no effort to change the practices of the police.

Social Democratic Leaders Go to Prison

The authorities also carried on their campaign against the Social Democrats in the courts. During the summer of 1886, the Social Democrats lost one of the most significant cases of the period under the Socialist Law.

At the end of July 1886, nine Social Democrats, including the well-known leaders Auer, Bebel, Dietz, Frohme, Ulrich, Viereck, and Vollmar, and two minor persons, Philipp Mueller, a sculptor, and Stephan Heinzel, a master tailor, were tried and convicted by the Saxon State Court (*Landgericht*) at Freiberg for participation in a secret and illegal "association" (*Verbindung*). These were the Social Democrats who had been arrested as they returned to Germany in April 1883 from the party congress in Copenhagen. The official charges were not initiated, however, until September 1884.[28]

The prosecution constructed its case so badly that two trials were necessary in order to get a conviction. The evidence against the Social Democrats was collected entirely from their publications, especially the protocols of the party congresses and the *Sozialdemokrat*. Nothing was added to what was already public knowledge about the activities of the Social Democrats. At the first trial, before the Saxon State Court at Chemnitz on September 28–30, 1885, all of the accused were ac-

[26] Bernstein, *Berliner Arbeiterbewegung*, II, pp. 180–82, 194–96.

[27] *SB*, VI, iii (1886), vol. I, pp. 32–37, 41–42. A full account of the wave of police action against the labor movement in 1886 and following would demand too much detail. For some of the details, see Kampffmeyer, *Unter dem Sozialistengesetz*, pp. 206ff.; Auer, *Nach zehn Jahren, passim;* Fricke, *Bismarcks Praetorianer*, pp. 201ff.

[28] Schulthess, *1884*, p. 92.

quitted. The prosecution then revised the charges and made a successful appeal.[29]

The same Social Democrats were brought to trial again at the end of July 1886 before the Saxon State Court at Freiberg. The key to the revised charges focused on the relationship of the accused to the *Sozialdemokrat*. The circulation of the *Sozialdemokrat* as the official party organ, the prosecution argued, necessitated the existence of an illegal "association." Since the accused Social Democrats had all approved the report on the *Sozialdemokrat* at the Copenhagen congress, they were charged with being responsible for the illegal "association." In addition to this, the Freiberg court interpreted "association" in a much broader sense than the Chemnitz court had. It therefore sentenced Auer, Bebel, Frohme, Ulrich, Viereck, and Vollmar to nine months in prison, Dietz, Heinzel, and Mueller to six months. Immediately the Social Democrats appealed their case to the Imperial Supreme Court (*Reichsgericht*) at Leipzig, but it upheld their convictions.[30]

The conviction of so many needed leaders created serious threats for the Social Democrats. For years, the party had successfully avoided serious convictions by a scrupulous study of the laws in order to stay within the limits of legality. After the Freiberg decision, which would be a precedent for more convictions, the Social Democrats had to alter their legal relationship to the *Sozialdemokrat*. Therefore, acting as the party's executive, the Social Democratic Reichstag delegation dropped the *Sozialdemokrat* as the "official" party organ.[31]

The party members could easily understand the true meaning of the decision: legally they had no connection with the *Sozialdemokrat*; morally, however, it was still their paper. Only the Berliners took the decision literally. They falsely believed that the party's executive had shown cowardice by severing its official connection to the *Sozialdemokrat*. In a public declaration, the Berliners stated their determination to preserve the *Sozialdemokrat* as the "official party organ." They added

[29] For the record of the trial, see *Der Chemnitzer Monstre-Sozialisten-Prozess*, 2 parts (Munich, 1885), in the series published by Louis Viereck, *Sozialpolitische Zeit- und Streitfragen*, Nos. 20, 21.

[30] *Der Freiberger Sozialistenprozess* (Munich, 1886), *passim; Der Chemnitz-Freiberger Sozialisten-Prozess vor dem Reichsgericht* (Munich, 1886), pp. 5, 12–13, 31–35. Both of these pamphlets in *Sozialpolitische Zeit- und Streitfragen*, Nos. 32 and 35. For a more detailed secondary account of the trials, see Hellfaier, *Die deutsche Sozialdemokratie*, pp. 201–04.

[31] "Erklaerung," *SD*, No. 43, Oct. 21, 1886.

to this a severe criticism of the party's Reichstag deputies for over-energetic parliamentary activity. The Berliners were convinced that the disavowal was the work of the moderate parliamentarians who frequently had clashed with the editor and staff of the *Sozialdemokrat*.[32]

The impulsive action of the Berliners aroused the anger and suspicion of many of the Social Democratic Reichstag deputies. The Berliners' intransigence threatened to undermine the legal effectiveness of the decision to sever the official connection with the *Sozialdemokrat*. The Berliners, it seemed to some, were playing into the hands of the police. So Carl Grillenberger, the Nuremberger, expressed his anger in a letter to Bebel on November 13: "You did not believe me the other day when I wrote you about what was to be expected from the Berlin Gentlemen. Oh, I know with whom I am dealing [*Ich kenne meine Pappenheimer*]! First of all these fellows have *not the slightest* understanding of our situation, and also [they have] the least [understanding] of *that*, that was *in reality contained* in our declaration." [33] To Grillenberger, it seemed certain that the Berliners were acting in the interests of the police. He concluded with a warning to Bebel that "the whole Berlin C[entral] C[ommittee] consists of *unadulterated Ihrings*." [34] Grillenberger also criticized Bernstein sharply for having published the inappropriate declaration of the Berliners. From Bebel's marginal comments it is possible to see that he agreed with much that Grillenberger said. Wanting no more fuss from the Berliners, Bebel advised Bernstein to keep such declarations unprinted in the future.[35] This seems to have taken care of the matter. No more outcries were heard from the Berliners on the party's new relationship to the *Sozialdemokrat*.

The Freiberg court had prescribed that the convicted Social Democrats were to serve their sentences in the Saxon State Prison at Zwickau, beginning late in 1886. This prison at Zwickau was well-known to Bebel; he had lived there for nine months during 1874–1875. As a veteran prison resident, Bebel accepted his sentence with equanimity. He even wrote optimistically of the beneficial consequences of the Freiberg trial: "Some of our moderates have been brought to the

[32] "Sprechsaal," *SD*, No. 46, Nov. 12, 1886.

[33] Carl Grillenberger to Bebel, Nov. 13, 1886, Bebel Archive, IISH.

[34] *Ibid.*

[35] *Ibid.* Bebel sent Grillenberger's letter on to Hermann Schlueter, a staff member of the *Sozialdemokrat*. Schlueter, therefore, was to communicate Bebel's marginal comments to the other staff members.

desired mood through the sentences: thus Auer and Grillenberger, who are not beyond improvement [*an denen noch nicht Hopfen und Malz verloren ist*]."[36] The trial, therefore, offered proof of what Bebel had always told the moderates—that it was an illusion to believe that Social Democrats could cooperate with the existing German government. Imprisonment could do much to bring the moderates to a more militant posture, or it would winnow out the weak and faltering.

One can see considerable irony in the situation at Zwickau: Viereck and Bebel, the two most antagonistic intraparty foes, were to share imprisonment! There was Viereck, who had written with so much generosity about Bismarck's social reforms, sitting in a cell not far from Bebel, who never hid his hatred of all things connected with the Chancellor. Was there a chance that their common fate would obliterate old differences? It was hardly possible. It merely amused Bebel to think about Viereck in prison: "The thought of how this nervous, over-excitable, completely spoiled man will take the situation has something unusually comical for me."[37] Even in prison Bebel and Viereck found no basis for a friendly reconciliation.

The conditions at Zwickau were not entirely unbearable. Bebel encouraged his wife Julie by minimizing the hardships of prison life with the comment that "a journey to the German-African colonies, even if half so long, would be more unpleasant and infinitely more dangerous."[38] There was truth in that. Each week the prisoners could write one letter. Bebel always wrote to his wife, including messages which his daughter "Friedchen" would then relay to the other Social Democrats. Auer, Bebel, and Ulrich could stroll together for two hours each day. Since each subscribed to a different newspaper, they exchanged news and commentary as they walked around the prison yard.[39] In an old Social Democratic tradition, they passed the time in confinement by studying more intensely the doctrines which had led to their convictions.

The Freiberg trial marked a significant turn in the fate of the Social Democrats. It had a profound affect on the internal development of the

[36] Bebel to Engels, Sept. 7, 1886, in Bebel, *Briefwechsel*, p. 282.

[37] August Bebel to Julie Bebel, Aug. 26, 1886, reprinted in Heinrich Gemkow, "Briefe August Bebels aus den Jahren 1886/87," *Beitraege zur Geschichte der deutschen Arbeiterbewegung*, II (1960), p. 141.

[38] August Bebel to Julie Bebel, Aug. 4, 1886, in *ibid.*, pp. 140–41.

[39] August Bebel to Julie Bebel, Dec. 15, 1886, in *ibid.*, p. 144. Ulrich, *Erinnerungen*, p. 80. The correspondence between Bebel and Engels is broken completely for the period of imprisonment, November 14, 1886—August 14, 1887.

party. Combined with the other oppressive practices, the Freiberg trial destroyed much of the basis for the moderate socialist parliamentarians. Little hope remained for moderates such as Frohme and Viereck to cooperate with the government on social reforms while they sat in prison. Consequently, the more intransigent posture of the radicals suited the situation better when the party needed unity in the face of oppression.

For the relationship of the Social Democrats to German public opinion, the Freiberg trial had a slightly beneficial effect. The trial caught public interest. The fact that several well-known moderate "non-revolutionary" Social Democrats were sentenced created a widespread impression that many socialists were the victims of a cruel persecution. Because of the tenuous nature of the charges against them, the Social Democrats won appreciable sympathy among German liberals, whose sense of justice was violated by the results of the Freiberg trial. Such sympathy offered no immediate practical benefits to the Social Democrats, but it added to the accumulated feeling that Bismarck had taken the wrong course to solve the social problems of Germany.[40]

The greatest disadvantage for the Social Democrats was that the Freiberg trial set a precedent for a wave of legal proceedings against the party members. Never before had the party been subjected to such intense harassment in the courts. Between 1878 and 1886, there were a total of twenty-four trials in which Social Democrats had been charged with violating the Socialist Law, the Imperial Penal Code, or local state laws of association. Only eight of these twenty-four cases had ended with convictions. But from August 1886 to January 1889, there were fifty-five such trials. In thirty-three of these trials a total of 236 persons were given prison sentences; in ten cases the charges were dismissed, and eight ended with acquittals.[41]

In the cases after 1886, the prosecutors usually charged that socialists and workers had formed illegal associations on the local level. A number of such cases were initiated against the Social Democrats during

[40] The Social Democrats made practical use of the unfavorable reactions to the results of the Freiberg trial. Bebel edited an extensive collection of such opinions from liberal papers such as the *Berliner Boersen-Courier*, the *Berliner Zeitung*, the *Nationalzeitung* (the leading National Liberal paper), the *Berliner Tageblatt* (a leading *Freisinnige* paper), the *Frankfurter Zeitung* and many others. See Bebel (unlisted ed.), *Pressstimmen ueber das am 4. August 1886 vom Landgericht zu Freiberg gefaellte Urtheil wider die Angeklagten Auer, Bebel, Dietz, Frohme, Heinzel, Mueller, Ulrich, Viereck u. Vollmar* (Nuremberg, no date, but 1886 or 1887).

[41] Mehring, *Geschichte der deutschen Sozialdemokratie*, IV, p. 286.

and following the election campaign of February 1887. In Magdeburg, the socialist Reichstag deputy August Heine and thirty-five of his comrades were accused of forming a secret society. At the trial, on May 12–13, twenty-four of the accused were sentenced to a total of eleven years and four months in prison. At another large trial in Breslau during November 1887, twenty-nine out of thirty-seven accused persons each received from four weeks to one year in prison. Among those convicted was the Social Democratic Reichstag deputy Julius Kraecker, who had been arrested as he left the Reichstag building on June 18, 1887, held in custody for five months, and then sentenced to seven months in prison.[42]

Other cases were tried throughout Germany. The Social Democrats became seasoned courtroom defendants showing wit and great skill in handling the charges raised against them.[43]

The largest and most spectacular trial ran for almost six weeks beginning on November 18, 1889, before the Prussian State Court at Elberfeld. Ninety Social Democrats, including the Reichstag deputies Bebel, Grillenberger, Harm, and Schumacher, were charged with having participated in a national party organization which was a direct extension of the structure formed in 1875 at Gotha. According to the charges, that organization intended to bring about the "overthrow of the monarchy" and the "complete destruction of the present system of production and the society based thereupon." [44]

The Elberfeld trial proved to be the last gigantic effort of the Prussian prosecutors. From the beginning, Bebel believed that it would be a "fiasco" for the prosecution. He had reasons for optimism, as he told Engels that "the president of the court declared, privately to be sure,

[42] Auer, *Nach zehn Jahren*, pp. 259–60; *SB*, VII, ii (1887/88), vol. I, pp. 8–9; Schulthess, *1887*, pp. 179–80; *Berliner Volkstribuene*, No. 40, Oct. 6, 1888, p. 1.

[43] Grillenberger was being tried before the Bavarian State Court in Nuremberg in November 1887 for sending forbidden material through the mails. *SB*, VII, ii (1887/88), vol. I, pp. 8–9. In July 1887, the Berlin Central Committee was arrested. At their first trial on November 12, 1887, they were acquitted, but at a second, in March 1888, they were convicted. Bernstein, *Berliner Arbeiterbewegung*, II, pp. 224–26. A trial of Polish socialists, in Posnan, on April 16, 1887, sentenced eight out of twenty-two accused from two weeks to two years in prison. Schulthess, *1887*, p. 111. More Polish socialists were sentenced in January 1888. Schulthess, *1888*, p. 19. On the trial of twelve Munich socialists, see Auer to Hermann Schlueter, Oct. 14, 1888, *Kleine Korrespondenz*, IISH; and the socialist pamphlet, *Der erste Nichtgentleman auf dem Zeugenstande. Bericht ueber den Muenchener Geheimbunds-Prozess, am 26. und 27. Oktober 1888, vor dem Landgerichte Muenchen I* (Munich, n.d., [1888?]).

[44] *Berliner Volksblatt*, No. 272, Nov. 20, 1889, *Beilage*, I, p. 3.

[that he] wanted to meet us halfway in every way. . . ."[45] But the trial was not a complete fiasco for the prosecution. Although it failed to prove that a national illegal organization existed, it did gain forty-three convictions of persons involved in an organization in the Elberfeld area.[46] Pleased that the Social Democrats won on the main issue, Bebel observed that the court had been "very proper" in its judgment of individuals. In all of his experience, Bebel had never participated in a "more exciting proceeding" than the trial at Elberfeld.[47]

The trials cost the Social Democratic party dearly in time, energy, and money. A full chronicle of these legal prosecutions of the Social Democrats will probably never be written. Trials were so frequent that they almost lost their significance. And there were not only trials, but the Social Democrats had constantly to be alert for the infiltration of the police. The number of police spies exposed by the Social Democrats increased noticeably after the Ihring-Mahlow affair in 1886.[48]

In such an atmosphere, how did the Social Democrats react? They demonstrated as before that under pressure they would not collapse. Nor would they turn to extremes, to the use of violence and conspiratorial methods. There was no panic or great despair. Insofar as it was necessary for the preservation of the party, they continued illegal practices, but they always preferred the path of legality. In a manner which is almost unbelievable for its steadiness, those Social Democratic leaders who had eluded prison cells calmly carried on an active parliamentary policy. As before, that policy combined hostile criticism of Bismarck's regime with some positive legislative ideas for the reform of German society.

The Election of 1887 and its Consequences

Only a few of the twenty-four Social Democratic deputies were able to make their way toward Berlin for the opening of the Reichstag session on November 25, 1886. Imprisonment, arrests, minor judicial

[45] Bebel to Engels, Oct. 17, 1889, in Bebel, *Briefwechsel*, p. 368.

[46] For the leading figures the prosecution demanded the following prison sentences: fifteen months for Bebel, twelve months for Grillenberger and Harm, six months for Schumacher. Harm was the only one sentenced; he got six months because of his role in the local organization. *Berliner Volksblatt*, No. 299, Dec. 21, 1889, *Beilage*, p. 3, and No. 2, Jan. 3, 1890, pp. 3-4.

[47] Bebel to Engels, Jan. 2, 1890, in Bebel, *Briefwechsel*, p. 373.

[48] Cf. Fricke, *Bismarcks Praetorianer*, pp. 230ff., 263-71; Auer, *Nach zehn Jahren*, pp. 172-92; Ernst, *Polizeispitzeleien*, pp. 61-93. Bismarck authorized that 30,000 marks be used for the employment of agents to infiltrate the Social Democrats on June 6, 1887. The same authorization was given again on July 7, 1889. Lipinski, *Die Sozialdemokratie*, II, p. 100.

cases, and financial problems reduced the active delegation to about sixteen members. During the first part of the session, Liebknecht was in the United States with Edward and Eleanor Aveling collecting a sum of about 16,000 marks for the party's election fund.[49] Despite the hardships, the Social Democrats, under the leadership of Blos, Hasenclever, Grillenberger, and Kayser, were still on hand in the fall of 1886 with criticism and positive legislative plans.

This session saw the great clash between Bismarck and the Reichstag over the Chancellor's demand for an increased army quota for a period of seven years, the bill known as the *Septennat*. A crucial constitutional issue was contained in Bismarck's package, that is, the Reichstag's struggle for control over the finances of the Reich. In the larger picture, therefore, the *Septennat* only highlighted the Chancellor's long and bitter campaign against parliamentarism in Germany.[50]

The Social Democrats did not hesitate to support the cause of parliamentarism, by promoting the authority of the Reichstag. The issues, however, were entangled. To counter Bismarck's seven-year military bill, the *Freisinnige* party introduced a three-year plan, which in all other respects exactly paralleled the Chancellor's. The Social Democrats convinced themselves that at the moment they had an obligation to join Bismarck's opponents. Therefore, they endorsed the *Freisinnige* three-year military budget. On January 12, 1887, just two days before Bismarck dissolved the Reichstag, Hasenclever confessed that the Social Democrats could discover no essential difference between a three-year and a seven-year military budget. Nevertheless, he said, his party would support the three-year budget.[51] But this created a serious dilemma for the Social Democrats. They could not support the three-year budget, which made no changes in Germany's military system,

[49] When Puttkamer learned of Liebknecht's trip in the United States, he got Bismarck to direct the German Embassy in Washington, D.C. to employ an agent to follow Liebknecht. Puttkamer was especially interested in obtaining evidence that Liebknecht was making friendly contact with the anarchists. The agent sent two reports, but could provide no proof of an anarchist connection. The pertinent documents are in Germany, FM Archives, UM, R. 104: Puttkamer to Bismarck, Oct. 5, 1886 (frms. 744–45); Rantzau to Puttkamer, Oct. 8, 1886 (frm. 748); two reports from the unnamed agent with a covering letter by the German Ambassador in Washington, Zedtwitz to FM, Nov. 4, 1886 (frms. 755–59). What is most amusing is that the reports on Liebknecht's trip which were written up in the *Sozialdemokrat* before the agent's reports came in were far more complete. Cf. "Die Agitation unserer Genossen in Amerika," *SD*, No. 41, Oct. 7, 1886; "Sozialpolitische Rundschau," *SD*, No. 42, Oct. 14, 1886.

[50] Ziekursch, *Politische Geschichte*, II, pp. 391–92; Ludwig Bergstraesser, *Die Entwicklung des Parlamentarismus in Deutschland* (Laupheim in Wuerttemberg, 1954), pp. 13–14.

[51] *SB*, VI, IV (1886/87), vol. I, p. 366. In the committee meetings on the *Septennat*

without violating their traditional principled rejection of the standing army. At the very beginning of the *Septennat* debate, Grillenberger had clearly stated the socialist demand for a National Guard with one-year service to replace the existing system.[52] But now their tactical parliamentary alliance with the *Freisinnige* threatened to nullify the meaning of the larger principle.

There is no evidence what discussions actually took place within the Social Democratic delegation between January 12 and 14. There must have been a serious debate on the party's position, for the policy of the party was altered. On January 14, just before the Reichstag voted on the three-year budget plan, Paul Singer announced that the Social Democrats would take no part in the balloting. But he made no further explanation.[53] At the last minute the tactical defense of parliamentarism had to be subordinated to the preservation of the party's principles on militarism. The Social Democrats stood aloof from the balloting as a majority of the Reichstag rejected the *Septennat*.

Although the debate on the *Septennat* overshadowed everything else in the session, the Social Democrats introduced five measures, two of which reached the floor for short discussions. Their most important bill was designed to clarify and enlarge the meaning of two parts of the Imperial Industrial Code: Article 152, which insured the workers' right of association; and Article 153, which prohibited boycotts and gave strike-breakers the protection of the law.[54] The German labor movement had learned from experience that the police most often infringed on the right of association by using the local state laws on association to obstruct trade union activities. The Social Democrats intended, therefore, to insure that the more liberal Imperial Industrial Code would take complete precedence over the state laws. Although this measure was sent to a committee, it died like the other Social Democratic bills when Bismarck dissolved the Reichstag as soon as the *Septennat* was defeated on January 14, 1887.[55] Elections were set for February 21.

The Social Democrats demonstrated two things in the short session

the Social Democratic member voted for the three-year budget. Cf. Adalbert Wahl, *Deutsche Geschichte* (Stuttgart, 1929), II, p. 351.

[52] *SB*, VI, iv (1886/87), vol. I, pp. 98–99.

[53] *Ibid.*, p. 428.

[54] *Ibid.*, vol. II, *Anlagen*, No. 22, p. 221.

[55] Cf. Kayser's speech on Dec. 15, 1886, *ibid.*, vol. I, p. 199. The state Association Laws originated for the most part in the 1850's; for a discussion on how they affected the labor movement, see Schmoele, *Gewerkschaften*, I, pp. 131–34.

which ended so abruptly on January 14. First, that even under the most adverse circumstances of oppression they were not discouraged from pursuing a positive legislative policy.[56] Second, that they were inclined to make tactical alliances with radical liberals in the interest of defending and expanding the powers of the German Reichstag. The same conditions prevailed in the election which followed, and the Social Democrats had to plot a campaign for the defense of German parliamentarism while simultaneously fending off the blows of the police from all sides.

Sitting in his Zwickau prison cell, Bebel reflected on the meaning of Bismarck's *Septennat* bill and the dissolution of the Reichstag. The defeat of the *Septennat,* he concluded, had been only a pretext for sending the deputies home, because Bismarck could as easily get the military bill renewed in three as in seven years. The real intention of the Chancellor, Bebel reasoned, was to get a new Reichstag majority which would approve new tax projects, a revision of the constitution, lengthened legislative periods, and added restrictions in the Socialist Law and the Penal Code. Should Bismarck get his majority, Bebel believed that there would be such a mass of "insidious and embittered measures" against the socialists that the consequences would be "totally incalculable." [57] It followed from Bebel's analysis that the Social Democrats had to hope, and even to work for the victory at the polls of any party which would not entirely subordinate itself to Bismarck.

The Social Democratic campaign corresponded closely with Bebel's thinking, and one may assume that the candidates followed his advice. The party's campaign literature emphasized first its political opposition to Bismarck and second its obligation to rally support for a strengthened Reichstag. "We Social Democrats," the socialist Reichstag deputies wrote on January 14, "are no followers of the parliamentary government system, which currently can only correspond to the views and interests of the bourgeoisie; but since we strive for popular sovereignty, we must demand the utmost competence for the representatives of the people." [58] With words of fire, the *Sozialdemokrat* appealed to

[56] The following bills, found in *SB,* VI, iv (1886/87), vol. II, *Anlagen,* were also drafted by the Social Democrats: to strike from the budget all funds for the maintenance of colonial officials (No. 45, p. 304); to alter the Industrial Code on hours and working conditions (No. 26, p. 232); to strengthen the immunity of Reichstag deputies (No. 23, p. 221); and to demand a liberalization of the regulations on civil cases (No. 30, p. 246).

[57] August Bebel to Julie Bebel, Jan. 17 [1887], in Gemkow, "Briefe August Bebels aus den Jahren 1886/1887," p. 147.

[58] "An das deutsche Volk," *SD,* No. 5, Jan. 29, 1887.

the German workers to enter the battle in defense of universal suffrage against the treacherous attacks of Bismarck. The circumstances thus demanded that the Social Democrats concentrate more on the protest vote, and less upon the presentation of their own program, which had been possible in 1884.[59]

A slightly different tone is noted in the campaign in Berlin. There, the Social Democratic literature thundered at Bismarck, but did not worry too much about the rights of the Reichstag. In Berlin, the Social Democrats had to contend chiefly with the *Freisinnige* party, the principal defender of parliamentarism in Germany. In that context, therefore, the Berlin Social Democrats tried to keep their appeal distinct from that of the *Freisinnige* party, although both were chiefly interested in the fight against Bismarck.[60]

The Social Democrats were probably at a greater disadvantage in the 1887 campaign than in any other under the Socialist Law. Their ranks were depleted; the nine leaders sentenced at Freiberg could take no part in the campaign. Other obstructions stood in their path. The Minor State of Siege was imposed on Frankfurt am Main and vicinity on December 16, 1886, and on Stettin and the surrounding towns of Grabow and Altdamm on February 15. A great number of expulsions followed in both places. Everywhere the police seemed to be more diligent than before. Even when the police did not close meetings, the owners of inns and beerhalls were often afraid to let Social Democrats use their facilities. In Chemnitz, the Social Democrats could not use their usual meeting places. In Berlin, there were Social Democratic candidates in all six of the city's districts, but only one was permitted to campaign. The others, including Paul Singer, had all been expelled. These are but a few examples of the pressures under which the Social Democrats fought the campaign.[61]

The issue of the election, as defined by Bismarck, also put the Social Democrats at a disadvantage. When the Chancellor dissolved the Reichstag and called for new elections, he maintained that his military bill was absolutely necessary for the security of Germany because of

[59] "Zum 21. Februar!" *SD*, No. 5, Jan. 29, 1887; cf. also "Das allgemeine Wahlrecht und die Arbeiterklasse," *SD*, No. 6, Feb. 4, 1887; "Was die sozialdemokratische Stimmzettel bedeutet," *SD*, No. 7, Feb. 11, 1887.

[60] Five of the Berlin campaign leaflets are reprinted in Bernstein, *Berliner Arbeiterbewegung*, II, pp. 191–93, 195, 199–200, 202–03.

[61] "Sozialpolitische Rundschau," *SD*, No. 1, Jan. 1, 1887; Lipinski, *Die Sozialdemokratie*, II, p. 108; Heilmann, *Arbeiterbewegung in Chemnitz*, p. 204; Blos, *Denkwuerdigkeiten*, II, pp. 151–52; Bernstein, *Berliner Arbeiterbewegung*, II, pp. 207–10.

the danger from the *revanche* sentiment in France. The Social Democrats held views diametrically opposed to Bismarck's. They minimized the danger from France, but stressed their long-standing enmity for Tsarist Russia. To Bismarck, such sympathy for France was tantamount to a complete lack of patriotism.

The Social Democrats, on the other hand, looked upon themselves as patriotic Germans because of their total hostility to Russia. They always assured the German public that in case of an attack from Russia they would urge all of their followers to the front. Grillenberger made this clear in the Reichstag on December 4, 1886: "I do not hesitate to assure you, if at any time our [Germany's] actual life-and-death enemy [*Tod- und Erbfeind*], who in our opinion sits in the east, should consider bringing his culture to the west and threaten the existence of Germany, Gentlemen, we are prepared to approve immediately the necessary means for the defense against such an attack." [62] Radical and moderate Social Democrats all agreed on this issue, but the German public was not convinced that Russophobia was a counterpart of German patriotism. It was taken rather as evidence that the Social Democrats were consistently friends of Germany's enemies and enemies of Germany's friends.[63]

Despite the many disadvantages, the Social Democrats slightly increased their percentage of the popular vote over 1884, but their number of seats dropped. With 9.7 percent of the total in 1884 they won twenty-four seats; with 10.1 percent in 1887 they won only eleven seats. There were two reasons for this. First, the city districts, the centers of their strength, had grown rapidly in population since 1871. But since the Reichstag seats had not been reapportioned, the cities no longer had anything like an equal representation with the rural areas. The Social Democrats were already the chief losers from this antiquated electoral system. In twenty-three districts which were totally within cities, the Social Democrats received over 36 percent of the popular vote; the *Freisinnige* party was next with almost 20 percent.[64]

[62] *SB*, VI, iv (1886/87), vol. I, p. 101.

[63] On Jan. 12, 1887, Hasenclever was greeted with hisses and ridicule in the Reichstag as he elaborated on the Russian danger and minimized the threat of war with France. *Ibid.*, pp. 363–64. Cf. "Vaterland und Vaterlandsliebe," *SD*, No. 3, Jan. 15, 1887.

[64] According to the Imperial Constitution, there was to be one deputy for every 100,000 inhabitants. In 1871, the balance between the city and rural districts was fairly even. By 1885, however, the average population in the city districts had grown to 165,875, while in the rural districts it was only 107,073. In mixed districts, with some city areas, the average population had grown to 136,165. Schippel, *Die Sozialdemokratie und der deutsche Reichstag*, pp. 19, 21, 30.

This meant that the Social Democrats had no chance of getting seats equal to their popular support.

The second reason for the decline in seats in 1887 stemmed from the fact that the Social Democrats were unable to pick up many votes from other parties in the run-off balloting. In the run-off balloting, the Social Democrats were willing to support candidates of other parties in districts where no socialist was running, if the candidate opposed the Socialist Law and upheld universal suffrage. That proved a boon for the *Freisinnige* party.[65] Out of the thirty-two seats won by the *Freisinnige* party in the run-off ballots, the Social Democratic votes were absolutely essential in eleven districts and helped greatly in fifteen others. But in return the Social Democrats received significant *Freisinnige* assistance in only two out of eighteen districts.[66]

The small Social Democratic Reichstag delegation consisted of Bebel, Dietz, Frohme, Grillenberger, Harm, Hasenclever, Kraecker, Meister, Sabor, Schumacher, and Singer. All of these were experienced in parliamentary work, but some of the ablest leaders were missing, notably Auer, Blos, Liebknecht, and Vollmar. With less than fifteen deputies, the Social Democrats lost their rights as an independent *Fraktion.* That meant that they could no longer participate in committee work or initiate their own bills without the assistance of non-socialist deputies. The requisite conditions for the positive parliamentary policy begun in 1884 had vanished. The Social Democrats were thrown back into the situation where they could only comment and make minor amendments to bills already under discussion.

The small delegation posed some disadvantages but this did not disappoint Bebel. A large delegation, as the preceding years had shown, was difficult to control. If the Social Democrats had won thirty seats, then Bebel thought, they would have had at least "20 little 'Statesmen' " with which to contend.[67] With a small group, Bebel could look forward to his own control of the *Fraktion* as soon as he had completed his prison term.

[65] "An unsere Parteigenossen," *SD,* No. 10, March 4, 1887; "Zu den Stichwahlen," *SD,* No. 8, Feb. 18, 1887.

[66] The Social Democrats won six seats on the first ballot and five in the run-off. In the run-off, the *Freisinnige* votes helped Kraecker in Breslau-West; in Elberfeld, Harm won with some assistance from *Freisinnige* and Center votes. Compiled from "Ergebnisse der Reichstagwahlen," *SB,* VII, i (1887), vol. III. *Anlagen,* No. 73, pp. 615–79.

[67] August Bebel to Julie Bebel, Feb. 28, 1887, in Gemkow, "Briefe August Bebels aus den Jahren 1886/1887," p. 149.

Liebknecht became despondent at his failure to win a seat, and Bebel also regretted the loss. But Bebel thought it ironical that one who had been such a flamboyant anti-parliamentarian should take his exclusion from the Reichstag so seriously. "Previously," Bebel said, "he [Liebknecht] took so little to the Reichstag—in my view a bit too little—why now the fuss when he can not join in?"[68] Bebel's question is easily answered. Certainly Bebel realized that Liebknecht had shifted to a more sympathetic attitude toward parliamentarism. Furthermore, some form of parliamentary work had become tactically necessary during the Socialist Law for a leadership position within the party. And, Liebknecht's defeat in the Reichstag election added a personal drawback because he had already lost his Saxon Diet seat in 1885. For a few years Liebknecht had to wait on the sidelines of public parliamentary activity.

Neither the unfavorable election result nor the government's oppression discouraged the Social Democratic leaders from pursuing whatever parliamentary work remained open to them. There is hardly any doubt that Bismarck would have been pleased to see the Social Democrats abandon the parliamentary course for a more radical tactic. He always hoped that he could pin anarchist violence on the Social Democrats. For that very reason, the Social Democrats were careful not to give Bismarck any added justification for his policy of oppression. The Social Democrats would not abandon their parliamentary course, because to have done so would have appeared as evidence of an identity with anarchism. In 1886–1887, it was doubly necessary to be cautious lest the Social Democrats be implicated in the new flurry of anarchist activity in Europe and England which also touched Germany indirectly. They all believed it necessary therefore to remain absolutely distinct from anarchism. Parliamentary activity presented a sure sign of that distinction. In addition to the need for a sharp distinction from anarchism, the Social Democrats still held that parliamentary activity was tactically necessary, since it was the only means of guaranteeing their public role in German politics.

Only seven Social Democrats could take their seats in the Reichstag for the session from March 3 to June 18, 1887. Two of these seven, Kraecker and Singer, faced arrest during the session, but the Reichstag upheld their immunity so that they could attend most of the sittings.[69]

[68] August Bebel to Julie Bebel, March 7, 1887, in *ibid.*, p. 152.

[69] During April, the police arrested Singer for a violation of the Prussian Law

Despite all of the interference with their parliamentary work, the Social Democrats supported some moderate labor legislation initiated by the Center party. Since the socialists were not entirely pleased with the Center party's bills, they introduced their own amendments, but finally voted for a child labor law which was accepted by the Reichstag.[70] In this way, it is clear that the unrestrained hostility of Bismarck's government had not destroyed the lingering belief that their legislative cooperation contributed to a solution of labor's problems.

Although the oppressive circumstances of 1886–1887 did not alter the basic course of the Social Democratic party, they created a situation which made the former position of the moderate socialist deputies much less tenable than it had been in 1885. The moderates could hardly ask Social Democrats to consider cooperation with Bismarck's government while Puttkamer launched new repressions against the labor movement. Faced with the wave of harsh government measures, a new spirit of unity emerged among the deputies, giving the radicals the advantage over the moderates. The oppressive conditions led to some intraparty changes which proved to be immensely significant, not merely for the practical activity but also for the theoretical position of the party. The changes were all integrally related to the role of August Bebel, for these were the decisive months during which he arrived at a plateau of almost absolute party control.

on Association. The case was before a lower court, the *Amtsgericht,* in Goerlitz, Silesia. The Social Democrats asked the Reichstag to demand that Singer be freed to attend the sessions; the request, which was granted, was undersigned by several *Freisinnige* deputies. *SB,* VII, i (1887), vol. III, *Anlagen,* No. 72, p. 614. Julius Kraecker was threatened with arrest, and finally put under lock and key as soon as the session closed on June 18, 1887. He was then held for five months while the police tried to establish the charges against him. He was finally sentenced and spent several months in prison. Shortly after his release he was arrested again, but he died on October 2, 1888, before the proceedings were concluded. On Kraecker see the obituary in the *Berliner Volkstribuene,* No. 40, Oct. 6, 1888, p. 1, and Schulthess, *1887,* p. 179.

[70] The Center party called for a regulation of Sunday work, female and child labor, and a legalized working day of 11 hours. *SB,* VII, i (1887), vol. III, *Anlagen,* No. 21, pp. 281–82; No. 22, pp. 282–84; No. 23, pp. 284–85. For the Social Democratic amendments, see *ibid.,* vol. IV, *Anlagen,* No. 126, p. 1023. The Social Democrats wanted it stipulated that before a fourteen-year-old could work, his elementary schooling had to be completed and a physician had to affirm that he was in good physical health. For the final Social Democratic support of the Center party's Child Labor Bill, see *ibid.,* vol. II, pp. 850–53.

CHAPTER X · THE ST. GALL CONGRESS AND THE SUPREMACY OF AUGUST BEBEL

Opposition to Bebel Fades

WITHOUT EXCEPTION, the events of 1886–1887 enhanced the power and prestige of August Bebel in the Social Democratic party. For years, Bebel had been a very influential leader of the party, no doubt the most influential. But previously he always had to fight a powerful group of dissenters who often formed a majority of the leadership. He had been, therefore, the most articulate spokesman for a minority. By the end of 1887, that situation changed. Circumstances and his own driving will created a sufficient shifting of the ground so that Bebel became the spokesman for the majority. A whole cluster of events created this situation, but the party congress at St. Gall in Switzerland, October 2–6, 1887, is most easily identified as the turning point. For several years after St. Gall, until 1890, no dissenting voices of any significance were raised against Bebel's leadership. This was highly significant for the future formation of the party's practical and theoretical character. Bebel's supremacy, as this chapter attempts to show, solidified an attitude of ambivalent parliamentarism for the party's political action and smoothed the way for the acceptance of a Marxist creed in economic theory.

Gradually but steadily, Bebel's most articulate opponents lost ground in the party. It has already been noted that in general the views of the moderates were less tenable in face of the government's intensified campaign against the party after 1885. The moderates lost further ground when some of their leading parliamentarians—Auer, Blos, Geiser, Kayser, and Viereck—were defeated in the election of 1887. In that way the Social Democratic set-back in the election turned into an intraparty victory for Bebel. Likewise, Bebel's personal influence over several moderates, such as Auer, Dietz, and Frohme had increased noticeably after they shared imprisonment at Zwickau.

Other unfortunate circumstances favored Bebel's role in the party. Of the old Lassalleans, Hasenclever's influence was the most distressing to Bebel. But in 1887 Hasenclever suffered from a severe mental illness; by November he rested in a sanitorium, his political career finished. Bebel was almost indifferent to this tragedy, as he commented to Engels that Hasenclever's "influence" was past.[1] Even when misfortune struck, Bebel had no sympathy for Hasenclever, and he sharply reprimanded the kindhearted Liebknecht for having written a laudatory account of the old Lassallean's career.[2]

Bebel showed more compassion for Max Kayser, the bright young Jew from Breslau who died from a throat tumor on March 29, 1888. Although he was only thirty-five when he died, Kayser, because of his strong statist views, had challenged Bebel's ideas with wit and energy for over a decade.[3] Usually Bebel had accepted Kayser's criticisms with good humor. Hasenclever had been the oldest and most respected socialist in the Lassallean tradition; Kayser too was in that tradition, the youngest and the brightest. Now both were gone.

A slightly different kind of misfortune hit Louis Viereck, another of Bebel's intraparty foes. Until the end of 1885, Viereck had the most profitable socialist publishing business in Germany. But then disaster struck. One by one the police suppressed his newspapers. When, late in 1886, Viereck went to prison in Zwickau to serve his nine-month sentence from the Freiberg trial, he could no longer manage the publishing business himself. By February 1887, all but two of his newspapers were suppressed by the police. As soon as he left Zwickau on August 17, 1887, he faced another trial at Chemnitz; the charges filled ninety-two pages. With every passing month, his troubles had mounted.[4]

[1] Bebel to Engels, Nov. 12, 1887, in Bebel, *Briefwechsel*, p. 313.

[2] Bebel to Liebknecht, Dec. 29, 1887, Liebknecht Archive, IISH. In this letter Bebel maintained that Liebknecht's "praise" was "in contradiction" to the feelings of the majority in the party. But Bebel's view is hardly supported by the evidence. A Hasenclever Fund was started at the end of 1887 to assist him and his family. By March 2, 1888, the fund had 5,808 marks! Cf. *SD*, No. 15, April 7, 1888, p. 4. When Hasenclever died (July 3, 1889), there were not only obituary notices in the Social Democratic press but special poems and essays were written in his honor. All of this is sufficient evidence that throughout his life Hasenclever had the respect of many Social Democrats. Cf. *Berliner Volksblatt*, No. 154, July 5, 1889, pp. 1–2, and No. 156, July 7, 1889, *Beilage*, p. 1 (contains poem by Fritz Kunert); "Hasenclevers Begraebnis," *ibid.*, No. 157, July 9, 1889, *Beilage*, p. 1.

[3] Max Kayser to Bebel, March 16, 1888, Bebel Archive, IISH. Biographical sketch of Kayser in *Berliner Volkstribuene*, No. 14, April 7, 1888, p. 1. "Max Kayser todt," *SD*, No. 15, April 7, 1888.

[4] Louis Viereck to Carl Grillenberger, Aug. 25, 1887, *Kleine Korrespondenz*,

Hoping to avoid further legal complications, after leaving prison in August, Viereck declined to undersign the party executive's announcement of the congress to be held in the autumn of 1887. But Bebel demanded that everyone who had been a Reichstag deputy sign the announcement or else forfeit his rights as a party member. Viereck's explanations did not satisfy Bebel, who persuaded the delegates at the St. Gall congress to drop Viereck from the party. In that way Bebel succeeded in excluding one of his most persistent and dangerous opponents from the party. The same fate fell to Bruno Geiser, who also refused to undersign the announcement of the congress. Except that Geiser was Liebknecht's son-in-law, he was more of an irritant than a threat to Bebel's predominance in the party. Bebel was pleased that both were removed from the party.[5]

One more key figure looms important for Bebel's supreme role in the party—Wilhelm Liebknecht. Enough has been said in the previous chapters about the quarrels and differences of these old friends; to mention every incident would be burdensome. Bebel was often sharp and severe with Liebknecht, who very seldom retaliated with equal harshness. But Liebknecht had worked constantly to reconcile differences in the party when Bebel preferred to fight them out. This friction altered the nature of their relationship. As an old and respected socialist, politically active since 1848, Liebknecht felt no obligation to subordinate himself to Bebel. But when Bebel, strong willed and often inflexible, could not rely upon Liebknecht to do his bidding, he ceased to depend upon him. Gradually their old partnership lost much of its meaning, although their friendship remained. By 1887 Paul Singer had really replaced Liebknecht as Bebel's most trusted associate. Although

IISH. Hess, "Louis Viereck und seine Muenchner Blaetter fuer Arbeiter 1882–1889," pp. 30–33, 47–50.

[5] There were actually seven Social Democrats who were or had been deputies and who did not sign the announcement of the congress: Viereck, Geiser, Wiemer, Vollmar, Pfannkuch, Kraecker, and Ulrich. The last four were all excused because they were either in prison or on temporary furlough from prison. The published minutes of the St. Gall congress do not give much information on this matter. Some supplementary information is available from a secret report to the Berlin Police Presidium by an unidentified delegate to the congress who was in the pay of the police. The report shows that Wiemer also asked to be excused from signing the announcement because he was facing financial ruin, much as Viereck was. While Bebel defended Wiemer, he was unyielding in his attack on Viereck and Geiser. Cf. "*Bericht* ueber den Verlauf des in der Zeit vom 3ten bis 6ten October d. Js. in der Brauerei Schoenenwegen bei St. Gallen abgehaltenen sozialdemokratischen Parteitages," Germany, FM Archives, UM, R. 104, frm. 839; also the *Verhandlungen des Parteitags der deutschen Sozialdemokratie in St. Gallen* (Hottingen-Zurich, 1888), p. 48.

relatively new to the party (his work began about 1878), Singer was diligent, financially solvent, and deeply devoted to Bebel.

Engels, too, had contributed to the change in Liebknecht's role. For over a decade after Liebknecht returned to Germany in 1862 he served as the chief contact for Marx and Engels in Germany. By the early eighties, however, that was no longer true; Engels had developed a far greater confidence in Bebel and communicated chiefly with him. This added enormously to Bebel's prestige in the eyes of those who looked upon Engels as the party's great adviser. In a public sense, Liebknecht remained the Grand Old Man of the party, but in private he was more often blamed than praised, especially by Bebel and Engels, whose scornful comments are sometimes unbelievable.[6]

It would be unfair and inaccurate to imply that Bebel reached a supreme position in the party as the consequence of mere accident or ill-natured maneuvers against his comrades. Bebel, as few others, devoted his whole existence to the party. No one else matched his single-minded commitment to party affairs. The unique character of the man is even more amazing when one remembers that not only did he give so much time and energy to party work, but also that until the end of the Socialist Law he was an active partner in a wood-turning shop and traveled throughout Germany several times a year as the distributing salesman for the products of the business. But as his power in the party grew, it became increasingly difficult to carry on the dual role. "It is no longer fitting for me to be a commercial traveler," Bebel wrote to Engels, in May 1888, "and thus often to be hindered directly when my intervention in party affairs would be most necessary." [7] At every moment he felt that he had to be at the center of things, now more than ever.

It was not by accident that Bebel perfected an almost complete supremacy during the Socialist Law. At the foundation of his success

[6] At the end of 1884, when the steamship subsidy issue first arose, Engels wrote to Sorge about his confidence in Bebel. "Luckily there is Bebel, who always grasps the decisive point correctly, and thus I hope that it [the steamship issue] will be settled without disgrace. Since I have been carrying on the 'official' correspondence with Bebel instead of Liebknecht, not only is everything handled smoothly, but things get done, and my opinion reaches them intact. Bebel is quite a splendid fellow; I hope he doesn't ruin his shaky health." Dec. 31, 1884, in Marx and Engels, *Letters to Americans 1848–1895: A Selection* (New York, 1953), p. 144. For Singer's career see the laudatory sketch by Heinrich Gemkow, *Paul Singer, ein bedeutender Fuehrer der deutschen Arbeiterbewegung* (Berlin-East, 1957).

[7] Bebel to Engels, May 2, 1888, in Bebel, *Briefwechsel*, p. 326.

lay his long career as the most capable and energetic socialist deputy in the Reichstag. In this period, the public activity of the Social Democrats took place almost exclusively within the parliamentary bodies, and so the most skillful socialist deputy had the best chance of becoming the supreme commander of the party.

The Congress at St. Gall, October 2–6, 1887

The events that transpired at the Social Democratic party congress at St. Gall (October 2–6, 1887) reveal Bebel's solidified leadership of the party. It has already been noted that Bebel in particular demanded the expulsion of Viereck and Geiser from the party. The congress did his pleasure. It is not surprising, therefore, that his mood after St. Gall differed markedly from what it had been after the Copenhagen congress in 1883. After the latter, he had lamented that a number of delegates harbored a dangerous hostility to his views on party policy. But, after St. Gall, he expressed a victorious mood. "With the outcome of the congress," he told Engels, "I am very satisfied. I have not even one complaint; everything went according to wish." [8]

Bebel had led the move to call a party congress as soon as he left the prison at Zwickau on August 14, 1887. For two years he had been demanding a party congress. But in 1885, when he hoped for a decisive confrontation with the moderates, he had been voted down by the majority of the party executive, and in 1886 the Freiberg trial interrupted the plans for a congress.[9] Finally, in 1887, his plans could be realized. Engels, however, urged Bebel to visit him in England as soon as he left prison, before the congress would meet. "Such a rest," Engels admonished, "appears to me to be absolutely necessary for your health, so that you can breathe free air again. Here [in England] the air is as free as it can generally be in a capitalist society." [10] The invitation appealed to Bebel, but party affairs came before pleasure; he did not go to England until after the congress.[11]

The seventy-nine socialists who met in secret at the *Brauerei Schoenenwegen*, a few miles outside of St. Gall, focused their attention on the problems related to the party's parliamentary activity. It was

[8] Bebel to Engels, Oct. 14, 1887, in *ibid.*, p. 312.
[9] Bebel to Engels, July 5, 1885, in *ibid.*, p. 230; Bebel to Motteler, March 13, 1886, Bebel Archive, IISH.
[10] Engels to Bebel, Aug. 13, 1887, in Bebel, *Briefwechsel*, p. 306.
[11] Bebel to Engels, Sept. 24, 1887, and Nov. 12, 1887, in *ibid.*, pp. 309–10, 313.

the first opportunity for the most trusted leaders to discuss collectively the rather extensive parliamentary work of 1884–1887. They had a special need for a general discussion of parliamentary work. An anti-parliamentarian current still flowed within the party, not very strong to be sure, but gaining some momentum, particularly in Berlin.

These anti-parliamentarians, who still drew very much of the justification for their position from Liebknecht's speech of 1869, had engaged in a short debate with Max Kayser late in 1886 and early in 1887.[12] The debate continued without too much spirit during 1887. In May, one of the young Social Democratic intellectuals, Max Schippel, warned that the party overlooked the dangers implicit in parliamentarism. At that time, the *Sozialdemokrat* answered Schippel by stressing the tactical need for a strong socialist delegation in the Reichstag.[13]

The anti-parliamentarian current threatened to blur the distinction between Social Democracy and anarchism. The anti-parliamentarians among the Social Democrats did not, however, agree with the anarchists that socialists should disengage themselves completely from parliamentary work. The anti-parliamentarians merely demanded that the Social Democratic party limit itself to a totally agitational and negative posture in the Reichstag.

In 1887, these anti-parliamentarian expressions had particular significance because throughout Europe and America the anarchists had been especially vocal during the preceding year. Anarchist influence was still meager in Germany, but the German anarchist clubs in London had stepped up their propaganda late in 1886.[14]

Spectacular events, starting with the Chicago Haymarket riot in

[12] Bernstein, *Berliner Arbeiterbewegung*, II, pp. 199–201; "Korrespondenzen," *SD*, No. 2, Jan. 8, 1887.

[13] Max Schippel, "Die Arbeiter, der Parlamentarismus und die buergerlichen Parteien in Deutschland," *Die Gleichheit* (Vienna), May 1887, cited in Bernstein, *Berliner Arbeiterbewegung*, II, p. 227. "Die Stellung der Sozialdemokratie zum Parlamentarismus," *SD*, No. 21, May 20, 1887.

[14] There were three German-speaking anarchist clubs in London. The *Communistische Arbeiterbildungsverein, I. Sektion*, had been led by Johann Most and the Belgian anarchist, Viptor Dave. By 1887, however, it was rather weak, with about thirty members. The strongest was the group *Autonomie*, whose leading spirit was the Austrian Josef Peukert. The membership was largely Austrian. The third, the *Club der Morgenröthe*, had been very active but suffered a serious blow when its most articulate leader, Karl Theodor Reuss, was exposed as an agent of the German police! See the unsigned article "Gegenwaertiger Stand der anarchistischen Bewegung," *Neue Freie Presse* (Vienna), No. 8264, Aug. 30; No. 8265, Aug. 31; No. 8272, Sept. 7; No. 8273, Sept. 8; No. 8293, Sept. 28; and No. 8294, Sept. 29, 1887.

May 1886, focused public attention on the anarchists. On February 21, 1887, for example, John Neve, a German anarchist from the London circle, was captured in Belgium and turned over to the Prussian police. Since Neve's trial before the Supreme Court at Leipzig began on October 3, 1887, the German public was reading the reports of anarchist activities at the same time that it first learned that the Social Democrats were holding another secret congress in Switzerland.[15] In such an atmosphere the Social Democrats at St. Gall were again alerted to the need to distinguish themselves from anarchism.

The congress thus spent most of its time on subjects related to parliamentarism and anarchism. The delegates subjected the whole socialist parliamentary record to review. The moderates were questioned about their support of the steamship subsidy; the Central Election Committee was reprimanded by some for its support of non-socialist candidates in the 1887 run-off elections; Vollmar and the Bavarians were rebuked for their compromises with the National Liberals, and voices were frequently raised against all compromises in elections.[16] Despite the many criticisms of particulars, there was no general objection in principle to a positive parliamentary policy.

The anti-parliamentarians still had no significant influence in the party as a whole in 1887. A few years later, however, in 1890, when they were known as the *Jungen* (the Young Ones), the anti-parliamentarians gathered strength and made a serious bid for party influence. By that time, Bebel, who had gained such great control, emerged as the chief defendant of the established policy of the majority.

The intraparty shift which made Bebel the leading advocate of the party's parliamentary policy was already indicated at St. Gall. This became clear in the discussion of the activities of the Social Democrats in the Saxon Diet. While Bebel reaffirmed his belief that the ultimate goals of socialism could not be achieved by the "parliamentary-constitutional path," he nevertheless emphasized the positive results of the Social Democratic parliamentary work, especially in the Saxon Diet. He maintained, for example, that the condition of Saxon miners had been improved as a result of the Social Democratic demands in the diet.[17]

Bebel also faced an embarrassing situation at St. Gall. He had to ex-

[15] For the most detailed account of the John Neve affair, see Rocker, *Johann Most*, pp. 250–92.
[16] *Verhandlungen . . . St. Gallen* (1887), pp. 14–15, 17, 28–33.
[17] *Ibid.*, pp. 12–13.

plain why the Social Democrats, under his leadership in the Saxon Diet, had supported the Saxon government's Schneckengruen Labor Colony. A number of Bebel's comrades believed that such labor colonies, designed to give temporary housing and work to unemployed wanderers, had no place in a socialist program. Bebel conceded the point, and obviously distressed by the matter, tried to explain that he and his comrades in the Saxon Diet had no illusions about the value of labor colonies. In the future, he admitted, such projects should not be supported. Later, when some delegates wished to discuss Schneckengruen further, Bebel impatiently declared that the whole matter was closed and should not be discussed.[18]

When Bebel could not defend his action, he arbitrarily insisted that there was nothing to discuss! And he succeeded in restricting the discussion. Even Bebel would have had to admit that Bismarck's insurance programs, which the Social Democrats rejected on the ground that they were inadequate, had a closer relationship to the socialists' aims and a much greater significance for the improvement of the workers' economic conditions than the labor colonies. Because his position was so completely untenable, he admitted his error and then asserted his power to prohibit an extensive discussion. Had some old Lassalleans, such as Hasenclever and Frohme, committed the same error in judgment, there is no doubt that Bebel would have been the first to insist upon a full review. By 1887, however, no one could force a full review of Bebel's mistakes.

The delegates at St. Gall took their stand on parliamentarism by passing a resolution which approved of the parliamentary record of the party deputies, but also recommended that the focus be on the "critical and agitational side" of Reichstag work and that "positive legislative activity" be carried on in a way as not to create "doubt" or "illusion" about its ultimate value.[19] The delegates also resolved that the Social Democrats should enter candidates in all elections for the Reichstag, the diets, and the municipal councils, but not in combination with other parties. Where no socialist was running in a run-off election, the congress "recommended" that the Social Democrats withhold their votes.[20] This indirectly condemned the policy followed by the party in the 1887 election.

[18] *Ibid.*, pp. 14–15.
[19] *Ibid.*, p. 19.
[20] *Ibid.*, p. 34.

After the parliamentary problems were settled, the delegates had to clarify once again the party's relationship to anarchism. Liebknecht undertook the role of enlightening the delegates on the subject. During the summer of 1887, he had synthesized revolutionary socialism and parliamentarism; at St. Gall, he sought to demonstrate the incompatibility between revolutionary socialism and anarchism. Two factors, according to Liebknecht, created the incompatibility: the extreme individualism of the anarchists and their use of "violence" (*Gewalt*). Because of its extreme individualism, Liebknecht interpreted anarchism as the logical outcome of bourgeois liberalism, a "bourgeois ideal in a revolutionary lion's skin." The delegates then debated a resolution, obviously drafted by Liebknecht, which explained that "violence" had more often been used as a "reactionary" than a "revolutionary" factor. Although a few voices challenged aspects of the resolution, it was unanimously adopted as an effort by the delegates to demonstrate their total repudiation of anarchism.[21]

The German government scrutinized carefully all of its available evidence on the St. Gall congress, and especially the repudiation of anarchism, which it did not accept at face value. According to the government's evidence, the extremists controlled the congress and the party. One of the delegates at the congress, whose identity is still unknown, was in the pay of the Berlin police; he sent confidential reports which were analyzed by the Prussian authorities and Bismarck.[22] In his last report, he observed that the course of the congress showed that Bebel, Liebknecht, and Singer were the "decisive" leaders of the party, but added that "Bebel is to be looked upon as the actual chief, whose position is exactly equal to that of a dictator." [23] The German Am-

[21] *Ibid.*, pp. 40–45.

[22] The Social Democratic leaders at St. Gall suspected one of the delegates, Rohmann, a master bookbinder from Berlin, of being a spy. They were so convinced that they had Rohmann denounced in the *Sozialdemokrat*. Several years later, after Rohmann was ruined as a Social Democrat, he was cleared of suspicion. Cf. Hellfaier, *Die deutsche Sozialdemokratie*, pp. 209–10; Fricke, *Bismarcks Praetorianer*, pp. 267–68. Unfortunately, the files of the German Foreign Ministry, which contain the reports written by the spy, do not reveal his identity. Whoever he was, Berlin Police Director Krueger had complete confidence in him. In a memorandum, Krueger said that he was an "especially capable [*tuechtigen*] secret agent" who attended the congress as a delegate. Memorandum by Krueger, Oct. 31, 1887. Germany, FM Archives, UM, R. 104, frm. 824.

[23] "*Bericht* ueber den Verlauf des in der Zeit von 3ten bis 6ten October d. Js. in der Brauerei Schoenenwegen bei St. Gallen abgehaltenen sozialdemokratischen Parteitages," unsigned report without date, in Germany, FM Archives, UM, R. 104, frm. 841. The full report covers frms. 825–41. The earlier report by the spy

bassador in Bern, Otto von Buelow, also received information on the congress through the Swiss police. On October 5, he wrote that "the extreme social revolutionary group, under the leadership of Bebel and the silent influence of Vollmar, terrorized and oppressed the moderate participants in the congress. . . ." [24] The resolution against anarchism, Buelow added a week later, "was not taken seriously by intelligent people," who interpreted it as a maneuver to make the meeting appear "harmless." [25] This interpretation was seconded by Dr. Kayser, a councillor in the Political Division of the Foreign Ministry. In a special memorandum "Concerning the anarchist development of German Social Democracy," he concluded that "the difference between Social Democracy and anarchism is not qualitative but only one of degree." [26] These reports were undoubtedly a further basis for Bismarck's conviction that sooner or later he would find sufficient evidence to prove Social Democratic responsibility for anarchist violence.

The conviction, still prevalent in government circles, that Social Democrats were not truly distinct from anarchists was undoubtedly reenforced in the weeks after St. Gall when the *Sozialdemokrat* passionately condemned the legal procedures used to convict the Chicago anarchists of the Haymarket riot.[27] On November 9, two days before the condemned anarchists were to be executed, Bebel, Grillenberger, Liebknecht, and Singer pleaded that their lives be spared in a telegram to the governor of Illinois. The appeal appeared on the front page of the *Sozialdemokrat* with a black band over the article entitled "The Legal Murder in Chicago." [28] After this, the theoretical articles which were intended to distinguish anarchism from socialism were undoubtedly taken by the authorities as mere cover-ups for the real solidarity between the two movements.[29]

is on the same reel, frms. 800–09. Neither report makes any essential change in our knowledge of the congress.

[24] Otto von Buelow to FM, Oct. 5, 1887, No. 43, *ibid.*, frms. 782–84.

[25] Otto von Buelow to FM, Oct. 14, 1887, No. 44, *ibid.*, frms. 794–95.

[26] Memorandum by Dr. Kayser, "Betrifft die anarchiste [sic] Entwickelung der deutschen Sozialdemokratie," Berlin, Oct. 25, 1887, *ibid.*, frms. 810–11. Similar judgments can be found in the police records. Thus, in a summary report on the Social Democrats, Police President Richthofen wrote on Nov. 15, 1887, that the conclusions of the congress demonstrated "that by far the largest and most influential part of the party has taken a big and fateful step in the direction of the violent revolution." Quoted in Hoehn, *Die vaterlandslosen Gesellen*, I, p. 296.

[27] "Wider einen Justizmord," *SD*, No. 44, Oct. 28, 1887.

[28] "Der Justizmord in Chicago," *SD*, No. 47, Nov. 18, 1887.

[29] Cf. "Zur sozialen Doktrin des Anarchismus," *SD*, No. 49, Dec. 2, and No. 51, Dec. 16, 1887.

Bebel's Supremacy and Social Democratic Parliamentary Practice

The German government officials were quite correct in their conclusion that Bebel and his radical associates had achieved an upper hand in the party, thus reducing the influence of the moderates who had been so strong for many years. They were wrong, however, when they believed that this would mean a decisive radicalization of party activity and possibly even greater sympathy with anarchism. Even the liberal *Frankfurter Zeitung*, often perceptive about socialist affairs, wrongly concluded that because of the control of the radicals the Social Democrats would be less interested in parliamentary work.[30]

It is true that for the remainder of the Socialist Law epoch the Social Democrats had few opportunities for positive work in the Reichstag. They could do little about that. In the Reichstag, the Social Democrats were involved in a life and death struggle against Bismarck, whose Cartel majority threatened to intensify the Socialist Law rather than weaken it. Social Democratic parliamentary work, therefore, was defensive, not primarily legislative.

In the fall of 1887, the government introduced a more severe version of the Socialist Law, the most important alteration of which provided that persons who violated the chief prescriptions of the law, or who were guilty of participation in a secret organization, should be exiled from Germany with a loss of citizenship. Without a doubt, all of the leading Social Democrats would have been expatriated had this hardened version become law. In addition, fines and prison sentences were to be increased, especially for the distribution of forbidden literature. Bismarck wanted this version of the Socialist Law adopted for a period of five years.[31]

Bismarck counted on his Cartel majority to carry the parliamentary fight for the intensified version of the Socialist Law. The Social Democrats also recognized that it might pass.[32] But a great part of the German press did not reflect Bismarck's views. With the exception of the "extreme reactionary papers," the German press condemned the

[30] *Frankfurter Zeitung*, No. 285, Oct. 12; No. 286, Oct. 13; No. 289, Oct. 16, 1887. Clippings found in the Motteler Archive, XII, IISH.

[31] *SB*, VII, ii (1887/88), vol. III, *Anlagen*, No. 71, pp. 386–89.

[32] "Zur Frage der kuenftigen Taktik," *SD*, No. 3, Jan. 15, 1888; "Unsere Antwort," *SD*, No. 5, Jan. 29, 1888.

powers of expatriation included in the new version.[33] Even before the debate on the Socialist Law began, much of public opinion did not favor Bismarck's objectives.

Bebel and Singer then directed a masterful campaign against the Socialist Law. During the first week of January 1888, they were in Zurich gathering the evidence for a spectacular exposure of the agents employed by the Berlin Police Presidium. What they found, with the help of the ever-alert Julius Motteler, amazed them. Bebel was jubilant as he told Engels: "This time it will crack." [34]

When the debate on the Socialist Law opened on January 27, 1888, Singer, the first deputy to take the floor, literally staggered his audience with detailed and well-documented evidence on two agents provocateur, Karl Schroeder and Christian Haupt, employed by the Berlin Police Presidium. Even the most conservative members of the Reichstag came to attention as Singer read a letter from the Zurich Police Commandant, Fischer, which supported the major accusations of the Social Democrats against Schroeder and Haupt.[35] Against Singer's impressive evidence, Puttkamer could only insist upon the good faith of the Berlin Police Presidium. In frustration, he vented his wrath against Fischer, the Zurich Police Commandant. But the following day Puttkamer had to admit that Schroeder and Haupt were employed by the Berlin police. The *Freisinnige* leaders used Singer's evidence to ridicule Puttkamer. Bamberger noted that Puttkamer's defense was weak and ineffective. And Marquardsen announced immediately that the National Liberals would only support the renewal of the existing Socialist Law for a two-year period.[36] The repercussions of Singer's exposure continued as the National Liberal and *Freisinnige* press gave it special attention.[37] The exposure proved a helpful weapon in hindering the passage of the severe version of the Socialist Law.

The Social Democratic attack on the Socialist Law could not, however, prevent its renewal for another two years. Windthorst had renewed his efforts to ameliorate the harshest aspects of the law, especially the Minor State of Siege. But the National Liberals stood with

[33] Apitzsch, *Die deutsche Tagespresse*, p. 156.

[34] Bebel to Engels, Jan. 9, 1888, in Bebel, *Briefwechsel*, p. 319.

[35] *SB*, VII, ii (1887/88), vol. I, pp. 532–34. Fischer's letter made such a deep impression that the whole correspondence was reprinted in Schulthess, *1888*, pp. 16–17.

[36] *SB*, VII, ii (1887/88), vol. I, pp. 540–50, 571–73, 580–81, 586.

[37] Cf. Apitzsch, *Die deutsche Tagespresse*, pp. 133–34, 156, 161, 165.

the Conservatives; on February 17, the Socialist Law was renewed for a period lasting until September 30, 1890.[38]

Until after the election of February 1890, the Social Democrats in the Reichstag were limited to speechmaking with critical comments on legislation before the house. This suited Bebel's disposition very well. Under his leadership, the Social Democrats used the budget debates to criticize the government's restrictions on the use of margarine, the high cost of the military establishment, the administration of the post office, the failure of the Interior Ministry to provide adequate housing for workers employed in building the North Sea Canal, and other similar subjects.[39]

When the government presented its draft of the Old Age and Invalid Insurance in the summer of 1888, the Social Democrats studied it carefully; their reaction fitted the pattern established in 1883–1884 when the Accident and Sickness Insurance plans were passed. They endorsed the broad goals of the Old Age Insurance, but rejected its organization. In principle they stood for an Imperial agency which would administer and subsidize the program from an income tax.[40] Secondly, they called for increased benefits for the workers and for payments beginning at sixty, rather than seventy years of age as specified by the government's draft. Without these improvements, which the socialists embodied in a bill of amendments,[41] they maintained that the Old Age and Invalid Insurance was nothing more than an extension of the Poor Relief system.[42] As before, they voted against the bill on the ground that it failed to provide an adequate system of insurance.

The limited possibilities for legislative work in the Reichstag during the last years of the Socialist Law has given the impression that the Social Democrats had an entirely negative parliamentary policy. To be sure, under Bebel's dominance the party's deputies appeared more consistently intransigent than during the period of great moderate influ-

[38] *SB*, VII, ii (1887/88), vol. II, pp. 859–62, 898–99, 991.

[39] *SB*, VII, iv (1888/89), vol. I, pp. 76–77, 101–11, 464–66, 534–37.

[40] Cf. "Keine Landes-, sondern eine Reichsversicherungsanstalt," *Berliner Volksblatt*, No. 159, July 10, 1888, p. 1.

[41] *SB*, VII, iv (1888/89), vol. VI, *Anlagen*, No. 149, pp. 1184–85; No. 199, p. 1232. Cf. also "Zur Alters- und Invalidenversorgung," *Berliner Volksblatt*, No. 165, July 17, pp. 1–2, and No. 166, July 18, 1888, pp. 1–2.

[42] Grillenberger summarized the Social Democratic position in the Reichstag on Dec. 6, 1888. *SB*, VII, iv (1888/89), vol. I, pp. 145–60. Cf. also August Bebel, "Das Gesetz ueber die Invaliditaets- und Altersversicherung im deutschen Reich," *Neue Zeit*, VII (1889), pp. 385–400.

ence. But the intransigent posture in the Reichstag somewhat clouds the picture. If we wish to know more precisely what Bebel's supremacy meant for the party's parliamentary policy the best evidence comes from the Saxon Diet, where the actions of the Social Democrats were less in the public eye.

Bebel's supremacy did not result in any change in the moderate and practical approach of the Social Democrats to their work in the Saxon Diet. Their hostility was evident, but never to the degree apparent in the Reichstag. Small things show again that they were not so seriously alienated from the existing society and government in Saxony as in the Reich as a whole. On December 13, 1887, for example, Stolle expressed his pleasure that the Saxon Minister of Culture had apparently responded favorably to an earlier socialist request that the "Artistic Institutions" of Saxony should be looked upon as the "common property" of the citizens. Free museum passes, Stolle noted, had been distributed to various groups, including 1,060 passes to "Trades Societies" (*Gewerbevereine*). And three days later the Saxon Finance Minister, Koenneritz, assured Vollmar that his government had been building covered cabooses for train brakemen as the Social Democrats had suggested several years earlier.[43] Such incidents, though small in themselves, gave the Social Democrats, even during a period of fairly severe repression, the grounds to believe that more gains in social legislation were still possible in the Saxon Diet.

Previous to the Saxon Diet session which began on November 15, 1887, the Social Democrats had little chance to work out their own legislative initiatives. Bebel had just returned from his visit with Engels in London in time to attend the opening of the session. For the 1887–1888 session, therefore, they limited themselves to a participation in the debates.[44]

At the next session, which began on November 14, 1889, the Social Democrats, who had just won two more seats in the diet, appeared with four major pieces of legislation. First, they reintroduced their bill of 1886 for cost-free education and a new bill for a graduated income tax. Next, they brought in two pieces of labor legislation. The first called for the abolition of all Workmen's Books (*Arbeitsbuecher*) in

[43] Saxony, *LT. Mitt.* (1887/88), vol. I, pp. 203, 222.

[44] In their only written motions, the Social Democrats suggested a minor change in the administrative regulations of the Accident and Sickness Insurance and asked that a certain workers' petition be sent to the Saxon state government. Saxony, *Lt. Acten* (1887/88), vol. I, No. 99; vol. II, No. 125.

the mining operations; such books were often used to force a worker to carry a full record of his employment history. Finally, the Social Democrats wanted to free workers and lower-class civil servants employed in Saxon state operations from the obligation to pay contributions to the Sickness and Old Age funds.[45] Previously the Saxon Diet had relieved teachers, clerics, and the higher civil servants from these contributions. In discussing the last measure, Liebknecht claimed that Social Democratic influence in the Saxon Diet had helped to bring improvements in labor relations in Saxony. In fact, he characterized Saxony as a "model state" in labor relations, which brought great laughter from the right side of the house.[46]

Although none of the Social Democratic bills were accepted by the diet, the party's deputies had once again, as in the previous sessions, concentrated on those aspects of legislation which were largely consistent with their program but were also moderate and practical. All the indications are that they introduced their legislative proposals in the Saxon Diet with the expectation that they would be influential, if not immediately successful. The fact that Bebel and his radicals won supremacy by the time of the St. Gall congress did not lead to a radicalization of party tactics nor to any anti-parliamentary tendencies among the party's chief leaders.

The practical and reformist Social Democratic policy revealed in the Saxon Diet was equally evident in the Hessian Diet, where Carl Ulrich and Franz Joest represented the socialists. Until 1888, the parliamentary activity of these two Social Democrats had been seriously hampered by arrests and imprisonment. But beginning in 1888 they made a favorable impression on the deputies in the Hessian Diet with a bill to divide Hesse into two factory-inspection districts with appropriate personnel.[47] From Joest's discussion of this bill, it is easy to see that he believed the existing state capable of achieving great social reforms. After Joest noted that a Hessian Minister of State had said that as civilization advanced further it was necessary for the state to intervene more, he added: "From that I have concluded that at least some of our socialist views and demands have already become governmentally acceptable [*regierungsfaehig*]." [48] Ulrich in turn assured the diet

[45] Saxony, *LT. Acten* (1889/90), vol. 1, No. 6, No. 9, No. 29, No. 30.
[46] Saxony, *LT. Mitt.* (1889/90), vol. 1, p. 318.
[47] Hesse, *Verhandlungen der Zweiten Kammer der Landstaende des Grossherzogthums Hessen* (1888–91), *Beilagen*, vol. 1, No. 67.
[48] *Ibid.*, *Protokolle*, vol. 1, p. 70.

that the experience with the factory inspectors in Offenbach had increased the confidence of the workers in the state's willingness and desire to protect their interests. One of the government officials also commended Joest for the tone in which he had presented the Social Democratic bill.[49] A year later, in May 1889, the government of Hesse did in fact present a bill for two factory inspectors, almost identical with the Social Democratic bill, and the Hessian Diet adopted it.[50] For this measure, Ulrich declared, the government of Hesse could count upon the "thanks" of the workers.[51]

Although Bebel had no direct control over the deputies in the Hessian Diet, their legislative "success" was not inconsistent with his thinking. It was not by accident that Ulrich and Joest had put special emphasis on factory inspectors in 1888. For some time the *Neue Zeit* and the other Social Democratic publications had turned special attention to factory inspection. Bebel, in fact, spent much of his time by 1887–1888 studying and reporting on the result of factory inspection. As a means for genuine social reform, he demanded a more effective and widespread factory inspection for Germany. Joest and Ulrich were very much in Bebel's tradition, although they did not exhibit his intense hostility to the existing social-political structure.[52]

For the practical political work of the party, therefore, Bebel's supremacy did not mean radicalization but the victory of ambivalent parliamentarism. Out of the tactical necessity to use the Reichstag for agitation grew a deeper attachment to parliamentary work in the hope of influencing legislation. Although a strong and positive parliamentary policy was not possible with so few deputies in the Reichstag between 1887 and 1890, the evidence from the state diets shows that the Social Democrats not only hoped to influence legislation but believed that they had already done so. Such minor success, however, was not sufficient to insure that the underlying hostility to parliamentarism as an institution of Germany's anemic liberalism would be overcome in the Social Democratic party. Alongside active work in the parliaments, their hostility to parliamentary institutions remained.

[49] *Ibid.*, pp. 77, 79–81.

[50] *Ibid.*, *Beilagen*, vol. II, No. 97.

[51] *Ibid.*, *Protokolle*, vol. III, p. 47.

[52] Bebel wrote four articles from the reports of factory inspectors for the *Neue Zeit* in 1889. Cf. especially, A. B., "Die saechsische Fabrikinspektion im Jahre 1888," *Neue Zeit*, VIII (1889), pp. 544–56.

Theoretical Marxism and Social Democratic Politics under Bebel

Bebel's personal supremacy held significant implications for the theoretical position of the party. It meant, in an important way, that there were no more personal barriers against the acceptance of Marxism as the party's official creed. As long as old Lassalleans and moderates had been strong in the party it had always been necessary to recognize publicly the great contributions of Lassalle.

The old Lassalleans would never have encouraged a revision of the Gotha program. But at St. Gall in 1887 they could no longer stand in the way. For the first time since the Gotha congress (1875), the delegates demanded that a program revision be undertaken. The motion was carried; Auer, Bebel, and Liebknecht were appointed as a committee to make a "revision" (*Durcharbeitung*) of the party program.[53] It is significant that although only twelve years had passed since the Gotha program was adopted, no Lassalleans were appointed to the committee for the revision of that program.

Conditions for the next three years were so difficult for the Social Democratic leaders that the committee had no chance for a serious discussion of program changes. There was no opportunity for the party as a whole to discuss program changes at a congress. Nevertheless, the move at St. Gall laid the groundwork for the adoption of a Marxist program.

It is not enough to show that the path for the official acceptance of Marxism had been opened. It is more important to ask: What did Marxism mean to those who thought of themselves as Marxists, and how did that meaning relate to the practical political life of the party?

To understand what meaning Marxism had for the Social Democrats it is necessary to examine briefly the contents of the organs which disseminated Marxism to the party as a whole. The chief source for this is the *Neue Zeit*, the journal founded by Karl Kautsky in 1883 with the assistance of Bebel, Liebknecht, Engels, and a leading Social Democratic publisher, Johann Dietz. Primarily, it was Kautsky's journal, and it reflected his interests and ideas. From the early 1880's, Kautsky resolved to overcome the eclecticism in Social Democracy with a journal devoted to the dissemination of a consistent Marxist theory.[54] He went to London in 1881 in order to study near Marx and

[53] *Verhandlungen . . . St. Gallen* (1887), p. 47.
[54] Kautsky, *Erinnerungen und Eroerterungen,* pp. 436–39, 514–17, 523–26.

Engels and lived there for much of the decade. The *Neue Zeit*, therefore, was very close to the thought of Marx and Engels. Of course, Marxism was also spread through the *Sozialdemokrat*, the speeches of some of the Social Democrats, and the writings of Marx and Engels. But of the writings of Marx and Engels it was only the *Communist Manifesto* and Engels' *Anti-Duehring* and the extracts from it in *Socialism: Utopian and Scientific* which were read very widely. The *Neue Zeit*, however, became the chief interpreter of "Scientific Socialism" for German Social Democracy.

One primary fact is strikingly clear not only from the *Neue Zeit* but also from the other sources: Throughout the 1880's, Marxism was presented and understood chiefly as a system of economic analysis with no immediate consequences for the politics of the Social Democratic party. Marxism provided both the motivation and the framework for intensive theoretical and concrete economic study; those who were the purest Marxists of the time, such as Karl Kautsky, concentrated almost exclusively on economic theory, with little concern for either political theory or political action.[55]

The reason for the exclusive concern with economic theory is not difficult to find. Marxism spread extensively at a time when Germany passed through a period of rapid capitalist development. The process of capitalist development which Marx had analyzed in the first volume of *Capital*, largely from the previous experience in England, was now taking place in Germany at a rapid pace. The phenomena of capitalist crises, of periods of depression following prosperity were now well-known. The explosive capitalist expansion of 1871–1873 had ended in a frightening crash and a prolonged depression which was not fully relieved until 1896. Within this era, there were shorter periods of upswing and downswing. Throughout German business and industry, an actual process of concentration was taking place, bringing with it the collapse of smaller operations. Because of technological advancement, handicraft production in several trades succumbed rapidly to the superior productivity of power machines. Urban centers grew as people moved into the cities to seek work in the mushrooming factories.

[55] In a very perceptive analysis, Erich Matthias points out that Kautsky's understanding of Marxism was limited by the natural-scientific assumptions which characterized his generation. Kautsky accepted the assumptions of Darwinism and sought in Marxism a theory for society and history which was equivalent to a natural science. Erich Matthias, "Kautsky und der Kautskyianismus," *Marxismusstudien*, II (1957), pp. 152–54.

Urbanization created a housing problem which was very acute by the middle of the eighties.[56] All of these, and more, were the signs of a capitalist society in the turmoil of industrial growth.

The *Neue Zeit* did not miss any of the signs of capitalist development. It looked for, and found, the internal contradictions which according to Marx would eventually bring the collapse of capitalism. That was the chief Marxist theme of the journal. The indications of economic concentration and of the accumulation of capital were recorded in its pages. Concomitantly, the decline of handicraft production as a consequence of capitalist economic organization and technological advance was repeatedly studied. These economic problems were all interpreted as being the consequences of the insoluble contradictions which characterized the development of capitalism as it moved irresistibly toward a series of severe crises and its predestined disappearance.[57]

That was the Marxist message of the *Neue Zeit;* it was economic and deterministic. It was Marxist to be sure, but without any special political thrust. The fact that political problems were not discussed is an interesting and important point. The more dangerous political subjects were no doubt avoided in part because they would have drawn the attention of the authorities and the journal might have been banned. It was necessary to deal with subjects which could be treated scientifically. Abstract economic theory and even concrete economic studies more easily preserved a scientific tone. The irony, therefore, is that the one journal intentionally founded for the dissemination of Marxism, generally believed to be a most dangerous revolutionary system, was never banned during the Socialist Law!

[56] Hans Rosenberg, "Political and Social Consequences of the Great Depression of 1873–1896 in Central Europe," *Economic History Review,* XIII (1943), pp. 58–73; Gustav Stolper, *German Economy, 1870–1940* (New York, 1940), pp. 83–85; Sombart, *Die deutsche Volkswirtschaft,* pp. 85–86, 178, 298–306, 313–17.

[57] Cf. the following articles in the *Neue Zeit:* "Nochmals des Einkommen der saechsischen Bevoelkerung," II (1884), pp. 126–29; "Die Konzentration des Kapitals und die Steuern," III (1885), pp. 142–43; "Das Bier und die Bierproduktion in Deutschland," III (1885), pp. 257–61; "Die Akkumulation des Kapitals," V (1887), pp. 47–48; P. Kampffmeyer, "Kleine Beitraege zur Geschichte der ursprunglichen Akkumulation des Kapitals in Deutschland," VI (1888), pp. 385–403, 433–49. There were frequent notices and articles in the *Neue Zeit* on the decline of handicraft production, e.g. "Der Rueckgang der Kleinbetriebe," VIII (1890), pp. 30–35. If an author happened to draw unsatisfactory conclusions on the subject, Kautsky added a "Postscript" to explain the Marxist position. Cf. Max Quarck, "Die thueringer Hausindustrie," III (1885), pp. 351–61, and Kautsky's "Nachwort," pp. 359–61.

One can see still a deeper reason for the exclusion of politics from the *Neue Zeit:* Karl Kautsky was not primarily interested in political problems. From his earliest participation in the Austrian socialist movement in 1875, Kautsky had focused his attention on historical and economic theory. His memoir shows that his admiration for his socialist comrades was directly proportional to their theoretical ability, not to their practical abilities as leaders of a working-class movement. He always considered himself a theoretician. His correspondence with Engels, which extends over fifteen years, shows only slight awareness of the importance of practical political questions, as well as of theoretical political problems.[58] As of the late 1880's, Kautsky did not have the experience or the desire to fashion the political course for the Social Democratic party which was integrally related to the Marxist philosophy he sought to disseminate. Kautsky began, and for the most part remained, a professor of Marxist economic theory for the socialist movement.

Kautsky rapidly won a position as the teacher of the Social Democratic party, especially of the young intellectuals. During the late eighties, a few intellectuals, some with university degrees, joined the Social Democratic party. Their intellectual guide, as Paul Kampffmeyer has testified, was Karl Kautsky. It was Kautsky who helped turn almost all of these young intellectuals to economic studies.[59] Many of them, such as Kampffmeyer, Max Schippel, Bruno Schoenlank, Paul Ernst, Heinrich Braun, and Emanuel Sax were well acquainted with Marx's published works, and they collaborated with Kautsky on the *Neue Zeit.*[60]

The interesting fact is that although a few of these young intellectuals went through a short radical phase in 1890, most of them drifted to the party's right wing in the years before the turn of the century. Some of them even disassociated themselves from Social Democracy. Obviously, an understanding and acceptance of economic Marxism did not necessarily produce political revolutionaries. From the perspective

[58] Kautsky, *Erinnerungen und Eroerterungen,* pp. 325, 337–38, 374–75, 442–43, 451–52. Cf. Engels and Kautsky, *Friedrich Engels' Briefwechsel mit Karl Kautsky, passim.*

[59] Paul Kampffmeyer, "Die Gruendung der 'Neuen Zeit' und die Intellektuellen. Eine persoenliche Erinnerung," in *Die Gesellschaft. Ein Sonderheft der Gesellschaft zu Karl Kautskys 70. Geburtstag* (Berlin, 1924), pp. 86–91.

[60] Schippel, Schoenlank, and Kampffmeyer were the most productive of the young intellectuals. As editor of the *Berliner Volkstribuene,* Schippel was able to initiate a series of socialist studies in 1889 devoted to economic and social subjects under the title *Berliner Arbeiterbibliothek.*

of an underlying economic determinism, the study of Marxism by the Social Democrats had no precise and necessary political implications for the action of the party.

Although the leading Marxist intellectuals in German Social Democracy were not concerned with political problems, their economic theory could be, and was, translated into political terms. As long as they understood Marxism to be a science of economic determinism, the logical consequence threatened to undercut the faith of the Social Democrats in the efficacy of their own political action. When the Social Democrats learned from Marx that the political superstructure of society rested upon basic economic relationships, they had no theoretical justification for the expectation, once quite seriously held, that they would gain power and then change the social structure to fit the prescriptions of socialism. From the *Neue Zeit*, the Social Democratic politicians learned that certain economic developments were necessary before their political action could become effective. One possible and serious consequence, therefore, of the Social Democratic understanding of Marxism was political passivity.

It would certainly be unjustified to say categorically that German Social Democrats concluded from their study of Marxism that the correct policy was to be politically passive. At most, this sometimes operated as an implicit, rather than an explicit conclusion for the party leaders. Nevertheless, some did make this an explicit conclusion. Such was the case with Maximilian Schlesinger (1855–1902), a Social Democrat from Breslau who had been very active in the party prior to 1878.[61] In 1889 Schlesinger published a small book on the social question. He professed to be a "student and admirer of Karl Marx," but he was also prepared to criticize Marxism as he understood it.[62] Earlier, in the seventies, Schlesinger had been an opponent of the Eisenachers, but there is no evidence that he had special hostility to Marxism in 1889. He even admitted that previously, in an article for Hoechberg's *Staatswirthschaftliche Abhandlungen*, he had misunderstood Marx's value theory.[63] Furthermore, in his 1889 study he made use of Kautsky's book on *The Economic Doctrines of Karl Marx*, first pub-

[61] Material on Schlesinger in Theodor Mueller (ed.), *45 Fuehrer*, pp. 47–50; and, Theodor Mueller and Georg Kaul (eds.), *Die Geschichte der Breslauer Arbeiter-Bewegung*. Erster Teil: *Bis zum Erlass des Sozialistengesetzes* (Breslau, 1915), pp. 100, 142–43.

[62] Maximilian Schlesinger, *Die Soziale Frage. Eine volkswirtschaftliche Untersuchung* (Breslau, 1889), p. 190.

[63] *Ibid.*, p. 3.

lished in 1887. He had, therefore, in 1889, a good knowledge of Marxist theory as it was understood at the time. All of this makes his observations extremely pertinent.

What must a believing Marxist answer if asked what socialism should do in the present? Schlesinger answers: "The Marxist who judges correctly will declare that the socialists have nothing more to do and also that they can not do otherwise than *to wait* peacefully with folded arms until the time when the great law which controls the accumulating ability of the stronger capitalist is fulfilled and the ground is prepared of itself for socialism. . . . Therefore, the economic slogan of the Marxist school is '*wait*'."[64]

Schlesinger genuinely believed this to be the correct consequence of Marxist economic theory. Nor did he find this conclusion particularly undesirable. Schlesinger, moreover, was not the first to call attention to this point. Hoechberg emphasized it, but as a criticism of the Marxists, in a private letter to Bernstein in 1884. At that time Hoechberg complained that the Marxists answered every problem with the proposition that "time" would bring the solution (see Chapter V). By 1889, when Marxism had gained much more ground in the socialist movement, Schlesinger's observation became even more meaningful. He had openly drawn the conclusion which seemed implicit in so much of the Marxist literature of German Social Democracy.

The inner circle of Marxists—Kautsky, Engels, Bernstein, and Bebel—found Schlesinger's book infuriating. The specific reason for their anger, however, did not stem from the passage quoted in the above paragraph. Although Schlesinger characterized himself as a "student and admirer" of Marx, he quarreled with several aspects of the empirical work in *Capital*. Schlesinger presumed to challenge Marx! Kautsky found that to be nothing but an outrageous "arrogance."[65] But even more maddening, Schlesinger's book had been published by Bruno Geiser in a series called the *Volksbibliothek*, which carried the name of Wilhelm Liebknecht as one of the editors! Its appearance in conjunction with Liebknecht's name left the impression that the German Social Democratic party implicitly endorsed Schlesinger's book.

[64] *Ibid.*, p. 158.

[65] Kautsky to Engels, April 3, 1889, in Engels and Kautsky, *Friedrich Engels' Briefwechsel mit Karl Kautsky*, p. 238. Cf. also Kautsky to Engels, April 17, 1889; and Engels to Kautsky, April 20, 1889, *ibid.*, pp. 239, 240–41.

The appearance of Schlesinger's book dropped a bombshell on Liebknecht, who actually had little to do with its publication. Liebknecht, always in financial trouble, had purchased a part-interest in the *Volksbibliothek*. It improved his financial situation, as well as that of his son-in-law, Geiser. Liebknecht himself did none of the editorial work. But for this connection Liebknecht received wrathful rebukes from Engels and Bebel.[66]

What is most interesting about the whole episode, however, is that those who cited the weakness of Schlesinger's book, never specifically commented on his conclusion that the correct Marxist policy for Social Democracy was to sit and wait. This does not mean that Kautsky and Bebel necessarily agreed with Schlesinger on this point. But in 1889 they did not attack it as the chief weakness of the book. What angered them was not Schlesinger's conclusion, but the fact that criticisms of Marx had appeared in association with a leading member of the Social Democratic party.

How then was the economic and deterministic understanding of Marxism, as illustrated primarily by Karl Kautsky and the *Neue Zeit*, related to Bebel and his predominant position in the Social Democratic party? As the chief politician of Social Democracy, Bebel had to formulate a course for the party in the interests of the working class. It was impossible for Bebel, as a politician, to conclude that a Marxist had nothing to do but wait. Such a negative conclusion, followed to its logical end, would even make the Social Democrats superfluous as a political party. But nothing new had been said in the eighties about Marxist politics which could be the basis for a more intense and direct action by the party. Marxism, as understood and interpreted in the *Neue Zeit*, in no way challenged the established parliamentary course of Social Democratic practice. In fact, it is possible to say that Marxism justified Bebel's own ambivalent approach to German parliamentarism, an attitude which pre-dated Bebel's serious acquaintance with Marx's writings. That ambivalent attitude said simply that the existing political influence of Social Democracy rested on its parliamentary activity, but that parliamentary activity would not be an effective instrument

[66] Liebknecht was forced to disavow the Schlesinger book in the *Sozialdemokrat* and to give up his material interest in the *Volksbibliothek*. Cf. Bebel to Liebknecht, April 15, 1889, Liebknecht Archive, IISH; Liebknecht to Engels, April 19, and Oct. 26, 1889, in Liebknecht, *Briefwechsel mit Karl Marx und Friedrich Engels*, pp. 337–38, 350.

for the transformation of society. Bebel was simultaneously attracted and repelled by parliamentarism. At St. Gall he put it in the following way:

> At no time has there existed a doubt among the party comrades that the power of the Social Democratic party rests fundamentally upon its parliamentary activity and its participation in the elections. Thus, it is not the participation in elections which harms the party, but only the over-estimation of parliamentarism which is dangerous. Whoever believes that the final goals of socialism can be reached by the existing parliamentary-constitutional road either does not know the goals or is an imposter.[67]

Within a Marxist system of economic determinism, ambivalent parliamentarism did not matter. The transformation would come with time. While Bebel waited for the basic transformation to come, he could carry on tactical maneuvers in a parliamentary anteroom. The problem was that the theory of ultimate goals could not be unified with the practice of day-to-day politics. The needed harmony did not exist.

Thus, despite the fact that Bebel had little confidence in the efficacy of parliamentarism, he turned his energy more and more to the practical problems of labor legislation which rested implicitly upon a parliamentary base. Not only had he drafted the Workmen's Protection Bill of 1885 but also, during the years that followed, Bebel studied intensely the reports of factory inspectors. In the latter years of the 1880's, no one else in the party equaled him in knowledge of legislative problems. This is a perplexing development in a man who professed to have no great faith in the effect of legislation.

But something was happening to Bebel's thinking, so gradually that one hardly notices it. In the last years under the Socialist Law, Bebel sometimes spoke more positively than before of the benefits of parliamentarism. While he waited for the economic development to take its course, he also had to be active, and legislative problems were to him the most promising. At the first meeting of the Second International in July 1889, Bebel spoke of how the German Social Democratic party more and more had turned its attention to the practical questions of

[67] *Verhandlungen . . . St. Gallen* (1887), pp. 12–13.

what improvements should be made immediately.[68] Such practical questions, Bebel admitted, assumed that the party wanted to change society through legislation. "German Social Democracy," Bebel told the delegates, "strives not only to spread its own ideas, but also places on itself the task of improving the working and living conditions of the workers by way of legislation, to create for the worker an existence in which he may more easily take up the struggle for emancipation and with greater prospect of success." [69]

Bebel's view on how socialism would be achieved thus had two aspects. First, the economic development of capitalist society would necessarily lead toward a socialist society. That was, in essence, the meaning of revolution. The real transformation would be economic and gradual. That did not exclude the possibility that at some time violence might break out. But force and violence were not necessary; they could in fact destroy the real revolutionary development. Second, to solve immediate problems, the Social Democratic party had to work for the improvement of the working-class condition through legislation. Revolution, therefore, did not enter into the practice of the Social Democratic party. Revolution came as inherent in the course of history, and the Social Democratic party was revolutionary because it identified itself with the class which represented the coming stage in the development of society. The Social Democrats, therefore, could never be the instruments of revolution, but only the beneficiaries of the changes which revolution would bring.

Although Bebel could not say in detail what the revolutionary development would be like, he believed that as history proceeded the Social Democrats could promote legislation which would embody the changes. Sometime in the future, then, it would be possible for the Social Democrats to introduce a fully socialistic program at the appropriate moment. When that moment would come, no one knew, but when it came there would no longer be an effective resistance to a socialist society. Therefore, a Marxist political party quite properly promoted legislation with a socialist tendency in all seriousness. When the historical development had reached a certain stage, the legislation would be accepted.

This in brief summarizes the manner in which Bebel synthesized

[68] *Protokoll des Internationalen Arbeiter-Congresses zu Paris* (Nuremberg, 1890), p. 24.

[69] *Ibid.*, p. 28.

Marxism and Social Democratic parliamentarism. He embodied it all in a Reichstag speech on December 11, 1890. As the abuses of capitalist society increased, Bebel said, so would a spirit of indignation increase in the mass of people. Then he continued:

> In the same degree [as indignation increases] the great majority of people will be permeated with socialist ideas and will be convinced of the absolute necessity for a different order of things. Then one day, without the application of any means of force, control will come into their hands. I could be in error, but with the presently rapid development of matters and thought, one can assume this to be correct. The force which will be used is the same force that you [the ruling classes] use, the force of legislation, the power of the great majority. At some time the great majority will issue its decree, the force of which will obliterate the present social order as it now exists. Peacefully we let this development take its course. We would be mad to precipitate the dangers which a policy of force would have for us and for everyone else. We permit matters to go as they go; in this respect we are the most perfect Manchesterites; in any case, we profit most of all from the course of things. . . .[70]

Two things stand out in this speech: the deterministic course of economic and social development (the end of which favors the Social Democrats) and the introduction of socialism by some kind of legislative action without the use of force. To his own satisfaction, Bebel had unified his knowledge of Marxist economic theory with the parliamentary political practice of the Social Democrats. Although he delivered this speech shortly after the fall of the Socialist Law, it represents the position he had arrived at several years earlier. In that way it illustrates the meaning of Marxism for Bebel and the meaning of Bebel's supremacy for the Social Democratic party.

Conclusion

By 1887, Bebel held the supreme position in the German Social Democratic party, a position which was not challenged until 1890. Bebel's supremacy affected not only the practical political course of the party but also its theoretical tendencies. Since his supremacy meant

[70] *SB*, VIII, i (1890/91), vol. II, p. 868.

that the previous strength of the Lassalleans and moderates had vanished, the path was open for the acceptance of Marxism as the party's official creed. What the party understood by Marxism was derived from the interpreters, the best of which were clustered around Karl Kautsky and the *Neue Zeit*. As of 1890 Marxism was understood almost exclusively to be a system of economic analysis based upon a deterministic theory of history and economic development. The implicit consequence of such a determinism was that a true Marxist party had nothing to do but await the coming of a socialist society. No political party, however, could explicitly draw such a conclusion without also destroying its own *raison d'être*.

As a politician, Bebel could not accept a passive role. Nevertheless, he accepted the premise that political action would not be the means to bring about the basic transformation in society. That transformation would come with the predetermined development in capitalist society. The revolution about which the Social Democrats spoke was economic and would be achieved by the objective development; the political action of the Social Democratic party, Bebel believed, was powerless to accelerate this development.

The political role of the Social Democratic party, therefore, could be limited to the promotion of legislation appropriate to the level of economic development at any one time. In this conception, political action, Social Democratic or any other, could only be a peripheral factor in the coming of socialism. Parliamentary politics fitted perfectly into such a scheme. In Germany that meant that Social Democracy fashioned its practical work after the pattern of the liberal parties. Concrete legislative work forced itself into the foreground and dominated the lives of the leading Social Democrats. Legislative activity became the proper, in fact the only possible sphere of Social Democratic work. All of this was very consistent with their Marxism.

A serious obstacle remained, however, which further crippled the party's hopes for political action. The German Reichstag was not the sole center of power, in fact it was hardly a center of power at all. Therefore, the German Social Democrats could not even feel satisfied that in parliamentary action they had an effective instrument for genuine social reform. Pushed toward parliamentarism by tactical necessity and a theory of history which allowed them no other sphere of action, they were simultaneously pulled away from parliamentarism because of its weakness in the German state. This ambivalence, so evident in

August Bebel, also dominated the party as a whole.[71] That was the ideological and practical meaning of Bebel's supremacy in the party.

[71] The ambivalent parliamentarism on the party level is illustrated in the following resolution passed in 1889 at a provincial Social Democratic election conference. The first part of the resolution is not easily harmonized with the second, and yet the whole accepts parliamentary action as essential. "In consideration of the fact that no thorough-going reforms, either in the political or economic area, are to be expected for the whole of the people from the German Reichstag in its present form (proof: Old Age and Invalidity Insurance, Socialist Law, Grain Tariff, etc.), the congress of Social Democratic voters from the Rhineland-Westphalia, meeting on Sunday, November 10, 1889, at the 'Johannisberg' in Elberfeld, declares that it is the duty of every party comrade to campaign forcefully in the next elections for the Social Democratic Candidates." From: *Sozialdemokratischer Parteitage fuer die Rheinprovinz und den Niederrhein von 1889–1909* (Elberfeld, 1910), p. 8.

CHAPTER XI · THE END OF THE SOCIALIST LAW: SOCIAL DEMOCRACY'S VICTORY AND CHALLENGE

A Year of Great Changes

DURING THE final phase of the Socialist Law, the established policy of German Social Democracy, as expressed in the views and actions of August Bebel, was both magnificently victorious and seriously challenged. Four events of 1890 were associated directly or indirectly with the victorious course of Social Democracy: the refusal of the Reichstag to renew the Socialist Law on January 25; the spoken support of Wilhelm II for the principle of protective labor legislation; the Social Democratic victory at the polls on February 20 (the party received 19.75 percent of the popular vote); and finally the resignation of Bismarck on March 18.

The demonstration at the polls was the most significant Social Democratic victory. It seemed to show beyond the slightest doubt that the party's parliamentary policy was an effective weapon. But such electoral success had dangers. With thirty-five deputies in the Reichstag, the Social Democrats could not just make speeches. Hopes of parliamentary reformism would certainly be aroused. But those opposed to parliamentarism were also aroused to speak more forcefully. The anti-parliamentarians in the Social Democratic party had to make a move at this moment if ever they were to challenge seriously the party's established policy. Their problems, however, were many. Their most serious obstacle was that Bebel, who at a previous period of great Social Democratic parliamentary activity (1884–1886) stood opposed to the majority, now in 1890 was the chief defender of the majority position in the party. In order to understand the nature of the anti-parliamentarian challenge let us first see the context of the events into which it fits.

The Miners' Strike (1889) and Wilhelm II's Social Policy

In 1888 the German economy began an upswing which lasted until 1891. Its best months came in 1889 and 1890. On the highest organizational level of the economy, this short period was marked by the formation of many of the cartels which still existed decades later. On the workers' level the increased prosperity was slight but noticeable, chiefly by creating new employment opportunities and stimulating a rise in wage rates. By 1889 the average gross money wages in industry had nearly regained their previous high of 1874. In agriculture, workers' wages had already surpassed the previous high. In such a period of boom, however, wages could not keep up with the cost of living.[1]

The economic boom naturally stimulated the demands of the workers for better working conditions and higher pay. For the trade unions this meant excellent opportunities for organizing workers. Not only because of the boom but also because Puttkamer's campaign against the labor movement had been relaxed (Friedrich III turned Puttkamer out of office in 1888), the trade unions experienced a spectacular rise in membership. Judged in terms of membership, 1889 and 1890 were the best years for the trade unions until a new boom came after 1896. Simultaneous with the rise in trade union membership came the demand for higher wages. A new era of strikes hit Germany in the summer of 1889.[2]

[1] Sombart, *Die deutsche Volkswirtschaft*, pp. 86, 316; Juergen Kuczynski, *A Short History of Labour Conditions under Industrial Capitalism*, III, Part I (London, 1945), pp. 128–29. Since Kuczynski is the only scholar who has attempted to construct a comprehensive wage index for the whole period between 1871 and 1913, his data are also used by Bry, *Wages in Germany*, pp. 329–30. See also Kuczynski's *Die Geschichte der Lage der Arbeiter unter dem Kapitalismus*, III, pp. 297–98, 302, comparing real wages and costs of living.

[2] For the period of the Socialist Law, there are no really reliable records on trade union membership. The following figures, compiled by W. Kulemann from the police records and the estimates of the *Generalkommission der Gewerkschaften Deutschlands* give the best estimate of the trade unions associated with Social Democracy.

1885/86	100,356
1887/88	103,330
Spring, 1889	135,353
Spring, 1890	277,098
End, 1890	320,213
Spring, 1891	277,474
End, 1891	269,988

The increase thus reached its peak at the end of 1890 and then fell off in 1891 with the general downswing of the economy.

The most spectacular strike of the whole Socialist Law era broke out among the coal miners in the Ruhr on May 2, 1889. Within a few days, it spread throughout Germany until not less than 120,000 miners were on strike by May 20. The strike erupted as a spontaneous grass-roots expression of discontent, not even planned by the recognized leaders of the miners. They had in fact previously arranged a conference for June 2 on means to secure shorter working hours. But almost without warning the miners in the Essen district struck on May 2 and the strike wave surged throughout Germany.[3]

Like everyone else in Germany, the Social Democratic leaders were taken completely by surprise by the miners' strike. There was in fact very little Social Democratic influence among the miners, especially in western Germany. Prior to the Socialist Law period, Hasselmann had sought to draw the miners in the Rhineland and Westphalia into the socialist movement. The results had been extremely limited. After 1878, socialist influence vanished almost completely, since the miners, mostly Catholic in faith, subscribed only to organizations which were sympathetic to Christianity. As of 1889, the Social Democrats had no organizational strength among these miners. However, one of the leaders of the 1889 strike movement, Ludwig Schroeder, had been an associate of Hasselmann during the 1870's. To lead the miners in 1889, Schroeder had to hide his previous Social Democratic affiliations. Only in 1890, when he ran for the Reichstag as a Social Democratic candidate, were his convictions fully known.[4]

The Social Democratic party remained aloof from the miners' strike and protested quite honestly that it did not approve of the walkout.

The Hirsch-Duncker unions, although never harassed during the Socialist Law, only increased their membership immediately following the passage of the Accident and Sickness Insurance plans in 1883–84; the upswing of 1888–91 did not help them. The Hirsch-Duncker membership:

1878	16,500
1885	51,000
1891	63,000

These figures are from W. Kulemann, "Die Gewerkvereine in Deutschland," *Handwoerterbuch der Staatswissenschaften* (2nd ed.), IV, pp. 649, 659.

[3] Schulthess, *1889*, pp. 64, 66–67; Kulemann, *Die Berufsvereine*, II, p. 326.

[4] Kulemann, *Die Berufsvereine*, II, pp. 323–26; R. Oldenberg, "Studien ueber die rheinisch-westfaelische Bergarbeiterbewegung," *Jahrbuch fuer Gesetzgebung, Verwaltung und Volkswirthschaft im Deutschen Reich*, XIV (1890), pp. 917–19, 954–55. Although it was generally recognized that the Social Democrats were weak among the miners, the Berlin Police President sent four detectives of the political police to the area to keep a special watch for socialist influence. Fricke, *Bismarcks Praetorianer*, p. 275.

Shortly after the strike began, an unidentified miner privately addressed an appeal to Bebel for funds from the Social Democratic "colleagues abroad." Bebel not only replied that no assistance would be forthcoming from the Social Democrats but he also advised the strikers to find an "acceptable compromise" with their employers.[5] At a moment when employee discontent had risen to an unprecedented level for the period of the Socialist Law, Bebel thus cautioned the workers to be moderate and "compromise" with the employers. His position harmonized with the generally accepted party view that the trade unions were valuable primarily as organizations in which the workers could learn the need for solidarity and class consciousness. Social Democrats did not expect significant economic gain from trade union activities, strikes or otherwise.[6]

The miners were not so pessimistic about their chances of economic gain. Furthermore, they were willing to appeal to any source which might help them. For that reason, three representatives of the striking miners, Ludwig Schroeder, Friedrich Bunte, and August Siegel, had an audience with the young Kaiser, Wilhelm II. While Wilhelm seemed to give them a sympathetic hearing, he also warned them to stay clear of all Social Democratic influence, "since for me [Wilhelm II] every Social Democrat is the same as an enemy of the Reich and the Fatherland." [7]

At first the miners succeeded; representatives of the mine owners guaranteed an eight-hour shift. Within a few days, however, the miners complained that the employers had already broken their promises. The owners had regained their confidence, and the further course of events went badly for the miners. The Social Democrats took this as justification of their original low estimation of the strike.[8]

The miners' strike proved a decisive event in prompting Wilhelm II's demand for labor legislation. The strike dramatized Germany's industrial problem at a time when the need for labor legislation had be-

[5] Open letter by Bebel, quoted in "Sozialpolitische Rundschau," *SD*, No. 23, June 8, 1889.

[6] In 1887 the *Sozialdemokrat* expressed the opinion that in the industrial states of Europe trade unions would soon cease to be an organizational form for the class conflict! "Die Grenzen der Leistungsfaehigkeit der Gewerkschaften, *SD*, No. 27, July 1, 1887. Cf. also "Ein lehrreiche Streik-Statistik," *SD*, No. 17, April 21, 1888, and No, 19, May 5, 1888; "Streiks," *Neue Zeit*, VIII (1890), pp. 47–48.

[7] From the minutes of the audience, quoted in Schulthess, *1889*, p. 64.

[8] *Ibid.*, pp. 71–74; "Verrathen und verkauft!" *SD*, No. 22, June 1, 1889.

come a frequent topic of public discussion, not merely with socialists but also with the governmental authorities of the continent. Early in 1889, the Swiss government had suggested an international conference on labor problems. As the young Kaiser was drawn directly into the negotiations with the striking miners, he gained a new awareness of the distressing problems faced by Germany's laboring class. He held the view, in contrast to Bismarck, that the state had an obligation to regulate in greater degree the working conditions in German industry. Wilhelm II, therefore, moved in that direction until it brought him into a direct and insoluble conflict with Bismarck.[9]

At the same time that Wilhelm II turned his attention to labor legislation, it was also the chief topic on the agenda for the first meeting of the Second International (Paris, July 14–20, 1889). The most important discussions and resolutions of the Paris congress called upon all of the industrialized nations to pass labor legislation embodying the eight-hour day, the abolition of child labor, and the other usual demands. Bebel collaborated with Jules Guesde, the French Marxist, to draft the congress's resolution on labor legislation. A more activist resolution, calling upon all parties associated with the International to demonstrate on May 1, 1890, for the eight-hour day was the sole work of the French delegates. The delegates at the congress did not place the emphasis on the demonstration, but on the legislation which they demanded be passed in each state.[10]

The year 1889 thus revealed an interesting and significant development: For the first time some agreement emerged between the head of the Reich government and the Social Democrats on what direction state action should take in order to be most helpful to the working class. That did not mean that the two camps could reconcile their basic differences, but a new phase was entered. The government, if it fol-

[9] Ziekursch, *Politische Geschichte*, II, pp. 431–35. The minutes of the *Staatsministerium* meeting on May 12, 1889, show that Bismarck, in contrast to Wilhelm II, was willing to see the miners' strike continue in order to "educate" the liberals in view of the coming debate on the Socialist Law. Paul Grebe, "Bismarcks Sturz und der Bergarbeiterstreik vom Mai 1889. Ein Beitrag aus den Akten des Staatsministeriums," *Historische Zeitschrift*, 157 (1937), pp. 90–91.

[10] *Protokoll des Internationalen Arbeiter-Congresses zu Paris* (1889), pp. 121–23. An unsigned article in *Schmoller's Jahrbuch* noted with proper bourgeois pleasure that from the conclusions of the Paris congress it was clear that reformism had won out. "Die internationalen Arbeiterkongresse des letzten Jahrzehntes und ihre Bedeutung fur die Arbeiterschutzreform," *Jahrbuch fuer Gesetzgebung, Verwaltung und Volkswirthschaft im Deutschen Reich*, XIV (1890), pp. 1262–64.

lowed Wilhelm II, now willingly recognized the legislative principle upon which the Social Democrats had built their previous labor protection bills as the best approach to social reform.

Bismarck realized that Wilhelm's growing support for protective labor legislation meant also that the harsh version of the Socialist Law would not be acceptable. The old Chancellor, therefore, fought desperately throughout January 1890 against the new orientation of the Kaiser. But Wilhelm II would not give in to Bismarck. At the decisive moment, in a Crown Council meeting on January 24, 1890, Wilhelm would not retreat even when Bismarck threatened to resign if the harsh version of the Socialist Law were not supported.[11]

The antagonism between Wilhelm II and Bismarck added to the differences among the Cartel parties on what to do about the Socialist Law. Only the conservative parties stood behind Bismarck's demand for a severe and permanent Socialist Law. The National Liberals were willing to accept a permanent Socialist Law only if it excluded the most severe measure, the Minor State of Siege. On this issue, Wilhelm II agreed with the National Liberals. The Center party now had a large majority entirely opposed to the law. And the parties to the left were all opposed to a renewal of the Socialist Law. On January 25, 1890, the Reichstag voted on a version of the Socialist Law which did not include the Minor State of Siege. The conservative parties, finding this version too soft, voted against it, while the National Liberals supported it. The parties from the Center party through the left voted against it. In this way the Socialist Law failed, but no one was sure at the end of January whether the elections in February would bring another strong Bismarck majority which would write a new law against the socialists.[12]

Immediately following the Reichstag's refusal to renew the Socialist Law, Wilhelm II publicly announced a significant change in government policy on labor questions. On February 4, he outlined in brief his reform plans and called for an international conference to discuss problems of protective legislation for labor. The statement indicated a decisive turn in government policy, based, however, upon much the same hope that had motivated Bismarck when he first promoted workmen's insurance. The government still hoped to draw the workers away from

[11] Ziekursch, *Politische Geschichte*, II, pp. 436–38.

[12] *Ibid.*, pp. 434–35; Pack, *Das parlamentarische Ringen*, pp. 230–35. For press opinion from the various parties see Apitzsch, *Die deutsche Tagespresse*, *passim.*

Social Democracy. Nevertheless, Wilhelm II's new policy also implied a recognition that many of the demands of Social Democracy were entirely justified, especially as they had been embodied in the labor protection bills of 1877 and 1885.[13]

The Social Democrats did not miss the fact that Wilhelm's statement conceded at least an indirect victory for their principles. Therefore, they greeted his policy statement with an unusual amount of goodwill. "What we wish to affirm above everything else," commented the *Berliner Volksblatt*, "is the moral victory which Social Democracy has gained in the shift of government policy. . . ." [14] The *Sozialdemokrat* hailed the announcement of February 4 as an "event of world history" and continued:

> No one can charge that we feel excessive respect for monarchs or attach too much significance to their activities. But here is an action whose significance can be sooner underestimated than overestimated.
>
> We are not joking. We are completely serious when we say that we believe that our evaluation [of the statement] is as great as its promoter's, Wilhelm II.[15]

These are certainly conciliatory words coming from the *Sozialdemokrat*. They are almost reminiscent of Viereck's sympathetic expressions for Bismarck's support of the "right to work" in 1884. Viereck believed in 1884 that Bismarck had conceded an important point. And so in 1890 the *Sozialdemokrat* believed that Wilhelm II had conceded an important point. The difference was that the "right to work" was not a principle or demand of the Social Democratic program (see Gotha program, Appendix A). Nevertheless, the cases are somewhat parallel, for the Social Democrats relaxed their political opposition when the powers above showed some sympathy for the economic problems of labor.

The Kaiser's concession on the principle of labor legislation was therefore a boon to anyone in the Social Democratic party who believed that the social problem could be solved by the cooperation of the monarch and the Reichstag. Wilhelm II had admitted that the principle of the Social Democratic labor legislative initiatives was now

[13] Eyck, *Bismarck*, III, pp. 564–65, 574–76.
[14] *Berliner Volksblatt*, No. 32, Feb. 7, 1890, p. 1.
[15] "Vor dem Siegeswagen der Sozialdemokratie," *SD*, No. 7, Feb. 15, 1890.

regierungsfaehig. This victory for Social Democracy, however, simultaneously generated more hope and enthusiasm for a strictly parliamentary party policy. The other Social Democratic successes in 1890 also enlarged the possibilities of parliamentary action.

February 20, 1890: 1,427,298 Social Democratic Votes!

The chances for an intense parliamentary policy were greatly enhanced by the election results of February–March 1890, which brought the Social Democrats thirty-five seats in the Reichstag.

In the election campaign, the Social Democrats emphasized their role as an opposition party to Bismarck and the "reactionaries." As an opposition party, the *Sozialdemokrat* declared, it was important that the Social Democrats win not only votes but also as many seats as possible.[16] The concentration on the number of mandates appears in 1890 as something new in the Social Democratic attitude toward elections; previously it had been argued that the number of mandates was not important. And, because the Social Democrats were in opposition to Bismarck, the *Sozialdemokrat* declared that they had no interest in seeing the numbers of the *Freisinnige* party weakened. They summed it all up in the slogan: "A defeat of the government parties, or, in other words: a victory for the opposition parties." [17]

The campaign literature also shows how the economic and gradualist interpretation of revolution was popularly used by the leaders of the party. They accepted the Kaiser's proclamation of February 4 on labor legislation as evidence of an inevitable movement of society toward socialism. Commenting on the proclamation, the *Berliner Volksblatt* concluded that our "present society is growing into socialism. . . ." [18] Even the young radicals such as Bruno Wille, one of those who later led an attack on Bebel's leadership, dismissed "overthrow" as irrelevant for Social Democracy since "evolution" would bring a solution. Wille observed happily, "So out of the present capitalist mode of production the socialist will evolve." [19] The economic and gradualist interpreta-

[16] "Zu den bevorstehenden Reichstagswahlen, I," *SD*, No. 2, Jan. 12, 1890.

[17] "Zu den bevorstehenden Reichstagswahlen, II," *SD*, No. 3, Jan. 18, 1890. On the need for the opposition parties to find a common basis for action, see *Berliner Volksblatt*, No. 25, Jan. 30, 1890, *Beilage*, p. 3, and No. 37, Feb. 13, 1890, p. 3.

[18] "Auf zur Wahl," *Berliner Volksblatt*, No. 42, Feb. 19, 1890, pp. 1–2.

[19] *Berliner Volksblatt*, No. 38, Feb. 14, 1890, *Beilage*, p. 3.

tion of revolution had become a commonplace. It was highly appropriate for a party with parliamentary ambitions.

For the Social Democrats, the election results were astounding. Not even the most optimistic Social Democrat would have predicted that the party would take almost 20 percent of the total with a popular tally of 1,427,298 votes. In the popular vote, this made the Social Democrats the strongest party in Germany. After winning twenty mandates on the first ballot, the Social Democrats picked up fifteen more on the run-off ballot; that gave them a Reichstag delegation of thirty-five.[20]

It is as difficult to give precise reasons for the great popular vote of the Social Democrats in 1890 as it is to explain the growing strength of the party throughout the period of the Socialist Law. Quite obviously, the Social Democratic growth related directly not only to the political but also to the deeper social and economic changes taking place in Germany. Some of the victory in 1890 must certainly have come from the rising discontent with the policies of Bismarck. But as a cause for Social Democratic success this cannot be taken very seriously. Political opposition to Bismarck could be expressed more easily in a vote for the *Freisinnige* party, which represented the purest political opposition. In fact, the *Freisinnige* vote did increase in 1890, so that instead of thirty-two seats the party had seventy-six. The south German People's party, totally defeated in 1887, also reappeared in 1890 with two seats. It is fair to assume that those Germans who merely wished to vote against Bismarck cast their votes for these parties. A purely protest vote cannot account for the great Social Democratic rise in 1890.

The basic cause of Social Democratic electoral success must be sought among those Germans, mostly workers, who for various reasons were increasingly alienated from the dominant German culture as defined by the traditions of *Bildung und Besitz* (education and prop-

[20] Those who won on the first ballot were: Auer (Glauchau), Bebel (Hamburg I), Dietz (Hamburg II), Frohme (Altona), Foerster (Greiz), Geyer, (Leipzig-Land), Grillenberger (Nuremberg), Harm (Elberfeld-Barmen), Hickel (Muelhausen i. Alsace), Horn (6th Saxon District), Liebknecht (Berlin VI), Metzger (Hamburg III), Schippel (Chemnitz), Schmidt (Mittweida), Schumacher (Solingen), Seifert (Stollberg-Schneeberg), Singer (Berlin IV), Stolle (Zwickau-Crimmitschau), Vollmar in two (Magdeburg and Munich II), and Wurm (Gera). "Der 20. Februar," *SD*, No. 9, March 1, 1890. On the second ballot the following won: Birk (Munich I), Blos (Brunswick), Bock (Magdeburg), Bruhns (Bremen), Dreesbach (Mannheim), Heine (Aschersleben), Joest (Mainz), Kunert (Halle), Meister (Hannover), Molkenbuhr (Pinneberg), Schmidt (Frankfurt a. M.), Schultze (Koenigsberg in Prussia), Schwartz (Luebeck), Stadthagen (Niederbarnim), Tutzauer (Breslau-East), Ulrich (Offenbach). Neumann-Hofer, *Die Entwicklung der Sozialdemokratie*, p. 47.

erty). This was both a social and an intellectual alienation. It characterized not only the new factory worker but all of those people whose way of life was disrupted or threatened by the process of industrialization. As mechanization increased in many trades, the handicraft worker discovered that the value of his labor had fallen. The search for work and the demand for a large concentrated labor force led to rapid urbanization. The working population of the growing cities such as Berlin and Hamburg was cut off from its old traditions. For these people the Social Democratic party offered a way both to express their alienation from German society and to identify with an organization in which the worker could find friendship and assistance.

The significance of the alienated German for Social Democracy is highlighted if we observe that the party failed to penetrate those areas in which Catholicism was strong. Catholicism, it may be suggested, offered the worker two essentials also given by Social Democracy. First, because of the *Kulturkampf* in the seventies the Catholic worker already felt estranged from the Reich in a cultural-religious sense. He could express this politically by voting for the Center party. A Catholic worker had no driving need to find another party of opposition. Second, even as a worker, a Catholic had no difficulty in maintaining his religious-political identification because from the time of Bishop Ketteler's first social teachings in the sixties both clerical and lay Catholics had developed a fairly articulate social consciousness. Thus, despite the highly industrialized character of the Ruhr by 1890, the Catholic worker there was not attracted to the Social Democratic party.

On the other hand, in the heavily Protestant areas of Saxony, where the consequences of mechanized weaving were first experienced, the Social Democrats maintained a strong hold even in towns of small population. In contrast to the worker with a Catholic tradition, the worker from a Protestant tradition had no opportunity to express a feeling of dissension through a confessional political party. Further, the worker from a Protestant tradition found that he could not identify fully with his inherited religion without endorsing the political supremacy of those who had social and economic control over him. The Protestant faith, therefore, offered no institutional forms through which he could dissent from the political establishment and still keep an identification with religion.

The electoral success of the Social Democrats in 1890 must also be related to the economic upswing which began in 1888. Trade union statistics for Germany show that membership rose concurrent with this upswing. That is not surprising since prosperity brought a demand for more labor power. What is startling, however, is that trade union membership (in those unions associated with Social Democracy) reached a peak by the end of 1890 which it did not regain until another economic upswing in 1896. From the beginning of 1889 to the beginning of 1890, trade union membership rose from 135,353 to 277,098. By the end of 1890, it reached 320,213. After that it declined for several years, and then rose until by 1896 it once again surpassed 300,000. These figures reflect a most feverish trade union activity concurrent with the elections of 1890.[21]

None of the factors mentioned completely explains the rise in strength of Social Democracy by 1890. One must say, almost as a tautology, that the Social Democrats were saying the right thing at the right time. Even the Kaiser had publicly admitted a need for protective labor legislation in his announcement on February 4. And the Kaiser made his announcement just two weeks before the election! What other party with a tradition of intransigent opposition could justifiably say that it had just won the Kaiser over to a principle which had been opposed for years by the Iron Chancellor? Without any awareness of the political implications of his declaration on February 4, Wilhelm II had enhanced the prestige of the Social Democrats, although he believed naïvely that his apparent goodwill toward the workers would wean them away from the socialists. After the election, Bebel commented on the meaning of the Kaiser's new policy for Social Democracy: "He [Wilhelm II] has the ambition to become a great social reformer. This ambition does not hurt us. Rather it is a very significant advantage for us because it puts him [Wilhelm II] on bad terms with the bourgeoisie and provides gigantic support for our endeavors among the masses." [22]

May 1: "We Shall Seek to Do Our Duty"

During the first three months of 1890, the Social Democrats passed from one exhilarating experience to another until all seemed capped by the resignation of Bismarck on March 18. Within a few months the party faced a situation greatly improved over what had existed in the

[21] Kulemann, in *Handwoerterbuch der Staatswissenschaften* (2nd ed.), IV, p. 659.
[22] Bebel to Engels, March 7, 1890, in Bebel, *Briefwechsel*, p. 383.

middle of 1889. The last great trial against the Social Democrats at Elberfeld in November–December 1889 had ended in a virtual defeat for the prosecution. The miners' strike had turned the Kaiser toward a positive labor legislative policy. The Cartel bloc had been weakened beyond repair by the elections of February. That insured, for all practical purposes, that the Socialist Law would not be renewed. The trade unions, enjoying both the economic upswing and the relaxation of pressures against them were going through a period of unprecedented boom.

The government's oppressive heel had also been lifted from the Social Democrats in many areas during 1889. In the fall of that year, provincial party congresses were held in Saxony, Rhineland-Westphalia, Baden, Hesse, and Silesia. Some 3,000 persons attended the Rhineland-Westphalia meeting on November 10, 1889 at Elberfeld.[23] All of this activity created an atmosphere of throbbing excitement in the labor movement. The momentum carried on past the election in February; everywhere rank-and-file Social Democrats expected that something more would be done. But what?

Those who wanted a further demonstration of the buoyant strength of the Social Democratic movement had a ready-made issue. The first meeting of the Second International at Paris in July 1889 had resolved that a "great international demonstration" for the eight-hour working day should take place on May 1, 1890. The labor leaders in each country were left to decide the specific form of the demonstration.[24]

In Germany it was up to the Social Democratic Reichstag deputies to spell out what should be done about May 1. But the newly elected delegation had no reason to convene during March and April since the Reichstag was not called into session until the first week of May. No word came from the party executive throughout March. The most powerful leaders of the party, such as Bebel, Liebknecht, and Singer, were all silent. But other voices were heard. During the first week of March, the *Berliner Volkstribuene*, edited by Max Schippel, discussed the possibility of a general holiday (*Feiertag*) for May 1, without specifically endorsing such a plan.[25] In the middle of March the same paper reported that 90,000 workers in Hamburg had demanded that

[23] *Sozialdemokratischer Parteitage fuer die Rheinprovinz und den Niederrhein von 1889–1909* (Elberfeld, 1910), pp. 3, 7.

[24] *Protokoll des Internationalen Arbeiter-Congresses zu Paris* (1889), p. 123.

[25] "Was soll am 1. Mai geschehen?" *Berliner Volkstribuene*, No. 9, March 1, 1890, pp. 3–4; "Zum 1. Mai 1890," *ibid.*, No. 10, March 8, 1890, p. 2.

May 1 be observed as a general *Feiertag* when no one would report for work.[26]

The workers thus set a course of their own, independent of the Social Democratic party leadership. Then the momentum increased. One week later, representatives of the Berlin Social Democrats publicly announced that they called for a general work stoppage on May 1.[27] This shifted the center to Berlin, the home of the most radical Social Democrats. At the end of March, the *Berliner Volkstribuene* fully endorsed the plan that the Social Democratic party call upon all German workers to celebrate May 1 with workers' meetings in the morning and festivities in the afternoon.[28] Still no word came from the executive committee.

The silence of the executive committee was not entirely accidental. In truth, the established Social Democratic leaders had no taste for a gigantic demonstration on May 1. Work stoppages and huge demonstrations throughout Germany, they feared, would become uncontrollable and open physical conflict might ensue. They preferred to draw back, even though a mass of German workingmen clamored for a show of strength.

The supreme commander of the party, Bebel, reflected all of these fears. He showed how much he preferred order and regularity to wild excitement and spontaneity. The masses, he admitted to Engels in a letter on March 31, had to be restrained before they jeopardized the orderly development of matters. Engels had already warned the German Social Democrats not to fall into Putsches, because "the increase of Social Democratic votes proceeds forward at every new election with the irresistibility of a natural process. . . ." [29] Here are Bebel's views on the same subject:

> I agree completely with you [Engels] that we in Germany find ourselves in a situation which demands the greatest tact and skillfulness. For this reason we have every cause to hold the masses within bounds in connection with the demonstration on May 1, so that no conflicts arise. Should we give the people free reins such conflicts would be inevitable, for the elections have turned the heads of the

[26] *Berliner Volkstribuene,* No. 11, March 15, 1890, *Beiblatt,* p. 3.
[27] "Was soll am 1. Mai geschehen?" *Berliner Volkstribuene,* No. 12, March 22, 1890, p. 4.
[28] "Zum 1. Mai," *Berliner Volkstribuene,* No. 13, March 29, 1890, p. 1.
[29] Friedrich Engels, "Was Nun?" *SD,* No. 10, March 8, 1890.

lesser trained masses and they believe that all they need is an act of will and anything can be achieved. Some people [meaning Social Democratic leaders], who certainly have no reputation for anxiety and over-cautiousness, even complain that they can hardly keep the reins on the masses.

Since now the course of business, by and large, is such that it creates a demand for workers, the strike fever is general and the noisiest possible demonstration on May 1 would lead immediately to strikes in unthought-of dimensions.

. . . .

Yesterday's *Volkszeit*[*ung*] was completely correct when it wrote that February 20 was a demonstration of the German workers which could not be outdone in magnificence. Nevertheless, we shall seek to do our duty on May 1.[30]

Bebel aptly expressed the general view of his colleagues: They viewed the May 1 demonstration as a "duty" which they would have to perform despite their obvious preference to back away from it. Their attitude is not surprising. During the Socialist Law, they had learned how to handle the orderly routine of parliamentary activity, but they had practically no experience with really mass activity. For years they had learned that prudence called them to avoid situations which could lead to violence. The Social Democratic tactic, Bebel wrote to Engels on April 9, would be to avoid all "provocations" by assuming a "waiting posture" at least until the Socialist Law had definitely expired on September 30.[31]

The Social Democratic Reichstag delegation finally met on April 13 to formulate party policy for May 1. It flatly rejected all plans for a general walkout on the grounds that the walkout would not succeed, and further, that the government had no greater wish than to see a conflict provoked so that force could be used against the labor move-

[30] Bebel to Engels, March 31, 1890, in Bebel, *Briefwechsel*, pp. 384–85. This is an answer to a letter which Engels wrote to Bebel on March 19, 1890, which unfortunately, is not extant. We can assume that the content of that letter was consistent with his article "Was Nun?" and with what Bebel made reference to. From all the evidence it is not clear that Engels agreed with everything Bebel did during 1890. The *Volkszeitung*, to which Bebel refers, was the radical liberal paper edited by Franz Mehring, who had not yet joined openly with the Social Democrats.

[31] Bebel to Engels, April 9, 1890, in Bebel, *Briefwechsel*, p. 387.

ment. The deputies stressed the greatness of the election victory on February 20. The enemies of labor, they said, were waiting for a chance to destroy the "fruits of the victory of February 20. . . ." "After the great mobilization [*Aufmarsch*] and victory of February 20, German Social Democracy has no need to hold a military parade [*Heerschau*]." The deputies therefore called upon the workers to celebrate May 1 by holding workers' meetings and festivities in the evening at which resolutions for the eight-hour day could be passed. If in some places, walkouts could be carried out without conflicts, the leaders did not forbid it.[32] In this way, the deputies had performed their "duty," and also sought to keep the reins on the mass of workers.

Throughout Germany, May 1 passed without any disturbing incidents. After working hours, meetings and festivities took place at which resolutions were passed. Order had been maintained in the labor movement.[33]

The Jungen: *Critics of the Established Leadership*

The May 1 issue brought into focus some deep dissension within the Social Democratic party. The party's executive committee (the Reichstag *Fraktion*), by its original hesitation and then its call for restraint and moderation, had frustrated the plans of those Social Democrats who wanted a gigantic demonstration of strength. Criticism of the May 1 policy led to criticism in other areas, until finally the whole orientation of the party came under attack.

The onslaught was led by a group of young intellectuals soon known as the *Jungen* (the Young Ones). Most of them were in their twenties or early thirties. They were an entirely different generation from the older leaders Auer, Bebel, Grillenberger, Liebknecht, and Singer, all of whom had already passed their fortieth year. Unlike the older generation, the *Jungen* included a great number of university-trained intellectuals, Max Schippel, Bruno Wille, Paul Kampffmeyer, Hans Mueller, Paul Ernst, and Bruno Sommer. Only a few of the leading *Jungen*, such as Wilhelm Werner and Karl Wildberger, were handicraft workers. All of the *Jungen* who played leading roles were connected with socialist

[32] "Zum ersten Mai," *SD*, No. 16, April 19, 1890.

[33] From throughout Germany the Prussian Interior Ministry received reports on what had taken place on May 1. Since nothing much happened, these reports are very short and unanimously report that everything was quiet and orderly. Cf. Germany, FM Archives, UM, R. 104, frms. 360–431.

newspapers. In Berlin they centered around the *Berliner Volkstribuene*, in Magdeburg around the *Volksstimme* (Mueller and Kampffmeyer), and in Dresden around the *Saechsische Arbeiterzeitung* (Sommer and Ernst). All of them, however, as a result of their conflict with Bebel and the older leaders, were removed from these papers before 1890 had passed.[34]

The intellectuals among the *Jungen* did much to set the character of the attack on the established party policies. These intellectuals had grown up and gone to school at a time when discussion of the "Social Question" had come into vogue. Like Karl Kautsky, who was a few years older, the *Jungen* intellectuals had focused their studies on economic problems. Several of them, Schippel, Kampffmeyer, and Ernst, wrote for the *Neue Zeit*. Although they were young and relatively new to the Social Democratic party, they had on the whole a much better knowledge of Marxism than the established party leaders. At least Schippel, Kampffmeyer, Ernst, and Mueller had plunged into serious study of the first two volumes of *Capital*, which was more than most party leaders, excluding Bebel and perhaps Liebknecht, had done. The *Jungen* believed with some justification that they knew as much about "Scientific Socialism" as the older Social Democrats.[35]

In addition to social and economic studies, several of the *Jungen* had literary interests, notably Paul Ernst and Bruno Wille. Both were members of a Berlin circle of young avant-garde writers known as *Durch*, which started in 1886. In their revolt against the dominant social, religious, and political values of German culture as depicted in its literature, the younger generation had turned to the naturalism of Zola and Ibsen. The *Durch* circle included an array of brilliant young poets, dramatists, novelists, and actors, who for the most part were not yet widely known in the 1880's. The circle included Arno Holz, the first

[34] Cf. Bernstein, *Berliner Arbeiterbewegung*, II, pp. 316–21; Paul Kampffmeyer, "Die Bewegung der Magdeburger 'Jungen'," in *Von Fehden und Kaempfen. Bilder aus der Geschichte der Arbeiterbewegung Magdeburgs* (Magdeburg, 1910), p. 42. Bebel was the direct cause behind the dismissal of Mueller and Kampffmeyer from the *Volksstimme* and Sommer and Ernst from the *Saechsische Arbeiterzeitung*. At a public meeting in Dresden on August 10, 1890, and a few days later in Magdeburg, he convinced the local Social Democrats who had control over these papers that the *Jungen* should be excluded.

[35] On the careers of these *Jungen* intellectuals through 1890, see Bruno Wille, *Aus Traum und Kampf. Mein 60 jahriges Leben* (3rd ed.; Berlin, 1920), pp. 15–30; Paul Ernst, *Juenglingsjahre* (Munich, 1931), pp. 166–78, 203–06, 260–65; Kampffmeyer in *Von Fehden und Kaempfen*, pp. 41–51. On Hans Mueller, see Victor Adler, *Briefwechsel mit August Bebel und Karl Kautsky*, edited by Friedrich Adler (Vienna, 1954), pp. 57–58.

German to articulate a theory of "consistent naturalism" for literature, Hermann Bahr, the radical young Viennese who had appeared earlier as an admirer of Rodbertus, and Gerhart Hauptmann, who drew much from Holz and who wrote the first successful social dramas in Germany.

This new generation had a full awareness of the changing society: the industrialization, the growing cities and the whole "Social Question." In the *Durch* circle they reflected a mixture of radical ideas, from atheism to anarchism. Most important, however, several harbored a strong sympathy for the Social Democratic movement. In addition to Ernst and Wille, several other *Durch* members were directly associated with the Social Democratic party at one time or another, including Arno Holz, Hermann Bahr (also a close friend to the Austrian socialist Victor Adler), Wilhelm Boelsche, who wrote popularizations of science, and Julius Tuerk, a young actor.[36]

The socialism of the *Durch* group, however, was not so much politically revolutionary as it was monarchically reformist, or possibly parliamentary reformist. In the mid-eighties, for example, Hermann Bahr simultaneously waxed enthusiastic for Bismarck's social reforms while he subscribed to the *Sozialdemokrat!*[37] The socialist tendency among these young writers from bourgeois backgrounds indicated their loss of faith in bourgeois liberalism, both politically and culturally. In their search for new values, however, these young writers had only a transitory relationship with Social Democracy; they could not wholly identify their case with that of the working class.

The political experience of the *Jungen* was far inferior to their social sensitivity. The German environment of the 1880's was in many ways a wasteland for political inspiration. As the *Jungen* grew up, they observed an anemic parliament trying half-heartedly to preserve some elements of liberal government in a conservative *Obrigkeitsstaat* (authoritarian state). In such a political atmosphere they easily learned to scorn and ridicule parliamentary institutions. From their political environment, they had no source from which to develop an admiration for democracy and radical liberalism. The democratic enthusiasm of

[36] Adalbert von Hanstein, *Das juengste Deutschland*, 3rd printing (Leipzig, 1905), pp. 71–79, 186–88; Ernst, *Juenglingsjahre*, pp. 135–36, 140–42; Annemarie Lange, *Berlin zur Zeit Bebels und Bismarcks* (Berlin-East, no date [ca. 1960]), pp. 358–68; Arno Holz, *Briefe. Eine Auswahl*, edited by Anita Holz and Max Wagner (Munich, 1948), pp. 66–67.

[37] Bahr, *Selbstbildnis*, pp. 171–72, 188–89.

the 1848 tradition, from which even Bebel derived a democratic political faith, had vanished completely in Germany.

Bebel's generation had watched the spiritual demise of German democratic liberalism; the *Jungen* came on the scene only after it had died. That created a decisive difference between the two generations. Bebel's generation had been rooted in democratic liberalism and believed vaguely that parliamentary institutions could be democratic and useful to the working class. The *Jungen* seemed never to have that faith. Without a strong belief in democratic liberalism, the *Jungen* had no feeling for the sentiments of the Bebel generation. And of course, the fact that for decades the Bebel wing of Social Democracy held parliamentarism in low esteem added to the *Jungen's* scorn for that institution.[38]

The political goals of the *Jungen* were therefore vague. At no time in 1890 did they present a program based on the basic principles of a democratic political faith. During 1890, the *Jungen* produced only a set of criticisms of the principles, tactics, and composition of the Social Democratic party. Most of their points were related in some way to a central anti-parliamentarian theme. Their over-all charge stated that the party had fallen into a "petty-bourgeois parliamentarism" which was "corrupting" the leaders and the masses in the party. The Social Democratic Reichstag deputies, the *Jungen* clamored, were corrupted by an over-estimation of their own value, by a "belief in their authority [*Autoritaetsglauben*]."[39] The *Jungen* reproached the *Fraktion* for having called upon Social Democrats to support the *Freisinnige* party in the run-off ballots in 1890, a decision which violated a resolution of the St. Gall congress. They denounced the timidity of the May 1 directives. The socialist Reichstag deputies were rebuked for participating in Reichstag committee work and chided for having introduced legislation for a ten-hour, rather than an eight-hour working day.[40] The *Jungen* denounced the original draft of a new post-Socialist Law

[38] To my knowledge none of the accounts of the *Jungen* note this lack of a political-democratic tradition. The most detailed account of the movement is by Hans Mueller, *Der Klassenkampf in der deutschen Sozialdemokratie* (Zurich, 1892). Mueller maintained that within Social Democracy there was a class conflict between the "revolutionary-proletarian" and the "possibilist-petty-bourgeois" elements. What he overlooks is that there were no proletarians among the leaders of the *Jungen*. Even Werner and Wildberger were craftsmen who owned their own instruments of production.

[39] *Berliner Volksblatt*, No. 187, Aug. 14, 1890, *Beilage*, p. 2; and No. 198, Aug. 27, 1890, *Beilage*, pp. 2–4.

[40] *Berliner Volksblatt*, No. 230, Oct. 3, 1890, *Beilage*, p. 3.

organization for the party because it specified that the party's Reichstag *Fraktion* would be a control group over the executive.[41] All of these charges were thrown together with more impulse than system.

The open struggle with the *Jungen* began in July after Bruno Wille wrote an article assailing the "corrupting" influence of parliamentarism and the "petty-bourgeois" nature of the party's leadership. In his criticism, Wille attacked not only the policies of the party but the leaders themselves, who, he implied, harbored all of the reprehensible characteristics of the petty bourgeoisie.[42]

The charge touched the personal sensitivities of the older leaders, especially Bebel. He set out immediately to crush such impertinence. He demanded that Wille give the names of those leaders who were accused of "corruption." [43] And then Bebel moved swiftly and vigorously; the *Jungen* soon discovered what the older moderates already knew, that Bebel was a most formidable foe with an unequaled power of persuasion in mass meetings. At Dresden on August 10, Magdeburg on August 13, and Berlin on August 25, Bebel persuaded mass meetings of Social Democrats to adopt resolutions condemning the charges of the *Jungen* as unjust. Sommer, Ernst, Kampffmeyer, and Mueller were all forced to resign their editorial posts with the Social Democratic papers in Dresden and Magdeburg. Within a few weeks the *Jungen* were on the defensive; the counter-attack went even better than Bebel expected.[44]

The *Jungen* fought back but revealed their lack of sureness and the fact that they did not have a program for the party. Presumably their criticism of the party's parliamentary work was political, but they offered no substitute plan for political action. The single most important source for their anti-parliamentarism was Liebknecht's Berlin speech of 1869.[45] But Liebknecht made his speech of 1869 more as an

[41] Bebel to Liebknecht, Aug. 9, 1890, Liebknecht Archive, IISH.

[42] "Der erste Oktober," *Saechsische Arbeiterzeitung*, July 23, 1890, summarized in Bernstein, *Berliner Arbeiterbewegung*, II, p. 318; Mueller, *Klassenkampf*, pp. 6, 78–79.

[43] "Die 'Saechsische Arbeiterzeitung' und tutti quanti," *Berliner Volksblatt*, No. 181, Aug. 7, 1890, pp. 1–2.

[44] Mueller, *Klassenkampf*, pp. 84–90. Bebel had been a bit apprehensive before the meeting at Dresden on August 10. After the meeting, however, he reported privately that he had more success than expected. Bebel to Liebknecht, Aug. 11, 1890, Liebknecht Archive, IISH. Then he had some of the same fears before the meeting in Berlin on August 25. Immediately after the meeting in Berlin, he confidently wrote to Engels that the "brawl [*Krakeel*]" was past. Bebel to Engels, Aug. 27, 1890, in Bebel, *Briefwechsel*, p. 395.

[45] Kampffmeyer, in *Von Fehden und Kaempfen*, p. 43.

emotional outburst against Bismarck's North German Confederation than as a consistent theoretical statement of an anti-parliamentary revolutionary position. In 1869 Liebknecht's comments were also directed against Schweitzer, who had introduced positive legislative measures in the Reichstag of the North German Confederation.

The role of the *Jungen* in 1890 paralleled Liebknecht's role in 1869 only in form, not in substance. The *Jungen* affirmed, to be sure, that parliamentary practice corrupted the socialist movement and that it could not be an effective instrument for socialization. But they did not understand that Liebknecht based his anti-parliamentarism of 1869 on a deep devotion to political democracy. By contrast, the *Jungen* were merely anti-parliamentarian. Even in this position they were unsure of themselves and failed to push anti-parliamentarism to its logical conclusion, that is, the rejection of all activity associated with elections and parliaments. Bruno Wille, for example, said on August 12 that the Social Democrats should continue to enter elections, make speeches, and introduce bills in the Reichstag, but only for the purpose of propaganda, to "expose" the bourgeois parties. Werner expressed the same view; parliamentary activity should be exclusively negative, propagandistic, and agitational.[46] That resembled the view of parliamentarism that Bebel professed to hold throughout the Socialist Law. Like Liebknecht in 1869, the *Jungen* in 1890 were not prepared to break completely with parliamentarism. Unlike Liebknecht, they did not build the criticism on a devotion to a genuine democratic principle.

The *Jungen* thought that Marxism provided a basis for their criticisms. A denunciation of "petty-bourgeois parliamentarism" seemed completely consistent with Marx's view that the working class had to emancipate itself. They discovered, however, that Engels considered their criticisms of the party childish. When Paul Ernst wrote to Engels on May 31, 1890, about problems of the materialist conception of history, Engels warned him against using Marxist materialism as a "ready-made formula," a practice which would lead to the distortion of the facts.[47]

[46] Wille's speech was entitled "Gedanken ueber die Taktik unserer Partei," *Berliner Volksblatt*, No. 187, Aug. 14, 1890, *Beilage*, p. 2. For the speech by Werner see *Protokoll ueber die Verhandlungen des Parteitages der Sozialdemokratischen Partei Deutschlands. Abgehalten zu Halle a. S. vom 12. bis 18. Oktober 1890* (Berlin, 1890), pp. 99–100.

[47] Quoted from a letter by Friedrich Engels to the *Berliner Volksblatt*, No. 232, Oct. 5, 1890, pp. 1–2. Engels' letter is dated Oct. 1, 1890, quoting his letter to Paul Ernst in June 1890.

Engels had thus given the *Jungen* a gentle hint that they should not presume to speak in the name of Marx. But that did not discourage Ernst, not immediately at least. As he and Bruno Sommer were forced to resign their editorial posts with the *Saechsische Arbeiterzeitung*, they wrote: "The departing editors of the *Saechsische Arbeiterzeitung* hope with Friedrich Engels that just as the naïve State Socialism of Lassalle was overcome, so also the success-mongering parliamentary direction of present Social Democracy will also be overcome by the good sense of the German working class [*Arbeiterschaft*]." [48]

Engels could only be infuriated by this unauthorized attempt to associate his name with the *Jungen*. In a sarcastic reply, published in the *Sozialdemokrat*, he ridiculed the "literati and student revolt" of the *Jungen* with its "convulsively distorted 'Marxism,'" which, he said, was characterized by "gross ignorance" and a "violent misunderstanding of the [Marxist] way of viewing things." As he continued, Engels left no doubt that almost without reservation he supported the party's policy as directed by Bebel. It was completely unknown to him, he said, that a "petty-bourgeois-parliamentary socialism" dominated the Social Democratic party.[49]

This was the first time in decades that either Marx or Engels had entered directly and publicly into an intraparty fight in German Social Democracy. At other times, when they had been angered by events within the party, as for example in 1875 when the Gotha program was drafted and in 1879 when the *Sozialdemokrat* was founded, they protested violently, but always in private. Engels' public statement thus dealt a crushing blow to the endeavors of the *Jungen*. If they hoped to justify their criticisms of the party policy on Marx, they now had to overcome the unlimited opposition of the world's leading Marxist.

Failure of the Jungen *and the Problem of Parliamentary Democracy*

Within a few weeks after the *Jungen* opened their challenge it was clear that they had no issues on which to build a fundamental and effective opposition to the majority under Bebel's leadership. The accusation that the leaders were corrupted by parliamentarism was pre-

[48] Quoted in the open letter by Friedrich Engels, Sept. 7, 1890, in *SD*, No. 37, Sept. 13, 1890.
[49] *Ibid.*

cisely the kind of charge against which Bebel could most easily defend himself. In so doing he was also defending men like Auer, Blos, Grillenberger, and Frohme, exactly the same men who, Bebel had charged in 1885, were being corrupted by parliamentarism! But in 1885 Bebel had been in the minority. In 1890, he was in control.

The other *Jungen* charges were equally ineffective. The accusation that many of the party's leaders and members were petty-bourgeois was true beyond doubt. But what could be done? Should every petty-bourgeois soul be purged? The *Jungen* themselves hardly qualified as proletarians! If the *Jungen* demanded that the Social Democrats should enter parliament only for agitational purposes, Bebel could point to a long record of parliamentary agitation. And he could say, with a certain truth, that the Social Democratic legislative initiatives had served an agitational purpose. If the *Jungen* denounced the party's support of *Freisinnige* candidates in the 1890 run-off ballot as a violation of Social Democratic principles, Bebel had only to point to the collapse of Bismarck's Cartel and the great socialist vote to convince the party masses that any other tactic would have been utter foolishness. If the *Jungen* accused the party leaders of timidity on the May 1 issue, Bebel had no difficulty in convincing Social Democrats who remembered Hoedel and Nobiling that the government was waiting for an excuse to put its repressive machinery into operation.[50] If the *Jungen* based their arguments on Liebknecht's anti-parliamentary speech of 1869, the "Soldier of the Revolution" came forth to tell them that everything had changed since 1869, that the "North German Confederation was an abortive birth, a German Reich did not exist at that time."[51] And finally, when the *Jungen* tried to run their campaign under the Marxist banner, Engels was on hand to speak against them in the very name of Marx.

On every issue, the *Jungen* collided with the immovable convictions and seasoned leadership of August Bebel. Throughout the whole debate, Bebel demonstrated once again those characteristics which had carried him to the top of the Social Democratic party: self-confidence, an unswerving conviction that his feelings were the feelings of the

[50] All of these issues were debated by Bebel, Wille, and Wildberger at the mass meeting (ca. 4,000 present) in Berlin at the Friedrichshain Brewery on the evening of August 25. Singer, Baginski, and Werner also spoke. *Berliner Volksblatt*, No. 198, Aug. 27, 1890, *Beilage*, pp. 2–4; Bernstein, *Berliner Arbeiterbewegung*, II, pp. 322–25.

[51] *Protokoll . . . Halle* (1890), p. 96.

German working class, a single-minded devotion to the ideas he believed to be right, a master's touch at party infighting, and an unequaled power of persuasion in public speaking. The *Jungen*, on the other hand, lacked most of these qualities. Bebel described the situation perfectly to Engels: "The opposition was dead from the moment it showed that it did not know what it wanted." [52]

Despite the truth of Bebel's observation, the *Jungen* expressed a spontaneous, intuitive, and vague awareness within Social Democracy that twelve years of oppression had not intensified the revolutionary spirit of the party leaders, but rather had taught them to choose the moderate and orderly path of parliamentary practice. The tone, the style, and the general demeanor of the Social Democratic leaders, the *Jungen* sensed, had been sapped of much of the revolutionary élan which had been characteristic of these same leaders in their younger days.[53]

The *Jungen* were also painfully aware that the parliamentary careers of the leading Social Democrats had given them a new kind of prestige and fame. They had seen how parliamentarism could transform comparatively unknown party members into men of national reputation. They knew that once a comrade became a Reichstag deputy he entered the highest rank of the party, a rank itself created by parliamentarism. The eminence of the Reichstag deputies had introduced a new element of inequality into a party committed to the egalitarian principle for all society. In this way the *Jungen* reflected a fear of what would happen to the party as it became a more decisive factor in German political life. They had a sectarian conscience which rejected parliamentarism because it implied that the Social Democrats not only existed within German society but were a part of that society.[54]

[52] Bebel to Engels, Oct. 24, 1890, in Bebel, *Briefwechsel*, p. 401.

[53] Mueller, *Klassenkampf*, p. 19, erroneously maintained that prior to the Socialist Law German Social Democracy was a "pure proletarian movement with a distinct revolutionary character." He thought that only with the Socialist Law had the petty bourgeoisie become important. There is some truth in his charge that during the Socialist Law petty-bourgeois members had become more important. They were the only persons who could afford to devote time to politics. *Ibid.*, p. 21. Although his history was inaccurate, he could see that parliamentarism tended to increase the influence of Social Democrats who had sufficient money so that they could take time off from work for politics.

[54] The *Jungen* spoke bitterly about how parliamentary work was an instrument for social climbing. Talking on August 12, 1890, Bruno Wille said, "The *Fraktion* is thus the gate through which the comrades can enter into political activity. By this means the hypocrit, the flatterer and the place-hunter [*Streber*] become big men." *Berliner Volksblatt*, No. 187, Aug. 14, 1890, *Beilage*, p. 2. For a good con-

No doubt their sectarian fears were justified. Parliament provided the one significant institution through which the Social Democrats could be linked positively with German political life. But the *Jungen* seemed naïvely to believe that once the party was aware of its weaknesses it would return to what they believed was its original purity. And when they failed many of them became discouraged, gave up the fight, and returned to their studies.

What is most perplexing about the *Jungen* movement is that none of its intellectual leaders remained on the radical wing of the Social Democratic party. Some of them moved farther right than others, but they all moved to the right. Hans Mueller moved to Switzerland, took out Swiss citizenship, and became a chief advocate of the moderate consumers' cooperative movement. Kampffmeyer remained in the party, but moved to its reformist wing. Schippel, who had never fought out in the open, moved to the extreme right wing of the party with strong imperialist and nationalist leanings. Wille soon lost direct contact with the Social Democrats; but he carved out a significant career as the leader of the "Free Thought Congregation" and as a promotor of popular performances of modern drama. Paul Ernst left the party, collaborated on a book with Rudolf Meyer, the close friend of Rodbertus, and then turned his energy to writing poems and novels glorifying agrarian life. He ended on the extreme nationalist right wing of German politics with strong sympathies for Hitler before he died in 1933.[55]

Why did all of these young radical intellectuals abandon their leftist positions so soon? Part of the answer may be that their radicalism was fed merely by an immature enthusiasm and youthful rejection of the older generation. But a more satisfactory answer is needed. What is extremely important, it seems, is that the anti-parliamentarism of the *Jungen* intellectuals had no basis in a democratic political philosophy. The *Jungen* did not share the assumptions of an earlier anti-parliamentarism in Germany, that of Moritz Rittinghausen, for example, who was anti-parliamentarian because he believed in direct democracy. Although Liebknecht did not agree with Rittinghausen, they were closer

temporary analysis of how parliamentarism created inequalities within the socialist movement, see Hugo Preuss, "Die Sozialdemokratie und der Parliamentarismus," *Staat, Recht und Freiheit. Aus 40 Jahren deutscher Politik und Geschichte* (Tuebingen, 1926), pp. 144–72. The essay was first published in *Der Zeitgeist, Beilage z. Berliner Tageblatt*, Sept. 21, 28 and Oct. 5, 1891.

[55] Ernst, *Juenglingsjahre*, pp. 270–71, 275–77, 282–86.

to each other than they were to the *Jungen*. Liebknecht had despised German parliamentarism in the sixties because through a clever manipulation of universal suffrage Bismarck had made a farce out of the institutions of democratic liberalism.

The *Jungen* had based their anti-parliamentarism on different sources. Despite obvious difficulties in delineating the influences that worked on them, a few suggestions may be given. In Germany, an anti-parliamentary position was by no means the monopoly of some radical Social Democrats. Almost all conservatives, even those who sat in the Reichstag, despised parliaments. The conservative economist, Rodbertus, whose work, as noted above, enjoyed popularity in the 1880's, had little patience with parliaments. The *Jungen* intellectuals were acquainted with Rodbertus; Schippel in fact had mastered the work of the Pomeranian economist. In 1890, the *Jungen* were not followers of Rodbertus, but here, at least, was another anti-parliamentarian voice with which they had contact.

Something may also be said of the Lassallean tradition. Lassalle has often been held responsible for engendering reformism into German Social Democracy. That is undoubtedly true, but a distinction must be made. Lassalle's reformism was as much monarchical as parliamentarian. Just as he believed that Bismarck could decree universal suffrage, so he believed that social reforms could be decreed from above. Reforms from above did not require parliamentary initiative. Further, Lassalle's heaviest blows were reserved for the German liberals, the chief representatives of the parliamentary principle. Lassalle too had taught the workers to despise what was liberal, and the parliament was liberal.

The *Jungen*, it should also be noted, grew up at a time when the only social legislation passed in Germany came from the Kaiser through the hand of Bismarck, and that very legislation was most persistently opposed by the Manchesterian liberals who were also the chief advocates of parliamentary institutions. It is not surprising, therefore, that Bruno Wille, probably the most articulate of the *Jungen* intellectuals of 1890, combined anti-parliamentarism with great enthusiasm for Wilhelm II when the latter announced his support of protective legislation for labor.[56] All of this indicates, somewhat indefinitely to be sure, that the anti-parliamentarism of the *Jungen* was probably

[56] Wille, *Aus Traum und Kampf*, p. 26.

built from a variety of sources scattered throughout the political spectrum in Germany. What the *Jungen* anti-parliamentarism lacked, however, was precisely what Liebknecht's had: a firm root in the principles of political democracy. For that reason, the *Jungen* intellectuals did not have to shift their ground materially in order to move to the right in later years.

Although the *Jungen* failed to carry a significant portion of the Social Democratic party with them in 1890, they had raised a fundamental issue of party policy at a crucial time. In so doing they forced the party leaders to clarify and possibly rethink their position on the problems related to parliamentary practice and parliamentary government. Two tendencies are observable among those who attempted to defend the established policies of the party: a restatement of the same ambivalent parliamentarism by Bebel and a new statement in favor of an unreserved support of parliamentarism by Eduard Bernstein.

In the thick of the battle, Bebel still stressed his point that the Social Democrats had patiently to "enlighten" the workers, a task best accomplished through the Reichstag. In a debate with the *Jungen* on August 25, Bebel asserted,

> In the parliament we have the best ground for spreading our ideas among the masses. The political and economic development revolutionizes the masses and turns them to us. Our job is to enlighten the masses. We have no need to use revolutionary phrases which are displeasing [to people] in leading circles and positions. It is sufficient to spread clarity about the facts, which lead in any case to further and further extensions of socialization.[57]

Liebknecht easily agreed that the Social Democrats had to mesh their parliamentary activities with the course of political and economic development. Bourgeois society, Liebknecht said at the Halle congress, would not "collapse on decree from above, but through its own contradictions and its general harmfulness, and through our [Social Democratic] activity. . . ." A day later he summarized his general approach to the problems of socialism and the tasks of the party. "Our first duty," he declared, "is to bring knowledge to the masses. In knowledge there is power." [58] Then he turned to the inevitability of socialism in the future:

[57] *Berliner Volksblatt*, No. 198, Aug, 27, 1890, *Beilage*, pp. 2–3.
[58] *Protokoll . . . Halle* (1890), p. 169, 205.

The whole social and political development from which we have come is a necessity [*Nothwendigkeit*]. This necessity, which our enemies cannot destroy with cannons [and] police weapons, continues; we continue by its power. Social Democracy is a historical necessity, and our victory is a necessity. Not the irrational necessity of Greek fate, which plays with man as a cat with a mouse, but the necessity of the organic process of development, in which man as the most highly developed organism performs the decisive, determining labor. A misguiding writer said recently that Marxist teaching implies the danger of engendering the belief that we have only to stand with folded arms and wait peacefully while the evolutionary process realizes itself, until the Social Democratic soup is cooked. The man who wrote that has not read or understood a line of Marx. Marx said distinctly that man himself is a co-determinant, nay, the decisive factor, but that he can not arbitrarily change the laws of development and annul their effect. And if this theory were not correct it would never be possible for us to defeat our opponent.[59]

Both Bebel and Liebknecht had harmonized the educational work of parliament with the general economic development that was taking place in capitalist society. For that reason they did not have to abandon their professed disapproval of parliamentarism. They had not materially changed their ambivalent parliamentarism. They were not prepared to draw the obvious conclusion from the twelve years under the Socialist Law: that, whatever its economic theory, German Social Democracy, in political theory and practice, was in historical reality a party of radical democratic liberalism.

It was Eduard Bernstein, later the leader of revisionist reformism, who already in 1890 drew the consequences of German Social Democracy's historical position for its political role. He had, in effect, broken with ambivalent parliamentarism. In an open and forthright manner, he indicated, probably better than any of the other leaders, that Social Democracy was necessarily an extension of democratic liberalism. He wrote the following in May 1890.

The political constellation in Germany is such that the influence of the Reichstag upon the destiny of the German people will presumably experience a fundamental strengthening. That also increases in

[59] *Ibid.*, pp. 205–06.

the Reichstag the tasks of the party which is the natural champion of the exploited and the oppressed. In consideration of our fundamental opposition to the existing political and social order, we hold that to deny or underrate these tasks is one of the most dangerous precipices to be avoided.[60]

. . . .

The road to full political liberty leads through parliamentarism, not around it. With all of its failings, parliamentarism is still the most modern public institution in present-day Germany; no doctrinaire ground may induce us to overlook that. Certainly we have yet to accomplish a great part of that which was the actual concern of the preceding bourgeois parties, but which they left unfinished. Thus, the systematic struggle against militarism, against privileges by birth, and further, the abolition of obsolete legal institutions—all things, which above will signify an expansion of the power sphere of parliament, i.e., the Reichstag.[61]

Bernstein was in the process of making a clean break with the former declarations of the radicals that parliamentary activity was intended only for agitation and propaganda. As the editor of the *Sozialdemokrat* for almost a decade, he had customarily agreed with Bebel that socialist delegates did not enter the Reichstag as parliamentarians but as propagandists and educators. But in 1890 he did not hesitate to call upon the Social Democrats to be parliamentarians, both in tactics and in principle. What the *Jungen* denounced as a corruption, Bernstein defended as a virtue. The fact that the significance of Bernstein's articles went unnoticed in 1890 can only be explained by noting that no distinction was made between the views of those who fought as a bloc against the *Jungen*.

The struggle with the *Jungen* continued when for the first time in thirteen years the Social Democrats held a party congress on German soil at Halle, October 12–18. The fight at Halle, however, was anticlimactic. The case for the *Jungen* suffered because the most talented

[60] "Klippen, II," *SD*, No. 18, May 3, 1890.

[61] "Klippen, III," *SD*, No. 21, May 24, 1890. In later years, Bernstein thought enough of these articles to reprint them, along with one other, under the title "Die Stellung der Socialdemokratie in den Parlamenten," in Eduard Bernstein, *Zur Geschichte und Theorie des Socialismus. Gesammelte Abhandlungen* (4th ed.; Berlin and Bern, 1901), pp. 15–31.

of their leaders were not delegates. The *Jungen* cause had to be carried on by Werner and Wildberger, both of whom had great persistence but no great ability. Any one of the old party leaders, Auer, Grillenberger, Liebknecht, could have demolished the inconsistent arguments of Werner and Wildberger. That was hardly necessary, although much of the debate was taken up with the *Jungen.* Bebel had solidified the support of the great mass of party members by the end of August.

After Halle, the *Jungen* movement continued and even received a new impetus when Engels published Marx's *Critique of the Gotha Program* in the *Neue Zeit* early in 1891. The *Jungen* took Marx's theoretical statements about the necessity of a "Dictatorship of the Proletariat" as further proof that the party's parliamentary tactic was anti-Marxist. This carried the *Jungen* movement into a new phase, in which, however, most of the intellectuals so prominent in 1890 played no role.[62]

Enthusiastic celebration of the fall of the Socialist Law was not at all diminished by the internal party dissension. At the end of September, a dramatic era in the history of German socialism came to an end. At the stroke of twelve on the night of September 30, in beerhalls throughout Berlin's working-class districts, Bebel, Liebknecht, Singer, and others began speeches to commemorate a moment of victory in the life of their party. Old comrades returned to Berlin, Leipzig, Hamburg, and Frankfurt am Main after years of expulsion. In Berlin, the celebrations continued throughout the next day, October 1. Now the party could look forward to a greatly enlarged area of public activity. It was also possible for Social Democrats to reflect upon what the Socialist Law meant for the history of their movement.

[62] For the further phase of the *Jungen* movement through the Erfurt congress (October 14–20, 1891), when they were expelled from the party see: Landauer, *European Socialism,* I, pp. 295–98; Mueller, *Klassenkampf,* pp. 101ff.; Boris Goldenberg, *Beitraege zur Soziologie der deutschen Vorkriegssozialdemokratie* (Published Dissertation, Heidelberg [1932]), pp. 16–18; Harry J. Marks, "Movements of Reform and Revolution in Germany from 1890 to 1903, with an Epilogue: 1903–1914" (Unpublished Ph. D. Dissertation, Harvard, 1937), pp. 32ff.

CHAPTER XII · THE HERITAGE OF THE SOCIALIST LAW EPOCH FOR SOCIAL DEMOCRACY

MUCH HAD changed in the Social Democratic movement between the unification congress at Gotha in 1875 and the fall of the Socialist Law in the autumn of 1890. Almost every aspect of the movement's life had been altered to some degree: the electoral base had broadened, links with the trade unions were strengthened, parliamentary tactics had been refined, the role of the old Lassalleans had been eliminated, Bebel and the radicals won control, and Marxism emerged to dominate the ideological outlook. From the flounderings in economic thought of the seventies, the party had achieved a firm certainty in socialist economics through a commitment to Marxism. The adoption of the Erfurt program in 1891, drafted by the leading Marxist theoreticians of the party, seemed to settle the fundamental ideological questions. On the surface it appeared that the ideological quest of the seventies had reached its goal through the experience of the eighties. However, the sense of certainty in economic thought, gained from the adoption of a Marxist program, hid an equally important lack of certainty in the area of political tactics and theory. The devotion of leading Social Democrats to Marxism solved only a portion of the problems they faced when the Socialist Law fell. The situation of the Social Democrats in relation to economic and political principles had almost completely reversed itself. In the seventies, they were unsure about their socialist economic principles; by 1890, Marxism cleared up all of those perplexities. In the seventies they were committed to a goal of political democracy as the framework for a socialist society; by 1890 they lacked certainty about the political framework for a socialist society. These parallel shifts contain a certain irony, for the well-articulated democratic goals of the early socialist movement posed just as great a political danger to the German Reich as did the Marxism of the Social Democrats in 1890.

Political Uncertainty: Social Democratic Estrangement from Political Democracy

In the eighteen-sixties and seventies the socialists had faced a problem of integrating their social and political principles into a balanced whole. At that time one frequently heard the complaint that political considerations outweighed the social and economic principles in the formation of the party's practical policies. By 1890 this was no longer true. Years of study on social and economic problems, combined with a concentration on Marxist economics, had shifted the focus of the Social Democrats. Now economic and social questions dominated their writings and discussions, and political questions faded into the background.

The change had taken place so gradually that it was hardly noticed. Not only had the general interest in political questions faded, the socialist commitment to the political ideals of a democratic framework for the socialist society had also diminished. Despite their tremendous electoral growth, the Social Democrats suffered from an underlying uncertainty about their political tactics and principles. This uncertainty arose from the fact that they could not resolve the question of how they related to the principles of parliamentary democracy.

The experience of the Social Democrats under the Socialist Law added numerous complexities to the relationship of the party to parliamentary democracy. Although both Lassalleans and Eisenachers had separated themselves from bourgois liberals and democrats in the 1860's, both socialist groups had sustained a spiritual contact with their progenitors into the seventies. The conditions in the eighties further estranged the socialists from bourgeois liberalism. In the mind of the socialist, the Socialist Law gave added evidence that liberal parliamentary principles could not be realized in Germany. Except for the members of the Progressive party, the greater part of the bourgeois liberals in Germany had approved of the Socialist Law, and socialists could not help but view the law as a measure to legalize their *de facto* social isolation from German society. Socialist workers were no doubt justified in assuming that German liberals generally favored the repressive legislation. Thus, the German authorities destroyed the trade unions associated with Social Democrats but not the Hirsch-Duncker *Gewerkvereine* connected with the Progressives. Such discrimination added to the general hostility toward everything associated with German liberalism, including the idea of a political structure based on parliamentarism. The failure of the liberals in the sixties to draw German labor along with them turned into a catastrophe in the eighties. The practical experience of the Social Democrats under the Socialist Law did little to suggest that German liberalism would provide the groundwork for the implementation of a democratic system in Germany.[1]

The weakening of the Social Democratic linkage to political democracy is illustrated by the fate of the concept of the "People's state." In the sixties and seventies, the Eisenachers in particular had expressed their belief in political democracy through the use of this idea. The Gotha program of 1875 stated that the goal of the Social Democratic party was a "Free state," meaning the same as the earlier Eisenacher call for a "Free People's state." In the subsequent three years preceding the Socialist Law, the Social Democrats had focused a good part of their discussions on the idea of a democratic "People's state." By 1890, however, this concept had been dropped completely from Social democratic discussions; it became a museum piece.

The theoretical reason for dropping the "People's state" is indicated by the intellectual development of August Bebel, treated above (see Chapter II). In the letter of March 18/30, 1875, Engels had given a reasoned statement on the basis of the Marxist social analysis for dropping all reference to the "People's state" as a goal of Social Democracy. Although Bebel did not immediately follow Engels' advice—the "People's state" still appeared in the first edition of *Die Frau und der Sozialismus*—the term vanished from his vocabulary in the eighties.

The disappearance of "People's state" from the parlance of the Social Democrats meant more than the simple elimination of a term. By "People's state," the Social Democrats had meant a "republic." Bebel, Liebknecht, and Hepner had all affirmed this meaning of the phrase in their Leipzig trial for high treason in 1872.[2] They used "People's state" instead of "republic" because the latter term would have involved them in a direct confrontation with the monarchy. They saw no reason to aggravate their difficult position by the use of language that would further provoke the authorities. Marx and Engels both agreed in the middle seventies that it would have been inexpedient to call openly for

[1] On the failure of German liberalism to revitalize its political drive after 1871, see Krieger, *The German Idea of Freedom*, pp. 458–64.

[2] *Der Leipziger Hochverratsprozess vom Jahre 1872*, pp. 59, 61, 71.

a republic. No difficulty arose at the time, for the membership of the party understood clearly enough that the "People's state" was their euphemism for a "republic."

The situation had changed by 1890. Uncertainty about the political principles of the Social Democrats crept in, not simply because they dropped "People's state," but because they did not replace it with another concept. This was not the fault of Engels, for in his letter to Bebel he had also suggested that the Social Democrats should think in terms of the "Commune." Recognizing that the Social Democrats would invite retaliation by the use of "Commune," he had also suggested the term "*Gemeinwesen*" (community). Although Bebel publicly defended the Paris Commune in the seventies, and also introduced the idea that a socialist society would have features in common with those that had appeared in the Commune, he never pushed this very far.[3] Each year the *Sozialdemokrat* commemorated the Commune (along with the March uprising of 1848), but never with the suggestion that the Social Democrats should write the "Commune" on their banners as an ultimate goal.[4] In speeches, pamphlets, and fliers from the years of the Socialist Law, one finds no evidence that German Social Democrats sought to make the Commune a vital force among the rank-and-file members. This failure too is understandable, for the Commune raised visions of terror among the non-socialists in Germany.

The Social Democrats might have replaced "People's state" with "republic," which is what they had meant in the seventies. But "republic" also aroused fears and hatred in the bourgeoisie and aristocracy. An ironic twist emerges in connection with "republic" and the failure of the Social Democrats to use this term openly. The Erfurt program, drafted and adopted in 1891, has traditionally been interpreted as a document that marked the identification of German Social Democracy with revolutionary Marxism. The matter is not that simple. The first part of the program offered a brief exposition of Marxist economic and historical theory, as a popular form of the "scientific" analysis of capitalism. The second part listed the immediate goals, in essence almost the same as those that had appeared in the Gotha program. These were goals achievable within the framework of the existing monarchical-

[3] On March 10, 1876, Bebel defended the Commune at length in a debate with Bruno Sparig, a National Liberal. Cf. Bebel, *Aus meinem Leben*, II, pp. 348-69.

[4] See above, Chapter V, pp. 149ff.

parliamentary structure in Germany. The realization of these immediate goals would have brought about some widespread changes, and in that sense they might be called revolutionary. The Marxist theory included in the program, while it broadly predicted the future political control of the proletariat, posed no immediate dangers to the existing German political-economic system. The political demands in the program implied an immediate reform, but not through direct revolutionary action. One important item did not appear in the Erfurt program —a demand for a republic. It did not appear because an energetic Social Democratic appeal for a republic would have posed an immediate danger to the existing German political system. The genuinely revolutionary principle in the context of Germany never emerged in the Erfurt program.

When Engels read the draft of the proposed program, he wrote a long critique, including a significant discussion of the failures of its political aspects. He specifically questioned the exclusion of the term "republic" from the text. He tried to make it clear that the working class could only come to power through the "democratic republic," which, he added, is the "specific form for the dictatorship of the proletariat. . . ." [5] If "republic" had to be excluded from the program, then he advised that at a minimum it would have to call for the "concentration of all political power in the hands of the representatives of the people." [6] For Engels, these were all intermediate political goals for a socialist movement, but the Social Democrats in Germany remained reluctant to include his recommendations in the program.

Although ten years passed before Engels' criticism of the Erfurt program appeared in the *Neue Zeit,* Bebel had read the commentary in 1891. Bebel frankly admitted in private to Engels that "to lift up the Republic as a goal is not possible under our German conditions." [7] The dangers implicit in such a move were too great. But obviously, no dangers were feared from stating a summary of Marx's economic and historical theory in the first part of the program. The dangers arose only if the Social Democrats presented their immediate political goals in clear and unambiguous language. For that reason they did not include "republic" in the program, nor did they follow the suggestion of Engels and demand the "concentration of all political power in the

[5] F. Engels, "Zur Kritik des sozialdemokratischen Programmentwurfes 1891," *Neue Zeit*, xx, Part 1 (1901/02), p. 11.

[6] *Ibid.*, p. 11.

[7] Bebel to Engels, July 12, 1891, in Bebel, *Briefwechsel*, p. 424.

hands of the representatives of the people." Bebel tried to convince Engels that, as drafted, the program satisfied all of his criticisms, because no one could assume that the demands in the Erfurt program were compatible with the "*Koenigtum.*"[8] In this way, Bebel only avoided the problem that Engels raised. Engels tried to make it clear that the Social Democrats had to distinguish between an immediate demand for a "democratic republic" and their ultimate goal of a communist society. The Erfurt program, however, made neither of these points clear. It failed to do so because most of the Social Democrats themselves were not clear about their political goals. Unwilling to commit themselves to a republic, they would have been on better ground had they simply revived the concept of the "People's state." But that idea had died.

The uncertainty about political goals in the minds of the Social Democrats was compounded by the role that Marxism cast for a "democratic republic." In the sixties and seventies, the Social Democrats accepted the idea that socialism would fit into the political framework built by a "People's state" (i.e. a republic). But Marx and Engels urged the leaders within Social Democracy to think of a "democratic republic" as merely a transitional stage (the specific form of the "dictatorship of the proletariat") on the road to a communist society. For a theoretician, such a distinction in stages introduced no problems, but for practical leaders of a movement of working-class people it did present difficulties. How convincing a case could the Social Democrats make for a "republic" if they also had to tell the workers that they fought for it only as an institution of a transitional nature? Even Bebel seems never to have quite understood the distinctions in Engels' mind.

The problem of political goals—immediate, intermediate, and final—found no clarification at the end of the Socialist Law. Dropping "People's state" may have been a completely appropriate move for a party with Marxist asssumptions. However, the failure to replace it with a more suitable term illustrates the confusion. One can search fruitlessly through the essays and correspondence of the period to find someone who perceived clearly what Engels had in mind in recommending a "democratic republic" as a transitional stage. That need not have been so detrimental, if at least the Social Democrats had at that point clearly committed the party to a "republic." But they had become quite uncertain about how to relate themselves to the goal of a

[8] *Ibid.*, p. 424.

"republic." If they took Marx and Engels seriously they did not need a deep commitment to a "republic." Bebel had already in the middle years of the 1880's doubted that Germany would ever know a stage of a radical petty-bourgeois republic. He expected that somehow German development would move directly from the existing system to a socialist society (see above, Chapter VIII, p. 230). That analysis could not help but undermine Bebel's own feeling of loyalty to a democratic republic.

The experience of German Social Democracy fits directly into what Arthur Rosenberg said some years ago. In his book, *Democracy and Socialism,* Rosenberg observed that a great shift had taken place in the attitudes of European socialists toward political democracy. From the time of the French Revolution, when the earliest socialist voices hailed political democracy, the mood changed until a great part of the socialist movement by the end of World War I had nothing but scorn for political democracy. Rosenberg suggested that the crucial period for this great change lay between 1850 and 1880.[9] This study suggests that for German Social Democracy the critical period lay between 1875 and 1890. If the German Social Democrats were not scornful of political democracy by 1890, at least they were very little concerned with it. For them political democracy had lost its inspiration.

Lack of Unity between Theory and Practice: The Heritage of Ambivalent Parliamentarism

Given the uncertainty among Social Democrats about the ultimate political goals of their movement, it is not surprising that Bebel's ambivalent parliamentarism reflected a general sentiment in the party. Despite the frequent discussions of parliamentarism, the experience of the Social Democrats under the Socialist Law left a fundamental dualism in their response to this issue. As a matter of tactics, almost all Social Democrats agreed that the party had to participate in elections and in some positive legislative activity. As a matter of principle, however, they could not decide how to relate to parliamentarism.

The previous chapters of this study have shown repeatedly that the tactical use of parliamentarism had become an absolute necessity under the Socialist Law. Even Liebknecht, the author of the most thorough

[9] Arthur Rosenberg, *Democracy and Socialism,* translated by George Rosen (New York and London, 1939), p. 9.

attack on parliamentarism in 1869, concluded by 1886 that parliamentary action offered a genuine road to a socialist society. And Bebel reminded the delegates at the St. Gall congress in 1887 that the growth of the party in the seventies and eighties rested fundamentally on its policy of parliamentary participation.[10] The tremendous strength shown by Social Democracy at the polls in February 1890 reaffirmed this conviction in the minds of all the established leaders. The necessity of making tactical use of the Reichstag and the state diets thus produced the ironic consequence that during the Socialist Law the leaders of the party went through a significant period of parliamentary education and experience. This was especially evident in the Saxon Diet, where radicals such as Bebel and Vollmar carried on a policy of moderate reformism in the interests of the lower classes of German society. Tactical use of the legislative bodies therefore impelled the Social Democrats to lean toward parliamentarism.

The tactical use of parliamentarism also affected the organizational structure of the party. Both during and after the Socialist Law the Reichstag electoral districts formed the basic local units for the party organization. Perhaps the significance of this can be exaggerated, but it indicated that, for the Social Democrats, their organization was designed fundamentally for the battle of the ballot box.[11] It is true that the Social Democrats came closer to revolutionary action during the Socialist Law than at any other time. But apart from the smuggling system for the *Sozialdemokrat*, the party built no organizations oriented toward revolutionary action as against parliamentary participation. On one level party members constructed illegal organizations, but these were designed to support the legal structures for promoting candidates in national and local elections.

The implications of the tactical use of parliamentarism for the formation of the party leadership are even more significant. Although a Reichstag seat had always added to the significance of a leader within the party, during the Socialist Law such a position became almost a necessity for recognized leadership. Perforce, the party's Reichstag *Fraktion* assumed the role of an executive committee after October 1878, greatly increasing the importance of parliamentarism for every

[10] *Verhandlungen . . . St. Gallen* (1887), pp. 12–13.

[11] One author has claimed that even the party congresses had a parliamentary orientation because the delegates were elected on the basis of the Reichstag electoral districts: Marks, "Movements of Reform and Revolution in Germany from 1890 to 1903," pp. 112–13.

party leader. Thus the peculiar situation developed whereby the party's executive committee was selected via the Reichstag elections, meaning that non-party members could also have a voice in this process.[12] Likewise, a parliamentary seat became almost essential to preserve a preeminent role in the party. Although Bebel often fretted about the depressing parliamentary chatter, he could not afford to abandon his seat without undermining his position in the party as a whole. After the fall of the Socialist Law, the other paths to leadership in the party reopened—journalism, trade union leadership, party offices—but a Reichstag seat continued to transform a local figure into a national leader.[13]

Although all of these tactical considerations drew the Social Democrats deeply into parliamentary activity during the Socialist Law, other factors continued to repel them from parliamentarism. They followed a parliamentary practice in the present, but they were unsure about the relation of parliamentary institutions in a future socialist society. If they followed Marx and Engels, parliamentarism fit into the socialist future only as part of the transitional machinery during a period of the democratic republic. Thus, Karl Kautsky soon concluded that "a genuine parliamentary regime can be just as good an instrument for the dictatorship of the proletariat as it is an instrument for the dictatorship of the bourgeoisie." [14] That indicated that, at most, parliamentarism could be only an intermediate goal for the Marxist, not an ultimate goal. Marxism added new theoretical reasons for rejecting parliamentarism as an ultimate principle of Social Democracy.

Clearly, any rejection of parliamentarism as a principle of Social Democracy conflicted sharply with the increasing pressure to become parliamentarians through practical necessity. The Social Democrats worked in an institution in which they did not believe, and which they viewed as an instrument serving the interests of their enemies, the bourgeoisie. Ambivalence necessarily followed. No one felt this more deeply than Bebel, whose career from the late seventies was character-

[12] The leadership role of the *Fraktion* after 1890 is discussed by Nipperdey, *Die Organisation der deutschen Parteien vor 1918*, pp. 381–86.

[13] In a different context, Hugo Preuss rightly noted that the parliamentarism introduced differentiations between the common Social Democratic voter and the deputy, and thus an element of inequality, contradicting a fundamental principle of the movement. "Die Sozialdemokratie und der Parlamentarismus," in *Staat, Recht, und Freiheit*, pp. 146–48. The essay first appeared in 1891. The inequality created by parliamentarism had been raised by critics in the Social Democratic movement, especially the *Jungen*.

[14] Karl Kautsky, *Der Parlamentarismus, die Volksgesetzgebung und die Sozialdemokratie* (Stuttgart, 1893), p. 118.

ized by an ambivalent parliamentarism. He and many of the other radicals passed this attitude on to the whole party. Most of them were so ambivalent on this issue that they refused to exclude parliamentarism completely from their statements of the principles of the party. Liebknecht sought to make parliamentarism acceptable to Social Democrats in some degree by his pamphlets in 1886–1887. In this way, Liebknecht tried to bring some harmony between the parliamentary practice and the ultimate goals of Social Democracy. Bernstein took similar steps in 1890, when he affirmed that Social Democrats had to take up the tasks of democratization in the German Reich which the liberals had abandoned. At the same time, however, the anti-parliamentarism of the *Jungen* indicated that an underlying suspicion and hostility to the bourgeois representative system had not vanished from the Social Democratic movement.

The experience with parliamentary tactics during the Socialist Law left a heritage of ambivalent parliamentarism among the German Social Democrats. Had the Social Democrats never dropped their commitment to the "People's state," they could have accepted parliamentarism as an ultimate goal of their party. They might still have criticized the specific form of parliamentarism in Bismarck's Reich, but they could have worked for its perfection without hesitation. On the other hand, had they followed the recommendations of Marx and Engels without hesitation, then they could have defined their ultimate political goals with greater certainty.

As ambivalent parliamentarians, the Social Democrats were also ambivalent revolutionaries. Success in elections and the occasional hope of influencing legislation made it unnecessary for them to think in terms of direct revolutionary action. The influence of Marxism, however, obliged them to think of themselves as revolutionaries. But Marxism could be interpreted to give revolution an essentially evolutionary meaning. With this interpretation, a commitment to Marxism did not imply a rejection of parliamentary tactics, regardless of how insignificant the latter might be for bringing about socialism. Marxism, as understood by Bebel and the other leaders, simply helped to solidify their ambivalent parliamentarism.

Certainty in Marxist Economic Theory

The devotion of Social Democracy's theoreticians to Marxism easily overshadowed the political uncertainty of the movement as a whole. In the seventies, the Social Democrats had literally fumbled their way through the intricacies of economic thought, seeking assistance from almost any thinker who offered guidelines on the subject. Although German Social Democrats generally recognized Marx's *Capital* as a fundamental book for socialists, they also flirted with Eugen Duehring, Albert Schaeffle, Karl Rodbertus, and others. All that changed during the eighties. For over a decade the movement had been more and more saturated with an elementary instruction in Marxist economic and historical theory, through Engels' *Anti-Duehring* and *Socialism: Utopian and Scientific,* the writings of Kautsky and many others in the *Neue Zeit,* and numerous handbooks, essays, and articles in the popular press. In terms of education, this marked a significant step forward, for now even the rank-and-file of the party received an elementary but systematic introduction in economic theory.[15]

Since the focus of Social Democratic studies had shifted so heavily to social and economic problems, this aspect of Marxism was naturally emphasized. Reading the issues of the *Neue Zeit,* one could learn the details of current social and economic developments, but Kautsky had not introduced discussions of political matters into this journal. Likewise, although Bebel always scrutinized German economic development and sought to understand it in terms of Marx's analysis of capitalism, he had not drawn from this any special lessons about a particular political role for the party. Bebel began a career as a parliamentary politician in 1867, before becoming a Marxist, and he continued the same form of political action after being instructed by Marx and Engels. From some of Bebel's thought, discussed in the earlier chapters, it is possible to conclude that he did not believe that political action on the part of the socialists would be necessary for the achievement of socialism. The course of historical and economic development itself would bring about socialism. At other times, as in 1890, he suggested rather directly that the road to socialism would be achieved through parliamentary political action. The supremacy of the radicals under Bebel's leadership at the fall of the Socialist Law provided the basis for a permeation of this general ambiguity throughout the party. The

[15] The series known as the *Internationale Bibliothek,* started in 1887, specialized in books on social and economic subjects. Another series, the *Berliner Arbeiterbibliothek,* edited by Max Schippel, also focused its attention on these subjects. As of 1890, only one pamphlet in this series touched on a political subject; but this was a statistical report on the growth of the socialist Reichstag vote through 1887 with no attempt to treat it as a political problem.

Erfurt program made it clear that the working class could not "effect the passing of the means of production into the ownership of the community without acquiring political power." But the exposition of Marxist theory in the program also made it clear that the existing capitalist system could not sustain itself, regardless of what means it used. Viewed in the light of the intellectual development of the party during the eighties, the Erfurt program can also be understood as stressing the achievement of socialism through the development of history itself. The only political action intimated in the Erfurt program was parliamentary, but this lacked a powerful thrust because of the ambivalence of the leading Social Democrats toward parliamentarism.

Nevertheless, the quest for economic certainty, so typical of the seventies, reached its goal by the end of the eighties. The repression under the Socialist Law had intensified the feeling of social alienation among the socialist workers, and in this context the Marxist emphasis on the class conflict fit the objective conditions in Germany perfectly. Marxism thus offered a system of thought which explained the causes of the conflict and provided the hope that it would vanish.

Weakness and Greatness

The heritage of the Socialist Law for the Social Democratic movement proved to be many-sided. It left the party with a commitment to Marxism and a certainty in economic and social doctrines. But it also left the Social Democrats with less certainty about political goals and the nature of their own political action. The party emerged from this period with its own "heroic" tradition, but the battles of the epoch were fought at the polls, not on the barricades. Nevertheless, the Social Democrats did not fail to act courageously and even defiantly throughout the twelve years of the hated law. But when their year of victory arrived, they had to celebrate it as parliamentary heroes, an ironic fact in view of the traditional disgust the radicals had shown toward parliamentarism. The radicals had warned against overestimating parliamentarism in the early and middle eighties, but by 1890 they found themselves in complete control of the party and defending its parliamentary tactics.

Despite the ambiguities and uncertainties apparent among the Social Democrats, no one can justly deny their great achievements by 1890. If, hoping to avoid provocative acts, they floundered initially in October 1878, they soon gained courage and resilience as the authorities insisted on implementing the Socialist Law harshly and indiscriminately. They wisely shunned the excesses of an anarchist "Propaganda by Deed," just as they learned how to undermine the political appeal of Bismarck's welfare legislation with shrewdness and wit. If they preferred the path of legality, they did not shy away from illegality when necessary; they accepted expulsion, arrest, and imprisonment with astounding calmness and sometimes with pleasure, but they never sought to become martyrs. Although hated, despised, and condemned by the dominant classes of German society, they were increasingly loved, admired, and praised by the workers. When Bismarck fell from power in March 1890, the Social Democrats could rightly claim that they had contributed to his departure. On October 1, they justly felt that they had confronted a great challenge with courage, intelligence, and ultimate success.

APPENDIX A

THE GOTHA PROGRAM, 1875 *

I. Labor is the source of all wealth and culture, and since generally useful labor is possible only through society, the collective product of labor belongs to society, that is, to all of its members on the basis of a universal duty to work and according to equal right, each sharing according to his reasonable needs.

In contemporary society the means of labor are the monopoly of the capitalist class; the consequent dependence of the working class is the cause of all forms of misery and servitude.

The emancipation of labor demands the transformation of the means of labor into the common property of society and the cooperative regulation of collective labor to be utilized for the public good and with fair distribution of the proceeds of labor.

The emancipation of labor must be the work of the working class, in contrast to which all other classes are but one reactionary mass.

II. Proceeding from these principles, the Socialist Labor Party of Germany strives with every legal † means for the Free State and the socialist society, the destruction of the Iron Law of Wages through the abolition of the system of wage labor, the abolition of exploitation in every form and the elimination of all social and political inequality.

The Socialist Labor Party of Germany, although working primarily within the national framework, is conscious of the international character of the labor movement and is resolved to fulfill every obligation which this imposes upon the workers in order to bring about the brotherhood of man.

In order to pave the way for a solution of the social question, the Socialist Labor Party of Germany demands the establishment of socialist producers' cooperatives with state-help under the democratic control of the working people. The producers' cooperatives are to be called into being for industry and agriculture on such a scale that the socialist organization of all labor will arise from them.

* German text in Wilhelm Mommsen (ed.), *Deutsche Parteiprogramme* (Munich, 1960), pp. 313–14.

† The word "legal" was eliminated by the first party congress under the Socialist Law at the Castle Wyden in Switzerland, on August 22, 1880.

The Socialist Labor Party demands as the foundation of the state:

1. Universal, equal, direct suffrage, with secret ballot and obligatory voting for all citizens over twenty years of age in all elections in state and municipality. The election day must be on a Sunday or holiday.

2. Direct legislation by the people. Decision on war and peace by the people.

3. Universal military training. People's militia [*Volkswehr*] in place of the standing army.

4. Abolition of all exceptional laws, especially the laws on the press, association, and assembly; in general, of all laws which limit free expression of opinion, free investigation, and thought.

5. Administration of justice by the people. Free administration of justice.

6. Universal and equal public education by the state. Universal obligatory school education. Free instruction in all educational institutions. Declaration that religion is a private matter.

Within the present society the Socialist Labor Party demands:

1. The farthest possible extension of political rights and liberties in the sense of the above demands.

2. A single progressive income tax for state and municipality, in place of the existing [taxes], especially the indirect taxes which burden the people.

3. Unlimited right of combination.

4. A normal working day corresponding to the needs of society. Prohibition of all Sunday labor.

5. Prohibition of child labor and all female labor which is harmful to health and morals.

6. Protective laws for the life and health of the workers. Sanitary control of workers' dwellings. Inspection of mines, factories, workshops, and domestic industry by officials elected by the workers. An effective employers' liability law.

7. Regulation of prison labor.

8. Complete self-administration for all workers' Aid and Assistance Funds.

APPENDIX B

THE ERFURT PROGRAM, 1891 *

The economic development of bourgeois society leads by natural necessity to the downfall of the small industry, whose foundation is formed by the worker's private ownership of his means of production. It separates the worker from his means of production and converts him into a propertyless proletarian, while the means of production become the monopoly of a relatively small number of capitalists and large landowners.

Hand-in-hand with this monopolization of the means of production goes the displacement of the dispersed small industries by colossal great industries, the development of the tool into the machine, and a gigantic growth in the productivity of human labor. But all the advantages of this transformation are monopolized by capitalists and large landowners. For the proletariat and the declining intermediate classes—petty bourgeoisie and peasants—it means a growing augmentation of the insecurity of their existence, of misery, oppression, enslavement, debasement, and exploitation.

Ever greater grows the number of proletarians, ever more enormous the army of surplus workers, ever sharper the opposition between exploiters and exploited, ever bitterer the class-war between bourgeoisie and proletariat, which divides modern society into two hostile camps, and is the common characteristic of all industrial countries.

The gulf between the propertied and the propertyless is further widened through the crises, founded in the essence of the capitalistic method of production, which constantly become more comprehensive and more devastating, which elevate general insecurity to the normal condition of society, and which prove that the powers of production of contemporary society have grown beyond measure, and that private ownership of the means of production has become incompatible with their intended application and their full development.

Private ownership of the means of production, which was formerly the means of securing to the producer the ownership of his product,

* German text in *Protokoll ueber die Verhandlungen des Parteitages der Sozialdemokratischen Partei Deutschlands. Abgehalten zu Erfurt vom 14. bis 20. Oktober 1891* (Berlin, 1891), pp. 3–6.

has today become the means of expropriating peasants, manual workers, and small traders, and enabling the non-workers—capitalists and large landowners—to own the product of the workers. Only the transformation of capitalistic private ownership of the means of production—the soil, mines, raw materials, tools, machines, and means of transport—into social ownership and the transformation of production of goods for sale into socialistic production managed for and through society, can bring it about, that the great industry and the steadily growing productive capacity of social labor shall for the hitherto exploited classes be changed from a source of misery and oppression to a source of the highest welfare and of all-round harmonious perfection.

This social transformation means the emancipation not only of the proletariat but of the whole human race which suffers under present conditions. But it can only be the work of the working class, because all the other classes, in spite of mutually conflicting interests, take their stand on the basis of private ownership of the means of production, and have as their common object the preservation of the principles of contemporary society.

The battle of the working class against capitalistic exploitation is necessarily a political battle. The working class cannot carry on its economic battles or develop its economic organization without political rights. It cannot effect the passing of the means of production into the ownership of the community without acquiring political power.

To shape this battle of the working class into a conscious and united effort, and to show it its naturally necessary end, is the object of the Social Democratic party.

The interests of the working class are the same in all lands with capitalistic methods of production. With the expansion of world-transport and production for the world-market, the state of the workers in any one country becomes constantly more dependent on the state of the workers in other countries. The emancipation of the working class is thus a task in which the workers of all civilized countries are concerned in a like degree. Conscious of this, the Social Democratic party of Germany feels and declares itself *one* with the class-conscious workers of all other lands.

The Social Democratic party of Germany fights thus not for new class privileges and exceptional rights, but for the abolition of class domination and of the classes themselves, and for the equal rights and equal obligations of all, without distinction of sex and parentage. Setting out from these views, it combats in contemporary society not merely the exploitation and oppression of the wage-workers, but every kind of exploitation and oppression, whether directed against a class, a party, a sex, or a race.

Setting out from these principles the Social Democratic party of Germany demands immediately—

1. Universal, equal, direct suffrage and franchise, with direct ballot, for all members of the Empire over twenty years of age, without distinction of sex, for all elections and acts of voting. Proportional representation; and until this is introduced, redivision of the constituencies by law according to the numbers of population. A new Legislature every two years. Fixing of elections and acts of voting for a legal holiday. Indemnity for the elected representatives. Removal of every curtailment of political rights except in case of tutelage.

2. Direct legislation by the people by means of the initiative and referendum. Self-determination and self-government of the people in empire, state, province, and commune. Authorities to be elected by the people; to be responsible and bound. Taxes to be voted annually.

3. Education of all to be capable of bearing arms. Armed nation instead of standing army. Decision of war and peace by the representatives of the people. Settlement of all international disputes by the method of arbitration.

4. Abolition of all laws which curtail or suppress the free expression of opinion and the right of association and assembly.

5. Abolition of all laws which are prejudicial to women in their relations to men in public or private law.

6. Declaration that religion is a private matter. Abolition of all contributions from public funds to ecclesiastical and religious objects. Ecclesiastical and religious communities are to be treated as private associations, which manage their affairs quite independently.

7. Secularization of education. Compulsory attendance of public primary schools. No charges to be made for instruction, school requisites, and maintenance, in the public primary schools; nor in the higher educational institutions for those students, male and female, who by virtue of their capacities are considered fit for further training.

8. No charge to be made for the administration of the law, or for

legal assistance. Judgment by popularly elected judges. Appeal in criminal cases. Indemnification of innocent persons prosecuted, arrested, or condemned. Abolition of the death penalty.

9. No charges to be made for medical attendance, including midwifery and medicine. No charges to be made for death certificates.

10. Graduated taxes on income and property, to meet all public expenses as far as these are to be covered by taxation. Obligatory self-assessment. A tax on inheritance, graduated according to the size of the inheritance and the degree of kinship. Abolition of all indirect taxes, customs, and other politico-economic measures which sacrifice the interests of the whole community to the interests of a favored minority. For the protection of the working class, the German Social Democratic party demands immediately:

1. An effective national and international legislation for the protection of workmen on the following basis:

(a) Fixing of a normal working day with a maximum of eight hours.

(b) Prohibition of industrial work for children under fourteen years.

(c) Prohibition of night-work, except for such branches of industry as, in accordance with their nature, require night-work, for technical reasons, or reasons of public welfare.

(d) An uninterrupted rest of at least thirty-six hours in every week for every worker.

(e) Prohibition of the truck system.

2. Inspection of all industrial businesses, investigation and regulation of labor relations in town and country by an Imperial Department of Labor, district labor department, and chambers of labor. Thorough industrial hygiene.

3. Legal equalization of agricultural laborers and domestic servants with industrial workers; removal of the special regulations affecting servants.

4. Assurance of the right of combination.

5. Workmen's insurance to be taken over bodily by the Empire; and the workers to have an influential share in its administration.

APPENDIX C

"LAW AGAINST THE PUBLICLY DANGEROUS ENDEAVORS OF SOCIAL DEMOCRACY" *

#1. Societies [*Vereine*] which aim at the overthrow of the existing political or social order through social-democratic, socialistic, or communistic endeavors are to be prohibited.

This applies also to societies in which social-democratic, socialistic, or communistic endeavors aiming at the overthrow of the existing political or social order are manifested in a manner dangerous to the public peace, and, particularly to the harmony among the classes of the population.

Associations of every kind are the same as societies.

#2. In the event that a registered cooperative comes under the provisions of #1, par. 2, then #35 of the Law of July 4, 1868, concerning the legal status of cooperative associations for business and [other] economic purposes [*Erwerbs- und Wirtschaftsgenossenschaften*] (*Bundesgesetzblatt* pp. 415ff.) is to be applied.

In an analogous event, #29 of the Law concerning registered Assistance Funds [*Hilfskassen*] of April 7, 1876 (*Reichsgesetzblatt* pp. 125ff.) is to be applied to Registered Assistance Funds.

#3. In the event foreseen by #1, par. 2, Independent Fund Societies (not registered) [*Unabhaengige Kassenvereine (nicht eingeschrieben)*], which have the statutory purpose of mutual support for their members, are not to be immediately prohibited, but are to be put under extraordinary state control.

Where several independent societies of this kind form a union [*Verband*], and in the event that in one of these societies the endeavors described in #1, par. 2 are manifested, this society can be ordered excluded from the union and put under control.

Likewise, if the described endeavors manifest themselves in one branch of a society, control is to be confined to that branch.

#4. The authority invested with the control is empowered:

1. To attend all sessions and meetings of the society [*Verein*].

* The law was first passed on Oct. 19, 1878. It was effective until March 31, 1881. Following that it was renewed four times: In May 1880, effective until Sept. 30, 1884; in May 1884, effective until Sept. 30, 1886; in April 1886, effective until Sept. 30, 1888, and in Feb. 1888, effective until Sept. 30, 1890. German text in *SB*, IV, i (1878), vol. 1, No. 47, pp. 132–35.

2. To call and conduct membership assemblies.

3. To inspect the books, papers and cash assets, as well as to demand information about the affairs of the society.

4. To forbid the carrying out of resolutions which are apt to further the endeavors described in #1, par. 2.

5. To transfer to qualified persons the duties of the officers or other leading organs of the society.

6. To take charge of and manage the funds.

#5. In case the membership meetings, the executive committee, or another managing organ acts in opposition to the directives of the controlling authority issued within the scope of its powers, or in case the endeavors in #1, par. 2, are manifested after the introduction of the control, the society may be prohibited.

#6. The prohibition or the imposition of control are within the competence of the State Police Authority [*Landespolizeibehoerde*].* The prohibition of foreign societies appertains to the *Reichskanzler.*

The prohibition is in all cases to be publicized through the *Reichsanzeiger;* in addition, the prohibition by the State Police Authority is to be publicized through the designated newspaper for official notifications by the authority of the locality or district.

The prohibition is valid for the entire area of the Federation [*Bundesgebiet*] and embraces all branches of the society, as well as every ostensible new society, which in reality is to be regarded as the old one.

#7. With the prohibition, the society's cash assets, as well as the objects intended for the purposes of the society are to be confiscated by the authority.

After the prohibition has become final, the Administrative Authority [*Verwaltungsbehoerde*] designated by the State Police Authority must delegate the settlement of the affairs of the society (liquidation) to suitable persons and supervise the liquidation; the Administrative Authority must also make known the names of the liquidators.

The decision of the Administrative Authority takes the place of a resolution by the membership meeting provided for by the laws or statutes.

The liquidated property of the society is, without detriment to the legal claims of third parties and of the members of the society, to be utilized as provided in the statutes of the society, or in general laws.

The moment when the prohibition becomes final is to be considered

* For the definition of State Police Authority see #29.

the moment of the dissolution of the society (or the closing of the Fund).

Appeal against the decrees of the authority is permitted only to the Supervising Authority [*Aufsichtsbehoerde*].

#8. The prohibition decree by the State Police Authority, as well as the establishment of a control is to be communicated in writing, indicating the reasons, to the society's Executive Committee, in case one exists within domestic jurisdiction. Against such a decree the society's Executive has the right to make an appeal (#26).

The appeal must be made within one week after receipt of the notice of the decree; the appeal is to be directed to the authority which issued the decree.

The appeal has no postponing effect.

#9. Meetings in which social-democratic, socialistic, or communistic endeavors which aim at the overthrow of the existing political or social order are manifested are to be dissolved.

Meetings for which the assumption is justified by the fact that they are intended to further the endeavors described in the first paragraph are to be prohibited. Public festivities and processions shall be treated the same as meetings.

#10. Prohibition and dissolution are within the competence of the Police Authority.

Appeal is permitted only to the Supervising Authority.

#11. Publications in which social-democratic, socialistic, or communistic endeavors aimed at the overthrow of the existing political or social order are manifested in a manner calculated to endanger the public peace, and particularly the harmony among all classes of the population, are to be prohibited.

In the case of periodical publications, the prohibition may extend to further issues as soon as a single issue has been prohibited on the basis of this law.

#12. The prohibition lies within the competence of the State Police Authority, and, in the case of periodical publications appearing within the Reich, under the competence of the State Police Authority of the District [*Bezirk*] in which the publication appears. The prohibition of the further distribution of periodical publications printed abroad lies within the competence of the *Reichskanzler*.

The prohibition is to be publicized in the manner described in #6, par. 2, and is valid for the entire *Bundesgebiet*.

#13. The prohibition of publications by the State Police Authority is to be made known in writing, with the reasons of the same, to the publisher or editor, and in the case of non-periodic publications, to the author of the same, if these persons are within the Reich.

The publisher, editor or author has the right of appeal against the order (#26).

The appeal must be submitted to the authority which issued the decree within a week after receipt of notification.

The appeal has no postponing effect.

#14. On the basis of the prohibition, the publications concerned are to be confiscated wherever found for the purpose of distribution. The confiscation may include the plates and forms used for reproduction; in the case of printed publications in the proper sense, a withdrawal of the set types from circulation is to be substituted for their seizure, upon the request of the interested parties. After the prohibition is final, the publication, plates, and forms are to be made unusable.

Appeal is permitted only to the Supervising Authority.

#15. Before the decree of prohibition, the Police Authority is empowered provisionally to seize publications of the character described in #11, as well as plates and forms for reproduction. Within twenty-four hours, the seized publication is to be delivered to the State Police Authority. The latter must either order immediately the restoration of the confiscated material or issue a decree of prohibition within one week. If the prohibition does not ensue within this period the confiscation is voided and the various pieces, plates and forms shall be released.

#16. The collection of contributions for the furtherance of social-democratic, socialistic, or communistic endeavors aiming at the overthrow of the existing political and social order, as well as a public appeal for such contributions, are to be prohibited by the police.

The prohibition is to be announced publicly.

Appeal is permitted only to the Supervising Authority.

#17. Whoever participates as a member in a prohibited society (#6), or carries on an activity in its interest, is to be punished by a fine of not more than five hundred marks or with imprisonment not exceeding three months. The same punishment is to be inflicted on anyone who participates in a prohibited meeting (#9), or who does not depart immediately after the dissolution of a meeting by the police. Imprisonment of not less than one month and not more than one year is to be inflicted on those who participate in a society or assembly as chairmen, leaders, monitors, agents, speakers, or treasurers, or on those who issue invitations to attend the meeting.

#18. Whoever provides a prohibited society or meeting with a place of assembly is to be punished with imprisonment of from one month to one year.

#19. Whoever distributes, continues, or reprints a prohibited publication (##11, 12) or a provisionally confiscated publication (#15) is to be punished with a fine not exceeding one thousand marks or with imprisonment not exceeding six months.

#20. Whoever acts in violation of a prohibition under #16, is punishable with a fine not exceeding five hundred marks or with imprisonment not exceeding three months. Moreover, all that which has been received in consequence of the prohibited collection or invitation, or its value, is to devolve to the Poor Relief Fund [*Armenkasse*] of the locality.

#21. Whoever commits one of the acts prohibited by ##17, 18, 19 without knowledge of the prohibition, but after the notification of the prohibition in the *Reichsanzeiger* (##6, 12) is to be punished by a fine not exceeding one hundred and fifty marks.

The same punishment applies to those who act in violation of a prohibition under #16 after the publication of the prohibition. The concluding provision of #20 applies.

#22. In addition to the punishment of imprisonment, in case of a condemnation for acts in violation of ##17 to 20, a further judgment may be rendered as to the admissibility of a limitation of their right of residence against persons who make a business of the agitation for endeavors described in #1, par. 2.

On the basis of this judgment, the residence of a condemned person in certain districts and localities may be forbidden by the State Police Authority, only if, however, the condemned person has not resided in his place of legal residence for a period of six months. Foreigners may be expelled from the *Bundesgebiet* by the State Police Authority. Appeal to be permitted only to the Supervising Authority.

Acts in contravention are to be punished with imprisonment from one month to one year.

#23. Under the conditions described in #22, par. 1, innkeepers, barkeepers, persons carrying on a retail business in brandy or liquors, book publishers, booksellers, librarians in lending libraries and proprietors of reading rooms, may, in addition to imprisonment, be forbidden to continue their business.

#24. The State Police Authority may withdraw the license for the professional or non-professional public distribution of publications, as well as the license for an itinerant trade in publications from persons who make a business of furthering the endeavors described in #1, par. 2, or who have been legally sentenced to punishment on the basis of the provisions of this law.

Appeal is permitted only to the Supervising Authority.

#25. Whoever acts in contravention of a judgment pronounced under #23 or of a decision decreed under #24 is punishable by a fine not exceeding one thousand marks, or by arrest or imprisonment not exceeding six months.

#26. A Commission is to be formed to decide upon the appeals in the cases of ##8, 13. The Bundesrat elects four of its own members and five from the highest courts of the Reich or the individual *Bundesstaaten.*

The election of these five members is for the period of the duration of this law, and for the period in which they hold judicial office.

The Emperor appoints the chairman and his representative from out of the number of the members of the Commission.

#27. A quorum of the Commission consists of five members, of whom at least three shall belong to the judicial members. Before a decision on an appeal is given, the appellant is to be afforded the opportunity to plead in support of his motion either verbally or in writing. The Commission is empowered to collect evidence in the fullest scope, and particularly through sworn witnesses and experts, and to collect evidence through a demand upon an authority of the Reich or of the states of the Reich. With respect to the obligation to testify as a witness or as an expert, as well as with respect to the punishment to be inflicted for disobedience, the laws of judicial procedure of the locality where the Commission sits, or where the government official called upon resides, obtain. The decisions are based upon free judgment [*freiem Ermessen*] and are final.

In other respects, the Commission's conduct of business is to be regulated by rules prescribed by itself, which are subject to the approval of the Bundesrat.

#28. For districts or localities where the public safety is menaced by the endeavors described in #1, par. 2, the following regulations may be decreed, in case they are not already permitted by state law, with the consent of the Bundesrat for a period not exceeding one year:

1. that meetings may take place only after the consent of the Police Authority has been obtained; this limitation does not extend to meetings called for the purposes of an announced election to the Reichstag or to the diets of the states [*Landesvertretung*];

2. that the distribution of publications shall not take place on public roads, streets, squares, or other public places;

3. that the residence in districts or localities of persons from whom danger to public safety and order is to be feared may be forbidden;

4. that the possession, bearing, importation, and sale of weapons is to be forbidden, limited, or made conditional upon certain requirements.

The Reichstag must be informed immediately, that is, upon its first reassembling, about any decree that has been issued under the foregoing provisions.

The decrees are to be announced in the *Reichsanzeiger* and by whatever manner is prescribed for local police orders.

Whoever, knowingly or after public notice is given, acts in contravention of these regulations, or of the decisions based thereon, is to be punished by a fine not exceeding one thousand marks, or with arrest or imprisonment not exceeding six months.

#29. The Central Authority of each Federal State will announce to which authority the designation of State Police Authority applies.

#30. This law goes into force upon the day of its proclamation and remains in force until March 31, 1881.

BIBLIOGRAPHICAL ESSAY

The following essay is designed as an introduction to the sources and literature on the German Social Democratic movement in the period between the unity congress at Gotha in 1875 and the expiration of the Socialist Law in 1890. Within these limits, it is not intended as an exhaustive compilation, but seeks simply to discuss the nature of the sources, aspects of the movement covered by the existing literature, and the salient interpretations of Social Democracy during the period of the Socialist Law. No attempt has been made to treat the fairly extensive body of writing on the Lassalleans and Eisenachers prior to 1875, although much of it is cited in the footnote references in Chapters I and II. Likewise, since the bibliography on Marx and Engels is immense, only that literature which is specifically concerned with their relationship to the movement in Germany has been treated.

Bibliographies

The study of the German labor movement in the nineteenth century is increasingly facilitated by the appearance of useful bibliographies. Writings by and on Kautsky have been carefully catalogued by Werner Blumenberg, *Karl Kautskys Literarisches Werk. Eine bibliographische Uebersicht* (The Hague, 1960), while Ernst Schraepler has performed the same service for Bebel, *August-Bebel-Bibliographie* (Duesseldorf, 1962). In this same category, but much older, is Ernst Drahn, *Johann Most: eine Bio-bibliographie* (Berlin, 1925). For the bibliographies related to other prominent leaders, one may refer to the biographies discussed below.

Recent literature on the German labor movement is discussed in a variety of bibliographical articles, one of the most useful being Erich Matthias, "Zur Geschichte der deutschen Arbeiterbewegung," *Neue Politische Literature*, III (1958). For several years, Wolfram Fischer has been preparing encompassing bibliographical essays with varying titles on social and labor history for the *Blaetter fuer deutsche Landesgeschichte,* see volumes 93 (1957), 94 (1958), 97 (1961), and 99 (1963). Although the two following articles concentrate on the period after the fall of the Socialist Law in 1890, the materials discussed frequently overlap: William H. Maehl, "Recent Literature on the German Socialists, 1891–1932," *Journal of Modern History*, XXXIII (Sept. 1961), and Georg Kotowski, "Zur Geschichte der Arbeiterbewegung in Mittel- und Ostdeutschland: ein Literaturbericht," *Jahrbuch fuer die Geschichte Mittel- und Ostdeutschlands*, VIII (1959). In addition, there are several current journals of a specialized nature which are valuable for lists and reviews as well as articles: *International Review of Social History* (Assen, 1956ff., published by the International Institute for Social History, Amsterdam); *Archiv fuer Sozialgeschichte* (Hannover, 1961ff., published by the Friedrich-Ebert-Stiftung); *Beitraege zur Geschichte der deutschen Arbeiterbewegung* (Berlin-East, 1959ff., published by the Central Committee of the Socialist Unity Party); and *Annali* (Milan, 1958ff., published by the Giangiacomo Feltrinelli Institute).

The older literature on the labor movement in Germany, including references to contemporary publications by Social Democrats, is available through Joseph Stammhammer, *Bibliographie des Sozialismus und Communismus*, 3 vols. (Berlin, 1893–1909); Ernst Drahn, *Fuehrer durch das Schrifttum des deutschen Sozialismus* (2nd ed.; Berlin, 1920); and Edouard Dolleans and Michel Crozier, *Mouvements ouvrier et socialiste. Chronologie et Bibliographie. Angleterre, France, Allemagne, États-Unis (1750–1918)* (Paris, 1950). An extensive list of contemporary socialist publications prohibited under the Socialist Law (1878–1890) is given in Otto Atzrott, *Sozialdemokratische Druckschriften und Vereine verboten auf Grund des Reichsgesetzes gegen die gemeingefaehrlichen Bestrebungen der Sozialdemokratie vom 21. Oktober 1878* (Berlin, 1886).

Surveys of the considerable amount of literature on the German labor movement that has appeared in the German Democratic Republic (DDR) are given by Hildegard Scheffler and Lutz Noack, *Bibliographie zur Geschichte der deutschen Arbeiterbewegung. Eine Auswahl der seit 1945 im Gebiete der DDR erschienenen Veroeffentlichungen* (Leipzig, 1955), and *Historische Forschungen in der DDR. Analysen und Berichte. Sonderheft der Zeitschrift fuer Geschichtswissenschaft* (Berlin-East, 1960).

On newspapers and periodicals related to the socialist movement, the International Institute for Social History has conveniently listed its holdings of "Newspapers and Periodicals in the German Language of the Period from 1830 to 1890 in the Possession of the International Institute of Social History," *Bulletin of the International Institute of Social History, Amsterdam*, v (1950). Similarly useful is John L. Snell's "Some German Socialist Newspapers in European Archives," *Journal of Modern History*, xxiv (1952). Several bibliographical essays on the German labor press with some reference to the period before 1890 are to be found in the *Handbuch des Vereins Arbeiterpresse*, edited by the Vorstand des Vereins Arbeiterpresse, iii (1914). Two studies by Ernst Drahn are equally useful: *Zur Entwicklung und Geschichte des sozialistischen Buchhandels und der Arbeiterpresse* (Gautzsch bei Leipzig, 1913), and "Zur Quellenkunde einer Pressegeschichte der Sozialisten (Marxisten) Deutschlands," *Jahrbuecher fuer Nationaloekonomie und Statistik*, Series 3, lxxvii (Feb.–March, 1930). Finally, special attention should be drawn to the current studies sponsored by the Westfaelisch-Niederrheinisches Institut für Zeitungsforschung in Dortmund, which has published the work by Ulrich Hess, "Louis Viereck und seine Muenchner Blaetter fuer Arbeiter 1882–1889," in its series, *Dortmunder Beitraege zur Zeitungsforschung*, vi (1961). The director of the institute, Kurt Koszyk, has contributed an important work on the *Anfaenge und Fruehe Entwicklung der Sozialdemokratischen Presse im Ruhrgebiet* (1875–1908) (Dortmund, 1953).

Archival Sources

Students of German socialism are especially fortunate in having much of the archive of the German Social Democratic party (founded in the 1880's) preserved in the International Institute for Social History in Amsterdam. These materials, especially the unpublished correspondence of the Social Democratic leaders, are of special significance for a period when so much evidence was destroyed to keep it away from the police. Of primary value are the letters and other sources in the *Nachlass* of August Bebel, Eduard Bernstein, Karl Kautsky, Wilhelm Liebknecht, Karl Marx/Friedrich Engels, Julius Motteler, and Georg von Vollmar; the division labeled as the *Kleine Korrespondenz* also contains valuable correspondence, although of a more fragmentary nature. The extensive correspondence between Bebel and numerous of his comrades contains the most detailed evidence on the internal development of the party. In the last ten years, the International Institute has completed the publication of the correspondence between Marx and Engels and Bebel, Kautsky, and Wilhelm Liebknecht in its series entitled *Quellen und Untersuchungen zur Geschichte der deutschen und oeterreichischen Arbeiterbewegung* (see below under Published Correspondence). The use of the letters of the leaders within Germany to Marx and Engels helps to correct the mistaken impression that the latter always gave enlightened directives from their refuge in London, a notion stimulated by the fact that previously only their letters had been published.

Although a detailed description of the archive is not needed here, two unpublished documents in the Motteler *Nachlass* were particularly useful for the internal party history during the early eighties. The first is the *Handschriftliches Protokoll des Wydener Kongresses 1880* which adds some important supplementary material to the abbreviated record of that congress published by the party. Second, and even more important, is the *Zuericher Protokoll*, an abbreviated record of the highly secret conclave of party leaders in August 19–21, 1882; without it we would have only a few references from memoirs and letters about this conference. From the Motteler *Nachlass* also comes Motteler's own detailed description of the smuggling system for the *Sozialdemokrat*, now reprinted in Ernst Engelberg, *Revolutionaere Politik und Rote Feldpost 1878–1890* (Berlin-East, 1959).

The filming of much of the material from the German Foreign Ministry Archives (1867–1920) has made another archival source available with some secret reports on the Social Democrats. Under Bismarck's direction, the Foreign Ministry made use of secret agents, usually disgruntled socialists or anarchists, to obtain inside information on the Social Democrats. Although often long and detailed, these reports have limited value, for Bismarck especially desired information connecting the Social Democrats with anarchists abroad; the agents followed his directions and the results were often trivial. The reports are in the Foreign Ministry division, Europa Generalia, No. 82, and may be obtained through the microfilms of the Universities of California and Michigan. For precise references, see *A Catalogue of Files and Microfilms of the German Foreign Ministry Archives 1867–1920* (Oxford, 1959), prepared by the American Historical Committee for the Study of War Documents.

Documentary Sources

Due to the peculiarities of the Social Democratic position under the Socialist Law, the record of the Reichstag debates, the *Stenographische*

Berichte ueber die Verhandlungen des Deutschen Reichstages (Berlin, 1871ff.), becomes more significant than for other periods. Since the Social Democratic Reichstag *Fraktion* functioned also as the party's executive committee, the speeches of the deputies served numerous purposes: as propaganda statements to the whole nation, as guidelines for the party following, and sometimes as genuine legislative deliberations. Although the speeches of Social Democratic deputies do not often reveal the intensity of intraparty antagonisms, the minutes of the Reichstag, because of their exactness and continuity, actually offer a more valuable source than the fragmentary *Protokolle* of the three party congresses under the Socialist Law. And, the *Mittheilungen ueber die Verhandlungen des ordentlichen Landtags in Koenigreiche Sachsen. Zweite Kammer* (1877–1890) is an invaluable source for the party's political objectives on the state level, where practical reformist goals are far more evident than in the Reichstag. Of less value, because so few Social Democrats held seats, are the *Verhandlungen des Zweiten Kammer des Landstaende des Grossherzogthums Hessen. Protokolle* and *Beilagen* (1885/88, 1888/91). Unfortunately, minutes of the city councils on which Social Democrats had representation were not available, although for Berlin, Paul Hirsch, *25 Jahre sozialdemokratischer Arbeit in der Gemeinde. Die Taetigkeit der Sozialdemokratie in der Berliner Stadtverordnetenversammlung* (Berlin, 1908), reprints resolutions and parts of speeches.

The published minutes of the three secret party congresses during the Socialist Law were necessarily incomplete summaries, carefully edited to avoid exposing the party to the police and to underplay the degree of disagreement among the leaders. The names of participants and speakers are excluded from the *Protokolle* for the congresses of 1880 and 1883. Nevertheless, some of the missing information can be supplied from the manuscript in the Motteler *Nachlass* (see under Archival Sources) for the *Protokoll des Kongresses der Deutschen Sozialdemokratie. Abgehalten auf Schloss Wyden in der Schweiz, vom 20. bis 23. August 1880* (Zurich, 1880). Similarly, the *Protokoll ueber den Kongress der deutschen Sozialdemokratie in Kopenhagen. Abgehalten vom 29. Maerz bis 2. April 1883* (Hottingen-Zurich, 1883) may be enlarged somewhat by reference to police reports cited in the work by Karl-Alexander Hellfaier (see below under Histories and Interpretations). On the other hand, the various police reports do not add substantially to the *Verhandlungen des Parteitags der deutschen Sozialdemokratie in St. Gallen. Abgehalten vom 2. bis 6. Oktober 1887*

(Hottingen-Zurich, 1888), which gives a much fuller summary of the discussions with the names of the speakers. A handy reference volume, arranged topically, of resolutions and speeches is available in Wilhelm Schroeder, *Handbuch der sozialdemokratischen Parteitage von 1863 bis 1909* (Munich, 1910). For precise references to the protocols of congresses prior to 1878 one may refer to the footnotes in the text or to the bibliographies in the works by Roger Morgan and Erich Kundel (see below under Histories and Interpretations).

The variety of ideas expressed in Social Democratic electoral programs and appeals can be followed through the documents reprinted in Bebel's edition of *Die Sozialdemokratie im deutschen Reichstag. Taetigkeitsberichte und Wahlaufrufe aus den Jahren 1871 bis 1893* (Berlin, 1909). The record of the high treason trial of Bebel, Hepner, and Liebknecht, newly edited by Karl-Heinz Leidigkeit, *Der Hochverratsprozess von Jahre 1872* (Berlin-East, 1960), is still a useful source on the political and social ideas of the Eisenachers at the time of German unification. Although there were frequent trials under the Socialist Law, the records are not so rich in idea content; the footnotes in the text give the exact citations. One of the best documentary sources on the implementation of the Socialist Law and the function of the so-called Reichs-Commission, the board which heard appeals on behalf of suppressed publications and societies, is in Leo Stern (ed.), *Der Kampf der deutschen Sozialdemokratie in der Zeit des Sozialistengesetzes 1878–1890. Die Taetigkeit der Reichs-Commission*, published in two volumes as Vol. III, 1 and 2, in the series, *Archivalische Forschungen zur Geschichte der deutschen Arbeiterbewegung* (Berlin-East, 1956). An interesting collection of sixteen long summary reports by the Berlin Police President on the activities of European socialists and anarchists, illustrating police mentality and adding some new information, has been edited by Reinhard Hoehn, *Die vaterlandslosen Gesellen. Der Sozialismus im Licht der Geheimberichte der preussischen Polizei 1878–1914.* Band I: (*1878–1890*) (Cologne and Opladen, 1964).

Newspapers, Periodicals, Pamphlets

Although far fewer Social Democratic newspapers appeared between 1878 and 1890 than in other periods, the two most important, the *Sozialdemokrat* (Zurich and London, 1879–1890) and the *Berliner Volksblatt* (Berlin, 1884–1890), represent the radical and moderate views, respectively, and thus offer valuable evidence on the party's ideological development. The *Sozialdemokrat* and the *Neue Zeit* (Stuttgart, 1883ff.), the latter edited by Karl Kautsky, became the chief organs of regular appearance for the popular and systematic dissemination of Marxism. Although both may be viewed as "official" organs of the party, they did not represent the full scope of Social Democratic theory and opinion. Unfortunately, most of the other newspapers which appeared in the 1880's, including the so-called "colorless" papers and the publications of trade unions, were not available for this study. Many of these were short lived, lasting sometimes for only a few months or years, and, if preserved, are scattered throughout local libraries in Germany. The chief exception is Louis Viereck's weekly, *Das Recht auf Arbeit* (Munich, 1884–1891) (1884–1887 available for this study), only one of several newspapers founded by this leader of the moderates. A fairly complete list of the newspapers that appeared may be compiled from the bibliographies discussed above and the local histories of the labor movement. For the years immediately before the passage of the Socialist Law, *Vorwaerts* (Leipzig, 1876–1878), the official organ of the party, reflects the diversity of opinion in the movement at the time.

The ideological debates within Social Democracy toward the end of the seventies are best studied through the three periodicals edited by Karl Hoechberg and founded with his financial assistance. The first of these, *Die Zukunft* (Berlin, 1877–1878), was endorsed as an official organ of the party; it reflects the eclectic nature of Social Democratic thought in the late seventies, but also a definite concern with the problems of political democracy. Hoechberg's other two periodicals, although they did not have official party recognition, carried articles by the Social Democratic leaders and served much the same function: *Jahrbuch fuer Sozialwissenschaft und Sozialpolitik* (Zurich, 1879–1881; edited by Hoechberg under the pseudonym, Dr. Ludwig Richter), and *Staatswirthschaftliche Abhandlungen* (Leipzig, 1879–1880; edited by Hoechberg under the pseudonym R. F. Seyfferth). Both Karl Kautsky and Eduard Bernstein, subsidized by Hoechberg at the time, wrote extensively for these periodicals.

The Social Democratic literature in pamphlet and book form, discussed and cited in the text of this study, hardly needs a special commentary here. The repressive conditions under the Socialist Law obstructed the possibilities for the kind of open theoretical discussion that took place within the movement after 1890. Except in a few cases, notably Bebel's *Die Frau und der Sozialismus* (Zurich, 1879), Kautsky's *Karl Marx' oekonomische Lehren* (Stuttgart, 1887), and perhaps one should include Engels' *Herr Eugen Duehring's Revolution in Science* (first serialized in *Vorwaerts*, 1877–1878), most of the literary output of the Social Democrats during these years did not have a lasting significance. No single book or pamphlet offered a clear statement of the moderates' views, and so for that current of opinion one must make a composite account from the writings of men such as Wilhelm Blos, Karl Frohme, Bruno Geiser, and Louis Viereck. However, one should not overlook the significance of Albert Schaeffle's *Quintessence of Socialism* (first German edition, 1874) for the influence of State Socialism among the Social Democrats, although the author was a political enemy of their movement. Much of the Social Democratic literature, it should be noted, was published as part of several publication series, the following being the most important: the *Sozialdemokratische Bibliothek* (Hottingen–Zurich, 1885ff., published by the party); the *Sozialpolitische Zeit- und Streitfragen* (Munich, 1883–1886, published by Louis Viereck); the *Berliner Arbeiterbibliothek* (Berlin, 1887– , edited by Max Schippel); and the *Internationale Bibliothek* (Stuttgart, 1887– , published by J. H. W. Dietz in close cooperation with the party executive).

Published Correspondence

No reasonably complete history of the internal life of the Social Democratic movement between 1878 and 1890 would be possible without the availability of the unpublished and published correspondence of some of the party leaders. Until recently, however, few letters of the German leaders were published, because the practice was to publish letters written by Marx and Engels, with little or no attention to what their correspondents wrote. This created a tendency to view the party's development from the perspective of the two residents in London, rather than from that of the participants in Germany. Apart from the correspondence between Marx and Engels themselves, one of the earliest collections including letters from German party leaders was F. A. Sorge's edition of the *Briefe und Auszuege aus Briefen von Joh. Phil. Becker, Jos. Dietzgen, Friedrich Engels, Karl Marx u. A. an F. A. Sorge und Andere* (Stuttgart, 1906). After World War I, Bernstein edited the letters he had received from Engels (with some from Kautsky), *Die Briefe von Friedrich Engels an Eduard Bernstein. Mit Briefen von Karl Kautsky an Ebendenselben* (Berlin, 1925). These must be supplemented with Bernstein's letters still in manuscript in the Bernstein *Nachlass;* they reveal that Bernstein had considerable independence of mind even while under the direct tutelage of Engels. Subsequently, the Marx-Engels-Lenin Institute in Moscow, under the editorship of W. Adoratski, published Marx' and Engels' *Briefe an A. Bebel, W. Liebknecht, K. Kautsky und Andere.* Teil I: *1870–1886* (Moscow-Leningrad, 1933), but the project was never completed. When Kautsky undertook an edition of Engels' letters to himself, he could no longer locate the letters he had written, *Aus der Fruehzeit des Marxismus. Engels' Briefwechsel mit Karl Kautsky* (Prague, 1935). Twenty years later Benedikt Kautsky remedied this deficiency in a complete edition of the correspondence on both sides, *Friedrich Engels' Briefwechsel mit Karl Kautsky* (Vienna, 1955), documenting how consistently Kautsky sought the advice of his master. This correspondence is particularly valuable for theoretical matters, but for a picture of the party inside Germany the recent publication of the letters of Bebel and Liebknecht to Marx and Engels is far more significant. Georg Eckert edited Wilhelm Liebknecht's *Briefwechsel mit Karl Marx und Friedrich Engels* (The Hague, 1963), and, although some manuscript copies of Liebknecht's letters were not available, the volume illustrates the strained relationship between the two.

To date, the most valuable published correspondence for the internal history of the movement is Werner Blumenberg's excellent edition of *August Bebels Briefwechsel mit Friedrich Engels* (The Hague, 1965), supplanting in usefulness an earlier edition prepared by the Institut für Marxismus-Leninismus beim ZK der SED of Engels' *Briefe an Bebel* (Berlin-East, 1958). The full measure of Bebel's apocalyptic expectations, his practical political sense, and his growing mastery over the movement are revealed in this correspondence. Of lesser importance for the 1878–1890 period are the following collections: Georg Eckert (ed.), *Aus den Anfaengen der Braunschweiger Arbeiterbewegung. Unveroeffentlichte Bracke-Briefe* (Brunswick, 1955); Victor Adler, *Briefwechsel mit August Bebel und Karl Kautsky, sowie Briefe von und an Ignaz Auer, Eduard Bernstein, Adolf Braun, Heinrich Dietz, Friedrich Ebert, Wilhelm Liebknecht, Hermann Mueller und Paul Singer*, edited by Friedrich Adler (Vienna, 1954); and Heinrich

Gemkow (ed.), "Briefe August Bebels aus den Jahren 1886/1887," *Beitraege zur Geschichte der deutschen Arbeiterbewegung*, II (1960). For the history of Social Democracy under the Socialist Law, one significant deficiency remains, that is the scarcity of correspondence from the side of the moderates. The party archive itself has only scattered letters from this wing of the movement, making it difficult to arrive at a truly balanced account on the basis of the existing evidence.

Memoirs and Biographies

Of the leading German Social Democrats in the seventies and eighties, the bibliography is most extensive for the radicals, and of these Eduard Bernstein has the most adequate treatment, both in his own memoirs and in scholarly biographies. Two of his autobiographical accounts, *My Years of Exile. Reminiscences of a Socialist*, translated by Bernard Miall (London, 1921) and the *Sozialdemokratische Lehrjahre* (Berlin, 1928), describe events and personalities with candor, humor, and generosity. In addition to Peter Gay's fine study of *The Dilemma of Democratic Socialism: Eduard Bernstein's Challenge to Marx* (New York, 1952), there is now Pierre Angel's *Eduard Bernstein et L'Évolution du Socialisme Allemand* (Paris, 1961); however, both concentrate on the life of Bernstein after 1890. No adequate and complete study of Bebel's life exists. His own memoir, *Aus meinem Leben*, 3 vols. (Stuttgart, 1911–1913), unfortunately ends around 1882, and, although filled with considerable detail for the earlier years, it contains only a few hints about his intellectual development. Despite a great number of biographical essays and short studies on Bebel (see Schraepler's *August-Bebel-Bibliographie*) none deserves a special commentary, although two personal necrologies give some insights: Robert Michels, "August Bebel," *Archiv fuer Sozialwissenschaft und Sozialpolitik*, XXXVII (1913), and Paul Kampffmeyer, "August Bebel," *Biographisches Jahrbuch und deutscher Nekrolog*, VXIII (1913). Currently, the historians in the German Democratic Republic (DDR) claim Bebel as their own, often extolling his virtues as a revolutionary fighter against opportunism, reformism and militarism and as a great inspiration for a communist regime. As yet, however, this enthusiasm has not produced a complete scholarly study, although the popular biography, *August Bebel. Eine Biographie* (Berlin-East, 1963), prepared under the direction of Horst Bartel, outlines the fundamentals of their interpretation. The devotion of the DDR historians to Bebel was reflected in a special conference of 1963, as reported by Horst Schumacher, "Wissenschaftliches Kolloquium ueber August Bebel," *Beitraege zur Geschichte der deutschen Arbeiterbewegung*, v (1963).

Wilhelm Liebknecht has faired less well than Bebel, partly because many historians, especially in the DDR, have accepted the criticisms directed against him in the correspondence of Marx and Engels. One is thrown back on Kurt Eisner's *Wilhelm Liebknecht, sein Leben und Wirken* (2nd ed.; Berlin, 1906), and Paul Kampffmeyer's *Wilhelm Liebknecht. Leben und Werk* (Berlin, 1927), the latter not available to me. The great optimist and reconciler of the movement in its decades of troubles, despite all of his theoretical muddling, certainly deserves better than this. The attractiveness of Liebknecht as a person becomes more evident as one reads the laborious pages of intellectual self-esteem in Karl Kautsky's *Erinnerungen und Eroerterungen*, edited by Benedikt Kautsky (The Hague, 1960). Nonetheless, Kautsky's memoir is useful for details on the German movement between 1878 and 1883, when the book ends. Kautsky's intellectual biography is more fully traced in two dissertations: Richard W. Reichard, "Karl Kautsky and the German Social Democratic Party, 1863–1914" (Harvard University, 1950), not used in my study, and John Kautsky, "The Political Thought of Karl Kautsky. A Theory of Democratic, Anti-Communist Marxism" (Harvard University, 1951), which fails, it appears to me, to take into account some of Kautsky's less democratic tendencies in the eighties. The most perceptive analysis is in Erich Matthias, "Kautsky und der Kautskyanismus. Die Funktion der Ideologie in der deutschen Sozialdemokratie vor dem ersten Weltkriege," *Marxismusstudien*, II (Tuebingen, 1957). In a study built in part on the unpublished sources, Reinhard Jansen, *Georg von Vollmar. Eine politische Biographie* (Duesseldorf, 1958), rightly sees Vollmar's initial shift from radicalism to reformism taking place in the middle eighties, a reflection of his character as a man of practice. One of the other radicals, Paul Singer, is the subject of a popular laudatory sketch by Heinrich Gemkow, *Paul Singer. Ein bedeutender Fuehrer der deutschen Arbeiterbewegung* (Berlin-East, 1957), of limited scholarly use.

The biographical literature on the moderates of the eighties is extremely limited. The two autobiographies by moderates—Wilhelm Blos, *Denkwuerdigkeiten eines Sozialdemokraten*, 2 vols. (Munich, 1914, 1919), and Carl Ulrich, *Erinnerungen des ersten hessischen*

Staatspraesidenten, edited by Ludwig Bergstraesser (Offenbach a. M., 1953)—fail to elaborate the fundamentals of their thinking. The career of Ignaz Auer is neatly summarized with some insight into moderate thinking in the memorial sketch by Eduard Bernstein, *Ignaz Auer: eine Gedenkschrift* (Berlin, 1907). The victory of the radicals over the moderates by the end of the eighties has had consequences for the historiography of Social Democracy; in terms of the biographical literature currently available, it appears that the historians of German Social Democracy have nearly forgotten that men such as Karl Frohme, Wilhelm Hasenclever, and Louis Viereck at one time had significant roles in the party. The gap is only partially filled by the short sketches of many Social Democrats in Franz Osterroth, *Biographisches Lexikon des Sozialismus*, Band 1: *Verstorbene Persoenlichkeiten* (Hannover, 1960), and Werner Blumenberg, *Kaempfer fuer die Freiheit* (Berlin and Hannover, 1959).

Histories and Interpretations

The history of Social Democracy under the Socialist Law has not been the subject of a sharply defined interpretive controversy, in part because traditionally most party members preferred to view it as a "heroic epoch" when internal antagonisms had little meaning as the movement faced a common enemy with solidarity, courage, and ultimate victory. One year before the law expired, in 1889, Ignaz Auer compiled a still useful volume pervaded with this view, *Nach zehn Jahren. Material und Glossen zur Geschichte des Sozialistengesetzes* (2nd ed.; Nuremberg, 1913). The same spirit moved Franz Mehring in the late nineties as he concluded his *Geschichte der deutschen Sozialdemokratie*, 4 vols. (8th and 9th ed.; Stuttgart, 1919) with an account of this period. The "heroic epoch" assumed legendary characteristics, leaving the memory of a revolutionary spirit of solidarity for later years when conflict between orthodox Marxists and revisionists threatened the unity of the party. Various memoirs and articles embellished this theme, and none with more imagination than Joseph Belli's delightfully written memoir-history of *Die rote Feldpost unterm Sozialistengesetz* (Stuttgart, 1912), the first fairly detailed narrative of the romantic exploits of those who smuggled the *Sozialdemokrat* into Germany. Only a few voices were heard to deny this interpretation, most notably those of the *Jungen* in the early nineties. Their view was compactly argued in the highly polemical booklet by Hans Mueller, *Der Klassenkampf in der deutschen Sozialdemokratie* (Zurich, 1892), who accurately detected the role of petty bourgeois leaders during the eighties, but mistakenly assumed that before 1878 the party had had a purer proletarian character. The challenge of the *Jungen*, however, failed to undermine the party's vision of its "heroic epoch" between 1878 and 1890.

The troubled experience of Social Democracy during World War I cast its shadow on thinking concerning the Socialist Law era, raising doubts about the "heroism" in some minds and diminishing the importance of revolutionary Marxism in others. Even then the idea that the Social Democrats had acted heroically did not die, but it lost its inspiration. Some, like Kurt Brandis (a pseudonym for Karl Friedrich Brockschmidt), *Die deutsche Sozialdemokratie bis zum Fall des Sozialistengesetzes* (Leipzig, 1931), directly challenged the "heroic epoch" interpretation as a myth, and maintained that, during the Socialist Law era, the fundamentally petty bourgeois and reformist nature of the party, rooted in Lassalleanism, had only been changed on the surface. Others, probing new archival sources, elaborated the party's history more favorably; such was the work of those with reformist backgrounds, such as Paul Kampffmeyer and Bruno Altmann, *Vor dem Sozialistengesetz. Krisenjahre des Obrigkeitsstaates* (Berlin, 1928), and Kampffmeyer's *Unter dem Sozialistengesetz* (Berlin, 1928). In a similar vein, Ferdinand Toennies, *Der Kampf um das Sozialistengesetz 1878* (Berlin, 1929), and Gerhard Schuemer, *Die Entstehungsgeschichte des Sozialistengesetzes* (Inaugural Dissertation; Goettingen, 1929), briefly reexamined the origins of the Socialist Law, the latter especially on the basis of new archival materials. Still others, such as Richard Lipinski, turned out completely uninspired chronicles, with little insight or theoretical discussion, written for the historical education of party functionaries, *Die Sozialdemokratie von ihren Anfaengen bis zur Gegenwart*, 2 vols. (Berlin, 1928). The historical studies ceased as the Social Democrats entered a new epoch of persecution in 1933.

Since World War II, the old themes have appeared once again as historians in the DDR quickly revived the "heroic epoch" thesis to establish a long revolutionary tradition for the new German Communist regime; Rudolph Lindau explicated this view in "Die heroische Periode der deutschen Arbeiterbewegung and ihre Lehren," *Einheit*, v (1950). The new enthusiasm in the DDR has stimulated considerable archival research, along with some propagandistic writing; on balance, however, the historical study of the Socialist Law epoch has certainly benefited, particularly through the use and publication of sources. To my knowledge, Erich Kundel, *Marx und Engels im Kampf um die revolutionaere Arbeitereinheit. Zur Geschichte des Gothaer Vereinigungskongresses von 1875* (Berlin-East, 1962), presents the first complete history of the Gotha unity conference, although his case for the influence of Marx and Engels and for the theoretical sophistication of the Eisenachers is not convincing. Using numerous sources, including the archive in Amsterdam, Ernst Engelberg, *Revolutionaere Politik und Rote Feldpost 1878–1890* (Berlin-East, 1959), details the operations of the smuggling system for the *Sozialdemokrat*, but his argument that an "anti-secret society tactic" (the idea comes from Julius Motteler) necessarily embodied a "revolutionary character," has weaknesses, for the former could also lead to a purely reformist practice. Although no longer living in the DDR, Karl-Alexander Hellfaier, *Die deutsche Sozialdemokratie waehrend des Sozialistengesetzes 1878–1890* (Berlin-East, 1959), utilized a number of police documents to describe the "illegal organizations and agitation" of the Social Democrats on the various levels. Adding much more evidence from the Prussian archives, Dieter Fricke has produced the most complete history of the police and the Social Democrats in *Bismarcks Praetorianer. Die Berliner politische Polizei im Kampf gegen die deutsche Arbeiterbewegung (1871–1898)* (Berlin-East, 1962).

Each of the above works elaborates the "heroic epoch" thesis, usually with the concomitant theme that the "victory of Marxism" gave the period its true greatness. Thus, the relationship of Marx and Engels to the German movement has been a frequent topic with DDR historians, who always stress, and sometimes exaggerate, the direct influence of the two theoreticians. Heinrich Gemkow popularizes this thesis in a short booklet, *Friedrich Engels' Hilfe beim Sieg der deutschen Sozialdemokratie ueber das Sozialistengesetz* (Berlin-East, 1957), followed by Horst Bartel, *Marx und Engels im Kampf um ein revolutionaeres deutsches Parteiorgan 1879–1890* (Berlin-East, 1961), an effort to show that Marx and Engels had a central role in founding the *Sozialdemokrat*. On this particular issue, Kundel chronicles the relationship of Engels to the paper in detail, but the subject is treated with a more convincing balance by Gustav Mayer, *Friedrich Engels. Eine Biographie*, 2 vols. (The Hague, 1934).

Outside the DDR, the "heroic epoch" thesis is not so compelling, and the period of the Socialist Law itself has received only limited attention. The numerous memorial histories of Social Democracy that appeared in the Federal Republic around 1963 to celebrate the first centenary of the party's existence did not especially glorify the "heroic epoch," nor, for that matter, did they offer anything of scholarly value worth mentioning here. (There are, however, numerous valuable articles on Lassalle and the Lassallean movement in the 1963 volume (III) of the *Archiv fuer Sozialgeschichte*.) On the other hand, Wolfgang Pack, *Das parlamentarische Ringen um das Sozialistengesetz Bismarcks 1878–1890* (Duesseldorf, 1961), gives a thorough and balanced narrative of the legislative history of the Socialist Law and the relation of the parties to it. Bismarck's concern about the political revolutionary threat of the Social Democrats is stressed by the conservative-minded Gustav Adolf Rein, *Die Revolution in der Politik Bismarcks* (Goettingen, 1957), and by Werner Poels, *Sozialistenfrage und Revolutionsfurcht in ihrem Zusammenhang mit den angeblichen Staatsstreichplaenen Bismarcks* (Luebeck-Hamburg, 1960).

Most of the sociological studies of German Social Democracy, so well discussed by Carl Schorske in *German Social Democracy 1905–1917. The Development of the Great Schism* (Cambridge, Mass., 1955), do not apply directly to the period before 1890. However, Guenther Roth examines with considerable insight the whole sweep of the Social Democratic movement from the 1860's through World War I in *The Social Democrats in Imperial Germany. A Study in Working-Class Isolation and National Integration* (Totowa, New Jersey, 1963), interpreting the life of the movement in terms of a subculture that developed as a result both of the rejection of the working classes by the dominant classes and of a "self-isolation of the labor movement." Although I am inclined to believe that prior to 1890 the isolation of the labor movement was not self-imposed to any significant degree, Roth's study is one of the most interesting to appear for several years and special attention should be drawn to his explanation of "the role of Marxism in the Social Democratic Subculture."

The place of German Social Democracy in the larger context of European labor and socialism may be studied through Carl Landauer's encompassing *European Socialism: A History of Ideas and Movements from the Industrial Revolution to Hitler's Seizure of Power*, 2 vols. (Berkeley and Los Angeles, 1959), a work marked by the author's wide knowledge and balanced judgment on controversial issues. Although Landauer is not as detailed in most areas as G. D. H. Cole's multi-volumed *History of Socialist Thought* (London, 1953ff.), he achieves a greater integration of the material. In this same connection, one must mention the vast work by Juergen Kuczynski, *Die Geschichte der Lage der Arbeiter unter dem Kapitalismus* (Berlin-East, 1961ff.), of which volumes II and III provide an economic and social history of Germany between 1848 and 1900 with considerable reference to the development of the socialist movement. Although one may tire of Kuczynski's devotion to Marxist-Leninist explanations, his work contains invaluable statistical compilations on economic and social conditions. On the problem of the relationship of the German movement to the First International, Roger Morgan, *The German Social Democrats and the First International 1864–1872* (Cambridge, 1965), demonstrates that Johann Philip Becker achieved far more for the First International in Germany than Wilhelm Leibknecht, the man who has traditionally received the credit. A sweeping narrative of the internationalism of the labor and socialist movements by Julius Braunthal, *Geschichte der Internationale*, 2 vols. (Hannover, 1961, 1963), places Germany in the European context and exposes some myths about the size and resources of the First International. On the theoretical level, George Lichtheim, *Marxism: An Historical and Critical Study* (New York, 1961), provides a perceptive analysis of the cooperative work of Engels and Kautsky in formulating a "Social-Democratic Marxism" after 1883.

Special Topics: Local Studies, Trade Unions, Anarchism, etc.

Several substantial narrative histories cover local party activity during the Socialist Law period, but in most instances they are not strong either in social analysis or on theoretical issues. The most useful of these include: Eduard Bernstein, *Die Geschichte der Berliner Arbeiterbewegung*, 3 vols. (Berlin, 1907–1910), offering some details on Berlin radicalism; Heinrich Laufenberg, *Geschichte der Arbeiterbewegung in Hamburg, Altona und Umgegend*, 2 vols. (Hamburg, 1911, 1931), integrating the local movement with the national level better than most; Georg Eckert, *Die Braunschweiger Arbeiterbewegung unter dem Sozialistengesetz*. Teil I. (*1878–1884*) (Brunswick, 1961), revealing a strong reformist tendency in this area; Ulrich Boettcher, *Anfaenge und*

Entwicklung der Arbeiterbewegung in Bremen von der Revolution 1848 bis zur Aufhebung des Sozialistengesetzes 1890 (Bremen, 1953), concluding that the Socialist Law widened the gap between the bourgeoisie and the Social Democrats in Bremen; Rudolph Strauss and Kurt Finsterbusch, *Die Chemnitzer Arbeiterbewegung unter dem Sozialistengesetz* (Berlin-East, 1954), an interpretation by DDR historians that may be contrasted to the rambling book by the reformist Ernst Heilmann, *Geschichte der Arbeiterbewegung in Chemnitz und dem Erzgebirge* (Chemnitz, n.d. [1912]); and Georg Gaertner, *Die Nuernberger Arbeiterbewegung 1868–1908* (Nuremberg, n.d. [1908]), still a still basic: Josef Schmoele, *Die sozialdemokratischen Gewerkschaften in Deutschland seit dem Erlasse des Sozialisten-Gesetzes*, 2 vols. (Jena, 1896, 1898), and W. Kulemann, *Die Berufsvereine*, Erste Abteilung, Zweiter Band: *Deutschland II. Organisation der Arbeitnehmer II* (2nd ed.; Jena, 1908). Several recent studies focus on developments after 1890, but include references to the earlier period: Gerhard A. Ritter, *Die Arbeiterbewegung im Wilhelminischen Reich. Die Sozialdemokratische Partei und die Freien Gewerkschaften 1890–1900* (Berlin-Dahlem, 1959); Heinz Josef Varain, *Freie Gewerkschaften, Sozialdemokratie und Staat: Die Politik der Generalkommission unter der Fuehrung Carl Legiens (1890–1920)* (Duesseldorf, 1956); and Max Juergen Koch, *Die Bergarbeiterbewegung im Ruhrgebiet zur Zeit Wilhelms II (1889–1914)* (Duesseldorf, 1954).

On anarchism in Germany during the nineteenth century, the bibliography is not only limited but also highly partisan and thin in the use good source for the activities of the moderate Carl Grillenberger.

Although the above narratives are useful sources of information, often revealing moderate tendencies on the local level, a more fruitful approach to local history is employed by Wolfgang Koellmann, *Sozialgeschichte der Stadt Barmen im 19. Jahrhundert* (Tuebingen, 1960). By integrating the labor movement into the larger context of the social, economic, and political development of Barmen and Germany, Koellmann overcomes the narrow focus of so many local histories of socialism. Although limited to an earlier period, much the same may be said about Rudolph Strauss' *Die Lage und die Bewegung der Chemnitzer Arbeiter in der ersten Haelfte des 19. Jahrhunderts* (Berlin-East, 1960).

A comprehensive study of the trade unions under the Socialist Law would be of considerable value, expanding on two older works that are

of scholarly apparatus. The two most informative books are Max Nettlau, *Anarchisten und Sozialrevolutionaere. Die historische Entwicklung des Anarchismus in den Jahren 1880–1886* (Berlin, 1931), and Rudolf Rocker, *Johann Most. Das Leben eines Rebellen* (Berlin, 1924). Some aspects of the movement in Germany are touched on by J. Langhard, *Die anarchistische Bewegung in der Schweiz von ihren Anfaengen bis zur Gegenwart und die internationalen Fuehrer* (2nd ed.; Bern, 1909). On August Reinsdorf, the leading German anarchist in the eighties, Max Schuette's *August Reinsdorf und die Niederwaldverschwoerung* (Berlin, 1902) was not available to me and Johann Most's *August Reinsdorf und die Propaganda der That* (New York, 1890) is overflowing with exaggerations.

Although there is no recent, comprehensive treatment of the ideas of State Socialism in the nineteenth century, much the same purpose is served by Walter Vogel's compact discussion of the theoretical, personal, and institutional origins of *Bismarcks Arbeiterversicherung. Ihre Entstehung im Kraeftespiel der Zeit* (Brunswick, 1951). A similar contribution, but narrower in scope, is made by Wolfgang Saile, *Hermann Wagener und sein Verhaeltnis zu Bismarck. Ein Beitrag zur Geschichte des konservativen Sozialismus* (Tuebingen, 1958), and Ralph Bowen, *German Theories of the Corporative State* (New York and London, 1947) is informative on Albert Schaeffle and Adolf Wagner.

The ambiguities and shifts in the views of the Social Democrats on nationality questions are examined in great detail by Hans-Ulrich Wehler, *Sozialdemokratie und Nationalstaat: Die deutsche Sozialdemokratie und die Nationalitaetenfragen in Deutschland von Karl Marx bis zum Ausbruch des ersten Weltkrieges* (Wuerzburg, 1962). Some of the literature on the socialists and Christianity has been discussed in my own article on "August Bebel and German Social Democracy's Relation to the Christian Churches," *Journal of the History of Ideas*, XXVII (April/June 1966). On the Social Democrats and the military system, the unimaginative compendium by Reinhard Hoehn, *Sozialismus und Heer*, 2 vols. (Zurich-Berlin, 1959), is at least useful for reference. For the early Social Democratic agrarian policy, Fritz Schaaf, *Der Kampf der deutschen Arbeiterbewegung um die Landarbeiter und werktaetigen Bauern 1848–1890* (Berlin, 1962), was unavailable to me at the time of writing, as was Susanne Miller, *Das Problem der Freiheit im Sozialismus* (Frankfurt a. M., 1964). Numerous short monographs and unpublished dissertations on special subjects, such as the Social Democratic policies on foreign policy, finance, tariffs, etc., have not been discussed in this bibliographical essay; references to these may be found in the bibliographies cited above and in the annual lists of dissertations, the *Jahresverzeichnis der deutschen Hochschulschriften.*

INDEX